The Death Penalty

The Death Penalty

AN AMERICAN HISTORY

STUART BANNER

HARVARD UNIVERSITY PRESS
Cambridge, Massachusetts, and London, England 2002

Library of Congress Cataloging-in-Publication Data

Banner, Stuart, 1963–
The death penalty : an American history / Stuart Banner.
p. cm.
Includes bibliographical references and index.
ISBN 0-674-00751-4 (alk. paper)
1. Capital punishment—United States—History.   2. Capital punishment—Moral and
ethical aspects—United States.   3. United States—Social conditions.   I. Title.

HV8699.U5 B367 2002
364.66′0973—dc21
2001047047

For Tamara: *donec gratus sum tibi, Persarum vivo rege laetior*

CONTENTS

ABBREVIATIONS

AAS   American Antiquarian Society, Worcester, Mass.
CHS   Chicago Historical Society, Chicago, Ill.
CTA   Connecticut State Archives, Hartford, Conn.
CTL   Connecticut State Library, Hartford, Conn.
FDR   Franklin D. Roosevelt Library, Hyde Park, N.Y.
GAA   Georgia Department of Archives and History, Atlanta, Ga.
ILA   Illinois State Archives, Springfield, Ill.
JC   Jimmy Carter Library, Atlanta, Ga.
LC   Library of Congress, Washington, D.C.
LFP   Lewis F. Powell, Jr., Archives, Washington and Lee University School of Law, Lexington, Va.
MAA   Massachusetts Archives, Boston, Mass.
MDA   Maryland State Archives, Annapolis, Md.
MOA   Missouri State Archives, Jefferson City, Mo.
NA   National Archives, College Park, Md.
NCA   North Carolina State Archives, Raleigh, N.C.
NYA   New York State Archives, Albany, N.Y.
NYDT *New-York Daily Tribune*
NYHS New-York Historical Society, New York, N.Y.
NYL   New York State Library, Albany, N.Y.
NYT   *New York Times*
PAA   Pennsylvania State Archives, Harrisburg, Pa.
PG   *Pennsylvania Gazette*
SCA   South Carolina Archives & History Center, Columbia, S.C.
TXA   Texas State Archives, Austin, Tex.
VAA   Library of Virginia, Richmond, Va.
VG   *Virginia Gazette*

INTRODUCTION

STEPHEN CLARK WAS HANGED in Salem, Massachusetts, in the spring of 1821. No one had been hurt when Clark had set fire to a barn late one night the previous summer, but the fire had spread to some of the neighboring wooden houses, and arson of a dwelling during the night was a capital crime. Ever since his conviction in February, petitions had been presented to the governor seeking to have Clark's sentence commuted to imprisonment. Clark was easy to sympathize with. He was only sixteen years old, pale and thin, with no criminal record, from a respectable family. But clemency had been denied. "Those who have been so anxious to have him spared, would allow *mercy* to wink *justice* out of sight," one local newspaper insisted; "they do not take into their estimation the vast amount of anxiety, of distress and misery that has followed his crime."

The execution began around noon, when Clark was taken from jail to the gallows in a carriage, escorted by a military guard, along with the sheriff and his deputies, mounted and armed. The jailer rode with Clark, as did a few ministers, who raced the clock to ensure that Clark attained penitence, and thus the possibility of an infinite afterlife, before it was too late. Hundreds, maybe thousands, of spectators walked alongside the procession. They caught no glimpse of Clark until the carriage arrived at the gallows.

As the crowd watched quietly, Clark emerged and climbed the steps up to the scaffold. The ministers and the sheriff followed. Clark wobbled and nearly fainted from fear; he had to lean on one of the ministers while the sheriff read his death warrant to the crowd. When the time came for Clark to address the spectators, he was too shy to speak. Instead, at his request, the Reverend Mr. Cornelius read a few sentences Clark had composed in jail the day before. "May the youth who are present take warning by my sad fate, not to forsake the wholesome discipline of a Parent's home," Clark urged with the aid of Cornelius's voice. "May you all pray to God to give you timely repentance, open your eyes, enlighten your understandings, that you may shun the paths of vice and follow God's commandments all the rest of your days. And may God have mercy on you all." The Reverend Mr. Carlisle delivered a sermon. The two ministers joined Clark in private prayer for a few minutes. Then the ministers hurried down the steps, leaving Clark on the stage with the sheriff and his deputies.

The deputies tied Clark's hands behind his back and opened his shirt a bit so the rope would touch his skin. Clark submissively lowered his head to make it easier for the deputies to slip the noose around it. Up on the platform, surrounded by spectators, Clark seemed young, small, helpless before the assembled power of the state. Sighs and groans could be heard from the crowd. Like many executions, Clark's would inspire maudlin but evidently sincere poetry, placing in ironic juxtaposition the stern justice imposed on Clark the criminal and the widely felt tenderness toward Clark the human being. When the deputies drew the cap over Clark's head, obscuring his face, everyone knew the moment was near. The sheriff gave a signal, a deputy sprang the trap door in the floor, and Clark dropped, stopping with a sudden jerk a few feet down, "dangling between heaven and earth" as the nineteenth-century cliché put it.[1]

Executions are very different today. No one is hanged for arson. In fact no one is hanged for *any* crime—even most of our murderers are sent to prison, and for those we execute, the usual method is lethal injection. The execution does not come within months of the crime, but only after a decade or more of litigation over whether the trial was conducted in accordance with the Constitution. The crowds don't number in the thousands or even the hundreds, but rather around twenty or so, all that will fit into the small drab concrete-block rooms deep within the state prison. No children watch. There may be a minister, but the condition of the condemned person's soul and his chances of entering heaven are not among the government's major concerns. There are no afternoon sermons or speeches—just a group of grim prison employees, shortly after midnight, trying to finish the job as quickly as they can. In 1821, when

Stephen Clark died, an execution was outside, open to the public, and embedded in ritual; now it is behind closed doors, accessible only to a few, with as little ceremony as possible.

The execution itself has been hidden from public view, but the issue of capital punishment has grown extraordinarily visible. Death was once the standard punishment even for nonviolent crimes like burglary and counterfeiting, and few judged the law too severe. For the past two centuries, however, the death penalty has been the subject of some of our most bitter debates. Whether phrased in philosophical, political, or economic terms, the arguments have been rooted in a basic moral question: Are there any crimes so grave, or any criminals so evil, that death is the only just punishment? Is it right for the state, acting in our name, to put criminals to death? From Stephen Clark to Gary Gilmore, from Bruno Hauptmann to Timothy McVeigh, Americans have argued passionately about the purposes, methods, and effects of capital punishment. As the annual number of executions in the United States approaches one hundred, and as swelling death rows in many states promise to push the execution rate sharply higher, the debate will only grow in volume and intensity of feeling.

This book is about the many changes in capital punishment over the years—changes in the arguments pro and con, in the crimes punished with death, in execution methods and rituals, and more generally in the way Americans have understood and experienced the death penalty. Many aspects of capital punishment today appear paradoxical without an appreciation of its history. Americans pride themselves on their commitment to human rights, but the United States is virtually alone among Western nations in putting its criminals to death, and in some parts of the world America's use of capital punishment is considered inconsistent with human rights. The death penalty is intended in part to deter others from committing crimes, but we inflict it in private. It is often justified in retributive terms, and yet we take great care to make it as painless as possible. We can resolve these apparent paradoxes only by looking back at how they came to exist.

The execution of Stephen Clark was not soon forgotten. Fifteen years later, when a committee of the Massachusetts House recommended abolishing the death penalty, Clark's case was the committee's primary evidence that the state's criminal code was too severe. A decade after that, when the reformer Charles Spear needed an example of the harshness of capital punishment, he too turned to Clark.[2] Had Clark been imprisoned for his fire no one would have remembered him a year later, but because of his death sentence Clark dangled in public memory far longer than he had lived on earth, as an image invested with meanings of which he himself could never have dreamed. He was not the first person converted into a debating point after having been punished with death, and he would certainly not be the last.

1

TERROR, BLOOD, AND REPENTANCE

ENGLISH COLONISTS of the seventeenth and eighteenth centuries came from a country in which death was the penalty for a list of crimes that seems shockingly long today. Treason, murder, manslaughter, rape, robbery, burglary, arson, counterfeiting, theft—all were capital crimes in England. All became capital crimes in the American colonies as well.

Today even capital punishment's most ardent supporters would recoil at the notion of executing thieves or counterfeiters. We have a consensus that if the death penalty is to be used at all it should be reserved for those who commit the gravest crimes. Until the late eighteenth century, however, the consensus was very nearly the opposite. Colonial Americans put crimes in the same hierarchy we do—everyone agreed that murder was more serious than theft, for instance—but there was scarcely any disagreement that death was the proper punishment for many of them.

How can we understand a society—*our* society—that executed burglars and horse thieves? The standard approach to the history of the death penalty in the United States has been a smug condescension to the past, a refusal even to try to understand. The times were rude and life was cheap, we tell ourselves. The people of the seventeenth and eighteenth centuries did not think as independently as we do; they were still shackled by oppressive political and religious traditions they were not yet able to throw off. But this story is a caricature of early modern thought, invented (as we will see) by capital punishment's later opponents. Executing a fellow human being was just as momentous in the seventeenth and eighteenth centuries as it is today. Colonial Americans were not blindly following tradition. They pondered the death penalty and the purposes it served, just as Americans do today. But because of the institutional structure and prevailing religious beliefs of their time, capital punishment could serve a broader set of purposes than it serves today.

The Bloody Code

England's North American colonies exhibited significant regional variation in their criminal codes right from the beginning.[1] The early northern colonies were far more lenient than England for crimes against property. Burglary and robbery, for instance, were not capital crimes under the initial criminal statutes of Connecticut, Massachusetts, Plymouth, or Pennsylvania, and were capital only on the third offense in the initial codes of New York, New Hampshire, and New Haven. Arson was not a capital crime in early Connecticut, Massachusetts, New York, or Pennsylvania. The law in the early northern colonies was closer to English law for crimes against the person, but was less harsh in several respects. Murder was capital everywhere, but rape was not capital in the first codes of Massachusetts, New York, or Pennsylvania, and even manslaughter was not capital in the early Quaker colonies of Pennsylvania and West New Jersey, which for a time gave the Delaware Valley the most lenient punishments in the English world.[2]

For what would today be called consensual crimes or crimes against morality, by contrast, the early northern colonial penal codes were often harsher than English law, because of the religious origins of many of these colonies. Blasphemy and idolatry were in principle capital crimes in Connecticut, Massachusetts, and New Hampshire; adultery was capital in early Connecticut, Massachusetts, and New York; sodomy and bestiality were capital throughout the region, even for the animals involved. In practice, however, these statutes were rarely enforced. Massachusetts executed four Quakers in the mid-seventeenth century who returned to the colony after having been banished, but these are the only people known to have been hanged in the colonies for their religious beliefs. James Britton and Mary Latham, hanged by Massachusetts in 1643 for adultery, are the only two known to have been executed for the offense in any of the colonies. As the New England colonies lost their original sense of a religious mission, they abandoned the death penalty for some of these moral crimes. Massachusetts decapitalized blasphemy, adultery, and incest in the late seventeenth century, and New Hampshire decapitalized blasphemy in the early eighteenth. Hangings for sodomy or bestiality were more common; there were at least three in Massachusetts, four in Connecticut, and three in New Jersey. The last American jurisdiction to hang someone for one of these crimes was the state of Pennsylvania, which executed Joseph Ross for "buggery" in 1785.[3] South of Pennsylvania, with the exception of a single execution for sodomy in Virginia in 1624, there are no known executions for any of these crimes against morality.

Except for a very brief period in early seventeenth-century Virginia, the early southern colonies did not enact criminal codes as the northern colonies did, but simply used English law. In the seventeenth century the law in the southern colonies thus included capital punishment for more property offenses and fewer morality offenses than in the northern colonies. As the northern colonies gradually decapitalized blasphemy and the like, the southern colonies were left with the greater number of capital crimes, particularly where property was concerned. Property tended to be distributed less evenly in the South than in the North—the southern pattern of wealth distribution was closer to that of England—which may have caused southern elites to see a need to maintain the English capital property offenses. Southerners also tended to come from regions of England that were more violent than the regions from which northerners emigrated, a cultural difference that possibly reinforced southerners' preference for a greater number of capital offenses.[4]

The period of American colonization coincided with a stiffening of English criminal law, as Parliament created myriad new capital offenses in the late seventeenth and eighteenth centuries. Most of these were for crimes against property that in retrospect seem trivial, and indeed seemed trivial to many at the time—poaching deer, stealing small sums of money, and so on. By the second half of the eighteenth century English lawyers counted nearly two hundred capital statutes, although most of these defined very narrow and local property offenses with no application to the colonies. But while a simple count of statutes could overstate the severity of the law, that law became more severe in substance as well as form. Over the course of the eighteenth century England's criminal code became the harshest in Europe.

The American colonies experienced a milder version of this trend. The newer southern colonies, established while this process was under way in England, began their existence with many capital crimes. The older colonies, both northern and southern, all added to their list of capital crimes. Massachusetts made robbery a capital crime upon a third conviction in

1642, upon a second in 1711, and upon a first in 1761. New Hampshire reduced the number of burglary convictions necessary for the death penalty from three to two in 1682, and then to one in 1718. Connecticut and Massachusetts both made arson a capital crime in the second half of the seventeenth century. In Pennsylvania, where murder had been the only capital crime for over three decades, pressure from the imperial government resulted in 1718 in the introduction of the death penalty for manslaughter, rape, highway robbery, maiming, burglary, arson, witchcraft, and sodomy. Later in the century the colony would add counterfeiting, squatting on Indian land, and prison-breaking to the list. New York added piracy, counterfeiting, and certain forms of perjury. Actual practice often lagged behind legislative change. Pennsylvania took eighteen years and nine capital burglary convictions, for instance, before hanging its first burglar.[5] But practice often caught up: in the next twenty-eight years, twenty-two more Pennsylvania burglars are known to have died on the gallows.

In the South the colonies followed England in capitalizing minor property crimes. Virginia imposed the death penalty for all sorts of crimes relating to the tobacco trade—including embezzling tobacco, fraudulently delivering tobacco, altering inspected tobacco, forging inspectors' stamps, and smuggling tobacco—as well as for stealing hogs (upon a third conviction), receiving a stolen horse, and concealing property to defraud creditors. Delaware made it a capital offense to steal £5 from a house, and then imposed the death penalty upon the third conviction of any theft, regardless of location or amount. South Carolina copied the English statute providing death for those convicted of burning the timber intended for house frames.[6] By the end of the colonial period both northern and southern colonies punished many more offenses with death than they had in 1700, and the southern codes were still harsher than the northern.

England's "bloody code" (as it was widely called by its detractors) had its eighteenth-century American counterpart in the swelling number of capital statutes applicable only to blacks. The first of these appears to have been enacted in New York, which in 1712, alarmed by a slave revolt, capitalized attempted murder and attempted rape committed by slaves. Most of these race-dependent capital crimes, unsurprisingly, were created in the southern colonies. Slaves made up more than half the population of South Carolina by 1720 and nearly half that of Virginia by 1750. To manage these captive workforces the southern colonies resorted to ever-increasing lists of capital statutes. In 1740 South Carolina imposed the death penalty on slaves and free blacks for burning or destroying any grain, commodities, or manufactured goods; on slaves for enticing other slaves to run away; and on slaves maiming or bruising whites. Virginia, fearing attempts at poisoning, made it a capital offense for slaves to prepare or administer medicine. The Georgia legislature determined that crimes committed by slaves posed dangers "peculiar to the condition and circumstances of this province," dangers which meant that such crimes "could not fall under the provision of the laws of England." Georgia accordingly made it a capital offense for slaves or free blacks to strike whites twice, or once if a bruise resulted. "The Laws in Force, for the Punishment of Slaves" in Maryland, its legislature found, were "insufficient, to prevent their committing, very great Crimes and Disorders." Slaves were accordingly subjected to the death penalty for conspiring to rebel, rape a white woman, or burn a house.[7]

Colonies with large numbers of slaves expedited the procedures for trying them. As early as 1692 Virginia began using local justices of the peace rather than juries and legally trained judges to try slaves for capital crimes. South Carolina adopted a similarly streamlined procedure in 1740. These systems remained intact as long as slavery existed. Execution rates for slaves far exceeded those for southern whites. In North Carolina, for instance, at least one hundred slaves were executed in the quarter-century between 1748 and 1772, well more than the number of whites executed during the colony's entire history, a period spanning over a century.[8]

The long list of capital crimes for slaves is, paradoxically, more readily understandable today than the shorter list for whites. Harsh punishments were obviously useful to those in power for disciplining a captive labor force. People who were already enslaved had little to lose and were understood to have less incentive than whites to follow the law. People who were believed to have less faith than whites in the Christian system of eternal rewards and penalties were thought to need more conspicuous penalties in this life. But how can we explain the death penalty for so many crimes committed by whites?

See and Fear

In 1700 the governor and Council of Maryland considered the fate of two men sentenced to death for burglary. It was the first offense for both. "What they have Stollen is but a Trifle," the governor noted, in suggesting that clemency might be appropriate. The Council disagreed. Members urged the governor to inquire whether the two were guilty of "any other evil Practices" that might allow him, in good conscience, to let the execution proceed. "So many Burglarys are Dayly comitted in this Province," the Council concluded, "that it is absolutely necessary some publiq Example should be made to deterr others from the like Crimes for the future."[9]

Criminologists would likewise call it *deterrence*, but eighteenth-century Americans usually had blunter words for the primary purpose they ascribed to capital punishment. "There are but few who are made without fear," explained James Dana a few hours before Joseph Mountain's execution in Connecticut for rape. The punishment that awaited Mountain was "calculated and designed to put the lawless in fear." The *Virginia Gazette* observed that capital punishment was a way of "counterbalancing Temptation by Terror, and alarming the Vicious by the Prospect of Misery." An executed criminal was "an Example and Warning, to prevent others from those Courses that lead to so fatal and ignominious a Conclusion: — and thus those Men whose *Lives* are no longer of any Use in the World, are made of some Service to it by their *Deaths*." Fear, terror, warning — whatever one called it, the main purpose of the death penalty was conceived to be its deterrent effect, its power to prevent prospective criminals from committing crimes. "Suppose our ministers of justice, in their superabounding mercy, should spare the vilest criminals," the minister Aaron Hutchinson imagined. "Vice would be daring, and the wicked walk on all hands."[10]

To convey that message of terror to the greatest number required careful management of the process by which criminals were put to death. Most clearly, an execution had to be a public event, open to anyone wishing to attend. "A principal design of public executions is, that others may fear," argued Noah Hobart before an audience gathered in Fairfield, Connecticut, to see Isaac Frasier hanged for burglary. "One end of the law," the minister Nathaniel Fisher proclaimed at a similar occasion, "in ordering him to suffer, in this public and ignominious manner, is to alarm and deter others." By locating executions in open spaces affording views to large numbers of people, and by scheduling them in the daytime to maximize visibility and convenience for spectators, officials sought to broadcast terror as widely as possible. Death "should be publicly inflicted on the wicked," Nathan Strong declared, so "that others may see and fear."[11]

The message was conveyed in several ways simultaneously. Americans in the seventeenth and eighteenth centuries knew in the abstract, even if they had not witnessed any actual executions, that death was the consequence of serious crime. Executions were reported in newspapers and discussed in sermons and were the talk of any county where one occurred, so the public would have been well informed about capital punishment even without the opportunity to see it put into practice. But there was something uniquely terrifying about *seeing* an execution. One could usefully meditate on the death of the burglar Philip Kennison, for instance, but it was only "the Sight of this unhappy *Criminal*" actually dying that could "give an Edge to these Meditations, and fix them with *lasting Impressions* on all our hearts." Those who *saw* Samuel Smith, another burglar, dropped from the scaffold would never forget that the "connexion between the crime and gibbet, is much nearer and more natural, than many suppose." Condemned criminals were well aware that their role at an execution was to be seen by as many as possible. Valentine Dukett was said to have pondered "the awful spectacle which this body of mine will in a short time exhibit." The burglar Levi Ames is supposed to have rhymed on the morning of his execution:

> Ah! what a Spectacle I soon shall be,
> A Corps suspended from yon shameful Tree.[12]

The death penalty was understood as something that had to be seen in order to have its maximum effect.

Not just seen, but seen properly. An execution needed to be "accompanied with circumstances of solemnity," because solemnity "would make a lasting impression on all ages, ranks, and characters—particularly on children and youth," who turned up in large numbers, and who could be expected to take the lesson of terror most to heart. The condemned person had to be transported from jail to the gallows, normally a long distance because a jail was in town but a gallows needed unobstructed space for spectators, and the trip offered the opportunity for a carefully orchestrated procession that could be seen by many, even those who did not attend the execution itself. People occasionally proposed modifying the ceremony to make it even more frightening—for instance, by staging the ceremony at night. "Night naturally brings with it a kind of Dread that strongly operates upon the Heart of Man," urged one newspaper editor. "Night introduces a mental Horror, and throws a saddening Awe upon the World."[13] It was precisely this dread, this horror, this awe that an execution, when seen properly, was thought to provoke.

And not just seen properly, but seen properly by the kind of people considered most likely to commit crimes. Mark and Phillis, slaves in Charlestown, Massachusetts, were hanged in 1755 for poisoning their master. Mark's dead body was then placed on display. Those who could read might have seen the broadside printed for the occasion:

> Let servants all in their own Place,
>   the Masters serve with Fear,
> Lest God should leave them to themselves
>   As these poor Creatures were.

But one did not need to read to understand the message Mark conveyed, a message that endured in the consciousness of many far longer than the printed word. Three years later, when Dr. Caleb Rea was passing through Charlestown, he found Mark still hanging, a bit decomposed, but with his skin largely intact. In 1798, forty-three years after the execution, Mark was long gone, but locals still remembered him well. That year, when Paul Revere described his famous ride of 1775, he said: "After I had passed Charlestown Neck, and got nearly opposite where Mark was hung in chains, I saw two men on horseback under a tree."[14] If Paul Revere could assume in 1798 that people would know the place he was referring to by the mere mention of Mark's name, the display of Mark's body must have had a powerful effect on the area's slaves and servants in the late 1750s, when Mark was still there.

One common way of directing the terror of capital punishment to its appropriate targets was to stage an execution as close as possible to where the crime had been committed. John Whitney and Michael Kennedy, members of "a Gang of notorious Thieves" based in Fredericksburg, Virginia, were tried and sentenced in Williamsburg, but were taken back to Fredericksburg to be hanged, in the expectation that a local execution "would be attended with better Effects to the Community than if transacted at a Distance, and might probably deter their Accomplices" — many of whom in fact attended. Hangings in eighteenth-century Maryland were normally conducted "as near the publick Road as conveniently can

be where the fact was committed," for the same reason. Two Indians convicted of murder in New York in 1672 were ordered to be hanged "in som
eminent Place near the Towne, soe to strike the greater terror in the rest
of their Companions." When two or more people were to be executed at
the same time for the same crime, they could be profitably allocated to
more than one location for maximum effect. Two servants were hanged
as accomplices in piracy in Virginia in 1729, for example, "one at
Rappahannock River, near the Place from whence they ran, and the
other at York River, near the Place where they committed the Piracy."[15]
The first location would drive the point home for other local servants, the
second for any prospective pirates.

If capital punishment was expected to deter prospective criminals, it
was certain to prevent existing criminals from repeating their crimes. The
murderer Samuel Frost was told by his spiritual counselor immediately
before his execution: "You have made yourself vile, and are become unworthy longer to be a member of the community. Your life and liberty are
dangerous to the peace of society, dangerous to the lives and liberties of
your fellow citizens." Chauncy Graham used a common metaphor to explain that the execution of a criminal was like "the cutting of a Wart or a
Wen from the Body," an operation that "does not only free it from that
troublesome and deforming Excrescence, which to the Loss of the whole,
drew off so much Nutrition to maintain its useless and troublesome Bulk;
but it may prevent the Growth of many more, that would in Proportion,
rob the Body of proper Nourishment."[16] Today criminologists call this
function "incapacitation," but in an age before the invention of the
prison there was no way to incapacitate a criminal short of killing him.
England and its colonies had *jails*, to hold suspects awaiting trial, but the
prison, as a punishment for those convicted of crimes, was a development
of the late eighteenth century. Before then, incapacitation and deterrence could not be separated. Both depended on the same show of force.
The primary purpose of capital punishment was the emphatic display of
power, a reminder of what the state could do to those who broke its laws.

Blood It Defileth the Land

Most colonial Americans assigned responsibility for crime to the criminal
himself rather than to his environment. Among writers on the subject,
humankind was often understood as intrinsically depraved, as having a
natural tendency toward evil. "Why; is every natural man a murtherer?"

asked Increase Mather. "Truly he hath a *murderer's heart within him*, and he would quickly shed bloud, he would actually commit murder, if God did not restrain him." If the spectators at an execution had not yet committed any crimes themselves, it was "no thanks to our own hearts, for we have the *same* nature that they [the condemned criminals] have." Anyone was liable to commit a crime at any moment.

> And shortly, reader, thou must follow me,
> And drop into a vast eternity!

So warned Robert Young, a rapist and maybe a poet as well.[17] While Young had raped an eleven-year-old girl and his readers had not, he saw no fundamental difference between them.

If humans were innately depraved, and if a criminal was someone who had failed to control a natural tendency that everyone shared, then the commission of a crime was an act for which blame properly attached to the criminal. The criminal had neglected to maintain the required degree of vigilance over his own conduct. He was responsible for his own crime. For those with a more benign view of human nature, the commission of a crime was still an exercise of free will that justified the assignment of responsibility to the criminal. Either way, the community took on a corresponding obligation to punish him, as a means of retribution that was not just legitimate but morally necessary.

The obligation was usually expressed in biblical terms. "Blood it defileth the land," God had instructed in the Old Testament, "and the land cannot be cleansed of the blood that is shed therein, but by the blood of him that shed it." Capital punishment was understood as necessary to purge society, not just of a bad member, but of a guilt that would otherwise be shared by everyone. "You are now to Dy," Cotton Mather advised the murderer Joseph Hanno, because "the Land where you now Live, would be polluted, if you should be spared from *Death*." Josias and Joseph, Indians convicted of murder, were executed in 1709 because "the Land which we inhabit, ought to be cleansed from that defilement, which the Voluntary and Unjust taking away of the Lives of men doth bring upon it." Thomas Starr was hanged in Haddam, Connecticut, so "that God, the God of our salvation would deliver us, and our land from blood-guiltiness."[18] Guilt belonged to the land as well as the criminal. Execution was the only way to expiate that collective guilt.

This was a prominent theme of the poetry printed to be sold at hangings in the eighteenth and early nineteenth centuries. Spectators at the 1734 execution of John Ormsby could read:

> No hope of Favour can he have,
>   from any human Hand,
> The Blood which he has spilt must be
>   purged from off the Land.

And for John Harrington, in 1757:

> Go Murd'rous Wretch, deep-drench'd in Gore;
>   With human Blood prophan'd;
> Thy Life we must admit no more,
>   A Burthen to the Land.[19]

The execution of a criminal was thus not merely a forward-looking exercise in deterrence, a way of preventing crimes in the future; it was also a backward-looking effort at purging the community of guilt for crimes committed in the past.

Expiation was so widely accepted as a goal of capital punishment that it was felt even by criminals themselves, who were sometimes moved to plead guilty to capital offenses, a step that was close to suicide. Patience Boston was executed in 1735 for drowning an eight-year-old boy in a well. According to the minister who attended to her in her final days, she explained that she had pleaded guilty to a crime she knew to be capital, despite being advised to the contrary, because "I was so pressed in my Conscience to take the Guilt of Blood from the Land, on my self; that nothing could prevail with me to deny the Fact."[20]

The goals of deterrence and retribution were both furthered by the speed with which capital trials were conducted. On March 15, 1673, Virginia's General Court tried Richard Thomas and Mary Blades from start to finish, in two separate trials for unrelated murders, and then sentenced them to death, and that was only a small part of the day's business, which also included ruling on some land claims and a civil suit. On June 17, 1675, the Massachusetts Court of Assistants ran through four capital trials for piracy before turning to other cases. The length of time between the apprehension of a suspect and the trial was more variable, but only because the courts of the era sat intermittently. When a court session was scheduled soon after the criminal had been found, the trial would proceed without delay. William Linsey, executed in Worcester, Massachusetts, for burglary in 1770, stole a pillowcase full of items from a house while the occupants slept on the night of September 8. He was caught on September 9 and held for the next court sitting in Worcester, on September 22, when he was indicted by a grand jury, tried by a petit jury, convicted, and sentenced to death. "Thus have I been hurried on from one step to another," Linsey complained.[21]

Capital trials could be quick because they were not conceived of as adversarial proceedings, as they would come to be understood in the late eighteenth and early nineteenth centuries. Witnesses typically testified only on the government's behalf. The only lawyer normally involved in the case represented the government. Samuel Guile's 1675 rape trial in Massachusetts lasted only so long as was necessary to read "the Indictment & evidences" to the jury, which promptly convicted him. When a slave named Harry was tried in West New Jersey for "Buggering a Cow," the entire trial consisted of the testimony of two witnesses. Mary Myers related that she "saw him ride upon the Cow And that he was in Action as Buggering the Cow," and that "the Cow had the usuall Motions of Cows when they had taken the Bull." Her daughter said the same thing, whereupon Harry was convicted and sentenced to death. Only then was he asked whether he had anything to say.[22]

Speed served the twin purposes of retribution and deterrence. It meant that trials normally took place when the community's memory of the crime was still vivid and when the connection between the crime and the resulting legal proceedings was still perceived to be strong. It meant that trials focused on a single question, the guilt or innocence of the defendant, without any consideration of the multiple issues that crowd into a modern-day trial—the character of witnesses, the admissibility of evidence, the validity of searches and arrests, and so on. The link between cause and effect, between the commission of the crime and the imposition of the death sentence, was made as conspicuous as it could be.

It Concentrates His Mind

Capital punishment was also understood in the seventeenth and eighteenth centuries to facilitate the criminal's repentance. It was of paramount importance that one should die in the proper frame of mind, because on that mental state depended, in large part, one's eternal fate after death. One had to achieve a proper consciousness of God before it was too late. This was not an easy task for anyone, much less a criminal. Any person facing the prospect of this internal struggle was likely to procrastinate, on the assumption that death remained far in the future. The living often "squander away precious time in hopes of long Life," one minister lamented, "that should be bestowed in laying up Treasure in Heaven for a future and an eternal Estate." Criminals, who had to start from a deficit in this sort of treasure, were even more prone to delay.[23]

In this respect a death sentence was of inestimable value. We may remember Samuel Johnson's comment—"when a man knows he is to be hanged in a fortnight, it concentrates his mind wonderfully"—as satire, and when Johnson, one of the most prominent of the early English penal reformers, said it in 1777 it was taken that way, but in the seventeenth century and for most of the eighteenth it was no joke. Unlike other people, a condemned criminal knew well in advance the exact date of his death. He had a deadline, and the state was eager to help him meet it. "There is no Place in the World," marveled one minister, "where such Pains are taken with condemn'd Criminals to prepare them for their Death; that *in the Destruction of the Flesh, the Spirit may be saved in the Day of the Lord Jesus.*" The condemned person was normally allowed at least a week or two, and often several weeks, to get ready to die. If one took the long view, executed criminals were the lucky ones. Unlike ordinary people, "they were not snatched into eternity, from their wicked courses, in a moment, without time or opportunity to reflect on, and repent, of their misspent life, and the disregard they had paid to the commandments of God, or the laws of man."[24]

From the government's perspective, a delay of several weeks after sentencing had the added advantage of allowing time for publicizing the scheduled execution by word of mouth and in the newspapers, permitting interested spectators to make plans to attend. But the government also paid a price for the delay, a set of implicit costs high enough to suggest a consensus on the importance of the criminal's salvation. Delay between conviction and execution weakened the deterrent and retributive effects of capital punishment by attenuating the link between the crime and the punishment. Simply housing and feeding a condemned criminal in jail during the interim was a significant expense for units of colonial government that never took in much money. Risk of an even greater cost was posed by the likelihood that the condemned person would escape. Jails tended not to be very secure. Condemned criminals had very little to lose. Eighteenth-century records are full of inmates escaping after being sentenced to death. In Georgia alone between 1790 and 1805, at least nine people escaped from jail after being condemned to death—two for murder, two for forgery, and five for horse-stealing. (In the same period at least six more escaped while awaiting trial for a capital offense.) The burglar John Brown, sentenced to death in Connecticut, escaped from the Litchfield county jail twice. Escapes like these forced the government to pay people to pursue the prisoners. The expenses of twice recapturing John Brown, for example, formed a major part of the bill submitted to the Connecticut Assembly by William Stanton, Litchfield's jailer.[25]

Yet governments continued to allow sufficient time for repentance, and even to lengthen that time for individual criminals. When "Bristol a Negro Boy," sentenced on October 11, 1763, to be hanged on November 17, petitioned the governor of Massachusetts that he was "desirous of further time being allowed him to prepare for death," his execution was put off another two weeks. Knowing the importance that those in authority placed on repentance, condemned prisoners desperately seeking to delay their executions were careful to include appropriate references to their efforts in that direction. Moses Paul, awaiting his death in New Haven, pleaded with the Connecticut General Assembly "at least to postpone the time, the dreadful time of his execution which now seems near at Hand; that he may have a longer space for repentance, that he may, if possible, (tho' he escape not punishment from men) escape the Punishment of God thro' the merits of Christ and Faith in his Blood." It worked. Paul's execution was put off from May until September.[26]

While in jail awaiting execution, the condemned person was not alone. A steady stream of ministers came to call, armed with advice on how to prepare for the death and the afterlife that awaited. "The compassionate *Judges* always allow a considerable Time (commonly a *Month* at least) after the Sentence is pronounc'd, before the Execution is proceeded in," one Boston writer noted in 1733. "All this while they are visited, it may be every Day, by some or other of the *Ministers* of the Town, to instruct them, direct them, and pray with them." Ministering to those condemned to death was so routine that in 1791 William Smith could publish a guidebook for ministers—*The Convict's Visitor: or, Penitential Offices, (in the ancient way of liturgy) consisting of Prayers, Lessons, and Meditations; with suitable devotions before, and at the time of Execution*—made up largely of scripted dialogue between the minister and the condemned prisoner. The prison cell of a condemned person was in effect the minister's emergency room, the place where he believed his services to be needed most urgently. Between sentence and execution, "constant attention is given by some clergyman, or more, to the religious instruction of the convict . . . And scarce a murmur is ever heard, that too much is done for such an important object."[27]

As might be expected, the gist of the ministers' message was the need to repent before it was too late. "If you want pardon, look to a crucified Christ," Joshua Spalding pleaded with the murderer Isaac Coombs. "What thou doest, do quickly!" Ministers emphasized that while little remained of this life, there was still opportunity for forgiveness in the next. William Shaw "would die as a condemned criminal," his counselor told him, "yet being in Christ, you may be pardoned of God, and acquitted in the final judgment."[28]

These sessions were often successful, at least by the ministers' own accounts. When a condemned criminal could be brought to Christ, it was an occasion for singing and celebration. Christopher Flanagan reported that his last meeting with the murderer John Young was "more like a rational congratulatory visit to a bridegroom, or a man about to be put in possession of great earthly happiness, than a visit to one, who in a few hours was to suffer an ignominious death." When Francis Personel was sentenced to death, he recalled, "I saw myself out of Christ. I saw that I was under the curse of a broken law, that I was a child of hell, a bond slave to the Devil." But after a week of visits from ministers, "I saw that the blood of Christ was fully sufficient to cleanse from all sin and iniquity." Prisoners were often allowed to attend church on the day of worship preceding the execution, where they would find themselves the subject of the sermon. Sometimes the condemned person was allowed to choose the biblical text upon which the sermon was based. Jeremiah Fenwick, who chopped up his neighbor with an ax in 1717, asked for Matthew 10:28—"fear not them which kill the body, but are not able to kill the soul; but rather fear him which is able to destroy both soul and body in hell"—and Cotton Mather was happy to oblige him.[29]

The condemned prisoners could also turn these visits to their own short-term advantage. There were few things as useful in obtaining executive clemency as a conspicuous repentance, especially one achieved in the company of ministers who had the ear of the government. Once sentenced to death, a prisoner had little to lose by confessing his guilt and proclaiming his newfound faith. This incentive casts some doubt on the sincerity of many of the execution-eve conversions so prized by the ministers. Every so often the strategy was revealed. John Morrison, condemned for robbery in Pennsylvania in 1751, "pretended to be a Quaker, and sent for some Preachers of that Profession to discourse with and pray by him; hoping by their Interest he might find Favour" with the colony's Provincial Council, which considered applications for clemency. The preachers "soon discover'd that he had never really been a Quaker, and that his present Pretensions and Desire of their Prayers, were with a View rather of being sav'd in this World than in the next." Morrison's application for clemency was denied.[30]

If ministers considered themselves indispensable advisors, that view was not unanimous, least of all among the condemned prisoners. After hearing a sermon about himself, Hugh Stone muttered "diverse things very Scandalous; and I could wish there had been more exactness in his *Repentance*," Cotton Mather admitted. "I do not think he is fit to preach," protested Rose Butler about one insistent clergyman, whose primary advice to Butler, a nineteen-year-old slave soon to be executed for the arson of her owner's house, was that she was sure to go to hell. Ministers were often perceived, one of their own number realized, as meddlers "who created all that contempt for religious pretentions . . . which their hypocrisy excites, & which weakens all regard to true religion."[31] Repentance required acknowledgment of one's crime, so ministers found it necessary to press the condemned prisoners to confess, but for those who believed themselves to be innocent, such persistence felt more like accusation than comfort.

Stuck in a jail cell, unable to stem the tide of clerical visitors, prisoners who did not share the ministers' opinions fought back as best they could by giving voice to their own views of death, sin, and the value of the clergy. "Don't you imagine that men of liberal education are more intriguing, and do more frequently deceive the world than illiterate farmers," Thomas Goss asked the ministers who tried to attend to him. "And will you not allow that there are as many bad clergymen, in proportion to their number, as of any other sect?—As this is my opinion, why should I request their advice or prayers, in preference to others?" When asked whether he wished to have a sermon preached at his execution, Samuel Frost replied "that he did not care any thing about it . . . and said he believed the Devils wore large black wigs—and many other such expressions of folly and absurdity." The pirate William Fly flatly refused to attend church to hear the sermon preached about him. Sarah Smith, who killed an infant conceived long after her husband had been taken captive to French Canada, held firm in her view that there was nothing sinful about sex outside marriage, in the face of repeated prison lectures to the contrary.[32]

The ministers were flabbergasted when a condemned prisoner rejected their consolation. What thinking person, on the precipice of eternal suffering, would spurn the only path to salvation? "When we consider the great Advantages you have had, since your Trial and Condemnation," John Webb remonstrated with John Ormsby and Matthew Cushing, "in the unwearied pains which some of the faithful Ministers of Christ have taken with you . . . to lay before you the miserable State you are in," Webb could only conclude that "the Grace of God has been bestowed upon you in vain." "Since your Imprisonment, nay, since your Condemnation," complained Increase Mather to another uncooperative prisoner, "the Gospel has been offered to you . . . How shall you escape the forest Damnation, if you regard not this offer of mercy."[33]

Ministers were not the only visitors. Practically anyone wishing to enter the cell of a condemned prisoner was allowed to do so, and many prisoners had constant company in the days leading up to their deaths. The numbers of visitors often increased as the execution drew nearer. "No Place upon Earth does equal this Place for that Exercise of *Charity*," boasted Cotton Mather. "And this poor Creature"—Margaret Gaulacher, soon to be executed for infanticide—"has had a very particular Share thereof: Not only have the *Ministers* of the Gospel done their Part, in Visiting of her, but also many Private Christians have done theirs." Mather bestowed particular praise on the many "Young Gentlewomen here in their Turns, [who] have Charitably gone to the Prison every Day for diverse Weeks together, and because of her not being able to Read, have spent the Afternoons in Reading Portions of the Scriptures, and other Books of Piety, to this *Condemned Woman*."[34]

As with the ministers, there could be a fine line between Christian fellowship and curiosity, between welcome sympathy and haughty moralizing. Twelve-year-old Hannah Ocuish, sentenced to death for murder, had to endure a succession of "persons who made severe remarks upon her." So many tried to visit the New York prisoners Sinclair and Johnson, "some through idle curiosity—others to commiserate and pray with them," that guests had to be admitted in shifts of twenty. Many visitors badgered the condemned person for a confession, not to facilitate the criminal's repentance but to provide gossip for themselves. Condemned prisoners were also visited by their friends, people presumably more welcomed by the prisoner if not by his ministers. "Too many persons coming to" the murderer Jeremiah Meacham, one minister regretted, "and some of them none of the best, nor upon the best designs, very much hindered the well improvement of his flying time." The burglar Matthew Cushing, another complained, was visited by "vain and inconsiderate people that resorted to the prison yard," who "were almost continually calling to and talking with him, . . . so that he was once or twice sadly overcome with strong drink."[35] A condemned person's final days could thus lack time for what they were intended to accomplish—reflection on a life of crime and proper preparation for death.

Today one virtually never hears anyone cite the facilitation of penitence as an object of capital punishment, or indeed of any kind of punishment. We still call our prisons "penitentiaries," but we no longer think of them as sites of penitence. Penitence can be valued only by those who view criminals as people not fundamentally different from themselves. If criminals are thought of as alien, as not fully members of the human community, we have little reason to worry about the state of their souls. Before the late eighteenth century Americans tended to understand criminals as people like themselves, human beings who had been overcome by the same tendency toward evil that afflicted everyone, so the criminals' penitence was an object of common concern. During the nineteenth century, as Americans became more likely to see themselves as inherently virtuous, and accordingly to view criminals as more alien, the interest in criminals' penitence correspondingly waned.[36] At the same time, religion was beginning to occupy a sphere apart from public, political life. States disestablished religions, Christianity was ceasing to be considered a foundation of the law, and faith was gradually being redefined as a private matter, separate from the state and the government. To the extent that Americans were still interested in facilitating the repentance of criminals, they were less likely to want the official criminal justice system to play a part in that process. Penitence became the province of private ministries, not public institutions.

Capital punishment could command widespread support in the seventeenth and eighteenth centuries as a punishment for all serious crimes because it served three important purposes. One was deterrence. American officials used a variety of corporal and financial punishments for lesser crimes, and they resorted to banishment for more serious offenses, but in an era before the invention of the prison, virtually everyone agreed that such punishments were insufficient to deter the gravest crimes. A second purpose was retribution. When the cause of crime was widely conceived as the criminal's failure to control a natural human tendency toward evil, capital punishment was accepted as a legitimate act of retribution directed at a person responsible for his own actions. A failure to punish the crime would spread the criminal's guilt to the entire community. The third purpose was penitence. Repentance before death was widely considered indispensable, and a death sentence was thought uniquely able to facilitate repentance. Given these three premises, capital punishment made a great deal of sense.

The death penalty circa 1700 was the equivalent of prison today—the standard punishment for a wide range of serious crimes. Today people criticize our prisons for not working as well as they should, and colonial Americans sometimes leveled the same kind of criticism at the death penalty. But for all the faults of prisons, no one seriously proposes that we do without them. The same was true of capital punishment before the late eighteenth century. It fulfilled the moral expectations of most colonial Americans most of the time, and that was enough to make it the standard penalty for all serious crimes. Hardly anyone suggested that it be used more sparingly, much less that it be abandoned.

2

HANGING DAY

UNTIL THE NINETEENTH CENTURY, hangings were conducted
outdoors, often before thousands of spectators, as part of a larger ritual including a procession to the gallows, a sermon, and a speech by the
condemned prisoner. Hangings were not macabre spectacles staged for a
bloodthirsty crowd. A hanging was normally a somber event, like a
church service. Hanging day was a dramatic portrayal, in which everyone
could participate, of the community's desire to suppress wrongdoing. It
was a powerful symbolic statement of the gravity of crime and its consequences. The person hanged had been condemned in court weeks earlier, but hanging day was a second, more collective condemnation—of
the individual and of crime in general. We have no comparable ritual
today.

The ceremony surrounding an execution could take several hours. It
began in jail, where the condemned person, sometimes dressed in a special robe, began the procession to the gallows. The prisoner was accompanied by ministers, by the sheriff and his deputies, and sometimes by a
military escort as well. The time and the route of the procession were
public knowledge, so any condemned person could expect large crowds
all the way from jail to the gallows, where an even larger crowd awaited.
The sheriff read the death warrant aloud and sometimes added his own
comments. At least one minister, and sometimes several, gave a sermon.
The condemned prisoner typically delivered a speech of his own. The
people on the scaffold might lead the audience in the singing of a hymn.
Finally a cap was pulled over the prisoner's face, the rope was adjusted,
and the prisoner dropped. The whole ceremony was public, outdoors,
and as conspicuous as any event could possibly be.

An Odd Sort of Curiosity

Because a hanging was open to anyone who wished to attend, there was no reliable way to count the spectators, but that did not stop contemporaries from trying. Esther Rodgers was hanged for infanticide in Boston in 1701 before a crowd of at least four or five thousand, her minister estimated, at a time when Boston's population was only around seven thousand. Joshua Hempstead, a farmer and justice of the peace in New London, Connecticut, watched the execution of Sarah Bramble in 1753 and guessed the crowd to number ten thousand, more than three times the number of New London's inhabitants. Daniel Wilson, a Providence rapist, drew more than twelve thousand in 1774, nearly three times the population of Providence. These crowds would grow even larger in the early nineteenth century. Over thirty thousand spectators watched from the surrounding hills as Jesse Strang was hanged in Albany, New York, in 1827, and fifty thousand were said to have watched the murderer John Johnson hanged in New York City in 1824.[1]

These were among the biggest crowds Americans had ever seen. The New London gallows that hanged Katherine Garret, an Indian convicted of infanticide in 1738, "was surrounded with a Vast Circle of people," marveled Eliphalet Adams, "more Numerous, perhaps, than Ever was gathered together before, on any Occasion, in this Colony."[2] The only other reasons so many gathered in a single place were to wage war and to hear celebrated ministers. Well into the nineteenth century, execution crowds still outnumbered crowds gathered for any other purpose.

One reason crowds were so big was that in any given area an execution was a rare event. When Sarah Simpson and Penelope Kenny were hanged for infanticide in Portsmouth, New Hampshire, in the winter of 1739, the ceremony "drew together a vast Concourse of People, and probably the greater, because these were the first Executions that ever were seen in this Province." Much of York County, Maine, flocked to the hanging of Joseph Quasson in the summer of 1726, "there having been no such Example in the County for more than seventy Years." In rural areas, hanging day was a rare occasion for the gathering of large numbers of people. In more thickly settled areas, executions were more frequent, but the pool of people within traveling distance was also bigger, so the numbers of spectators could mount. The 1686 hanging of James Morgan in Boston was considered "a Piece of News," one witness reported, so much so that "some have come 50 miles to see it." Richard Doane, hanged in Hartford in 1797, was the first person executed there in seven years, long enough to draw "a large concourse of people collected from the neighbouring towns."[3] Nearly all Americans in the seventeenth and eighteenth centuries could have seen a hanging at some point in their lives, but outside the largest towns it would have been a rare experience, and even in the largest towns several years might pass between executions.

Execution crowds could be so large that many of their members had little hope of actually seeing the events on the scaffold. A broadside commemorating the 1734 hanging of John Ormsby and Matthew Cushing included a wry comment on the ceremony's logistics:

> Then they arrive at th' Gallows Tree,
>   While Spectators lament and cry;
> Alas! how hard it is to see,
>   Much more to feel their Destiny.

Hearing the speeches was even more difficult. The sheer distance between the scaffold and the farthest members of the crowd, coupled with the noise made by spectators themselves, meant that even many of those who could see were doubtless unable to hear. Olivia Robbins of Troy, New York, went to a hanging in 1811, but, as she told her sister, "I did not hear enough of the discourses to give you any statement of them."[4]

Closer to the front, however, spectators at an execution had a degree of contact with the condemned person that would be unimaginable today. Participation in the ceremony was not limited to those with an official role to play. Spectators who were close enough could ask questions of the prisoner and hope to get them answered, take their final leave if he was a friend, or join him in prayer. Sometimes they could even inspect his body after the hanging was over.

In the larger cities, crowd sizes posed a dilemma for the officials responsible for staging the ceremony. Hangings had to be in open spaces that could accommodate several thousand spectators, but they could not be so far from settled areas that mass attendance would be impractical. The Common Council of the City of New York wrestled with this problem for decades. In 1784, after execution crowds trampled their property, the residents of Chatham Street and Tryon Row pleaded with the Council to move the city's gallows farther away from their houses. The Council complied, but in 1811 the issue arose again. At the city's first execution in five years, spectators had sat on and destroyed the fences and tree branches of one Elizabeth Glover, who demanded that the city reimburse her for the damage. The 1824 hanging of John Johnson, said to have attracted an audience of fifty thousand, prompted similar claims. New York had only recently stopped hanging burglars and robbers, men who did not have sufficient respect for the rights of private property, so it would hardly do for the hanging ceremony itself to commit the same offense. Officials began staging executions on uninhabited islands in the harbor, where spectators could watch from boats without trespassing on private property. (The federal government had already conducted at least one hanging on a ship moored in the East River, and would continue to use islands long after the state had moved its executions into the jail yard.) In Philadelphia, where hangings were often held on an island in the Delaware River, the crowds along the wharves could grow so large that the people living near the river would abandon their homes for the day.[5] Without sufficient open space, it was not easy to strike the appropriate balance between public instruction and private rights.

Public executions would be widely criticized in the nineteenth century, and much of the criticism would be directed at the crowd, who would be accused of drunkenness, irreverence, rowdiness, and similar sins. Respectable Americans of the nineteenth century would come to feel embarrassment at the idea of attending an execution, and a superiority to the sort of person who would attend. Those sentiments were rare in the eighteenth century. People occasionally complained about the crowd's behavior, as in this broadside poem written a few days before the 1773 hanging of Levi Ames:

> See! round the Prison how the Throng
>   From every Quarter pour;
> Some mourn with sympathising Tongue,
>   The ruder Rabble roar.

John Bryson recalled attending a hanging in Fredericksburg, Virginia, in the late eighteenth century at which one spectator was caught picking the pocket of another just as the cart drove off. This kind of anecdote would become commonplace in the nineteenth century. But so far as one can tell today, eighteenth-century American execution crowds were usually not noisy or drunk or disrespectful. Indeed, when the earliest American opponents of capital punishment wished to argue that frequent public hangings instilled in spectators a lighthearted attitude toward violence, they had to cite examples of *English* execution crowds, for want of appropriate examples at home.[6]

An execution was "a most sad mellancholly scene," as one spectator put it. The diaries of upstanding citizens mention watching executions with the same matter-of-fact tone they use for describing the weather. "At Townhill to See Kate the Indian Woman Hanged for murdering her Bastard Infant at Saybrook last year & thn home," the Connecticut justice of the peace Joshua Hempstead noted in his diary in 1738. "By the way," the Baptist minister Isaac Backus wrote in his, "Mr. Reed at Abington told me that he was at Boston yesterday and See Willm. Wicer hanged for murdering one Chism last April."[7] There was nothing unseemly about going to an execution.

Indeed, a hanging was considered an especially wholesome experience for children. The midwife Martha Ballard sent her daughter Dolly and her son Ephraim to see Edmund Fortis hanged in Maine, two years after she had helped Fortis's wife deliver their first child. "Only 13 boys were in school," the lawyer Henry Van Der Lyn's son reported the day George Denison was hanged in Chenango County, New York. "The rest had gone to see the execution." Ministers and condemned criminals often went out of their way to speak directly to "the *Younger Sort*, wh[o] usually appear on such an Occasion."[8]

The ministers emphasized the pedagogical value of attending an execution, but everyone knew that much of the motivation for attendance was simple curiosity. Death itself was a common enough sight—family members died in the home, not in hospitals—but not death in such a spectacular form. "From the vast Numbers of People who constantly attend at all publick Executions, and from thence return, either indolently indifferent, or extremely commiserating," said a pamphlet published in Boston, "'tis evident to common Observation, that there is an odd Sort of Curiosity, implanted in the Nature of some People, which prompts them to see, with a kind of Pleasure, the Sufferings of their Fellow Creatures."[9] A hanging was *fascinating*, in a way that aroused no embarrassment. Today we perceive no shame in attending films that use special effects to simulate death; in the eighteenth century people felt the same way about attending hangings that caused real death. And the hanging was only a small part of the ceremony, which included a parade, a sermon or two, sometimes delivered by men who were celebrities in their own right, and a dramatic speech by the condemned person, who was on the verge of death and so worth hearing regardless of his or her level of eloquence. What could be more interesting?

What criticism of execution crowds existed in the eighteenth century tended to come from ministers, who were unhappy not with the crowd's deportment but with its state of mind. The clergy wanted to teach a moral lesson, not to entertain, but they were afraid they were doing more of the latter than the former. "Here is a vast number of people met together this day," Ephraim Clark observed at the hanging of the murderer Solomon Goodwin, "and God and your own consciences know best what ends you have in view in coming; whether to satisfy your curiosity, or that you might reap some good to yourselves from the heart-affecting scene." The ministers' enemy was not frivolity but curiosity. "Now, tho' *Curiosity* might move many Persons to come and behold those sad Objects," William Shurtleff conceded, "I would charitably hope that many came from a *better Principle*." The "numerous Audience of Christians" addressed by William Williams "are together, not out of Curiosity, we trust, but in a serious Frame, with their Hearts affected, to consider the sorrowful Effects of Sin."[10] Williams's tone suggested that he was not optimistic.

Curiosity was often accompanied by sympathy. The ceremony focused public attention on a fellow human being who would shortly die. Much of the ceremony was devoted to displaying the condemned person's penitence and readiness for the afterlife. As a result, a criminal who had been despised weeks earlier could find a very different reception at his hanging. Ebenezer Mason killed his brother-in-law W. P. Allen, but at the execution the mourning was not for Allen:

> Mason, alas! we mourn for you;
> Sentenc'd to die, as murderers do.

Condemned prisoners had a forum in which to dramatize their humanity. Esther Rodgers murdered her baby, but several months later, before four or five thousand spectators, she demonstrated such "Composure of Spirit, Cheerfulness of Countenance, pleasantness of Speech, and a sort of Complaisantness in Carriage towards the Ministers" that memories of the murder were superseded by very different feelings. Rodgers "melted the hearts of all that were within seeing or hearing, into Tears of affection, with greatest wonder and admiration."[11]

The broadside poetry sold at hangings was awash with this sort of sympathy. A typical verse was inspired by the hanging of the burglar Hugh Henderson in 1737.

> O HENDERSON! unhappy Man!
> How did'st thou feel, when in thy Ken,
> The best was Horror, like Despair,
> Amazing Doubt, or anxious Fear?
> What Pangs, what Extasys of Smart
> Convuls'd thy poor, thy bleeding Heart,
> When in that State, were bro't to Mind
> Th' unnumber'd Crimes of Life behind?

Sympathy could only have been increased by the recognition that all concerned worshiped a God who, in his terrestrial form, had himself been publicly executed. The metaphor of the hanging tree allowed one poet to compare Christ with the burglar Levi Ames:

> He died the death of the accursed tree,
> That from the sting of death you might be free.

"Unhappy wretch!" began one sympathetic fictionalized account of a hanging, "This day thou must be launched into eternity!"[12]

The ceremony broadcast deterrence, but the message was one of sympathy as well. "Methinks there is none of you, but what must find your bowels yearning towards him," Thaddeus Maccarty observed.[13] The object of this yearning was a twenty-one-year-old black rapist named Arthur, not the sort of person likely to have attracted much sympathy in any other context. The execution ceremony, with all attention focused on the prisoner, facilitated the perception of the condemned person as a victim of sorts himself.

Public sympathy for condemned criminals did not, in the colonial period, translate into opposition to capital punishment. One could deplore the fate of an individual person without criticizing the general laws under which all were governed.

To see her when she's just condemn'd
does make my heart to ache,
But God I know is just and true
and this just law did make.

So concluded one spectator at the 1744 hanging of Elizabeth Shaw, with whom one could sympathize without casting any doubt on the justice of the death penalty for infanticide. And at the execution of the murderer Ebenezer Ball:

But though we pity this poor BALL,
Which we all do, I trust,
Yet when we know for what he dy'd,
We own his sentence just.[14]

This would begin to change in the late eighteenth century, as more and more spectators would translate their sympathy for the condemned prisoners into opposition to capital punishment generally.

In the seventeenth and eighteenth centuries hangings were genuinely popular. All kinds of people came to watch—old and young, rich and poor, white and black, male and female—in numbers that were enormous for the era. For the spectators there were at least three reasons to see an execution. First, violent entertainment has been popular in all cultures, and colonial America was no exception. Hangings were occasions for the vicarious experience of violence, a niche occupied today by television, movies, sports, video games, and the like. *Why* people enjoy watching violence is a difficult question, one that has only recently begun to receive much study. Violent entertainment does not appear to have a cathartic effect; that is, spectators tend to be more aggressive, not less, after watching violence. Spectators don't seem to feel a need to purge themselves of violent feelings; rather, they enjoy those feelings and seek low-risk opportunities for experiencing them, for reasons that are not well understood.[15] The ministers' repeated references in their execution sermons to the spectators' "curiosity" suggests that the appeal of violence was part of the attraction of a hanging.

Second, an execution was a dramatic portrayal of community at the moment when the fear of danger to the community was at its highest. Crime, then as now, prompted a terror of disorder. At a hanging, where the criminal's repentance and God's forgiveness took center stage, the instigator of that terror could be symbolically reintegrated into society. Reintegration was only symbolic, of course—it took place just before the criminal was dropped from a height with a noose around his neck—and so it was of no terrestrial benefit to the condemned person himself, but the gain to the spectators was the demonstration that the rupture had been repaired and the community was back to normal. This was not just an intellectual experience for audience members. There could be no more viscerally powerful way to banish the terror of crime than to feel a genuine sympathy for the criminal, an emotion that was possible only because the staging of a hanging allowed sympathy to be experienced at a safe distance. No one sympathizes with a killer on the loose, but anyone can sympathize with a killer on the gallows.

Because sympathy for the individual did not translate into opposition to that individual's punishment, sympathy was not inconsistent with a third reason for spectators to attend executions. Watching a hanging allowed spectators to signify, in the strongest possible way, their disapproval of crime and the criminal. The ritual of hanging day put the words of the criminal law into practice, in the clearest and most dramatic way possible. By attending, a spectator could witness and participate in a depiction, literally in the flesh, of the community's most important norms, those proscribing grave crimes. For each person in the crowd, the ceremony reinforced the community's concern with crime. At the same time, each spectator by his simple presence in effect declared his membership in that same community and his adherence to those same norms. Despite their sympathy with the condemned prisoner as a person, spectators were not there to take his side against the state. If they had been asked to declare their allegiance, the vast majority would have sided with the government. Hangings were not the only public ceremonies with these symbolic effects. People watched the infliction of lesser kinds of public punishment, and they flocked to courts to watch the proceedings there. But hangings were bigger, rarer, and more exciting. There was no other occasion on which the community's interest in crime and its consequences was made so manifest.

A Very Profitable Spectacle

"There are certain miserable People to bee executed on the morrow," Cotton Mather noted in his diary in 1681. "A Man, for a Rape; and Two

Negroes, for Burning of Houses, and Persons in them. What use am I to make of this?"

Mather knew very well how he would use the hangings. They would provide an occasion for him to consider his own nature and the spiritual tasks that lay ahead. "Lett mee, with deep *Humiliation* reflect on the Vileness of my own Heart," his diary entry continued. "Alas, I have the Seed of all Corruption in mee." Such reflection would be of immeasurable benefit to Mather at the moment of his death, but Mather doubtless also had an eye on the more tangible gains to be had in the short term. An execution was an occasion for a sermon, and not just any sermon, but a sermon delivered before a crowd that could be hundreds of times larger than normal. The scaffold was the minister's stage, the gallows his spotlight. With a single sermon, heard by thousands and then perhaps published and read by thousands more, a minister could inject more good into the world than on any other occasion. Not incidentally, he could also make a career. Mather rejoiced when, "by a very strange Providence, without any Seeking of *mine*," an execution was rescheduled to permit him to speak. "I did then with the special Assistance of Heaven, make and preach, a Sermon," Mather recalled. "Whereat one of the greatest Assemblies, ever known in these parts of the World, was come together." "I may never have another opportunity of addressing so immense an assembly," another minister realized. For minister and spectators alike, an execution could be "a very *miserable*, but . . . also a very *profitable* Spectacle."[16]

The profit to the spectators was understood by the ministers to reside in the uniquely clear view an execution provided of the consequences of sin. Execution sermons consistently urged spectators to seize the opportunity to reflect on their own sinfulness, and thereby to profit from the mistakes of others. "When you see this sad consequence of indulging vice," exhorted Andrew Eliot, "let it make you watchful against your own corruptions."[17]

Ministers frequently sermonized about the particular sins most likely to be practiced by members of the audience. Few spectators had committed murder, but many were drinkers, so at the hanging of a murderer there was more to be gained by addressing the evils of drink than those of murder. "And indeed, *Drunkenness* has bin a bloody sin," Increase Mather lectured; "it has bin the cause of many a Murder." Few had committed infanticide, as Abiel Converse had, but infanticide was the product of fornication, and fornication was a much more popular offense, so it was the theme adopted by Aaron Bascom at Converse's hanging. "The practice of young people of both sexes keeping company together," said Bascom, "I think is a detestable practice: It is carried on in many instances no doubt, to gratify lust." Few were rapists, like the free Negro Anthony, but "the transition in the crime of lewdness, from little to great, is alike easy, and almost unavoidable."[18] The message was repeated in countless execution sermons: small sins lead inevitably to big ones, which carry grave penalties, so it was important to avoid even the small.

Sin was on stage, but so too was forgiveness. An execution was an unparalleled opportunity to display the power of salvation. The sermons routinely described the condemned prisoner's efforts at repentance, if there were any to describe, and assured the spectators that those efforts could not have been made in vain. If even condemned criminals, the worst sinners in the world, could find forgiveness in Christ, then members of the audience were reminded that they could do the same. The sermons carried both a negative and a positive message: avoid sin, and don't waste any opportunities to seek forgiveness.

With thousands listening, the ministers could hardly have been expected to stop there. Many used the occasion to buttress their own positions. A consistent message delivered in execution sermons was the importance of paying attention to ministers—not just at hangings, but every day. "Shall we begin, with the mention of that, which is the usual Beginning of all Wickedness?" asked Cotton Mather. "That is to say, Sabbath-breaking . . . Yes, By breaking the *Fourth Commandment* they come to the vilest Breaches of all the rest." In Dedham, Massachusetts, Thaddeus Harris cautioned his listeners against reading "idle and romantic books . . . written with a design to contradict the evidences and destroy the authority of religion." In New York Hezekiah Woodruff addressed "the friends of the prisoner, if any are present," to persuade them of "the importance of cultivating, more particularly, an acquaintance with Christian people" like himself.[19] An execution could be a splendid occasion for reinforcing religious authority.

And with the power of the state on display, an execution was perfect for underscoring secular authority as well. Spectators were urged to "reverence, then, in silence the majesty of the laws—and consider that the existence of your comforts, privileges and advantages depends on the execution of them." At the 1819 hanging of Rose Butler, a New York City slave convicted of setting fire to her owner's house, the Baptist minister John Sandford directed his remarks to the black spectators. "The wings of the Constitution of America are extended to defend and foster the property, the liberties, and the lives of all its citizens, without exception," he began. "In this inestimable privilege, our fellow citizens of *color* enjoy a mutual share with us; and this unquestionably should dictate to them a corre-spondent spirit of gratitude and the practice of every social virtue. It is therefore deeply to be regretted that persons of color should either envy or attempt to destroy the safety and comfort to which we are justly entitled."[20] Hierarchies of all kinds could be explained and justi-fied at hangings by ministers who worked such messages into their sermons.

Even apart from their substantive message, the sermons were a form of drama in their own right. "You deserve to suffer the eternal pains of hell, it is just in God to send you to the hopeless regions of the damned," Tim-othy Pitkin screeched at the murderer John Jacobs before an appreciative audience. Spectators did not need to agree with the theology to be enter-tained by the rhetoric. "The Horrors of bloody & cruel *Murder* have is-sued in public, infamous strangling & Death," ranted Ebenezer Parkman before Bathsheba Spooner's execution for killing her husband in 1768, "and such cruel, unnatural loathsome *Murder* has been preceded by de-testable uncleanness, by *repeated*, if, I say, not *multiplyd* acts of unfaith-fulness to the conjugal Bonds, & defiling the Marriage Bed."[21] Speeches rarely got this racy in the eighteenth century, except at executions. That alone must have accounted for some of the popularity of execution ser-mons. A great deal of private life saw the light of day in these speeches, behavior to which the community had access on few other occasions. The ministers' persistent reminders to the crowd that a hanging involved more than just entertainment suggest that the ministers themselves had some doubts about how the spectators were profiting from the event.

The sermon remained a standard part of the execution ceremony as long as executions were held in public, through the first half of the nine-teenth century in the North and well into the twentieth in parts of the South. After executions were moved into the jail yard and the sermon was abandoned, ministers would remain on hand to counsel the condemned prisoners and to lead those present in prayer. Even today, when execu-tions are attended by only a few carefully chosen spectators and officials, there is often a clergyman in the room, a vestige of a time when the clergy played an important role in political life, when the line between secular and religious power was not drawn as sharply as it is today.

The Hangman's Office

Ministers had the luxury of restricting themselves to the execution's spiritual aspects. They did not have to build the gallows, or adjust the rope, or pull the lever that would release the trap door. These physical tasks—the actual steps toward death—typically fell to the sheriff of the county in which the prisoner had been tried. A sheriff was "to make Execution, in Cases Civil and Criminal," instructed George Webb's 1736 manual for Virginia justices of the peace. For "Executing a Person condemn'd," Virginia sheriffs were to receive 250 pounds of tobacco.[22]

In England and elsewhere in Europe, death sentences were carried out by professional executioners, specialists loathed by the public. Massachusetts began with professionals. The "executioner Thomas Bell" appears in government records beginning in 1649, when by virtue of his office he was excused from taking his turn on the night watch. Maryland found it so difficult to appoint an executioner that the colony turned to a succession of criminals, each of whom was reprieved from a death sentence in exchange for agreeing to serve as hangman for a term of years or life. The first of these was apparently the murderer John Dandy, who became Maryland's executioner in 1643. Later hangmen included Pope Alvey, sentenced to death for stealing a cow; John Oliver, sentenced to death for the theft of seven shillings sixpence; and James Douglas, sentenced to death for stealing a horse bridle and saddle. But this system did not last long in Massachusetts or Maryland, and if it existed in other colonies it did not endure there either. By 1693 responsibility for Massachusetts executions rested with the county sheriff.[23] Other colonies were already conducting executions through their local sheriffs.

The duties of a sheriff encompassed the entire execution, from the erection of the gallows to the disposition of the corpse. (Because hangings were rare events in most places, few counties had a permanent gallows. Gallows were typically constructed for a hanging and dismantled afterward.) The sheriffs tended to delegate these responsibilities when they could. When Caleb Gardner was sentenced to death in Albany, New York, the sheriff promptly placed an advertisement in the local newspaper soliciting applications from persons willing to undertake the execution.[24]

The bills submitted by sheriffs for reimbursement often included entries for payments to several other people for actually carrying out the hanging. It was not easy to kill a fellow human being, even when the law required it.

Some of the surviving bills are soaked so thoroughly in liquor as to suggest that hangings were far from somber backstage. For the 1669 hanging of Angle Hendricks in New York, the sheriff, John Manning, disbursed one pound five shillings in "French wine to the Carpenters" and another eleven shillings in "Brandy to the Carpenters," for building the gallows; three pounds in money and eight shillings in brandy and wine to "the Executioner" for hanging Hendricks; two pounds in brandy and two pounds four shillings in wine "to the Carrmen & Porters" for carrying Hendricks and her coffin from jail to the gallows and from the gallows to her grave; as well as another pound spent on "more Wine and Beere." John Reynolds, in charge of Philadelphia's Walnut Street Jail, submitted a bill in 1780 that included "3 bowls of punch at putting up the gallows to Hang Dawson and Chamberlain," "3 bowls and a half of Toddy after the Execution," "3 bowls of Toddy at putting up the gallows on the island," and "Toddy for the Constables for hanging Sutton."[25] The managers of most hangings were not experts; they were local officials and contractors who typically had little opportunity to acquire any experience. The ever-present liquor must have been intended in part to strengthen the nerve of the participants in a difficult and gruesome task.

When a sheriff could find no one willing to carry out the work for money and drink, he might induce another condemned prisoner to do the job in exchange for a reprieve. Sheriffs did not have the authority to grant reprieves themselves, but the courts and governors that did possess that authority were willing to cooperate. Isaac Bradford, sentenced to death in Pennsylvania for robbery, was relieved of his own sentence in exchange for hanging two burglars. "A *very hard choice*," the newspaper called it. In Massachusetts John Battus was hanged by a fellow prisoner. A Maryland slave named Tony was sentenced to be the executioner of his four co-defendants, fellow slaves, who had been convicted of killing their owner.[26]

When the sheriff could find no hangman, the job fell to him. "Last week one Robert Roberts was hanged" in Somerset County, New Jersey, the *Pennsylvania Gazette* reported in 1731, "and the Sheriff not being able to procure an Executioner, was necessitated to perform the Office himself." But not all sheriffs were willing to conduct hangings themselves. In New York one 1762 double hanging had to be postponed when the sheriff could not find anyone to act as hangman. "The Sheriff informs me that he has taken all Possible Measures that the Time will allow to procure a Hangman for the two Persons that were to have been executed this morning & that he can procure None," Chief Justice Benjamin Pratt informed Governor Cadwallader Colden. "I think it would be hard to oblige the Sheriff to act the Hangman's Office in Person if it could be avoided." Before the hanging of Patience Boston in Maine there was considerable uncertainty as to who would do the work, so Boston made her own preferences known. She was "unwilling the common Whipper should Execute her, because he is an idle Man, and will misspend the Money he gets," she explained, and added that "*Sambo* a Negro should not do it, because it would be a dishonour to the Church of which he is a Member."[27] The sheriff himself was not even in the picture.

American officials of the seventeenth and eighteenth centuries were often not as severe as the penal codes they were charged with enforcing. With a few early exceptions they were not the experienced professional executioners of Europe, a caste traditionally shunned by others. They were ordinary citizens. They avoided the job of hangman when they could, and when they could not they dissolved their apprehensions in liquor. When the hanging was over, they were ordinary citizens once again. In the American colonies responsibility for conducting hangings was, for want of a better word, democratized. It was moved from a small set of specialists to a diffuse group of amateurs, where it would remain as long as executions were conducted by hanging. This diffusion of responsibility to nonprofessionals would contribute, in the late nineteenth and early twentieth centuries, to the United States assuming the lead in developing alternatives to hanging. In the seventeenth and eighteenth centuries the amateur hangmen reinforced the communal nature of capital punishment. Executions were often conducted by true representatives of the community, men without any specialized training, men who were known to the spectators as friends and neighbors. A professional executioner might be seen as an agent of the central government, but an American sheriff was a member of the local community. Acted out through the sheriff or his hired hand, the hanging ceremony embodied norms that were truly popular.

But if the death penalty was almost universally supported as just punishment, the difficulty of finding executioners suggests that it could prompt revulsion in specific instances. There was a tension between the general and the particular, between the approval of death as a punishment and a strong reluctance to carry out the distasteful steps necessary to put that punishment into practice. The tension would only intensify in later years. In the nineteenth and twentieth centuries it would result in the abolition both of public execution and of hanging itself.

A Very Sensible Trembling

And what did the ceremony mean to the condemned prisoners? The murderer Barnett Davenport was terrified. The burglar Levi Ames literally trembled with fear. "No Mortal, except the Sufferer, can form any adequate Conception of that Terror which seizes the Soul of a Person doomed to suffer such an exquisitely shocking and shameful Death," John Shearman is supposed to have said, and if the precise wording is too flowery to credit, the sentiment was widely enough shared to be taken as accurate. At the sight of the gallows the counterfeiter David Reynolds "burst into Tears," and even hardened pirates "seemed much distressed, and continued crying to God." The Annapolis robber James Powell fainted away in his cart at the conclusion of the sermon, and had to be revived in order to be hanged.[28] The stars of the execution ceremony could look forward to pain and death under the close inspection of thousands. Many were understandably frightened.

Many others were angry. One Boston pirate "broke out into furious Expression" laden with profanities. A woman hanged in Maryland for eating her own child in the midst of famine "cried out to the people, in the presence of the governor, that . . . what she had done she did in the mere delirium of hunger, for which the governor alone should bear the guilt," because his military expeditions were the cause of the famine. John Young, who murdered a deputy sheriff who was trying to serve process on him, took advantage of his moment on the scaffold to decry New York's "oppression of the Unfortunate" in the form of laws facilitating the collection of debts.[29] Many of the condemned prisoners had spent months in jail, nursing grievances that exploded on hanging day.

The public display of emotion was limited in many cases by an ethic, inherited from England and widely shared, of "dying game" — of putting up a front of conspicuous unconcern as a way of defying the authorities. The Pennsylvania murderer John "McDonald died game, as it is called by such wretches," recalled Charles Biddle. "A gentleman present when he was led pinioned and put in the cart for execution, observed he believed he had seen him before, wheeling oysters about the streets of Philadelphia. 'Yes,' says he, 'you may have seen me before, wheeling oysters, and if you will wait until Jack Ketch has done with me, I'll turn round, that you may see me behind and know me better at our next meeting.'" The condemned person, surrounded by force, could not offer any meaningful physical resistance, so this sort of psychological resistance was all he had. The pirate William Fly, hanged in Boston in 1726, "seem'd all along ambitious to have it said, *That he died a brave fellow!*" remembered a disbelieving Cotton Mather. Fly "pass'd along to the place of Execution, with a *Nosegay* in his hand, and making his *Complements*, where he *thought he saw occasion*. Arriving there, he nimbly mounted the Stage, and would fain have put on a Smiling Aspect." Fly even "reproached the Hangman, for not understanding his Trade, and with his own Hands rectified matters."[30]

The condemned prisoner had to acknowledge that the state had won his body, but he could do his best to demonstrate that he had not lost his spirit. "I shall go to the gallows, just as free as any other person would take a pinch of snuff," John Banks asserted. An unnamed slave hanged in Annapolis "behav'd with as much resolution and unconcernedness as possibly could be: As he rode to the gallows he sung all the way with the executioner (who was one of his colour) a Negro Song . . . about war and fighting in their own country." Elizabeth Atwood, who was hanged for infanticide in Ipswich, Massachusetts, in 1725, believing that the executioner would be given her clothing, dressed her worst, and on the way to the gallows exclaimed, "I am laughing to think what a sorry suit the hangman will get from me."[31] Lurking beneath all the bravado, however, was an unmistakable terror, which sometimes showed through the mask. After William Fly's execution, it was Cotton Mather who could have the last laugh. "In the midst of all his affected *Bravery*," Mather noted, "a very sensible *Trembling* attended him; His hands and his *Knees* were plainly seen to *Tremble*."[32]

The condemned prisoners knew they were expected to address the crowd. "It is customary for Wretches under my unhappy Circumstances to say something at the Place of Execution, to satisfy the World," John Lewis recognized. The horse thief John Clarkewight acknowledged that "it may be expected that I will give some short account to the world." Few passed up the opportunity. For some, it was the last chance to declare their innocence. "I solemnly declare I had no enmity against Capt. Drowne, nor do I know how it happened," proclaimed Elisha Thomas, convicted of Drowne's murder. "I never had any intention of taking the life of any fellow mortal, whatever." *"I am innocent of what is laid to my Charge,"* pleaded John Ury, convicted as one of the conspirators in New York's 1741 "Negro Plot." The gallows speech provided an occasion for getting back at the witnesses whose testimony had sent the condemned person to his death. "As my Life is short I have one Thing to say that Isaac Miller, who swore against me was FALSE," argued John Smith just before he was hanged for counterfeiting. One could accomplish the same end more subtly with a sarcastic display of charity. "Four of the Men, who perjur'd themselves, and are the only Means of my Blood being innocently shed, I heartily forgive, and pray God to forgive them likewise," Joseph Lightly announced at his hanging for the murder of his female companion; "and as to the Woman who was my reputed Wife, she died with a Lie in her Mouth, but I freely forgive her."[33]

Genuine charity was not absent. George Burns and two other men were condemned for robbery in Charleston, South Carolina, but just before his hanging Burns exonerated the other two, who were later pardoned. The Virginia murderer John Sparks attested to the innocence of the man who had been sentenced to die with him, whose execution was then called off.[34] On the gallows a condemned criminal had nothing to lose by helping a colleague.

The hope of clemency was often present to the end. If they were to have any hope of avoiding death, the condemned prisoners could not say or do anything to detract from a conspicuous display of good character. As a result, the gallows speech was for the most part the most formulaic of genres, with near-obligatory recitals of a life's misdeeds and warnings to the audience to stay on the right path. The genre was a staple of English executions, at which the condemned prisoners faced the same set of incentives, and it became common in North America as well.[35] On the verge of death, condemned criminals felt the force of convention more strongly than ever.

The moral of the gallows speech, echoing that of the sermon, was that small malefactions would lead inevitably to grave ones. "I know not where to begin the black Catalogue of my Sins," Matthew Cushing declared, "except with my undutifulness to my Parents, which is enough to lead on to all others." The condemned person was accordingly expected to provide a full criminal record, which served as evidence both of penitence and of credibility to deliver the warning that would follow. "I was guilty of many small Thefts while very Young," began the burglar Stephen Smith, who then traced the progression of his career to bigger burglaries and robberies. "When I was about ten Years old I betook myself to stealing small Things, such as Fruit, Knives and Spoons," admitted William Welch, to demonstrate how theft could lead to robbery and robbery to murder.[36]

The message of the inevitable progress of sin was reinforced by the poetry published in connection with executions, much of which was written in the voice of the condemned person (although most was not likely to have been written *by* the condemned person).

> The dreadful Deed for which I die,
> Arose from small Beginning;
> My idleness brought poverty
> And so I took to Stealing.

Such was the tale attributed to Levi Ames, hanged in 1773 for burglary. A generation later, readers could learn the same lesson:

> But those who deal in lesser sins,
> In great will soon offend;
> And petty thefts, not check'd betimes,
> In murder soon may end.

No matter how small, and whether or not he had been caught, every sin ever committed by the condemned prisoner was understood as a predictor of his eventual fate. Even activities that seemed harmless at the time could be recognized in retrospect as seeds of crime. Samuel Smith's road to burglary had begun, he now saw, when "I fell in company with a female of whom I was foolishly and extravagantly fond, but at length I found her heart was corrupt." The disappointment led to liquor, and the liquor led to capital crime.[37]

After completing his own history, the condemned person was expected to warn those spectators who might be starting down the same road. "Avoid bad company, excessive drinking, prophane cursing and swearing, shameful debaucheries, disobedience to parents, the profanation of the Lord's day, &c." advised three murderers. In that "&c.," probably inserted by the publisher, was a recognition of how routine these warnings could be. "I am sensible that there are many Houses in this Town, that may be called Houses of Uncleanness," Rebekah Chamblit advised. "O shun them, for they lead down to the Chambers of Death and Eternal Misery."[38]

When the warnings were directed at particular groups of people, they tended like the sermons to reinforce the standard hierarchies of race and gender. "I would solemnly warn those of my own Colour, as they regard their own Souls, to avoid Desertion from their Masters," a slave named Arthur declared. Rachel Wall, one of the rare women executed for highway robbery, took special care to warn other women against a similar career. "Until we convince ourselves that we are by nature the children of wrath," the Mohegan Moses Paul was advised by a fellow Mohegan, "Hell must be our eternal home." At Paul's execution, the famous Indian minister Samson Occom is reported to have said, in substance if not in these exact words:

> My Kindred Indians pray attend and hear,
> With Great Attention and with Godly Fear,
> This Day I warn you of that cursed Sin,
> That poor despised Indians wallow in.
> 'Tis Drunkenness, this is the Sin you know,
> Has been and is poor Indians overthrow.

On the scaffold, Paul duly exhorted the many Indians in the crowd "to shun those Vices, to which they are so much addicted, viz. Drunkenness, Revenge, &c." Despite the fact that some of the condemned prisoners had flouted social convention most of their lives, the opportunity afforded by the gallows speech for critical social commentary was rarely taken.[39]

It *was* taken every so often. Cato, a New York slave, blamed his criminal career on the mistreatment he had received as a child from his master, "a man of very corrupt and immoral habits," and urged slaveowners to "learn the necessity of paying due attention to the instruction of their servants." The free black man Abraham Johnstone, hanged in New Jersey, spent his last days in jail placing his execution in the context of American race relations at the close of the eighteenth century. Johnstone was concerned that his case would "be made a handle of in order to throw a shade over or cast a general reflection on all those of our colour, and the keen shafts of prejudice be launched against us by the most active and virulent malevolence." He pointed out that if one compared the numbers of blacks and whites executed with the racial composition of the population, "it will be found that as they claim a pre-eminence over us in every thing else, so we find they also have it in this particular, and that a vast majority of whites have died on the gallows." He concluded "that there are some whites (with all due deference to them) capable of being equally as depraved and more generally so than blacks or people of colour."[40] Johnstone followed with an argument for abolishing slavery. But social commentary was a rare commodity on the scaffold. With very few exceptions, if you had heard one gallows speech, you had heard them all.

After the speech, a hood was pulled over the face of the prisoner and the rope was adjusted around his neck. There might be a final prayer, inaudible to spectators except those right in front. And then came a riot of motion.

Turned Off

Hanging was the ancient and familiar English method of executing criminals. Not until the late nineteenth century would Americans begin to ponder whether other methods might be better, and even then hanging would continue to have its partisans, because it had some undoubted advantages over other conceivable ways of putting people to death. It required no equipment beyond a rope and a high structure sturdy enough to support the weight of a human body. It called for no expertise apart from the ability to tie a knot. In most cases it caused little damage to the exterior of the corpse. These were the benefits that had institutionalized hanging in England, and they did the same in the American colonies.

The earliest American criminals were hanged from tree branches. Within a short time after settlement, most communities switched to gallows specially constructed for the purpose. Boston, for example, built a gallows sometime before 1650, when the governor ordered "that the gallowes be taken doune from the place where it now stands, and forthwith removed into a convenient place of common." A gallows was often no more than a simple structure made of two vertical poles and a horizontal crossbar, around which the rope could be tied. The hanging tree lived on in common speech as a metaphor. Owen Syllavan, hanged in New York in 1756 for counterfeiting, declared on the gallows that he hoped his confederates would not "die on a Tree as I do." A broadside poem commemorating the 1732 execution of the Boston burglar Richard Wilson referred to the instrument of death as "the Gallows-Tree."[41]

A hanging required some method of dropping the condemned person from a height. In the seventeenth century the drop was commonly achieved by means of a ladder placed against the tree or the gallows. The prisoner, with a rope tied around his neck and his hands tied, would climb the ladder. When all was ready, the executioner would simply turn the ladder away, depriving the prisoner of support. A person hanged in this manner was said to be "turned off." Ladders remained in use for some time, despite some evident shortcomings. Dorothy Talbye, hanged in Boston in 1639 for murdering her daughter, swung away from the ladder and then swung back, enabling her to catch it with her legs. More often, the fall from the ladder was too gradual to be fatal, because the ladder, removed horizontally, allowed the prisoner let him- or herself down slowly. After one Massachusetts woman "was turned off and had hung a space, she spake, and asked what did they mean to do." Cotton Mather found a mysterious message in the execution of Mary Martin: "She acknowledged, her *Twice* Essaying to Kill her Child, before she could make an End of it; and now, through the Unskilfulness of the Executioner, she was turned off the Ladder *Twice*, before she Dyed."[42]

By the eighteenth century the drop tended to be accomplished by having the condemned person stand under the gallows in a horse-drawn cart, which could be pulled away at the designated moment. But even the cart was not foolproof, because it too had to be removed horizontally. Anthony Dittond, hanged by means of a cart near Williamsburg, Virginia, in 1738, was still alive three minutes later, causing the executioner to pull on his legs to create a downward force greater than that provided by gravity. The executioner's efforts broke the rope, and Dittond, not yet dead, tumbled to the ground.[43]

Dissatisfaction with the efficacy of ladders and carts prompted some communities to build the gallows on top of a scaffold, the floor of which contained a trap door. The condemned person would stand on the trap door until its supports were pulled away. Boston had such a device as early as 1694, when Samuel Sewall attended the hanging of seven pirates. "When the scaffold was let sink," he reported, "there was such a Screech of the Women that my wife heard it sitting in our Entry next to the Orchard, and . . . our house is a full mile from the place." Boston's scaffold predated the use of scaffolds in England by several decades. A scaffold could be built up to a greater height than a cart, and the falling trap door made it impossible for the prisoner to let himself down gradually, so his fall was more likely to reach a velocity that would kill him. The scaffold's efficacy, along with, presumably, the difficulty of driving a horse and cart away from a gallows surrounded by spectators, made scaffolds common by the nineteenth century. With the routine use of a scaffold, the condemned prisoners were gradually no longer said to be "turned off." A new expression became commonplace, one referring to the speed of the process. "He was led to the *scaffold*," one account of a 1797 execution read, "the *supporting* line unfastened, and the *malefactor launched into Eternity*."[44]

But even with a scaffold, hanging might not kill on the first try. Ropes ripped apart with the sudden downward jerk. The drop might still be too short to kill. Thomas Lee, dropped from a scaffold in New York in 1787, hung by the chin for two minutes before saying "It does not choak me."[45] Occasional failures would remain associated with hanging throughout its existence, well into the twentieth century.

The technology of hanging was simple, so simple that nearly anyone could conduct a hanging, even of him- or herself. Hanging was a common method of suicide in the American colonies. The *Pennsylvania Gazette* reported at least ten suicides by hanging in the Philadelphia region in the 1730s alone, including three in Chester within a two-week period. Eight of the ten were slaves or indentured servants, most very young. One was a five-year-old boy, who hanged himself from a fence stake in Burlington, New Jersey, a few days after he had watched the execution of two local men. "It is said," the *Gazette* reported, "that he dreamt much of that Execution the Night before, and telling his Dream in the Morning, added, *and I shall die today*."[46] Of all the conceivable ways of killing, hanging was one of the easiest. Only in the military, where firearms were relatively plentiful and speed often essential, were significant numbers of seventeenth- and eighteenth-century executions conducted by means other than hanging.

Death by hanging could be fast or slow, apparently painless or obviously excruciating, depending on the actual cause of death. If the prisoner was lucky, the force of the drop would fracture the vertebrae of his neck and sever his spinal cord, typically between the second and third vertebrae. This is an injury often seen today—and still colloquially known as "hangman's fracture"—usually after head-on automobile accidents in which the victim's body is thrown forward but his head is snapped back by the windshield. Death by this mechanism was nearly instantaneous and thus caused little or no pain. It was also unusual. A mass autopsy of English murderers executed between 1882 and 1945 and exhumed during prison construction found only six cervical fractures in thirty-four cases. An older study of sixty-five hangings conducted in the United States between 1869 and 1873 counted only six complete fractures and four partial fractures.[47]

Most people who were hanged died more slowly, as the rope encircling their necks either cut off the supply of blood to their brains or prevented them from breathing, or as the force of the drop wrenched the larynx away from the trachea, again preventing breathing. All these methods of dying took several minutes. The loss of blood to the brain was the least painful, producing unconsciousness within seconds. Asphyxiation, in contrast, left the conscious victim writhing and gasping through the last several minutes of his life. His mouth and nose would turn dark purple, and his eyes would bulge monstrously wide. Convulsions would gradually extend throughout his body, spreading from contortions of the eyes to violent kicking with the legs. He might urinate or defecate. His penis might become erect. Such displays accompanied a significant percentage of hangings. The study of sixty-five executions mentioned earlier catalogued their number and severity: *"Throes and Contortions—Severe and Continuous 23, Moderate 14, Feeble and Evanescent 18. Chest-heavings* (indicative of persistent sensation) 8."

Since at least the seventeenth century, Anglo-American lore had held that the crucial determinant of the means of death was the placement of the knot. A knot under the ear, it was thought, would exert sufficient leverage on the jawbone and temple to fracture the spinal column; a knot on the throat or the back of the neck would not. "Yes," said one prison superintendent, responding to a remark that the condemned man under his charge had died easily, "there is every thing in knowing how to fix the knot." Considering their personal interest in the issue, it is not surprising that some condemned prisoners were familiar with this lore, and were careful to instruct their executioners to put the knot in its proper place. "Let's see, where does the knot go, under the right ear?" asked the murderer Harry Hayward, in what would prove to be his last words. "Please pull it tight. That's good."[48]

The infrequency of cervical fractures is difficult to square with the apparently wide knowledge of knot lore unless that lore was wrong, as it may well have been. While there has understandably been little research on the point, the authors of a study of a 1993 hanging in the state of Washington (the first execution by hanging in the United States since 1965) suggest that knot placement probably made no difference at all. The English study found that the incidence of fracture was unassociated with hangman or hanging technique, a finding that suggests that the pain of being hanged was unlikely to have been mitigated by any skill possessed by one's executioner.[49] Whether a hanging was painless or painful seems to have been largely a matter of chance.

In the middle of the nineteenth century, when technological change would make it possible to minimize pain, more and more spectators would begin to find hanging too gruesome a method of execution. Until then, death by asphyxiation was understood to be unfortunate but inevitable. Accounts of evidently painful hangings written before the mid-nineteenth century tend to betray only resignation, not shock. Executions were not *supposed* to be painful. None of the reasons for favoring capital punishment made spectators or government officials want to inflict suffering along with death. There was just not yet any known way of eliminating the pain.

The Inquisitive Public

The crowd went home, the condemned person was cut down and usually buried, the gallows was dismantled, and everyday life picked up where it had left off, but the execution lived on in three genres of literature: the sermon, the last words, and the account of the prisoner's life of crime and public death. The dying speech and the criminal biography had already been popular literary forms in England, but the stand-alone execution sermon may have been an American invention. These genres overlapped. Last words and accounts of the criminal's life were often appended to published sermons in order to boost sales. Criminal biographies often culminated in the condemned criminal's last words. All three genres were published in greatest number in the North, especially in New England, which in the eighteenth and early nineteenth centuries accounted for the overwhelming majority of published material of all types. They found a ready market. The sermons, ostensibly published for didactic purposes, could enrich writer as well as reader. By Cotton Mather's own reckoning, his sermon *The Valley of Hinnom*, delivered before the 1717 hanging of the murderer Jeremiah Fenwick, sold nearly a thousand copies in five days.[50] Criminal biographies were printed as inexpensive broadsides and sold to spectators at hangings. Accounts of last words and executions, often set in rhymed verse for public reading or singing, were advertised in newspapers. Published execution sermons remained popular in the North through the first quarter of the nineteenth century, after which changing attitudes toward the place of religion in public life and the move away from public executions caused the genre to disappear. Criminal biographies and accounts of last words held on longer; both were still being published in the second half of the nineteenth century.

The eagerness with which publishers pressed condemned prisoners to provide last words in advance of the execution is sure proof of the profits that could be had from selling them. The publisher of Matthew Cushing's "Declaration & Confession" tried his best to get a comparable statement from John Ormsby, who was executed alongside Cushing, but failed. Ormsby "appear'd very stupid at the time of his receiving Sentence," the publisher reported, "and remain'd very much so till the Day of his Execution; and we could get nothing from him worthy of any publick Notice." Lack of material was no deterrent to other publishers, who went ahead and wrote the last words themselves, then attributed them to the condemned person upon publication. One account of Whiting Sweeting's final days denounced "the *spurious* publication, by Mr. Barber," of a competing version, which "is supposed to have been in consequence of a *merited* denial of his application, hoping thereby to injure the sale of, and bring into disrepute, the *true* work." But how could a reader be sure that Barber's was not the true account, and the second one the pretender? The 1733 hanging of an Indian named Julian produced a battle of broadside "final warnings," each claiming to be the only authentic version. One broadside, bearing the oddly spelled title *Poor Julleyoun's Warnings to Children and Servants*, insisted that it was "Published at his Desire, in Presence of two Witnesses." That drew a sharp rebuke from the publisher of *Advice from the Dead to the Living*, who alleged that the other was "false and spurious, and disowned by the said Julian in the Presence of three Persons." The publisher of another version, *The Last Speech and Dying Advice of Poor Julian*, included a statement supposedly from Julian himself: "I do hereby utterly disown and disclaim all other Speeches, Papers or Declarations that may be printed in my Name."[51] The three broadsides bore no resemblance to one another. Two were in verse, one in prose; one of the verses was supposedly in Julian's voice, the other in the third person. At least two were spurious, and perhaps all three were.

Knowing that they were addressing a public rightly skeptical of the authenticity of these accounts, publishers of condemned criminals' last words routinely included an attestation that the prisoner really did speak words close to those attributed to him. "After I had penned it from his own Mouth, I read the same over to him, because I had not related it just in the very same numerical words," wrote the publisher of the biography and last words of Thomas Hellier, an indentured servant executed in Virginia for murdering his master's family. "After he had heard the same read over, he acknowledged this to be the true sense of his own Intentions." "The reader will take notice that I do not attest to the truth of Pomp's dying speech," conceded Jonathan Plummer, who purported to have interviewed Pomp, a Massachusetts slave, in his jail cell, "but I affirm that he related to me as matters of fact the particulars recounted in this speech."[52] But of course such affirmations were as easy to falsify as the content of the speeches. Most readers had no way to know whether the condemned prisoners had actually said what they were reported to have said. Two centuries later, neither do we. Some of the accounts are written in a style probably too highflown to have been within the capacity of a person of average literacy, but of course some condemned prisoners, then as now, possessed literary skills far above the average. In other instances publishers may have embellished the style without altering the substance. Some publications were outright fraud. The published dying declaration unavoidably aroused doubts as to its authenticity.

From the condemned person's perspective, the opportunity to share in the profits of the enterprise, and thereby to provide some money for the family left behind, no doubt contributed to a willingness to cooperate. But money was not the only reason for publication. John Batter, hanged in Maryland for robbing a church, wrote out his confession in order to warn everyone about his accomplice "Dennis Hayes for he is the greatest Rogue in the World lest he bring them to the Gallows, as he brought me." Levi Ames pleaded with readers not to consider his execution any reflection on his mother or his brother, who already had troubles enough. A published declaration was also a final opportunity to declare one's innocence, even from the grave. "If the word of a dying man can be taken," said one New York counterfeiter who was probably already dead by the time his words could be read, "I am innocent of the crime imputed to me."[53]

Unlike dying declarations, criminal biographies did not necessarily depend for their authenticity on the cooperation of the condemned prisoner. The facts of the crimes could be obtained from other sources. Like sermons and dying declarations, accounts of crime were often published ostensibly as a means of instruction. Many, however, contained little or no text explicitly devoted to that purpose. Crime was simply interesting to read about. As one broadside sold at Moses Paul's hanging admitted, "it is expected that the inquisitive Public will be desirous to know some Particulars" of Paul's life and crime.[54] Information about crime was valuable enough in its own right for readers to cover the cost of publication and more.

An execution thus possessed a literary existence long after everyone had gone home. By the time the last pamphlet was sold, several months might have passed since the criminal had been sentenced to death. He had been the object of hatred, then fascination, and then sympathy, and all the while in the eye of a public much larger than the crowd that attended his execution.

W hy all the fuss? Convicted criminals could more easily have been killed without any ceremony at all. The procession, the sermon, the gallows speech—all of it must have served some purpose, or people would hardly have gone to the trouble. We may identify two reasons eighteenth-century officials would have found it useful to situate hangings within this kind of ceremony.

First, the ceremony provided a way to amplify the message of terror created by the hanging and to broadcast that message to the public. The infliction of death by itself might have drawn a crowd, but when death was placed at the end of a series of dramatic events that could have attracted spectators by themselves, the number of spectators was multiplied. Every additional member of the audience was one more person to be deterred from crime in the future. The hanging's message was intensified for each spectator by the context created by the procession, which could amount to a significant display of the armed power at the government's disposal, and by the speeches, which clarified why that power was being directed at a particular individual. If the primary goal of capital punishment was to make people fear the consequences of committing crime, the ceremony served the twin goals of increasing the number of people and the level of fear.

The ceremony served a second purpose as well: that of reinforcing order. One common way to underscore the importance or unusualness of an event is to surround it with proceedings that set it apart from everyday life.[55] To demonstrate the importance of marriage, many people embed the brief moment of declaring the marriage within a much longer wedding ceremony. The rituals associated with judicial proceedings, in the seventeenth and eighteenth centuries as now, lent weight to those proceedings by dividing them from events before and after. The ceremony of hanging day did the same for hangings. By setting the actual hanging apart from daily life, the ceremony demonstrated the separation of the legitimate violence inflicted by the state on this occasion from the illegitimate violence inflicted by anyone else, often including the condemned prisoner. By embedding the hanging within the ceremony, the state symbolically declared that the hanging was something very different from what one might see elsewhere. The sort of violence that *establishes* order was clearly marked off from the sort of violence that *disrupts* order.

The ceremony thus permitted what might otherwise have been paradoxical: the ritual display of violence as a means of dramatizing the community's disapproval of violence. The staging worked. Not until the late eighteenth century would critics discern any paradox. Until then, hangings were understood by all as participatory enactments of a collective interest in punishing crime. Government officials, ministers, ordinary citizens—all came together to make an emphatic statement of condemnation.

3

DEGREES OF DEATH

ELIZABETH RAINER WAS TAKEN from jail to the gallows. Eleven months earlier, in the summer of 1676, she had conceived a child. That in itself had been a crime because Rainer was unmarried; as the indictment filed in a Special Court of Oyer and Terminer in Southampton, New York, put it, she had "played the whore, & become with childe by fornication." Fearing the disapproval of her neighbors, Rainer tried to conceal her pregnancy, and then when the baby was born in March 1677, in her father's house, she tried to hide that too. She took the child to a nearby cooper's woodshop, where, again in the words of the indictment, she "didst sinfully & wickedly leave it dead upon a piell of Chipps . . . And more like a bruit Beast than a mother did not acquaint any of the same, nor go in any way to save the life of it." Now, in May, she had been convicted. An audience gathered around the gallows to watch. No doubt many in the crowd knew her well. All knew of her crime and her sentence. Someone, probably the local sheriff, led her to the gallows and placed a halter around her neck. Elizabeth Rainer was ready for the execution of her sentence.

A half hour later that sentence had been executed. The crowd dispersed. The sheriff removed the halter from Rainer's neck. He did not need to carry her body away, because she was still alive. She was taken back to jail, where she would remain, probably frightened, probably embarrassed, pending further order of the court. Elizabeth Rainer had not been sentenced to death. Like many American criminals of the seventeenth and eighteenth centuries, she had been sentenced instead to "stand a full ½ houre on the gallowes with a halter about her neck."[1] She had been sentenced to play a part in the ceremony of capital punishment, but not to capital punishment itself.

No one was surprised. Rainer knew she would live, and the crowd knew it too. This sentence would have been nonsensical—pointless play-acting—had her contemporaries not believed that it would have some salutary effect on Rainer and the crowd, at best that it would deter infanticide, or at the very least that it would make all concerned think twice before fornicating. From Elizabeth Rainer's sentence we can begin to get a sense of the centrality of capital punishment in early American criminal justice.

Capital punishment was more than just one penal technique among others. It was the base point from which other kinds of punishment deviated. When the state punished serious crime, most of the methods at its disposal were variations on execution. Officials imposed death sentences that were never carried out, they conducted mock hangings (as in Rainer's case), and they dramatically halted real execution ceremonies at the last moment. These were methods of inflicting a *symbolic* death, a penalty that mimicked some aspects of capital punishment without actually killing the defendant. Officials also wielded a set of tools capable of *intensifying* a death sentence—burning at the stake, public display of the corpse, dismemberment, and dissection—ways of producing a punishment worse than death. Taken together, these provided a wide range of possible punishments for serious crime, within a penal system that in principle included only one.

Mercy

A death sentence did not necessarily result in an execution. It merely shifted the case from the judiciary to the executive, from the question of guilt to the question of mercy. There was no expectation that all or even nearly all condemned criminals would be executed. In eighteenth-century New York, for instance, just over half received pardons. In a sample of death sentences from eighteenth-century Virginia, between one-quarter and one-third were never carried out.[2]

Unlike us today, when executive clemency is very rare, Americans of the seventeenth and eighteenth centuries assumed that the written law provided only an upper limit to the punishment a criminal might receive. While every death sentence was the same, the circumstances of every capital crime were different, and so were the life histories of the condemned criminals. The power of clemency was understood as a means by which the state could tailor the sentence to the individual case.

Clemency was governed by no rules. It was purely within the discretion of colonial and state governors, who could grant or deny a pardon for any reason or no reason.[3] In a world of unequals, connections mattered. Dennis Kilsbye, coachman to the governor of New Jersey, raped a fifteen-year-old girl but was pardoned. "Some Circumstances appeared to be in his Favour," was all the newspaper reported, and it was clear enough what those circumstances were. Where an application came from "Sundry Gentlemen," as in the cases of the Maryland burglars Samuel Nollar and "Mulatto Dick," or "the respectable inhabitants of Fredericksburg," as in the case of the horse thief Joshua Night, a pardon was almost a certainty. When the greater part of the Richmond bar petitioned in behalf of Angelica Barnett, a free black woman convicted of murdering a white man who had tried to whip her, Barnett was pardoned. Without friends in high places, in contrast, the chances of clemency were much smaller. The Connecticut murderer Richard Doane found himself "destitute of property & connections to support or intercede for him," and accordingly had to appeal to the legislature directly. (In Connecticut the legislature rather than the governor had the power to grant pardons.) "Others have their friends to speak for and redeem them from death," lamented Charles O'Donnel shortly before his execution. "But there is none to speak a word in favour of the guilty O'Donnel."[4]

Influence was most important where inequality was greatest. The owner of a slave convicted of a capital crime short of murder virtually possessed the power of life or death. Landon Carter's slave Manuel was "the best plowman and mower I ever saw" until drinking and whoring turned him to burglary. "For this I prosecuted him and got him pardoned," Carter reported. When another of Carter's slaves set fire to his meathouse, Carter simply sent a letter to the governor, and the slave was likewise pardoned. In New York a slave named Jack was sentenced to death for burglary but was not executed because his owner, the bricklayer Dyrck Vandenburgh, said that Jack had cost him £60 and was very helpful in his trade. The *Virginia Gazette* summed up the power of slaveowners in its account of some runaway slaves awaiting their executions: "It may be supposed if their masters would come and interceed for a pardon it might be granted."[5]

Most of those who were condemned lacked a powerful patron, but for each there was at least one man of influence who knew something about his case—the judge or judges who had sentenced him. "Your Honor having presided at my Trial are better acquainted with all the Circumstances attending it than almost any other person," Levin Handley pleaded with the Honorable Nicholas Thomas from his jail cell in Cambridge, Maryland. "Let me then entreat you to lay my Case, my long and painfull Confinement, my numerous and suffering Children, my ready and willing Services rendered my Country . . . before his Excellency the Governor, these I hope joined to your Honors powerfull Intercession." The trial judge was often the only person the condemned prisoner knew who was likely to have access to the governor. At the same time, because governors and their advisors normally lacked any firsthand knowledge of the case, the trial judge was often the only person the governor knew who possessed accurate information about the condemned prisoner and his crime. The recommendations of trial judges were thus pivotal in determining who would receive clemency. Although a New York jury had convicted James McBride of murder, Justice Daniel Horsmanden was persuaded that McBride had not intended to kill, and so McBride was not executed. Although a Maryland jury had convicted Elizabeth Horner of horse theft, the judge thought it possible that she might be innocent, so Horner was not executed either.[6]

To say that decisions were discretionary and influence important is not to say, however, that clemency was purely a matter of connections. Many people with no apparent influential friends were pardoned. When the powerful intervened after conviction they did not simply rely on their influence; they found it necessary to state *reasons* for clemency. Although no written law regulated the decision to grant a pardon, decisions were in practice governed by stable unwritten conventions which enabled all concerned to form a sense of the types of cases appropriate for clemency. These conventions allowed clemency to serve several purposes in the seventeenth and eighteenth centuries, functions all served by other legal institutions today.

First, clemency was the only means available to correct legal errors occurring at trial. Today appellate courts perform that role, but there were no criminal appeals in the seventeenth and eighteenth centuries. "I was this moment informed of the case of a negro man named Phil, belonging to one Tyree," Edmund Randolph anxiously wrote to the governor of Virginia. Phil had been sentenced to death as a burglar, for "going into a house, in the day time, *while the door was open*, and stealing a considerable sum of money." As every lawyer knew, however, "*a breaking* was absolutely necessary to justify" a conviction for burglary, and because Phil had walked right through an open door, no breaking had occurred. "The court, who sat on the trial, were very respectable and sensible men," Randolph assured the governor, "but seem to have mistaken the law." Phil received a pardon the following week because of the error.

Condemned prisoners and their lawyers, if they had lawyers, knew that a legal error at trial was likely to result in a pardon, and they accordingly proffered the sorts of arguments that today would be directed at an appellate court. The lawyers for a Connecticut slave named Cuff, condemned in 1749 for raping fourteen-year-old Diana Parrish, argued (apparently without success) that the colony's statute establishing rape as a capital offense ought to be interpreted in the light of the Old Testament, which they asserted punished with death only the rape of a *betrothed* virgin, not that of an unbetrothed virgin like the victim. James Gibson, convicted of raping the elderly Mrs. Hubbard of Haddam, Connecticut, argued in his own behalf that his conviction had been procured unlawfully because the deliberating jury had been allowed to consult law books. Gibson's argument prevailed, although not without some cost; his sentence was commuted to castration.[7]

The most serious kind of trial error was, of course, the conviction of an innocent person. Governor Robert Hunter of New York arranged pardons for several of the slaves convicted of conspiring to revolt in 1712, "there being no manner of convincing evidence against them, and nothing but the blind fury of a people much provoked could have condemned them." Seventeen-year-old Margaretta Kirchin of Lancaster, Pennsylvania, was convicted by a jury of murdering her illegitimate infant in 1759, but when the judges at her trial reported that Kirchin's guilt was unclear, she was pardoned. In an era when all forms of scientific evidence still lay well in the future, it was not unusual for facts to come to light only after the trial was over. Clemency allowed such facts to make a difference. A slave named Bristo was convicted of raping young Hannah Beebe of Connecticut in 1756, upon Beebe's own testimony. As Bristo's execution date approached, Beebe admitted that she had falsely claimed to have been raped because she had been told that the claim would entitle her to obtain compensation from Bristo's owner. Bristo was immediately pardoned.[8]

Where the condemned person's guilt was clear and his trial conducted properly, youth or inexperience as a criminal might save him from being

hanged. This was a second function served by clemency, that of classify-
ing offenders according to what was often called their "character," which
tended to be synonymous with the perceived likelihood that they would
commit more crimes in the future. Today this sorting function is incorporated into sentencing itself. Maryland's governor learned in 1754 that two
condemned burglars "are both very Young and that this is the first offence
that either of them to Our knowledge has been arraigned for." The burglars were pardoned. James Mansfield and Samuel Hall were condemned for counterfeiting North Carolina's bills of credit, but a petition
signed by several of their neighbors demonstrated that "they are but
young Men and of a former good character," whose crime was "more ow-
ing to the Unsteadiness of Youth and the Attacks of an old and hardened
Offender, thoroughly hackneyed in the Ways of all Vice, than from any
Settled Principles of Viciousness in Themselves." Mansfield and Hall
were pardoned. Clemency served to separate such incidental criminals
from those like John Webster, who had "committed many crimes of the
most heinous nature," or James Duffy, whose single murder was "perpetrated in so unmanly and cruel a manner" as to leave no doubt as to his viciousness.[9] Some criminals were simply worse than others.

A third purpose served by clemency was that of encouraging criminals
to inculpate their colleagues. John Smith was sentenced to death for being the ringleader of a group of men who murdered a ship captain in
Maryland, for example, but because Smith provided the government
with evidence against his confederates, he was pardoned. The condemned Philadelphia burglar John Crow was pardoned after informing
on his accomplices. Today this sort of encouragement tends to be provided before trial, in the course of plea bargaining. Before there were police forces to investigate crimes, however, and before there was any
significant amount of plea bargaining, clemency was used as a tool of law
enforcement.[10]

The multiple purposes served by clemency put the condemned prisoner in a bind. A claim of innocence might make him a more appealing
candidate for clemency, but if the claim was not believed it would be
taken to demonstrate a lack of penitence indicative of a hardened criminal, and would thus make an execution more likely. To admit guilt and
show remorse, in contrast, would make manifest one's good character,
but it would simultaneously reinforce the appropriateness of the conviction and the ensuing sentence. As one defendant was paradoxically told,

"Unless he gave in a Petition wherein he Confest his Crime, he should have no Reprieve, but Execution would soon be put upon him."[11]

Caught in this dilemma, the prisoners made their choices. Some mounted displays of conspicuous repentance. His victim "was basely used by me," admitted the rapist Robert Young; "I humbly ask her forgiveness, and all others whom I have offended." The pirate Richard Barrick and the murderer Cassumo Garcelli, like many others, recited their prior records and conceded the justice of their sentences. John Ryer assumed a pose of prayer on the scaffold and remained motionless for three minutes, long enough to ensure that no spectator could miss the point.[12] Repentance may often have been genuine, but it was always useful.

Another way a condemned prisoner could demonstrate his good character was to show his appreciation for the services performed for him in the days leading up to his death. Three Boston pirates were careful to give thanks for "the humane and kind treatment they have met with ever since their Confinement, from every Person concerned with them, and from the many kind and charitable Citizens who have visited and comforted them." The burglar Dirick Grout thanked his jailer and the jailer's family "for their kind Attention to me while under Confinement." Bristol, a sixteen-year-old slave, "was very particular in thanking every Body that had taken Notice of him while in Prison."[13] Again, the gratitude may well have been authentic, but it was also prudent. There was good reason to show that one was not a hardened criminal.

Many took the opposite course, maintaining their innocence in the face of evidence to the contrary. Some of the strongest evidence against Moses Paul had been Paul's repeated threats to carry out the murder of which he was later convicted. Paul nevertheless insisted that although he "made use of some vile, threatening language; yet he begs leave to say that he had not any desire of murder in his Heart, and that his words and expressions at the time, whatever they might be, were but empty sounds without any meaning."[14] Innocence was probably as often genuinely felt as repentance, and it was always just as useful.

Other condemned people tried to avoid the paradox of clemency by finding ways to display innocence and repentance simultaneously. One might deny the crime but acknowledge that one deserved to die nevertheless, for leading a life of smaller sins like drunkenness and Sabbath-breaking. One might more plausibly project atonement for the *acts* constituting the crime but deny having committed the crime itself, for want of one of the elements making up its legal definition. "I have uniformly thought that the witnesses were mistaken in swearing to the commission of a *Rape*," Joseph Mountain was supposed to have said. "That I abused her in a most brutal and savage manner—that her tender years and pitiable shrieks were unavailing—and that no exertion was wanting to ruin her, I frankly confess." Mountain repented for his intent to commit rape, not for an actual rape. Sixty-eight-year-old John Jubeart "declared upon the word of a dying man, that it was more for the sake of trying an experiment than any fraudulent intention he had to impose upon the public" that he had melted down five Spanish dollars and mixed in an equal quantity of metal to coin ten new ones. Jubeart could use the law's requirement of intent to display penitence for coining fake money while simultaneously denying that he was a counterfeiter.[15] Legal argument allowed room for a condemned criminal to play both sides of an appeal for clemency.

Drink provided another middle path between the two sides of the clemency dilemma, because it allowed the condemned person to apologize for his conduct while disclaiming complete responsibility for it. "How I came to commit this Wickedness, I can give no Account," the murderer John Ormsby related, "unless it was the Effects of the Drink which had brought on my former Delirium." Ormsby could display repentance for an unintentional killing and for a life of drink, neither of which was a capital crime, without having to admit to murder in the technical sense. John Green, one of the few Americans ever sentenced to death for blasphemy, attributed his words to "an Excessive drinking of Rum the common strong drink of this land, which your Petitioner found by woful Experience operated upon him in an extraordinary & peculiar manner, causing him to be wild & frantick, noisy & turbulent little short of a madman." After fourteen years of abstinence, Green explained, "being not well your Petitioner thought he might prudently take a little strong drink thinking it would be for his health & comfort." But a nip of rum "alas whet & inraged your Petitioner's old appetite," and Green once again gave in to his addiction, "til frantick & wild with the fumes of large quantities of strong liquors your poor Petitioner, (as he is told for truly one half he cannot recollect) became more like a fiend than a human creature, hollering affronting words to God & man."[16] Green could portray himself as a weak man but not an evil man, and his blasphemy as fueled by drink rather than a godless character. The depiction probably worked, because while there is no surviving record of the action taken on Green's petition, there is also no surviving evidence that Green was ever hanged.

As the date of execution approached, many condemned prisoners resorted to desperate means of seeking clemency. A few minutes before his scheduled hanging for counterfeiting, Benjamin Cooper confessed that he had also been part of a major unsolved robbery, and promised to name his accomplices if he could only live a bit longer. Cooper's execution was postponed, and he was eventually pardoned. The Philadelphia counterfeiter Herman Rosencrantz, in a last-minute effort to gain favor, named so many innocent people as his accomplices that the publisher of his confession felt compelled to clear their names in an appendix. Some prisoners pleaded for alternative sentences. The horse thief William Barker begged to be "Transported to some of her Majesties Colonies abroad" or to "spend the remainder of his Dayes in her Majesties service either by Sea or Land." The slave Cuff pleaded that his death sentence might "be changed into whipping branding transportation or castration any or all so as his life may be spared."[17] As time ran out, the tools available to condemned prisoners became weaker.

The ever-present possibility of clemency suggests why the last words of condemned persons tended to be so formulaic. Condemned prisoners all faced a similar set of incentives. They needed to project two inconsistent images, one of innocence and one of contrition for the crime. In the effort to obtain a pardon, one could choose one route or the other, or one could try to walk the narrow path between them. There were no other strategies available. To vent one's frustrations, or to take the opportunity to criticize the criminal justice system, was to make one's bad character manifest. It was a decision, in effect, to give up hope of living. One can readily understand why few pursued that course. The condemned person was far more likely to live another day if he met the expectations of his audience.

That audience was a broader group than it is today. Community sentiment still plays a role in criminal sentencing, especially in cases potentially capital, but that sentiment tends to be formally channeled through a small number of community representatives, most obviously through juries in capital cases, but also through elected prosecutors and judges, and through the victims and others who are permitted to testify at sentencing hearings. And we tend to be suspicious when the role of community sentiment is too overt—when the prosecutor or judge favors the death penalty shortly before an election, for example, or when sentencing juries seem to be influenced by public opinion. Neither the formal channeling of community sentiment nor the suspicion of it was present in the seventeenth and eighteenth centuries. Whether the condemned person lived or died was *supposed* to reflect the will of the community. Who, after all, knew the criminal's character better? Who had a better sense of whether he had made a single mistake or was truly evil?

Those who were locally powerful had a disproportionate say in which prisoners would be pardoned, but that was an attribute of the politics of the era generally, not a feature unique to clemency. As politics became more democratic in the nineteenth century, so too did clemency decisions, as governors found themselves increasingly forced to consider the electoral consequences of the grant or denial of a pardon. But regardless of who spoke for the community, the community was understood to play a proper role in deciding which condemned prisoners would die. Sentencing was not a specialized function reserved for either a technically trained elite (as noncapital sentencing often is today) or a jury presented with information in a formal, restricted setting (as capital sentencing is today). Through clemency, capital sentencing in the seventeenth and eighteenth centuries was seen as a community decision.

Symbolic Execution

The state also had at its disposal a variety of means, short of a pardon, to mitigate a death sentence. By invoking the ancient legal doctrine of benefit of clergy, by conducting simulated hangings, and by staging dramatic reprieves under the gallows, officials could reap much of the benefit of the death penalty without actually having to kill.

Benefit of clergy was a relic of English law. It began with the separation of temporal and ecclesiastical courts after the Norman Conquest. Criminal trials of members of the clergy fell within the jurisdiction of the ecclesiastical courts. A clergyman charged with a crime in a temporal court would accordingly plead his status—his "clergy," as it came to be called—as a bar to prosecution. Over time the English courts developed a shortcut for assessing the truth of the claim that a defendant was a clergyman. Rather than conducting a full-scale inquiry into the defendant's career, the courts simply ascertained whether he could read, on the assumption, realistic at the time, that few people other than members of the clergy would know how to read. By the close of the fourteenth century, however, many of the people successfully claiming the benefit of clergy in English courts were in fact not clergymen at all but literate people pursuing secular occupations. One's status as a member of the clergy continued to be important only in successive prosecutions. Real clergymen could claim the benefit as many times as they needed, but literate laypeople were given only one opportunity. By the late fifteenth century laypeople pleading benefit of clergy were branded on the thumb to indicate that their immunity had already been used. Eventually the literacy test was abolished. A legal rule that had begun its life as an allocation of jurisdiction between different courts had been transmuted into a system of leniency for first offenders.[18]

Benefit of clergy was much more common in the southern colonies than in the northern because of the greater number of capital offenses in the South.[19] The doctrine was unavailable for the most serious crimes, and in the North these made up most or all of the capital offenses. Many of the criminals tried for the lesser capital crimes knew, if it was their first such trial, that the maximum penalty they could suffer was to be burned in the hand.

By tinkering with the scope of benefit of clergy, colonial governments could incrementally modify the severity of the criminal law in response to perceived patterns of crime. After the burning of the Kent County courthouse in 1720, the Maryland General Assembly was dismayed to realize that benefit of clergy was unavailable only for *residential* arson, and promptly withdrew the privilege for anyone thereafter convicted of setting fire to a courthouse. Nine years later, finding that "several Felons have feloniously broke and enter'd several Shops, Store-houses, or Warehouses, not contiguous to or used with any Mansion-house, and stolen from thence several Goods and Merchandizes," and discovering that only residential burglaries were exempt from benefit of clergy, the General Assembly likewise disallowed the privilege for burglars from commercial premises. In 1737, after a spate of burglaries from "Tobacco-houses, and other Out-houses"—structures neither residential nor commercial—the Assembly believed it necessary to prohibit these burglars as well from claiming the privilege. "Offenders have been encouraged to commit the said Crimes, by the Lenity of our Laws, and Expectation of having the Benefit of Clergy, when detected," the Assembly explained.[20]

The doctrine remained in place until the penal reforms of the late eighteenth and early nineteenth centuries. Massachusetts abolished benefit of clergy in 1785, upon a legislative finding that "it was originally founded in superstition and injustice," and that as a means of mitigating the rigor of the penal law it "in most cases operates very inadequately and disproportionately." New York abolished the doctrine in 1788. The U.S. Congress, when enacting the first federal criminal statutes in 1790, explicitly refused to make the doctrine part of federal law. Pennsylvania abolished it in 1794, Virginia in 1796, Maryland in 1810. The southern states were generally slower to undertake penal reform, and this divergence between North and South extended to benefit of clergy. South Carolina did not abolish the doctrine until 1869.[21]

To prevent offenders from pleading the benefit more than once, governments needed a means of keeping track of their criminals. Any single community would have no trouble remembering who had been granted benefit of clergy in the past, either by keeping written records or simply by holding that knowledge in memory. A year after Pope Alvey received the benefit of clergy for murder, he was back in court again, convicted of stealing a cow. The court had little trouble turning him down when he tried to plead clergy a second time. But people seeking to escape their pasts could be highly mobile. They could change their names. Without an effective way of transmitting criminal records from one place to another, a criminal might plead the benefit of clergy again and again. Governments exchanged that data by placing it directly on the body of the criminal, in the form of a permanent burn mark on the thumb. Convicted criminals carried their histories around with them. The mark placed court officials on notice. The *Boston Weekly Post-Boy* joked that John Stevens, sentenced to death as a previous recipient of benefit of clergy for counterfeiting New York bills of credit, "complains much of a Hurt in his Right Thumb, and it is tho't he will have it cut off for fear of a general Mortification." The mark served the same function for the world at large: a person branded on the thumb was immediately identifiable as someone convicted of a nominally capital crime, and thus someone unlikely to make much way among respectable company. "After I received those marks of infamy," recalled the burglar John Brown, "I was held as an Enemy by the public and shunned as a pestilence by Common Society."[22] The doctrine of benefit of clergy thus provided a first step in a graded scale of punishments, within a penal law that in principle included only a single punishment for serious offenses.

A second form of symbolic hanging made its first appearance in American statute books in 1693, when Massachusetts adopted a new scheme of punishments for burglary and robbery. A third offense would be capital, as before. But second offenders would merely be required to sit upon the gallows for an hour with a rope around their necks. After the hour was up, they would be whipped.[23]

Simulated hanging must have been widely perceived as a successful punishment, because Massachusetts returned to it repeatedly over the next several decades. When the colony decapitalized adultery in 1695, the penalty substituted for death was an hour on the gallows with a rope around the neck, plus whipping, plus the wearing of the letter A forever. (This last punishment, of course, was the basis for Nathaniel Hawthorne's novel *The Scarlet Letter.*) Massachusetts did the same for incest the following year, with only the letter I to distinguish the incestuous from the adulterous. Blasphemy was decapitalized in 1697, and several possible sentences were substituted, one of which involved sitting on the gallows. Duellists received the same penalty in 1729, provided their opponents did not die. (When his opponent died as the result of a duel, the winner was to be executed and then buried without a coffin, with a stake driven through his body.) In 1737 the second offense of theft, if of over 40 shillings, received an hour on the gallows, plus whipping and triple restitution. The last of these statutes was enacted by Massachusetts in 1785, when it abolished benefit of clergy. Simply abolishing clergy, without simultaneously redrafting the rest of the state's penal code to provide lesser penalties for first offenders, would have suddenly rendered that code much more severe. Instead, the state substituted simulated hanging.[24]

The practice of simulated hanging was known throughout early modern Europe. It must have been familiar to many of the seventeenth-century colonists of North America, because in some early instances they conducted fake hangings without any statutory authorization. One case involved a slave referred to in the Massachusetts court records only as Anna Negro, who was accused of killing her illegitimate child in 1674. Although Anna was accused of murder, and was found to have committed the charged acts, the jury chose the wording of its verdict carefully: "They found the said Anna Negro Guilty of having a Bastard child & privately convey[ing] it away." Faced with a verdict that stopped short of a formal finding of murder, apparently because the jury was reluctant to condemn Anna to death, the court fashioned an appropriate sentence: an hour on the gallows with a rope around her neck, to be followed by whipping and a month in jail.[25]

In the eighteenth century simulated hangings appear to have been most common in New England. New Hampshire adopted the punishment when it decapitalized blasphemy in 1718. Rhode Island did the same for adultery and bigamy in 1749. Pairs of adulterers were mock-hanged in Boston in 1731 and in Worcester in 1752. A pair of duellists, apprehended before they could fire a shot, suffered the same penalty in Charlestown in 1753. In 1754 Joseph Severance and Eunice Clesson of Springfield were convicted of incest, for which Severance sat on the gallows for an hour. Clesson did not, for what were expressed only as "special Reasons" — the court may have suspected that she had been an unwilling participant. Such had been the case in Connecticut in 1725, when the Assembly had relieved Sarah Pirkins of the same sentence, upon finding that "she was unnaturally forced . . . by her fathers . . . authority." When both parties appeared to have consented to incest, as in the 1778 case of Dudley Drake and Abigail Holcomb, both spent an hour on the gallows.[26]

In Massachusetts and Connecticut simulated executions were also conducted as acts of leniency in cases where the statutory punishment was death. Arson was a capital offense in Massachusetts in 1753 when Sarah Peake was convicted of setting fire to her master's house, but she was sentenced only "to be whipp'd Twenty Stripes under the Gallows" after an hour with the rope about her neck. Connecticut's General Assembly sometimes commuted real executions to simulated ones. Vans Skelly Mulley, for instance, had been convicted of raping ten-year-old Amy Palmer of Greenwich, but the Assembly found several reasons to mitigate his guilt. He had only recently been brought to Connecticut as a captive from French Canada in the French and Indian War. Having been "born and brought up under the Dominions of the French King & in a great measure Ignorant of the Law of God & Man always prevented & forbid the knowledge of Reading or Writing," he claimed to be astonished to discover that in Connecticut rape was thought to be an offense "of so high & aggravated a kind & called for so great a punishment as Death." Further inquiry of one of Mulley's jailers revealed that Mulley may not in any event have been particularly skillful at his crime. "Damon Luck one of the men who sarched the frenchman said that he and the other men did not think by what appeared to them that he ever entered her body," it was reported to the Assembly. They supposed instead that he "fumbled ther abouts till he satisfied himself by what appeared on his shirt." The men and women of the community, meanwhile, were watching Amy Palmer closely. In the immediate aftermath of the rape she was riding horses, carrying wood, playing with other children—in short, doing the same things she had always done. One man said that "he in pertickler tuck notis of the behaviour of the Girl and if he had not been told that was the girl he should not have thought any thing had ben the matter with her." One woman "wondered that Justus palmer [Amy's father] and his wife would let that girl go out in the wet if shee was so much hurt as they pretended." The Assembly accordingly commuted Mulley's sentence to a simulated hanging, followed by a whipping, "and then to have his right ear naild to a post & cut off," then a month in jail, then another whipping, and finally to be banished from the colony.[27]

With all this whipping and nailing, the hour on the gallows seems today to be scarcely a punishment at all. The scant surviving evidence of how these episodes were perceived at the time, however, suggests that they were intended and interpreted as serious punishment. The many statutes and newspaper accounts describing simulated executions always list them first, before the whipping or other punishment that would follow. This may be only an artifact of the order in which they were administered, but that order is itself indicative of the relative prominence of the punishments. A whipping or a term in prison could just as easily have come first, but it never did.

There is only one surviving visual representation of a simulated colonial hanging, on a broadside whose title deserves quotation in full as the best possible description of its contents: *Inhuman Cruelty: Or Villany Detected. Being a true Relation of the most unheard-of, cruel and barberous Intended Murder of a Bastard Child belonging to John and Ann Richardson, of Boston, who confined it in a small Room, with scarce any Victuals, or Cloathing to cover it from the cold or rain, which beat into it, for which Crime they were both of them Sentenc'd to set on the Gallows, with a rope around their Necks, &c.*[28] The title itself suggests the importance the author ascribed to the hour the Richardsons spent on the gallows. We know that similar cases were followed by corporal punishment, so we can assume that the Richardsons were sentenced to that as well, but the author relegated this part of the sentence to the "&c." at the end of the title, a choice that strongly implies that he considered the time on the gallows to be the primary part of the sentence. The broadside includes a standard picture of a hanging scene, with a large audience. The picture was probably not intended to be a representation of the actual event, but was rather a generic decorative element similar to those on many of the broadsides accompanying real executions. That a fake hanging would be thought a suitable occasion for publishing a stock picture of a real hanging suggests the perceived similarity of the two events. The text of the broadside suggests that the message a simulated hanging was intended to convey was exactly the one conveyed by a real hanging:

> Behold him, Sirs, with his inviting *Fair*,
> High on the gallows, see him seated there:
> Behold how well the pliant halter suits
> These harden'd monsters, and unnatural brutes.
>
> . . .
>
> Behold, ye Swains, how great their guilt has been;
> Then stand in awe, and be afraid to sin.

A symbolic execution, with all the trappings of a real execution save the death of the criminal, was evidently understood to bear the same message of terror as a real one.

A third kind of symbolic execution was carried out in the case of two Philadelphia burglars, James Prouse and James Mitchel, who were scheduled to be hanged on January 14, 1731. Prouse was only nineteen, and Mitchel was widely thought to be innocent. A bell was tolled at one in the afternoon to signify that they would soon emerge from prison to begin the trip to the gallows. A crowd gathered to watch. Outside the prison walls, the condemned men's irons were removed and their arms were bound behind them. Prouse cried all the while. "Do not cry Jemmy," Mitchel said softly, in a futile effort to console him. "In an Hour or two it will be over with us, and we shall both be easy." Prouse and Mitchel were placed in a cart, next to their coffins, and led through the city to the gallows. Upon the scaffold, the sheriff told them they were expected to confess their crimes to the crowd, and to exhort listeners to avoid the paths they had taken. Prouse admitted that he had committed the burglary. Mitchel asked only "What would you have me to say? I am innocent of the Fact."

Their brief speeches concluded, Prouse and Mitchel were instructed to stand up. The ropes were prepared, one end affixed to the crossbeam, the other around their necks. The sheriff reached into his pocket, took out a piece of paper, and started to read. "And whereas the said James Prouse and James Mitchel," the sheriff began. Prouse and Mitchel were barely listening to what they expected would be the routine reading of their death warrant. But then they began to hear some unexpected words: "have been recommended to me as proper Objects of Pity and Mercy." This was legal boilerplate too, the opening not of a death warrant but of a pardon. No one needed to hear the rest. Mitchel exclaimed "God bless the Governor" and immediately fainted. Prouse was overwhelmed with joy. Mitchel recovered consciousness in time to hear the crowd's acclamations for the governor's mercy. The sheriff had been carrying the pardon with him in his pocket all the way from the prison.[29]

Prouse and Mitchel's near-hanging was no doubt a "remarkable Transaction," as the *Philadelphia Gazette* put it, but it was by no means an unusual one. Government officials often withheld information about clemency until the last moment. By waiting until both the condemned prisoner and the audience were certain that an execution would take place, the government staged a drama of terror without having to take any life. Officials could simultaneously convey two opposing messages, the severity of the law and the kindness of the individuals administering it. Isaac Bradford was pardoned in 1737, "yet that his Crime may leave a more lasting Impression on him," Pennsylvania's Provincial Council ordered that Bradford's name nevertheless be included in an execution warrant, and that Bradford "be carried with the other Malefactors to the place of Execution, and there receive a Reprieve." The rapist Richard Shirtliffe was granted a pardon which the sheriff was "directed not to make known to him until he be taken under the gallows." John Cowman, condemned in Maryland for witchcraft, was ordered to be taken to the gallows, and, "the rope being about his neck, it be there made known to him how much he is beholding to the lower house of the assembly for mediating and interceding in his behalf."[30]

The practice persisted well into the nineteenth century. In 1820, when Ebenezer Dexter, the federal marshal in Providence, received a pardon for William Cornell, he promptly wrote back to Secretary of State John Quincy Adams with an urgent question: "Am I to understand that it is to be kept a secret until the day that he was to have been executed and every preparation to be made accordingly and to be made known under the gallows at the Hour appointed for his execution?"[31] Allocated judiciously, last-minute pardons provoked all the terror of full execution.

Allocated too often, on the other hand, the gallows reprieve would undermine the purposes served by the death penalty. If condemned criminals learned to expect that their executions would be called off at the last minute, they would neither experience the terror associated with the contemplation of death nor concentrate their minds on repentance. By the middle of the eighteenth century some condemned prisoners were approaching the gallows with this expectation. In Connecticut the burglar Isaac Frasier "behaved with a good deal of seeming unconcernedness, 'til a little before he was turned off," because "he had a secret hope of escaping his punishment." The burglar John Bly said, just before his execution, that watching others receive pardons "induced me to suppose, what many others vainly encouraged me in, that we should never be executed."[32] The practice of staging gallows reprieves began to come under criticism for raising the expectations of condemned criminals and thereby causing them to be too cavalier during their final days.

In benefit of clergy, simulated hangings, and gallows reprieves, the state had at its disposal a few forms of capital punishment that did not kill. Today we measure punishment in units of time in prison. Before prison became the standard method of punishment, the only available units of measurement for serious crime were degrees of deviation from an ordinary execution.

Worse Than Death

An ordinary death by hanging was not, however, the harshest penalty at the disposal of the seventeenth- and eighteenth-century state. Just as there were a few steps short of death, there were a few steps beyond it. "'Tis well known there are some kinds of Death more sharp and terrifying than others," one English writer noted. "An Execution that is attended with more lasting Torment, may strike a far greater Awe."[33] These more severe punishments were carefully handed out to apply terror where it was thought to be most needed.

Hanging, as we have seen, sometimes caused a quick and apparently painless death. When government officials wanted to ensure that death would be slow and painful, and thus all the more frightening to contemplate, they resorted to an alternative method—burning alive. Burning had a long history in English jurisprudence. In the late medieval period it had been a common method of execution for heresy and witchcraft.[34] By the time of the colonization of North America, however, burning was no longer used as a punishment for religious offenses. Those convicted of witchcraft at Salem were hanged, not burned, as were the other colonists executed for witchcraft in the seventeenth and early eighteenth centuries. Burning was reserved for two classes of offenders whose crimes were considered unusually disruptive of the social order.

The first of these classes was slaves convicted either of murdering their owners or of plotting a revolt. In Virginia a "Negro Woman who lately kill'd her Mistress" confessed to the crime, "and is since burnt." "He stood the Fire with the greatest Intrepidity," it was reported of a New Jersey slave who killed his owner in 1753. Thirteen of the black participants in the New York "Negro Plot" were burned at the stake; none of the whites was. The second and smaller class of offenders subject to being burned alive was women convicted of killing their husbands. Catherine Bevan was burned at the stake in Pennsylvania in 1731 for this offense. Her accomplice, Peter Murphy, was merely hanged. What these cases have in common is the reversal of the traditional hierarchy of the household, the revolt by slave against master or wife against husband. The legal name for such crimes, petit treason, suggests the strength of the analogy contemporaries drew between the household and the state. Treason denoted "not only offences against the king and government," explained William Blackstone, but also crimes "proceeding from the same principle of treachery in private life."[35]

Death by burning was always painful, and was for that reason alone a more fearful punishment than hanging, which was painful only sometimes. Burning also destroyed the body, unlike hanging, which usually left an intact corpse. Burning at the stake was thus a form of super-capital punishment, worse than death itself. Cotton Mather was at the 1681 burning of a slave the records call "Maria Negro," in the company of William Cheny, who was hanged for rape immediately afterward. Cheny had remained stoic through his trial and the period leading up his execution. He had protested his innocence, refused to listen to the sermon preached for him on his hanging day, and ignored the ministers who urged him to repentance. Only the sight of Maria being burned alive, Mather recalled, was enough to break Cheny down. "Never was a Cry, for *Time! Time! A World for a Little Time! the Inexpressible worth of Time!* Uttered, with a more unutterable Anguish."[36]

Burning was inflicted only rarely. Many slaves who killed their masters, and many women who killed their husbands, were sentenced to be hanged instead. Sheriffs conducting burnings were sometimes so reluctant to proceed that, as an act of charity, they hanged the condemned person first to spare some of the pain. Catherine Bevan's executioner hanged her above the flames, hoping she would be dead before the burning began, but the fire spread too quickly to the rope around her neck and burned it off, dropping her, still alive, into the fire. Sentences sometimes specified that the defendant should be hanged first, and only then burned, as a way to intensify a death sentence without increasing the measure of pain involved.[37]

Another way to inflict a sentence worse than death was to display the corpse in a public place. The body, covered with tallow or pitch to delay decomposition, was encased in a *gibbet*, an iron cage sturdy enough to hold it high above the ground and with large enough spaces between the bars to permit easy viewing. A gibbeted criminal was commonly said to be "hung in chains" or "hung in irons." The practice was intended to magnify the deterrent effect of capital punishment, in two senses. By keeping the execution in public view much longer than the ceremony itself, gibbeting allowed the state to repeat its message of terror, day in and day out, to those who passed near the site in their daily routines. And by denying the customary burial, permitting the condemned person's body to decompose in full view, subject to weather, insects, and birds of prey, the state could intensify the message of terror by exploiting the popular concern with the integrity of the body after death.

Hanging in chains was a penalty applied in an ad hoc fashion. The gibbet would be in order whenever officials perceived the need for an extra dose of terror. Slaves were often hung in chains for crimes like rape and arson, in a show of force to other slaves in their community. Indians were gibbeted too, for the same reason. In Woburn, Massachusetts, William Bradstreet noted in his journal in 1671, "an Indian knockt an English maid on the head with his hatchet. He was taken & hanged and so hung upon a gibbett." When whites were hung in chains, their crimes tended to be those considered extraordinarily grave. Pirates often received the gibbet. Murderers might be hung in chains for particularly egregious crimes. In 1751 residents of Annapolis could watch the decaying body of

Jeremiah Swift, who had killed a group of children; in 1754 they could see John Wright and "Mulatto Toney" gibbeted near the harbor for the murder of a ship captain.[38]

The public display of the dead body of a famous criminal, by all accounts, created a sensation, attracting a steady stream of spectators. Benjamin Colman saw the Massachusetts pirate William Fly gibbeted; he called it "a Spectacle for warning to others." The notorious pirate Joseph Andrews was hung high in chains "on the most conspicuous Part of the Pest-Island in New-York Bay." Pest Island is now called Liberty Island, and if one considers the visibility of the Statue of Liberty one can get a sense of how well Andrews's rotting corpse could serve "as a Spectacle to deter all Persons from the like Felonies for the future." The gibbet was rare enough in any given place that it was an object of curiosity, a magnet that drew spectators from all social classes and age groups. Jeremiah Bumstead of Boston described a pleasant 1724 outing in his diary: "My wife & Jery & Bety, David Cunningham & his wife, & 6 more, went to the castle to Governors Island, & to see the piratte in Gibbitts att Bird Island."[39] As mentioned earlier, the 1755 gibbeting of a slave named Mark was remembered distinctly by residents of Charlestown, Massachusetts, as late as 1798. One purpose of the gibbet was to reach the public, and the public appears to have taken notice.

The public-relations value officials perceived in the gibbet can be seen clearly in three unrelated episodes in late seventeenth-century New York, all involving the hanging in chains of people who were already dead when the decision was made to gibbet them. In 1682 an unnamed slave believed to have murdered three people, including two of his owner's children, was found dead in a river. His body was retrieved and gibbeted. In 1685 the body of a slave named Cuffy, executed for arson and then buried, was dug up and hung in chains. In 1697, when a murderer under sentence of death died of natural causes before his execution date, his body was ordered to be gibbeted.[40] In such cases, where officials manipulated the bodies of the dead as a warning to the living, the mere fact of death was evidently considered less important than the manner in which death would be publicly presented.

A poem published in Philadelphia in 1793 suggests that the fear inspired by the gibbet arose not so much from the prospect of having one's corpse seen as from that of having it torn to shreds:

He being hang'd, his body was conveyed
To hang in chains where he the murder did,
And the next day as for a truth 'tis well known,
His flesh the birds did pick from off the bone.

An experienced pirate, Joseph Andrews kept up an imperturbable front the night before his execution, except when his thoughts turned to the gibbet. "He was very desirous to know if his Body *really* was to be hung in Chains," one person present related. Andrews had been pressed to tell his life story for publication, and he grasped at that request, the only leverage he had, to bargain in vain with his jailers. If they would cancel the gibbeting, "he would give a particular account of the Transactions of his Life; but if, on the contrary, they persisted in their resolution to Hang him in Chains, the World should have little Satisfaction from him." English petitions suggest that the families of condemned criminals felt much greater disgrace from a gibbeting than from an ordinary hanging.[41] To have one's dead body exposed to the elements was to die dishonorably.

Hanging in chains was one way of intensifying the message of terror conveyed by an execution. The public display of a dismembered body was another. When tensions between colonists and Indians were running high, an Indian hanged for murdering a colonist might have his head "cutt off the next day and pittched upon a pole in markett place," as was the case with Nepaupuck, convicted of murder in 1639, shortly after the initial settlement of New Haven. In 1671, as war threatened, an unnamed Indian in Massachusetts "was hangd and his head sett upon a pole on the gallowes." When slaves threatened to rebel, their decapitated heads might be conscripted for the same public good. In 1763 a local court ordered that a slave named Tom from Augusta County, Virginia, who had been convicted of killing his owner, "be hanged by the neck until he be dead and . . . that then his head be Severed from his body and affixed on a pole on the Top of the Hill near the Road that lead from this Court House." Tom's head, high enough to be visible from a distance and close to a heavily traveled road, was no doubt seen by many, but probably not by as many as the body parts of another slave named Tom, also convicted of killing his owner, in Amelia County, Virginia, in 1755. This Tom was sentenced to have his head "severed from his body which is to be cut up in four quarters and disposed of in the following manner. His head is to be stuck up at the cross road near Major Peter Jones', one quarter near William Wiley's, one quarter at Farley's, and the other at any other public place within this County the Sheriff shall think proper."[42]

In 1729 the Maryland legislature found that "several Petit-Treasons, and cruel and horrid Murders, have been lately committed by Negroes, which Cruelties they were instigated to commit with the like Inhumanity, because they have no Sense of Shame, or Apprehension of future Rewards or Punishments." The ordinary manner of executing criminals, the legislature concluded, "is not sufficient to deter a People from committing the greatest Cruelties, who only consider the Rigour and Severity of Punishment." Maryland accordingly authorized its judges to sentence slaves in cases of murder or arson "to have the right Hand cut off, to be hang'd in the usual Manner, the Head severed from the Body, the Body divided into Four Quarters, and Head and Quarters set up in the most publick Places of the County where such Fact was committed."[43] Quartering, it hardly needs to be said, permitted four times as many people to see the criminal's dead body. While no early American theoretical discussion of the point has survived, we may surmise that further dismemberment, although allowing for a greater number of display sites, was thought to reduce the visual impact of each one. A severed head must have been considered a better deterrent than an ear, an arm better than a finger. The dead bodies of slaves were ripped into pieces, always four, on several occasions in the eighteenth century.

The harshest kind of dismemberment, preceded by disembowelment while still alive, was reserved for those believed to pose the greatest threat to public order—people found to have committed treason. Jacob Leisler and Jacob Milborne, convicted of treason in New York in 1691, were sentenced to be hanged "by the Neck and being Alive their bodys be Cutt downe to the Earth and their Bowells be taken out and they being Alive, burnt before their faces; that their heads shall be struck off and their Bodys Cutt in four parts." The sentence was carried out. The leader of the Regulators of North Carolina received the same sentence in 1771. So did a group of Maryland residents convicted of aiding the British in the Revolution. Disembowelment and quartering had been the common punishment for treason in England, and the practice was copied in the colonies.[44]

If many today would be horrified by such brutal punishments, so too were many in the seventeenth and eighteenth centuries, or else the punishments could not have been believed to serve as such emphatic deterrents to crime. But if today's horror would cause people to find fault with the criminal justice system itself, the horror of the seventeenth and eighteenth centuries did not. Before the later eighteenth century there is no record of anyone in British North America claiming that public dismemberment was too severe a penalty for crime. To the extent that popular attitudes before then are recoverable today, they may be exemplified by an article in the *Boston Evening-Post* from 1765, describing an execution in Paris from two years before. According to the article, a midwife found to have killed several babies was executed by hanging her, over a fire, in a large iron cage also occupied by sixteen wild cats. The cats attacked her while she was still alive, pulling out her entrails in 35 minutes of what the account called "unspeakable torture," until she and the cats all died. Whether or not the story is true, the interesting aspect of it for our purposes is the short comment the paper's editor appended to it. "However cruel this execution may appear with regard to the poor animals," he lectured (speaking of Massachusetts as part of England, which it still was), "it certainly cannot be thought too severe a punishment for such a monster of iniquity, as could proceed in acquiring a fortune by the deliberate murder of such numbers of un-offending innocents. And if a method of executing murderers, in a manner somewhat similar to this was adopted in England, perhaps the horrid crime of murder might not so frequently disgrace the annals of the present times."[45] The conspicuous show of state power might be gruesome, but sometimes it was necessary. This, so far as one can tell today, was common thought for the seventeenth and most of the eighteenth century.

Burning, gibbeting, and dismemberment all dwindled away toward the end of the eighteenth century, when they were replaced by a single method of intensifying a death sentence—dissection. The older forms of aggravated capital punishment were flamboyant public displays (sometimes literally so); dissection, by contrast, took place indoors, under the gaze of a small number of people. The abandonment of these most violent forms of public punishment was the first step in the abandonment of public punishment generally, a process that took place throughout North

America and Europe between the late eighteenth and early twentieth centuries.

The practice of dissecting dead bodies, both for ascertaining causes of death and for instructing medical students, had a long history in England and the colonies. As instruction in anatomy came to be understood as an essential component of a medical education in the eighteenth century, the demand for cadavers began to exceed the supply. In the eighteenth and early nineteenth centuries the demand for cadavers was primarily satisfied unlawfully, by grave robbers who dug up the bodies of people recently buried.[46]

In this context the dissection of executed criminals killed two birds with one stone. By adding dissection to a death sentence the state could simultaneously furnish bodies to physicians and deter crime. The dissection of English criminals dates back at least to the sixteenth century, and there is evidence of the practice in the earliest American colonies. The 1641 Massachusetts Body of Liberties included a requirement that executed criminals be buried within twelve hours "unless it be in case of Anatomie," which suggests that some were being dissected. The earliest condemned North American criminal actually known to have been dissected was an Indian named Julian, who was hanged for murder in Boston in 1733. Five years later, in Williamsburg, Virginia, the murderer Anthony Dittond was "anatomiz'd by the Surgeons," according to a local newspaper account.[47] While the evidence is not entirely clear, these early dissections appear to have been authorized after the execution rather than being part of the sentence itself. They do not seem to have been undertaken in a conscious effort to deter crime by adding an extra element of terror to the punishment.

Dissection became a formal arm of penal policy in 1752, when Parliament passed an act "for better preventing the horrid crime of murder." In order "that some further terror and peculiar mark of infamy be added to the punishment of death," bodies of English murderers were required to be given to physicians to be anatomized. Colonial practice was never as severe. Dissection remained the exception rather than the rule for colonial murderers. After independence, many states authorized judges to include dissection in a capital murder sentence, but these statutes were nearly always phrased in discretionary terms, to allow judges to sentence a murderer to be dissected only where the judge believed the added penalty appropriate. The first of the American dissection statutes, and apparently the only one not allowing judges discretion in this respect, was a Massachusetts law of 1784 that made the increased penalty mandatory only for those convicted of winning a duel. (The judge was given discretion to order the loser to be dissected as well.) New York gave its judges the discretion to have murderers anatomized in 1789, after a riot in New York City the previous year directed at grave-robbing surgeons. In 1790, in the very first federal criminal statute, Congress provided the same discretion to federal judges. Other states and territories followed suit: New Jersey in 1796, the Louisiana Territory in 1808, Maine in 1821, Connecticut in 1824 (after an anti-dissection riot like the one in New York), Illinois in 1833, Iowa in 1838, and Nebraska in 1858. As late as 1904 a new statute in Massachusetts reaffirmed the power of a court to sentence a murderer to be dissected.[48]

Accounts of capital trials suggest that dissection was included in a very small percentage of nineteenth-century murder sentences. Like burning, gibbeting, or dismemberment, dissection was an enhancement to a murder sentence, not a standard part of one. Often it was imposed on defendants convicted of murder as part of a shipboard mutiny, or individuals considered more culpable than the accomplices with whom they had been convicted, as a way of signifying that some murderers deserved a greater punishment than others. "We ought to proportion the terror of punishment to the degree of offense," James Madison argued in dissection's favor in the first Congress. As United States Supreme Court Justice James Iredell explained to a Georgia grand jury in 1792, dissection was only for cases "of very aggravating circumstances."[49]

There were also, however, many cases in which no reason for dissection is apparent from the record, where it seems likely that the idiosyncrasies of the judge, or the lack of local relatives to claim the body, or the social standing of the defendant's family, or the earnestness of the local medical community played a role in filling the anatomy table. At a New York sentencing proceeding in 1818, the judge "took occasion to say, that he considered a weak man in the administration of justice, as dangerous to the community as a wicked or corrupt man," and then to prove his strength sentenced James Hamilton to be dissected. In Massachusetts Dominic Daley and James Halligan were dissected because two justices of the Supreme Judicial Court believed them to "possess dispositions wicked, perverse, and incorrigible." The murderer Jesse Strang was spared dissection only because of the judge's "respect for the feelings of his aged and respectable parents."[50] Whether or not dissection would be part of a sentence was purely within the discretion of the trial court, and for that reason was often unpredictable.

In the debates on what would become the dissection provision in the first federal criminal statute, one representative cited "the very great and important improvements which had been made in Surgery from experiment" as an argument in its favor. But penal dissection failed miserably as a means of supplying surgeons with cadavers. The number of criminals executed was never anywhere close to the number of cadavers demanded for medical instruction. By the middle of the nineteenth century most states ensured a steady supply by donating to physicians the unclaimed bodies of the poor. Some of these unclaimed bodies belonged to executed criminals, so the connection between execution and dissection would never be totally severed. As a boy in 1881, John Motley Morehead attended the hanging of two black men and one black woman in Rockingham County, North Carolina. "There was no claimant for the body of one of the negro men," he recalled fifty years later, "and Dr. Wall of Madison bought it for $10.00. He embalmed it in some way and used it for dissecting and in the teaching of some students who intended to study medicine."[51] By the second half of the nineteenth century, however, if the bodies of hanged criminals were dissected, it was usually because when alive their possessors had been poor, not because they had been criminals.

But if dissection fell short of one of its objectives, it achieved the other. Dissection "was attended with salutary effects, as it certainly encreased the dread of punishment," one of its congressional proponents argued in 1790. The family and friends of Whiting Sweeting, hanged in Albany in 1791, pleaded in vain with the doctor who had been assigned the rights to Sweeting's corpse. Abram Antone, interviewed shortly before being hanged in Morrisville, New York, declared "that he is willing to die, and only complains of the *manner*. He is very anxious respecting his body, being fearful that it will be obtained for dissection."[52] Condemned prisoners were sometimes careful to instruct people they trusted to look out for their bodies, lest they be delivered to the surgeons. Michael Martin, executed in Boston in 1821, included such a clause in his will: "Feeling much repugnance that my body should be given over for dissection, or fall into the hands of the surgeons,—therefore, I do hereby bequeath my body to Francis W. Waldo, of Boston, Esquire, trusting to his friendship for me, that he will see it decently interred, and preserve it, as far as possible, from molestation." In 1878 John Ten Eyck of Pittsfield, Massachusetts, "worried lest his body should be dissected and his skeleton grace some museum, but his fears were set at rest" by his father-in-law, who volunteered to take custody of Ten Eyck's corpse. (The father-in-law did carefully remove Ten Eyck after the execution to another part of Pittsfield, where he began charging admission to see him. When the town government shut down the show, the father-in-law moved to a nearby town and netted fifteen dollars at ten cents a head. But Ten Eyck was never dissected.) Cases like these offered evidence in support of the view of one Boston judge that people had a "terror of dissection, greater even than the terror of death."[53]

Terror was not the only reaction to dissection. The conversion of a corpse into a commodity offered certain advantages to condemned prisoners, and some were quick to exploit them. Shortly before his death in 1772, the Massachusetts rapist Bryan Sheehen sold his body to a Dr. Kast of Salem, and in his last words he so instructed the hangman. In Somerset County, Maryland, a man named Rounds sold his body for dissection to a group of Philadelphia physicians. In New Hampshire Franklin Evans sold his white corpse to a Dr. Crosby of Dartmouth College for $50, but a few years later in Americus, Georgia, Charles Tommey could get only $3 for his black one. Amasa Walmsley found it necessary to dispel rumors that he had sold his body to the surgeons for rum. A New York arsonist named Will spent the proceeds of his own self-sale eating gourmet food in jail while waiting to be hanged. Jails of the eighteenth and early nineteenth centuries offered easy access to nearly anyone wishing to visit their inmates, so surgeons had ample opportunity to negotiate with the prisoners. Many condemned prisoners owned little or nothing apart from their own bodies. Many were leaving wives and children behind. In such circumstances the sale of one's cadaver to anatomists might be a prospect more attractive than any of the alternatives. But dissection was normally something to be feared, not welcomed. "To be dismembered by the *Greedy Knife*," as a late eighteenth-century poet put it, was to suffer a fate worse than the ordinary death.[54]

Burning, hanging in chains, dismemberment, dissection—these were four ways to make a death sentence more severe by destroying the physical body after death. Burning (if one was still alive) was also painful, but the other three were not. Their terror arose not from the prospect of pain but from the common concern for the integrity of the body, from the felt need for a proper burial.

Americans of the period knew that dead bodies decompose. They understood that they would all be reduced to skeletons within a short time after dying. Why then were they so afraid of having their dead bodies destroyed? It is easy to say that there was honor in a proper burial and dishonor in a mutilated corpse, but to call the phenomenon "honor" only gives it a name without explaining it. Why was honor equated with an intact corpse?

Part of the answer is not unique to colonial America. All over the world, in all eras of recorded history, people have cared deeply about the disposal of dead bodies. That concern persists in our own culture today. Many people, even those who consider themselves free of religious and mythical beliefs, place great importance in a proper burial, for reasons they may not be able to articulate. Punishments that mutilate the dead body or interfere with the undisturbed rest of the dead would be viewed as extraordinarily harsh today, just as they were in the seventeenth and eighteenth centuries. Scientific knowledge has barely dented our intuitive sense that an individual's personality is in some way connected with his or her physical body even after death, and that the improper treatment of a corpse is accordingly an insult to the person who inhabited it.

But these intensified forms of capital punishment could be effective in the seventeenth and eighteenth centuries—probably more so than they would be today—because colonial Americans had two additional reasons to be worried about the physical integrity of the dead body. First, most of the early Christian writers held that although the soul left the body at death, body and soul would be reunited at the last judgment. "If there be no resurrection of the dead, then is Christ not risen," Paul had told the Corinthians, and centuries of theologians interpreted that and similar passages to refer to the resurrection of the physical body. The precise details of how a decomposed corpse would be reassembled were a mystery, but the process was hardly beyond the competence of an omnipotent God, who had once created humans from nothing. "Our faith is not so fraile as to think that the ravenous beasts can deprive the body of any part to bee wanting in the resurrection," the Puritan John Weever affirmed; "where not a haire of the head shall be missing; a new restitution of our whole bodies being promised to all of us in a moment."[55]

Christian theology fused with older folk beliefs about the importance of undisturbed rest for the dead to create a powerful popular taboo against tampering with a dead body. All over early modern western Europe, it was widely believed that a corpse whose integrity had been violated would be denied resurrection at the final judgment. The confidence of the ecclesiastical writers in God's power of reassembly "did not succeed in convincing the people," Philippe Ariès concludes, "who had a very vivid sense of the unity and continuity of the individual and did not distinguish the soul from the body or the glorified body from the fleshly one." The dead body in early modern Europe was popularly understood as a sacred object, and the cemetery as a sacred place. This blend of elite and folk belief was carried by colonists to North America, where it persisted for some time (and indeed is still common today). It could be seen most clearly in the eighteenth and early nineteenth centuries in the widespread horror at dissection for anatomical instruction, a horror due in part to the methods by which cadavers were acquired, but largely due to the sense that something sacred was being defiled.[56]

Against this background of thought, a punishment that destroyed the body was especially terrifying. Even an executed criminal, if properly buried, might hope for bodily resurrection at the last judgment, but someone who had been intentionally burned beyond recognition, or whose body had been permitted to decompose in a gibbet, or who had been cut into quarters for display, or who had been carved up by surgeons, could never be resurrected. By merely hanging a criminal, the state could end this life, but it could not preclude the possibility of an eternal and perfect life sometime in the future. When the state killed and destroyed the body, however, the stakes were much higher. The Scottish merchant John Melish was on his way through Georgia in 1806 when his American companion "stopped to point out the spot where two negroes were executed for killing an overseer. The one was hanged, and the other was burnt to death." His friend explained to Melish "that this mode of punishment is sometimes inflicted on negroes, when the crime is very flagrant, to deprive them of the mental consolation arising from a hope that they will after death return to their own country."[57] In exercising its power to deny the afterlife, the state exploited the most powerful weapon in its arsenal.

Popular religious belief thus provides one reason why these forms of punishment inspired a terror worse than death. There was also a very practical reason. Simply stated, one could never be absolutely sure that a seemingly dead person was irrevocably dead.

Colonial Americans inherited an extensive European folklore concerning the danger of premature burial. People heard buried corpses moving about and making sounds like squealing pigs, phenomena attributed today to the emanation of gases in decomposition, but quite disturbing at the time. Fear of being inadvertently buried alive led to a variety of common precautions by the seventeenth century, most often a delay of several days between death and burial. These fears crossed the Atlantic to North America. The United States granted twenty-two patents for devices to be placed inside coffins to enable the erroneously buried to signal that they were still alive, typically by pulling a rope that ran up to the surface and rang a bell or raised a flag.[58]

The danger of being buried too soon was especially great when hanging was involved. Hanging often caused death very slowly, by strangulation. Death was often preceded by unconsciousness. If a hanged body was removed quickly enough and hastened to a physician, there was a possibility that the hanged person could be revived. Eighteenth-century American newspapers were full of such accounts. In 1736 the *Virginia Gazette* reported the miraculous story of Vernham and Harding, hanged in Bristol, England. "To the Surprize of every one," Virginians learned, "after hanging the usual Time, and being cut down, Vernham was perceived to have Life in him, when put into the Coffin; and some . . . who promis'd to save his Body from the Surgeons, carried him away to a House; and a Surgeon being sent for, immediately open'd a Vein, which so recovered his Senses, that he had the Use of Speech, sat up, rubb'd his Knees, shook Hands with divers Persons that he knew, and to all seeming Appearance, a perfect Recovery was expected." When the sheriffs heard the news, they retook Vernham to be hanged again, but Vernham died a few hours later, "in great Agony of Pain, his Bowels being very much convuls'd, as appeared by his rolling from one Side to the other, and often on his Belly."

That was worth reporting, but what made the event so remarkable was that Harding revived too, "and is actually now in Bridewell, where great Numbers of People resort to see him, particularly Surgeons, curious of Observations. He lies in his Coffin, covered with a Rug, has a Pulsation, breathes freely, and has a regular look with his Eyes." Harding had hung so long, with the rope's pressure preventing oxygen from reaching his brain, that he had apparently suffered brain damage. "He has not been heard to speak, only motions with his Hand where his Pain lies," it was reported. It was thought that Harding would not be rehanged, but would rather "be provided for in some convenient House of Charity, with Restraint, he being to all Appearance defective in his Intellects." Resurrection of the supposedly dead was common enough after hangings, but "two such resurrections happening at one Instant in the World, was never heard of in the Memory of Man."[59]

Stories like this one received wide circulation in eighteenth-century America. Several newspapers reprinted a 1767 account from Cork, Ireland, about the robber Patrick Redman or Redmond, who was cut down after hanging for twenty-eight minutes. Five or six hours later he was "actually brought to life by Glover the actor, who it seems is also a dexterous surgeon, and who made an incision in his wind pipe." Redman had been pardoned, and was still alive. The English newspapers published many more such accounts, enough to supply everyone with a stock of knowledge of the possibility of resurrection after execution.[60]

Americans also knew of equally thrilling episodes closer to home. The most famous may have been the story of Joseph Taylor, which was published in several editions between 1788 and 1790.[61] Soon before Taylor was hanged in Boston in 1788 for highway robbery, he was visited in jail by an unnamed doctor, who wished "to Bargain for My Body." Taylor recalled that the prospect of selling himself for dissection put him "in a cold sweat my Knees smote together and my Tongue seemed to cleave to the Roof of my mouth." Evidently feeling some sympathy for Taylor, the doctor offered to help "recover me to Life if my Body could be carried immediately after I was cut down to some Convenient Place, out of the Reach of the People."

The doctor hired a small boat, which would be ready to whisk Taylor to a larger boat moored at some distance from the wharf, upon which the doctor and his apprentice would be waiting. He supplied Taylor with instructions on how to minimize the physical damage wrought by hanging: "Taylor, everything depends on your presence of mind. Remember that the Human Machine may be set in Tune again if You preserve the Spiral Muscle from injury and do not dislocate the Vertebrae of the Neck . . . you must endeavour to Work the Knot behind your Neck and Press your Throat upon the Halter which will prevent the Necks breaking and likewise the Compression of the Jugular and preserve the Circulations in some degree." Taylor carefully followed these directions. While everyone else on the scaffold was praying, he "kept gently turning my head so as to bring the Knot on the Back of my Neck." When the trap fell, his "First Feeling after the Shock of Falling was a Violent strangling and oppression for want of Breath." That sensation "soon gave way to a Pain in my Eyes which seemed to be burned by two Balls of Fire which appeared before them and which seemed to dart on and off like lightning." After one last flash of light, "I sunk away without Pain like one Falling to sleep."

Taylor was unconscious when his friends carried his body to the doctor. He did not know exactly what the doctor did to him, but an hour and twenty-two minutes after being taken on the boat, two hours and forty-three minutes after being dropped from the scaffold, Taylor began to move slightly. Twenty minutes later "I gave a violent deep groan." He felt pain greater than the pain of hanging itself: "I cannot Describe the Intolerable agony of that moment Ten Thousand Stranglings are trifling to it." But under the doctor's care Taylor soon recovered. He fled to Sweden.

A similar but less detailed account, *The Wonderful and Surprising Resurrection of William Jones*, was published in New Jersey three years later.[62] Jones was hanged for murder in Newark in 1791, but appeared a week later with a story much like Taylor's. He had arranged ahead of time with a physician learned in "certain processes in the medical art lately discovered in Europe." Jones followed the physician's directions on how to avoid having his vertebrae broken. "At the moment of my suspension," Jones recounted, "I could hear a buzzing noise in the crowd, which was instantly succeeded by a total darkness in my faculties, accompanied by seeming flashes of fire." Jones remembered nothing else until he awoke to see the physician's face staring down at him. Like Taylor, he experienced excruciating pain upon being restored to consciousness. For four days his feet were paralyzed, but then they began working again. He too planned to leave the country to avoid being hanged a second time.

Were stories like these true? Two centuries later it is probably impossible to know for sure, but at the very least they are not implausible. Unconscious people, apparently dead, are sometimes revived today even after they have stopped breathing. One study of suicides by hanging found that death by asphyxiation typically takes five to twenty minutes, but that it is possible to restore life even to a person who has been suspended for half an hour.[63] Eighteenth-century doctors knew less than doctors do today, but the same was true of the local sheriffs who served as eighteenth-century executioners, so it would not be surprising if on occasion they ended a hanging too soon. The physicians may not have been skilled in any secret art but may simply have taken good care of the body and watched closely for signs of life that might appear in a small percentage of prematurely terminated hangings. It is certainly possible that some of the stories were true—and, more important for our purposes, contemporaries thought they were. Ascertaining death was a tricky business even when death arrived quickly, and it was doubly difficult when the cause of death was slow strangulation. Contemporaries almost certainly believed that every so often an executed criminal was not irrevocably dead. This belief would play a role in the growing dissatisfaction with hanging as a method of execution in the later part of the nineteenth century, and around the turn of the twentieth century it would give rise to a scientific controversy over the efficacy of electrocution.

The possibility of revival provided the second reason punishments like burning, dismemberment, and dissection were so terrifying. By destroying the body the state could snuff out whatever remnants of life remained. The gibbet allowed birds, insects, and weather to do the same. Just as the disassembly of the dead body prevented eternal resurrection at the final judgment, it prevented terrestrial resurrection in the hours after execution.

Beginning in the late eighteenth century the adoption of prison as the standard method of punishment would allow fine gradations in sentencing, calibrated by years or even days. Penal reformers would consider the death penalty too blunt an instrument for the wide range of crimes to which it applied, and they were partly right. Compared with prison, it was. But the reformers' rhetoric has obscured the fact that capital punishment was not just a single penalty in the seventeenth and eighteenth centuries. It was a spectrum of penalties, providing government officials with gradations of severity above and below an ordinary execution. Judges and governors had considerable discretion to tailor the punishment to fit the crime—not as much as they would have with the prison, but more than reformers would later acknowledge. Had that not been the case, the system of capital punishment in effect in the seventeenth and eighteenth centuries could not have been as durable as it was.

4

THE ORIGINS OF OPPOSITION

ASSIGNED IN 1793 TO WRITE an essay, Daniel Tompkins was having trouble settling on a topic. The Columbia College student spent hours searching for a fresh theme, but when the clock struck nine and he had not progressed past the first sentence, he gave up any hope of originality. "Want of time," he concluded, obliged him "to take refuge in some old thread bare subject as Capital punishment." He had nothing new to say about whether or not capital punishment ought to be abolished, he recognized, but "enough has been written by others to furnish us with materials for one side down and two or three lines at the top of the second page."[1]

Here lurked a revolution in public consciousness. Forty years earlier capital punishment had been uncontroversial. In the 1760s and 1770s that had begun to change, as many Americans started to question whether death was too great a punishment for property crimes like burglary and grand larceny. By the 1780s and 1790s the propriety of capital punishment for *any* crime, even murder, was a bitterly contested issue. Whether to abolish capital punishment completely was a subject taken up in debating societies and at college commencement ceremonies. Newspapers carried editorials and letters arguing for and against abolition. Some rising political figures, such as James Madison and the future governor of New York DeWitt Clinton, favored abandoning capital punishment altogether. Others, such as Thomas Jefferson and Benjamin Franklin, advocated eliminating the death penalty for all crimes other than murder. The Massachusetts minister Robert Nesbitt reported that "sentiment was spreading in his parts" to do away with capital punishment, even for murder. "Humanity and reason are likely to prevail so far in our legislature that a law will probably pass in a few weeks to abolish capital punishments in *all cases* whatever," predicted the Philadelphia physician Benjamin Rush, the leading American opponent of the death penalty, in 1793.[2]

Rush was wrong, but not by much. No state ended the death penalty completely in the eighteenth century, but several did away with it for crimes short of murder. The partial abolition of the death penalty was just one component of a broader set of penal reforms that included the elimination of lesser public punishments like whipping and the pillory and the adoption of the prison as the standard tool for punishing criminals. This dramatic transformation in penal thought and practice was an international phenomenon. Opposition to capital punishment began to spread throughout Europe, and some European nations even abolished the death penalty completely. To understand why many Americans began to question capital punishment in the latter part of the eighteenth century, therefore, we must consider issues beyond the death penalty and places other than the United States.

A Very Novel Experiment

Opposition to capital punishment was not without some Anglo-American precedent. English radicals of the 1640s and 1650s argued unsuccessfully for an end to the death penalty for property crimes like robbery and burglary.[3] Some of the Quakers went even further and advocated abolishing the death penalty for all crimes. In the colonies of Pennsylvania and West New Jersey, where for a time they had the numbers to put their views into practice, the Quakers did eliminate capital punishment for crimes other than murder, but they never went so far as to abolish it altogether. This experiment ended in 1718, when Pennsylvania adopted a penal code like those of the other colonies, with the death penalty for crimes like robbery, burglary, and arson. There would be no similar legislative experiments for nearly seventy years.

The law on paper had to be enforced through the verdicts of juries, however, which gave the propertied white male public a point at which to register its opposition to capital punishment in specific cases. Juries in eighteenth-century America, as in England, sometimes tailored their verdicts to avoid imposing the death penalty for lesser felonies. Thomas Gray, charged in North Carolina in 1726 with the capital crime of grand larceny for stealing twenty shillings worth of assorted goods, was convicted by a jury that valued the goods at only ten pence, a figure low enough to come within the definition of the noncapital offense of petit larceny. Another North Carolina jury exercised the same kind of leniency in the 1724 case of Mary Cotton, when it valued sixty shillings worth of stolen goods at ten pence. Whether in the form of acquittals or in the form of convictions for lesser, noncapital offenses, such jury verdicts indicated an undercurrent of dissatisfaction with the formal criminal law.

> And tho' his Crime so great may'nt be,
> Yet by the Law 'tis Burglary.[4]

So read a poem commemorating the 1734 hanging of the Boston burglar Matthew Cushing, a faint glimmer of an argument that Cushing's sentence was disproportionate to his crime.

That glimmer grew into a blaze in the 1760s and 1770s, as more and more Americans began to question the appropriateness of capital punishment for property crime. "Who can avoid pitying poor young fellows, whose existence is cut off in the prime and vigour of life, for the paltry theft of a handkerchief, or of a watch, or for writing a few words on a slip of paper, with a fraudulent intention?" asked the *Georgia Gazette* in 1767. "Surely, means of intimidation cannot be wanting, even tho' every gallows were chopped down." The *New-York Journal* complained in 1773 of the "great disproportion between the value of goods stolen, and the life that is forfeited by the theft." The hanging of Levi Ames for burglary that year prompted a Boston poet to reflect on the incongruity that the government hanged burglars while pardoning a good many murderers.

> Must Thieves who take men's goods away
> Be put to death? While fierce blood hounds,
> Who do their fellow creatures slay,
> Are sav'd from death? This cruel sounds.

At other executions for burglary, ministers took note of the widespread doubts as to the propriety of the sentence and attempted in their sermons to justify it. But doubts continued to multiply. "If I am not myself so barbarous, so bloody-minded, and revengeful, as to kill a fellow creature for stealing from me fourteen shillings," Benjamin Franklin wondered along with a great many others, "how can I approve of a law that does it?"[5]

Opposition to capital punishment for property crime thus originated in a changing morality of retribution. Death, many believed, was simply too harsh a punishment for theft. This moral sentiment quickly acquired urgent practical implications, because as belief in the disproportion of death for property crime grew, so did the difficulty of obtaining convictions. The propensity of juries to acquit defendants of property crimes rather than send them to their deaths began to be perceived as a serious problem in the 1760s. "Perhaps more villains escape punishment by the present rigour of the law than would otherwise if the penalty bore a greater proportion with the crime," reasoned one correspondent to the *Georgia Gazette* in 1767. Because "the law leaves no medium, but provides either death or no punishment at all" for theft, jurors with "a regard for the value of life, and above all for the value of souls," had no choice but to let thieves go free. The difficulty of obtaining convictions for the capital crime of horse-stealing caused New Jersey to substitute corporal punishment in 1769. The death penalty "has not answered the good Purposes thereby intended," the legislature explained; "but, on the contrary, from an Idea of its extreme Severity operating upon the Minds of the Inhabitants of this Province, has destroyed that Vigilance usually exerted by them in the apprehending of Criminals."[6] As dissatisfaction with the retributive aspect of capital punishment for property crime spread, concern about its deterrent aspect had to spread too, because a penalty from which juries were known to shrink could hardly deter prospective criminals.

In this climate of thought arrived one of the most influential books of the eighteenth century, the Italian philosopher Cesare Beccaria's *Essay on Crimes and Punishments*. Published in Italy in 1764, Beccaria's *Essay* was the first work to present a rigorous, sustained attack on the utility and the legitimacy of the death penalty. Within a few years of its appearance it was published in translation all over Europe. The first English translations appeared in London and Dublin in 1767. These circulated widely in the American colonies. Thomas Jefferson and George Washington bought copies, probably in 1769. Jefferson copied extensive passages into his commonplace book. John Adams quoted Beccaria in the opening sentence of his defense of the Boston Massacre soldiers in 1770. English editions were advertised in American newspapers as early as 1772. The first American edition was published in Charleston, South Carolina, in 1777, and two Philadelphia editions followed, one in 1778 and the other in 1793. The *Essay* was serialized in the *Worcester Gazette* in 1786. In the same year another serial version began in the *New Haven Gazette* and concluded in the *Connecticut Magazine*. Beccaria's ideas were meanwhile being repeated by English and American writers who were also widely read. For lawyers, the most important was William Blackstone, whose four-volume *Commentaries on the Laws of England* was the most popular jurisprudential work of the era. In his fourth volume, first published in 1769 (two years after Beccaria's initial publication in English), Blackstone called Beccaria "an ingenious writer" and summarized Beccaria's argument against capital punishment.[7]

Beccaria presented a two-part critique of the death penalty. He first questioned the state's authority to punish crime with death. "What *right*, I ask, have men to cut the throats of their fellow-creatures?" Relying on social contract theory, Beccaria reasoned that if the government possessed only those powers invested in it by the individuals who came together to form it, it could not claim any power over its members' lives, because in a pre-societal state of nature those individuals had not possessed power over their own lives capable of being delegated. "Did any one ever give to others the right of taking away his life?" Beccaria asked. "If it were so, how shall it be reconciled to the maxim which tells us, that a man has no right to kill himself, which he certainly must have, if he could give it away to another?" This argument was not original with Beccaria. Locke and Hobbes had raised and rejected it in the seventeenth century, on the ground that although one could not delegate a nonexistent right to commit suicide, a criminal forfeited his right to his own life, which could thus be legitimately taken by the community as a penalty. Rousseau did the same in 1762, only two years before Beccaria's *Essay*, in terms suggesting that the issue was already an old one.[8] But although the argument was not new, Beccaria's version of it would flourish in the newly independent American states.

The second and more original part of Beccaria's opposition to the death penalty rested on utilitarian reasoning. Death, he argued, was a less effective deterrent than imprisonment. "It is not the intenseness of the pain that has the greatest effect on the mind," he suggested, "but its continuance; for our sensibility is more easily and more powerfully affected by weak but repeated impressions, than by a violent but momentary impulse." The longer a punishment could endure, the more it would remind prospective criminals of the price they would pay for crime. Anglo-American governments had long experience with this principle in the form of the gibbet, which could make a single hanging echo for years. But Beccaria proposed something even better—a punishment that did not diminish in intensity over time. "The death of a criminal is a terrible but momentary spectacle, and therefore a less efficacious method of deterring others than the continued example of a man deprived of his liberty." Even the most hardened criminals, "who can look upon death with intrepidity and firmness," would be frightened by the prospect of lengthy incarceration.

But what made forced labor such a remarkable improvement, Beccaria suggested, was that while it would be a greater deterrent than death, it was in truth a less cruel sentence. "If all the miserable moments in the life of a slave were collected into one point," he conceded, imprisonment "would be a more cruel punishment than any other; but these are scattered through his whole life, whilst the pain of death exerts all its force in a moment." As a result, imprisonment was perceived by the observer, who "considers the sum of all his wretched moments," as a punishment more severe than death, while the prisoner himself, who "by the misery of the present, is prevented from thinking of the future," would perceive his punishment to be less severe than death.

Another utilitarian concern led Beccaria to the same conclusion. "The punishment of death is pernicious to society," he argued, "from the example of barbarity it affords." The spectacle of executions only encouraged citizens to violence by acclimating them to its use. Laws, "which are intended to moderate the ferocity of mankind, should not increase it by examples of more barbarity." Spectators, like criminals, would be rendered less likely to commit crime by the abolition of capital punishment.[9]

Beccaria was hardly the only mid-eighteenth-century European writer with harsh words for the death penalty. Virtually all the writers of the Enlightenment had something to say in favor of milder punishments, including Montesquieu and Rousseau before Beccaria and Voltaire after. "The accumulation of sanguinary laws is the worst distemper of a State," insisted the English lawyer William Eden in 1771, effectively summarizing Enlightenment thought. "Let it not be supposed, that the extirpation of mankind is the chief object of legislation."[10] But Beccaria was the first to organize this pervasive discomfort with capital punishment into a coherent framework encompassing virtually all that could be said in opposition to it. From the late 1760s until nearly a century later, Beccaria was a name familiar to literate Americans, a name synonymous with opposition to capital punishment.

Beccaria's influence was felt quickly in the debate over whether death was too harsh a penalty for property crime, but American reformers were not yet ready to follow him in advocating the abolition of capital punishment for all crimes. That tension is evident in an anguished essay published in the *Connecticut Courant* in 1768 on what the *Courant* called "*a very important Question,* viz. Whether any Community have a right to punish any species of theft with death?"[11] The *Courant* followed Beccaria in arguing that when individuals left the state of nature and formed a government they could invest that government with only those powers which they as individuals had possessed in a state of nature. The power to take one's own life was not one of them. "As a consequence," the *Courant* concluded, "we as individuals have no right to give up our lives to the community, to be taken from us, for any species of theft whatsoever."

Having gone this far, however, the *Courant* drew back from the obvious implication that capital punishment for murder, or indeed for any crime, was just as illegitimate. "I am sensible by this time the reader is impatient to ask, Whether a community has a right to punish murder with death, consistent with these principles?" the essay's anonymous author recognized. "I answer, they have, for there is an essential difference between murder and theft." The difference was that in a pre-societal state of nature a murderer had no right to live. "By the law of nature, he that had taken away the life of another wrongfully forfeited his own; not to any community, but to every individual man." It was this right to kill a murderer that individuals had delegated to the government when they entered into the social contract. Admiring Beccaria's methods but fearing their logical conclusion, the *Courant* was forced to assume a natural law that matched the positive law it urged on Connecticut's legislature. Locke and Rousseau had earlier responded to the social contract argument with a natural law in which *all* criminals forfeited their right to life; in keeping with developing American attitudes toward lesser felonies, the *Courant's* version of natural law limited that forfeiture to murderers.

Several of the state constitutions of the late 1770s and early 1780s included instructions to state legislatures to reduce the number of capital crimes. "The penal laws as heretofore used shall be reformed by the legislature of this state, as soon as may be, and punishments made in some cases less sanguinary," proclaimed Pennsylvania's constitution of 1776. Maryland and South Carolina followed soon after. The most explicit of the early state constitutions was the New Hampshire bill of rights of 1784, which instructed:

> No wise legislature will affix the same punishment to the crimes of theft, forgery and the like, which they do to those of murder and treason; where the same undistinguishing severity is exerted against all offences, the people are led to forget the real distinction in the crimes themselves, and to commit the most flagrant with as little compunction as they do those of the lightest dye: For the same reason a multitude of sanguinary laws is both impolitic and unjust. The true design of all punishments being to reform, not to exterminate, mankind.[12]

These constitutional provisions were aspirations, not actual changes in the law. The war years of the 1770s and 1780s understandably saw little move toward milder punishments.

But not everyone was too busy in the late 1770s to turn some attention to the subject. In November 1776 Virginia's House of Delegates appointed a committee, chaired by Thomas Jefferson, one of Beccaria's enthusiastic American readers, to revise the newly independent state's laws. The committee met in early 1777 to decide which aspects of English law needed revising. The very first item on the resulting list was a drastic reduction in the use of capital punishment: "Treason and Murder (and no other Crime) to be punished with Death." Most other crimes that had long been capital, including manslaughter, arson, robbery, and burglary, were to be punished by public labor.

Reform of capital punishment was only one of many projects undertaken by the committee, so it was not until late 1778 that Jefferson had drafted a "Bill for Proportioning Crimes and Punishments in Cases Heretofore Capital." The bill's lengthy preamble summarized much of what was crystallizing as progressive, Enlightenment thought. Governments have a duty "to arrange in a proper scale the crimes which it may be necessary for them to repress," Jefferson began, "and to adjust thereto a corresponding gradation of punishments." This was, in part, because "the reformation of offenders, tho' an object worthy of the attention of the laws, is not effected at all by capital punishments, which exterminate instead of reforming." Criminals kept alive might also "be rendered useful in various labors for the public," a particularly happy result in the new states of

North America, which were plagued by chronic labor shortages. Laboring criminals, meanwhile, "would be living and long continued spectacles to deter others from committing the like offenses." And by abandoning capital punishment for lesser felonies the state could boost conviction rates: "The experience of all ages and countries hath shewn that cruel and sanguinary laws defeat their own purpose by engaging the benevolence of mankind to withhold prosecutions, to smother testimony, or to listen to it with bias, when, if the punishment were only proportioned to the injury, men would feel it their inclination as well as their duty to see the laws observed."[13]

Here was a full catalogue of the emerging utilitarian arguments against capital punishment. The substitution of forced labor as the penalty for all but the gravest crimes would reduce crime rates in three different ways—by reforming criminals, by better deterring prospective criminals, and by encouraging the law-abiding to do their duty as witnesses and jurors—all while harnessing criminals' labor for public works. The public would win on all fronts simultaneously.

The bill was not introduced in the Virginia legislature until 1785, by which time Jefferson was in Paris as the American ambassador. In the interim the judges of the General Court had expressed their support for reform: "as men," they had informed the governor, "we cannot but lament that the laws relating to capital punishments, are in many cases too severe." The bill was nevertheless defeated in the House of Delegates by a single vote. James Madison, who presented the bill in Jefferson's absence, attributed its defeat to a widespread "rage against Horse stealers" which made the political climate a poor one for reducing criminal penalties.[14] Interest in penal reform subsided in Virginia for a time, but a decade later the state would once again be at the forefront of the movement against capital punishment.

While Virginia was rejecting Jefferson's bill, Pennsylvania became the first state to adopt something very close to it. With the end of the war, opposition to capital punishment for lesser crimes reentered public discourse in Philadelphia. "In some countries, the legislators, like Draco of old, seem to make sport of human life, and declare it forfeit on the most trivial occasions," declared the *Pennsylvania Evening Herald* in 1785. "We need go no farther than some of those European nations, which pride themselves on being patterns of refinement and civilization, for examples of this." The *Freeman's Journal,* another Philadelphia newspaper, followed Beccaria in arguing that prison and forced labor would be more effective deterrents than the death penalty. A decade after the state's post-independence constitution had voiced the aspiration to reduce the use of the death penalty, the legislature finally followed through. Legislators recognized, as one of them put it, that "we are about to try a very novel experiment."[15]

Pennsylvania's 1786 penal reform, the first of many that would follow in the United States over the course of the next century, abolished capital punishment for robbery, burglary, sodomy, and buggery.[16] "It is the wish of every good government to reclaim rather than to destroy," trumpeted the statute's preamble, and the statute accordingly provided for sentences of up to ten years, in the state's new prison, for those convicted of any of these formerly capital offenses. But the goal of reclamation was plainly eclipsed by that of deterrence. Capital punishment for these four crimes, the legislature explained, had failed "to produce such strong impressions upon the minds of others, as to deter them from committing the like offences; which it is conceived may be better effected by continued hard labour, publickly and disgracefully imposed on persons convicted of them." Murderers and those committing manslaughter, rapists, arsonists, and counterfeiters—all would continue to be hanged as before. These were crimes for which Pennsylvania juries were still willing to impose the death penalty, the legislators believed. Where capital punishment could survive in practice, it would remain an effective deterrent.

In the years following, reformers were confident that rates of robbery and burglary had declined as a result of the reform. "Our streets now meet with no interruption from those characters that formerly rendered it dangerous to walk out of an evening," exulted Caleb Lownes. "Our houses, stores, and vessels so perpetually disturbed and robbed, no longer experience those alarming evils. We lay down in peace—we sleep in security." A French visitor to Philadelphia reported that two of the first robbers tried under the new statute pleaded to be tried under the old instead, preferring the chance of an acquittal or a pardon to the certainty of a long prison sentence.[17] The choice seemed to confirm the reformers' belief that milder sentences, consistently applied, would be more feared by criminals than an unpredictable death penalty.

Support for the abolition of capital punishment for lesser felonies continued to spread through the early 1790s. "What shall we say of the injustice and barbarity of our present institutions?" asked one writer. "How can an American tell an inhabitant of Turkey, or of Persia, that for stealing an horse, or for purloigning to the amount of five pounds, we punish the offender with *death?*" Another lamented that "so many of our laws, like those of Draco written in blood, stand in this liberal and enlightened age, as monuments of ancient barbarity." By 1794 New York Governor George Clinton could report to the state's legislature that "the sanguinary complexion of our criminal code has long been a subject of complaint," because "little attention has hitherto been paid to a due proportion between crimes and punishments."[18]

Calls for reform were more numerous in the North than in the South, but southern voices were heard as well. "Where is the man of humanity," asked one North Carolinian in 1796, "who could endure to see his fellow creature struck out of the present state of existence by the operation of our present sanguinary law, merely because he had stole his horse or other like property?" The Democratic Society of Lexington, Kentucky, adopted a resolution in 1793 complaining of "the multitude of inferior crimes which are capitally punished," and appointing a committee "to draft a memorial to the General Assembly, requesting that a radical change be made in our criminal code."[19]

Between 1794 and 1798 five states abolished the death penalty for all crimes other than murder, and three of the five even abolished it for certain kinds of murder. The first was Pennsylvania, which in 1794 provided prison sentences in place of death for treason, manslaughter, rape, arson, and counterfeiting. Murder remained the sole capital crime, and even murder, for the first time in any jurisdiction with a legal system based on that of England, was divided into degrees. First-degree murder, the only kind to be punished with death, included murder "perpetrated by means of poison, or by lying in wait, or by any other kind of wilful, deliberate and premeditated murder" and murder committed in the course of arson, rape, robbery, or burglary. All other murders would constitute the new crime of second-degree murder and would be punished with a prison sentence. Two years later Virginia enacted a similar statute. In 1798 so did Kentucky, in a statute whose preamble was lifted nearly word for word from that of Jefferson's failed Virginia bill of 1778–1785. New York and New Jersey enacted reforms nearly as dramatic in 1796. Both states restricted capital punishment to treason and murder, the latter crime not divided into degrees.[20] As treason against a *state* government would be a rarity in the new United States, murder was in practice the only capital crime left in these two states.

Two of the five states that partially abolished capital punishment in the 1790s, Virginia and Kentucky, had large slave populations. In both the reforms were explicitly intended only for free people. Slaves, already in a prison-like environment, continued to be subject to a long list of capital offenses. Conceptions of appropriate punishment were changing, but in the South they changed only so far. The problem of managing large numbers of captives—in Virginia, nearly half the population—prevented any further reform.

Even in states that had not yet pruned their list of capital crimes, the small number of offenses carrying the death penalty relative to the English penal code became a point of pride for Americans of the late eighteenth century. "It doth honor to the wisdom as well as lenity of our legislators," said James Dana of Connecticut, that "not more than six crimes are capital by our law." "How few are the capital crimes, known to the laws of the United States," exulted James Wilson soon after his appointment as one of the initial Justices of the new United States Supreme Court, "compared with those, known to the laws of England!"[21] The gradual abolition of capital punishment for lesser crimes was increasingly understood as a mark of the new nation's progress.

As states partially abolished the death penalty, they resorted to prisons to fill the void. Several states, including Massachusetts, New York, and Pennsylvania, established their first prisons in the 1780s. When New Jersey, Virginia, and Kentucky partially abolished capital punishment in the 1790s, each state simultaneously appropriated funds for its first prison. These early prisons were a substitute for more than just the gallows. They replaced a host of lesser public punishments as well, including whipping, carting, and outdoor public labor. A variety of circumstances led to the birth of the prison, some of which had little to do with capital punishment. Increasing material wealth allowed governments to feed, clothe, and house prisoners for extended periods, a project that in an earlier era would have been prohibitively expensive. The development of the factory offered a model for imposing discipline on large numbers of people. But much of the motivation for the invention of the prison arose from the growing distaste for executing burglars, robbers, rapists, and the like.[22] Changing conceptions of the proper scope of retribution—the deepening sense that death was too harsh a penalty for crimes other than murder—had resulted in a new calculus of deterrence. The new prisons, it was widely thought, would prevent crime more successfully than did capital punishment.

Virtue and Disease

In the late 1780s American opposition to capital punishment for lesser crimes blossomed into opposition to capital punishment for all crimes. The earliest American argument for complete abolition may have been an editorial published in the *Pennsylvania Evening Herald* in 1785.[23] Debates over complete abolition became common in the Philadelphia press in the late 1780s and then spread to other cities, especially New York, in the 1790s.

If there was one point on which the advocates of abolition were unanimous, it was that they were living in an era of great progress but that penal policy was lagging behind. "The world has certainly undergone a material change for the better within the last two hundred years," Benjamin Rush observed in 1789. Humankind was improving, but the civilized inhabitants of the late eighteenth century were still saddled with criminal laws written in a ruder, more barbaric time. "If we examine history in general," argued one New Yorker in 1794, "we shall readily perceive, that as mankind became more civilized, and advanced toward refinement, punishments became less severe." Capital punishment might be backed by the authority of the Bible, but, as Pennsylvania's attorney general, William Bradford, contended, humanity had made great progress since then. "How dangerous it is rashly to adopt the Mosaical institutions," he suggested. "Laws might have been proper for a tribe of ardent barbarians wandering through the sands of Arabia which are wholly unfit for an enlightened people of civilized and gentle manners." The New York reformer Thomas Eddy found it impossible to believe "that a people enamoured of freedom and a republic, should long acquiesce in a system of laws, many of them the product of barbarous usages, corrupt society, and monarchical principles." The scientist Samuel Mitchill grouped capital punishment with slavery, duelling, and imprisonment for debt as vestiges of a lesser age, relics "which doubtless will be done away when right reason shall gain the ascendency over the human mind."[24]

In an earlier stage of society, reformers argued, capital punishment might have been necessary. But people were better than that now. "I am indeed surprised that capital punishment has not been totally abolished in this country," wrote the French penal reformer Brissot de Warville. "Morals here are so pure, material well-being is so general, and poverty is so rare! Is there any need of such terrible punishments to prevent crime?" When the Yale senior class debated the death penalty in 1784, the debate was not over its propriety in all places and at all times but over whether it was "too severe & rigorous in the United States for the present Stage of Society." New York, declared the physician Phineas Hedges, was a place where "the vindictive spirit of the laws, the implacable, intolerant disposition of the heart," in the form of capital punishment, "obscure the brilliancy of our revolution."[25] Hedges was speaking on the Fourth of July, but he was talking about a revolution deeper and more gradual than the one his listeners had gathered to commemorate. It was a revolution in human nature and in human understanding of the possibilities of further improvement.

The progress of society to a higher stage of civilization, the reformers believed, undermined each of the reasons for capital punishment. Now that Americans had built prisons, the death penalty was no longer necessary as a deterrent. "Every man of principle and honour would cheerfully sacrifice his life sooner than bend under the yoke of slavery," averred one writer. Capital punishment could only be justified on the ground that the criminal's death "is *necessary* to the future safety of society," posited one newspaper editor, but if "confinement will effectually answer this end, the question is decided *against all capital punishment*."[26] Here was one clear way in which progress, reformers believed, had rendered capital punishment a relic of a less civilized past.

Progress was also more subtly at work, they contended, in the minds of the key decisionmakers within the criminal justice system: the victims, jurors, and judges. Citizens had come to abhor harsh punishments, James Wilson told his Philadelphia law classes. As a result, where execution was known to follow upon conviction, "the criminal will probably be dismissed without prosecution, by those whom he has injured. If prosecuted and tried, the jury will probably find, or think they find, some decent ground on which they may be justified or, at least, excused in giving a verdict of acquittal." And even if convicted, the criminal would be in the hands of judges who would "with avidity, receive and support every, the nicest, exception to the proceedings against him; and if all other things should fail" would recommend him to executive clemency. "In this manner," Wilson summed up, "the acerbity of punishment deadens the execution of the law." Death might be more severe than prison in the abstract, Bradford explained, but for criminals banking on the humanity of judges and jurors, a hanging was the last thing on their minds. "Experience proves that these hopes are wonderfully strong," he reported, "and they often give birth to the most fatal rashness."[27] For this reason as well, the advance of civilization was gradually removing the deterrent value from the death penalty.

Capital punishment had been understood to facilitate the criminal's repentance, but this advantage was likewise undermined by the existence of the prison. The prison itself could be "a house of repentance," as Rush put it, a place for the regular religious instruction that was lacking in the world outside.[28] The very word reformers used to describe the prison—a "penitentiary"—emphasized the spiritual transformation they hoped would take place during the period of incarceration. There was no longer any need for a hanging to concentrate the mind on penitence. The prison could reclaim the spirit just as well, without killing the body in the process.

Progress, in the form of the prison, had thus weakened the deterrent and penitential justifications for the death penalty. But the early opponents of capital punishment discerned a far more fundamental result of progress, one that removed the death penalty's retributive justification as well. Ever since the earliest colonial days, Americans had tended to attribute crime to innate human depravity. Everyone had a natural inclination to evil, it was thought, and so a life of virtue required a constant exercise of the will. The commission of a crime represented a failure of will, a decision to neglect the vigilance required of all members of society. Capital punishment, in this way of thinking, served a legitimate retributive purpose. The criminal's lapse from virtue was properly blamed on the criminal.

Many in the late eighteenth century began to reject this understanding of the cause of crime because they adhered to a new conception of human nature, one in which humans were *not* born evil. If people began life as blank slates, or if they were inherently *virtuous*, as many were coming to believe, then how could one explain the existence of crime? The criminal began to be conceived as somehow *different* from everyone else.[29] By some means the criminal had acquired an unnatural mode of thinking and acting. But how? The answer contemporaries developed to this question—that crime was caused by malign influences beyond the criminal's control—began to undermine the retributive justification for capital punishment.

The concept was not entirely new. Youth and inexperience had long been common reasons to grant clemency, especially when the condemned person had been under the sway of an older, hardened offender, so the idea that a person might be induced to commit a crime by the influence of those around him was a familiar one. What was new in the late eighteenth century was the effort to attribute *all* evil to the criminal's environment. Some began to explain crime in terms of biological causation. When naturally healthy people became physically sick, it was because they had caught an infectious disease. Perhaps the same was true of the spiritual sickness that was crime. "Let every criminal, then, be considered as a person labouring under an infectious disorder," argued a resident of Maryland in 1790. "Mental disease is, indeed, the cause of all crimes: for to a sound mind, virtuous action is as natural and as necessary as breathing is to life." Speaking on the floor of the Virginia House of Delegates in support of the 1796 bill abolishing capital punishment for all crimes but murder, one legislator compared criminals to patients and the state to a physician. "What then shall we say of that system of law," he asked, which sends criminals "to the hands of the executioner, without a single effort for his cure?"[30]

If crime was a disease, the retributive justification for capital punishment, indeed for any punishment, virtually disappeared. How could society blame someone for catching a disease? A disease had to be *treated*, not punished. "To propose an hospital, for the reformation of criminals, is a new attempt, and may perhaps tend more to excite the ridicule, than the candid attention of those who estimate opinions by their antiquity," the Marylander recognized. But he nevertheless considered prison a hospital for crime, a hospital in which "fasting, hard labour, and bodily pain, may, in certain cases, be successfully applied in the reformation of criminals." Benjamin Rush, himself a physician, likewise drew an analogy between evil and disease, and spoke of prison routines as "remedies . . . for the cure of crimes."[31] To cure a disease one did not kill the patient.

If crime came not from within the criminal but from without, it followed that a naturally virtuous person repeatedly exposed to evil and violence might gradually become evil and violent himself. (A similar account is often given today of how crime is caused by exposure to pornography or violence on television.) On this view, executions did not deter crime; they *caused* crime. Capital punishment "lessens the horror of taking away human life," Rush insisted, "and thereby tends to multiply murders." One only had to look at the number of crimes committed at hangings, another Pennsylvanian agreed.[32] If crime was understood as a product of the environment, caused not by universal human nature but by the specific circumstances in which individual humans found themselves, circumstances largely beyond their control, capital punishment ceased to serve any retributive purpose.

American abolitionists challenged the death penalty's retributive underpinnings by repeating the social contract argument popularized by Beccaria. "Life is a natural blessing, not a political one," declared a correspondent to the *New-York Evening Post*; the right to take life "appertains alone to the creator that bestowed it." Another writer concluded, following Beccaria, that *"no man can surrender* or *transfer it,* consistently with the mandates of Nature, consequently Society cannot *receive it, nor does it exist* in any assembly of men whatever." Despite its origins, the belief was not confined to intellectual circles but began to appear in clemency petitions written by people evidently without much education.[33]

This sort of abstract political theory was common by the end of the eighteenth century. Rush was the first to take the far more difficult step of attempting to reconcile opposition to capital punishment with the Bible. As everyone knew very well, the Bible was full of passages in which people were instructed to impose capital punishment in retribution for various offenses. "I expect to meet with an appeal from the letter and spirit of the gospel," Rush admitted, particularly "the law of Moses, which declares, that 'he that killeth a man shall surely be put to death.'" Rush had several responses. Most of the Old Testament's provisions for capital punishment, he noted, were the ones transmitted by Moses, which were "accommodated to the ignorance, wickedness, and 'hardness of heart' of the Jews." God had not purported to be laying down rules applicable to all societies at all times. Rush immediately conceded that this argument would not apply to the most frequently cited of God's instructions concerning the death penalty, the command to Noah in Genesis 9:6 that "whoso sheddeth man's blood, by man shall his blood be shed." This order, all agreed, had been intended not just for the ancient Jews but for humanity in general. But was it an order at all? Rush drew upon a recently published lecture of the English cleric William Turner to suggest that Genesis 9:6 was properly interpreted not as a command but as a *prediction*, along the lines of parallel Biblical passages like "He that taketh up the sword, shall perish by the sword" or "He that leadeth into captivity shall go into captivity." If these were all to be treated as commands, Turner had pointed out, then a magistrate had as much of a duty to sell slave traders into slavery as to sentence murderers to death.[34] Rush enthusiastically agreed.

Rush then returned to the more numerous provisions for capital punishment in Mosaic law. These did not include just the crimes punished with death in late eighteenth-century America, he noted, but also crimes like adultery and blasphemy, offenses for which virtually no one wished to impose capital punishment. One could not plausibly believe oneself bound by some of the laws given by Moses but not others. If advocates of capital punishment wished to rely on Old Testament passages other than Genesis 9:6, they would have to swallow some unpalatable laws as well.[35]

While Rush's utilitarian arguments against capital punishment had a great deal of support in the late eighteenth century, the same cannot be said of his biblical interpretation. "Some of his explanations of texts, we think, are forced," one reviewer sympathetic to Rush's cause concluded. Abolition of capital punishment might be more easily reconciled with scripture, the reviewer suggested, by recognizing that "whatever might be done under former dispensations, the discontinuance of the punishment of death is most consonant to the human spirit of the religion taught by him who 'came, not to destroy men's lives, but to save them.'" The message of Christ could be a potent tool for rebutting biblical justifications of capital punishment.[36] But the Bible would always be an obstacle to opponents of capital punishment. Their opposition followed from Enlightenment ideas about human virtue and human progress, ideas not easily reconciled with ancient texts and institutions. They were confident that they could solve problems their ancestors could not, using techniques of which their ancestors could never have dreamed. They were sure of the possibilities for improvement, for the reformation of the individual criminal, and for the remaking of a rational society.

Their adversaries—who outnumbered them in the late eighteenth century, judging by the persistence of capital punishment in every state—were far less optimistic about the direction in which the new nation was heading. "Liberty in the united states is verging fast toward licentiousness," declared the Philadelphia minister Robert Annan in a passionate response to Rush's arguments for abolition. "Religion, the only sure basis of good government, is entirely set aside . . . Humanity is become the popular cry!" The death penalty had been ordained by God, and it was presumptuous to announce that God's provisions were no longer needed. "If capital punishments be such a crying iniquity as our author pretends," smirked another of Rush's critics, that "reflected very little credit on the justice and goodness of their God." Human nature could hardly change so fast, if indeed it could change at all, and even the reformers would become their old selves under pressure. Rush, Annan supposed, "has never had a brother, a wife, or a child murdered by the cruel hands of any ruffian. It is all theory with him." But if crime ever paid a visit to Rush's household, Annan predicted, "his fictitious humanity will evaporate before the strong and irresistible feelings of nature, and perceptions of justice and equity," and Rush's opposition to capital punishment "will evanish as chaff before the whirlwind."[37] Capital punishment's supporters doubted the possibility of improvement, whether of the individual or of the society as a whole.

The early reformers were motivated by Enlightenment visions of progress, but once having decided to oppose capital punishment, they drew upon other instrumental arguments. Abolition of the death penalty, Rush contended, would prevent those inclined to suicide from committing murder in order to be executed. No doubt this was not the reformers' strongest point, but neither was it as frivolous as it may seem today, when cultural and religious norms against suicide are much weaker than they once were. The Pennsylvania minister Henry Melchior Muhlenberg heard in 1765 of a New York man who cut the throat of his infant son because he lacked the courage to cut his own. A few months later Muhlenberg counseled a recent immigrant from Germany named Henrich Albers who, Muhlenberg concluded, "had purposely cut the throat of a twelve-year-old German boy in order that he might thus lose his own life."[38] The prevention of suicide was not what drove reformers to oppose capital punishment, but it was a collateral benefit they could claim once the decision had been made.

The same was true of another anticipated benefit, the possibility of forcing criminals to work to compensate their victims. If a murderer was kept alive rather than executed, the proceeds of his labor could be "applied to the use of the widow or children of the person murdered." The point was not uncontroversial; Robert Annan, for instance, thought it "one very shocking idea." Annan put a question directly to Rush: "Supposing a midnight robber were to murder him, while sleeping securely, as he vainly imagined, under the protection of the laws, how would his lady and children relish the food which, in this case, and on his plan, might be called the price of his blood?"[39] Again, this was more a side-benefit than an independent reason for opposing capital punishment, but it was one that appealed to the reformers' utilitarianism.

The debate over capital punishment broke out on many fronts in the late eighteenth century. The driving force behind all the biblical interpretation and the utilitarian calculus, however, was a new faith in humanity and in the possibility of progress. If people were virtuous at birth, if evil was an intruder arriving from outside rather than a part of human nature, one might design institutions to disinfect the criminal, to restore him to moral health. In this light the gallows seemed a product of ignorance and superstition.

Sympathy and Utility

The early United States was a particularly likely place for dissatisfaction with the death penalty to develop.[40] Many Americans adhered to a liberal theology emphasizing personal reformation and the possibility of universal salvation. Such beliefs created an intellectual climate congenial to the reformers' emphasis on innate human virtue and conducive to proposals for far-reaching changes in penal institutions. Especially after the Revolution, it was plausible to understand capital punishment as an outmoded institution, suitable only for monarchies or aristocracies, with no place in a more egalitarian republic. These strands of thought are detectable in the writings of some of the early American penal reformers, especially Benjamin Rush.[41]

But the emergence of opposition to capital punishment was not just an American phenomenon. It took place all over Europe too. The Grand Duke of Tuscany abolished capital punishment completely in 1786. Not long thereafter, so did the Austrian Emperor Joseph II. The Prussian General Law Code of 1794 limited the death penalty to murder and treason. Russia abolished capital punishment for all crimes but treason. France drastically reduced the number of crimes punished by death in 1791. There would be little legislative change in England until the nineteenth century, but the spirit of reform was very much in the air from the 1770s on.[42] The American reformers like Bradford and Rush considered themselves part of an international movement. They were avid readers of the accounts of travelers in Tuscany, Russia, and other European states that had reduced the use of capital punishment, and they cited these European reforms as models for Americans to follow.

This international wave of opposition to capital punishment was part of a larger change in sensibility. As confidence in the possibility of progress increased, so did the belief that misery of all kinds was not part of the human condition but might be eliminated. It seems no accident that significant opposition to the death penalty emerged at exactly the same time as significant opposition to slavery, or that sympathy for the suffering of criminals grew side by side with sympathy for the suffering of animals.[43] The era saw the rapid growth of forms of evangelical Protestantism that placed a premium on sympathy with others. Sympathy was on the rise, and so was utilitarianism, which when applied to the question of crime yielded a sense that the proper punishment was rationally calculable by reference to the perceived costs and benefits of committing a particular offense, rather than by reference to the Bible or any other form of authority.

The sympathy came first. We have seen that the earliest American critics of capital punishment for property crime spoke not of its inefficacy but of their own emotional identification with the condemned prisoners. They reported "pitying poor young fellows" hanged for burglary. After the reforms of the 1790s they celebrated "the humanity of the modern code of this country." The residents of Alexandria (then part of the District of Columbia) pleaded with President Thomas Jefferson to pardon the condemned burglar Samuel Miller on the ground that capital punishment for burglary was "something shocking to the sense of moral justice."[44] Spectators at executions had long sympathized with individuals who were executed without translating that sympathy into a general opposition to capital punishment, but that changed in the second half of the eighteenth century. More and more people felt that their moral responses to individual executions justified them in expressing dissatisfaction with the criminal law.

Since the publication of Michel Foucault's influential *Discipline and Punish* in the 1970s it has not been fashionable to credit the penal reformers' professions of sympathy and humanity. Foucault rightly pointed out that much of the systematic penological writing of the period was grimly utilitarian and betrayed very little concern for the actual people being punished. For many of the more philosophical reformers, the goal was, as Foucault memorably put it, "not to punish less, but to punish better."[45] But sympathy and utilitarianism are not mutually exclusive, and indeed here they went hand in hand. To "punish better" in the late eighteenth century required partially substituting prison for capital punishment only because capital punishment was widely thought to be causing too many people to sympathize with the criminals. A hundred years earlier, when there was less of this sympathy, there had been no reason to invent a new kind of punishment.

Sympathy came first, but utility was not far behind. Many of the early American opponents of capital punishment did, in fact, want to punish better, and often to punish *more*. The reformer Robert Turnbull favored prison over the death penalty because he thought capital punishment "evidently too mild for the crime of cool and deliberate murder." A life sentence lasted much longer than a hanging, so it could "be considered as the most painful." Rush proposed a prison in a remote location, one to which the road was "difficult and gloomy," where the clang of the iron gates would be "encreased by an echo from a neighbouring mountain, that shall extend and continue a sound that shall deeply pierce the soul." He envisioned a system in which the term of imprisonment would be unknown to all but government officials until the day the prisoner was released, in which visitors were strictly forbidden, and in which guards would never so much as smile at the prisoners. "I cannot conceive any thing more calculated to diffuse terror," Rush explained. "Children will press upon the evening fire in listening to the tales that will be spread from this abode of misery. Superstition will add to its horrors."[46] Here was a truly Foucauldian punishment, one that would insinuate itself deeply into the psychology of offenders and the innocent alike, a penalty that operated as much on the imagination as on the body. Rush was no humanitarian; he was interested in punishing better, not less.

Utilitarianism pervaded the early opposition to capital punishment in another sense as well. One aspect of punishing better was punishing more uniformly by eliminating the wide disparity in actual penalties caused by a system of wholesale capital sentencing and frequent pardons. Before the late eighteenth century clemency was valued as a way of fitting the punishment to the offender by separating the reclaimable from the irredeemably vicious. To the rationalists of the Enlightenment, however, this system looked hopelessly ad hoc. They agreed with Beccaria that the best deterrent was the certainty rather than the severity of punishment, that there would be less crime in a penal system that was inexorable and mild than in one that was harsh but unpredictable. "It is the universal opinion of the best writers on this subject, and many of them are among the most enlightened men of Europe," William Bradford argued, "that the imagination is soon accustomed to over-look or despise the *degree* of the penalty, and that the *certainty* of it is the only effectual restraint." For the same reason Rush declared that it "has long been a desideratum in government, that there should exist in it no pardoning power," and that the elimination of capital punishment was the only way to achieve uniformity in sentencing.[47] The substitution of prison for hanging was a way of punishing more effectively by punishing more systematically.

One precondition for the emergence of opposition to capital punishment was thus this broad change in sensibility. Americans, like Europeans, began to sympathize more with criminals, and began to believe that they could better shape the behavior of potential criminals by more subtly modifying the pattern of incentives potential criminals faced. But these intellectual changes might have had little practical effect had they not been accompanied by a crucial technological change—the invention of the prison. One could not credibly argue against the death penalty without proposing something else to take its place. In the late eighteenth century, for the first time, the idea of the prison provided American reformers with an alternative. The prison and the anti–death penalty movement went hand in hand: growing opposition to the death penalty caused growing interest in prison construction, while the existence of prisons strengthened the arguments of death penalty opponents.[48]

It was the emergence of the prison, combined with this Enlightenment conjunction of sympathy and utility, that gave rise to the first wave of significant opposition to capital punishment. The reformers understood utility and sympathy—"Reason and Humanity," as Bradford put it—to be twin facets of the progress they saw taking place all around them. "The voice of Reason and Humanity has not been raised in vain," Bradford proclaimed. "A spirit of reform has gone forth—the empire of prejudice and inhumanity is silently crumbling to pieces—and the progress of liberty, by unfettering the human mind, will hasten its destruction."[49] Humanity was what allowed reformers to understand the causes of crime; Reason was what enabled them to calculate how best to prevent it. In a country where people increasingly believed they possessed both sympathy for others and the rationality to influence others' behavior, reformers were sure that capital punishment would not endure much longer.

5

NORTHERN REFORM, SOUTHERN RETENTION

"SO MUCH HAS BEEN WRITTEN and said on the subject of capital punishments," noted a Philadelphia newspaper in 1812, "that it looks almost like presumptive vanity to pursue the topic any farther." But Americans throughout the northern states did pursue it. Looking back in 1854, a New York lawyers' magazine concluded: "There is no legal question which has been so thoroughly and extensively discussed as that concerning the death penalty; no law which has been enacted, repealed, and re-enacted, as has that of Capital Punishment." Within the previous decade alone, three states had abolished the death penalty completely. Several others had come close. Throughout the North capital punishment had been removed from crime after crime, until none of the northern states used it for any offense other than murder. These legislative changes sat atop a mountain of public debate that had filled books, magazines, newspapers, and speeches since the turn of the nineteenth century. Yet after all this arguing the issue was no closer to being settled than it had been fifty years before. "The expediency or inexpediency of most legal enactments, is determined by a comparatively short discussion, or, at the farthest, by a few years' experience," the magazine recognized. "But in the case of capital punishment, reason and experience seem alike in vain; each new statute leaves the question still open, and the discussion waxes louder and more earnest at each new step in legislation." After decades of confrontation, "neither party in the debate are able to see any reason on their opponent's side."[1]

In Louisiana, meanwhile, it was a capital crime to print or distribute material, or to make a speech or display a sign, or even to have a private conversation, that might spread discontent among the free black population or insubordination among slaves. Virginia provided the death penalty for slaves who committed any crime for which free people would serve a prison sentence of three years or more.[2] Throughout the South attempted rape was a capital crime, but only if the defendant was black and the victim white. The debate over capital punishment that engulfed the northern states in the first half of the nineteenth century was virtually absent from the South. The difference was a product of slavery.

The Northern Debate

Isaac Mickle, an apprentice to a Philadelphia lawyer, was part of an audience of nearly two thousand at an 1842 debate on what Mickle called "The Capital Punishment question which is now agitating the good people of the Commonwealth." Arguing for abolishing the death penalty was "the somewhat famous Charles C. Burleigh," who had become so for nothing but speaking and writing in favor of abolition. Burleigh's opponent was the minister William McCalla. After three consecutive evenings of debate, Mickle was won over to Burleigh's cause. The next year, when Mickle himself chaired another debate on the subject, he decided in favor of abolishing capital punishment.[3]

Similar scenes were repeated throughout the northern states. In Boston the Massachusetts Society for the Abolition of Capital Punishment put on all-star programs of speeches against the death penalty, with prominent reformers like Wendell Phillips and William Lloyd Garrison on the schedule. Debating societies in places as remote as rural Iowa considered whether government had any right to take human life. European visitors were astonished by what the English novelist and naval officer Frederick Marryat called "this aversion to capital punishment." "In no country is criminal justice administered with more mildness than in the United States," marveled Alexis de Tocqueville, who had been sent by the French government to report on the new American prisons. "The Americans have almost expunged capital punishment from their codes." The English tourist Harriet Martineau concluded that "in a short time capital punishments will be abolished throughout the northern States."[4] Reformers certainly thought so. They considered themselves on a crusade comparable to the simultaneous movement to abolish slavery.

The capital punishment debate in the North revolved around three issues familiar since the 1780s and 1790s. Was the death penalty necessary to deter crime, or would prison be a more effective deterrent? Was the death penalty a legitimate act of retribution, or did government—for reasons rooted in the nature of crime, the characteristics of criminals, or the limited power of the state—lack the authority to punish crime with death? Was the death penalty a useful means of encouraging repentance, of reforming the criminal's soul, or would prison do the job better? All three were contested issues throughout the North in the first half of the nineteenth century. The debate quickly crystallized into stock arguments for and against abolishing the death penalty, arguments that drew standard responses. When the debate reached its peak, from the 1830s through the 1850s, there were no new moves available to participants on either side.

DETERRENCE

Its opponents were sure that capital punishment was unsuccessful as a deterrent to crime. "Does capital punishment tend to lessen the number of those crimes for which it was instituted?" asked one in 1810. "Certainly not." They were confident that prison would deter more effectively. Supporters of capital punishment were just as sure of the opposite. "Murder never has been, and never can be checked, by a slighter penalty than death!" exclaimed a popular magazine. This debate has persisted up to the present, but what is striking about its contours in the early nineteenth century is the virtual absence of any attempt by either side to back up its claims with numbers. The *National Era,* a black newspaper in Washington that favored abolishing the death penalty, complained with some justification that reformers "seem to rely more upon abstract reasoning, than appeals to facts," in contrast with their English counterparts, who "investigate with great care the statistics of crime, and dwell upon the comparative effects upon its prevention" of different penalties. American reformers did on occasion use statistical evidence. A lengthy article published in 1838 in the *American Jurist,* a leading legal periodical, surveyed recent rates of execution and crime in several states and foreign countries in an effort to prove that a decrease in the number of hangings had not been accompanied by an increase in crime. Robert Rantoul, the leader of the reformers in the Massachusetts legislature, used data from Belgium to infer that reducing the number of hangings would reduce the number of murders.[5] But statistical evidence was unusual, on either side of the debate, before the late nineteenth century.

The combatants instead relied on competing understandings of human nature. Abolitionists contended that prospective criminals feared prison more than death. "Who would wish to live, if life offered no enjoyment?" one writer asked. A life in prison was worse than a thousand deaths, another averred. Retentionists believed the opposite: that most prospective criminals feared death above all else. A member of the New York Assembly noted that prisoners often asked to have death sentences commuted to prison terms, but never the opposite. "Do men request to escape from a milder to a more terrible punishment?" he asked. "Or is not this the spontaneous voice of the soul declaring which of these penalties is most dreadful, and hence most efficacious?" Abolitionists replied that the chance of acquittal or pardon was much smaller when death was not the sentence, and that a high chance of prison deterred more effectively than a low chance of death. In the absence of much information that could resolve the question one way or the other, the result was a standoff. "Whether the fear of capital punishments operates as a more powerful preventive of crime, than confinement for life to hard labor in the state prison, is rather a matter of conjecture or of argument, than of certainty," admitted one abolitionist. "There are not facts enough before the public to decide."[6]

In the debate over deterrence the incentives faced by jurors were no less important. It was a commonplace among abolitionists that jurors' reluctance to impose the death penalty caused conviction rates to be much lower in capital cases. "Jurors can no longer hold the scales of judgment with an even hand, when one man's blood is to be weighed against another's," concluded the *United States Magazine*, edited by the ardent New York abolitionist John O'Sullivan. "But if the punishment were of a nature less cruel, it would be more certain." In the twenty-nine murder trials conducted in Massachusetts between 1832 and 1843, one abolitionist observed, there had been only six convictions. In the sixteen capital arson trials there had been only four convictions. Charles Burleigh pointed to similar statistics in Philadelphia, where conviction rates were much higher in noncapital cases. The point was that a rarely enforced death penalty could scarcely serve as a deterrent.[7]

Retentionists had a ready response. That jurors were reluctant to convict in capital cases was undeniably true, they conceded, "but it is difficult to see how it can be regarded as an argument against the death penalty. If the law is a good one, and men are unwilling to execute it, there is greater reason why its friends should rally to its support." If capital convictions were becoming more difficult to obtain, they reasoned, that was due to the active promotional efforts of the abolitionists, who, if not engaged in jury-tampering in a legal sense, were up to something much like it on a far broader scale.[8] The debate over deterrence could not be resolved with facts. Despite its empirical surface, it was a moral debate at its foundation.

RETRIBUTION

Very few people in the early nineteenth century were prepared to argue explicitly that retribution was not a legitimate purpose of punishment. The abolitionist *United States Magazine* found the distinction between impermissible private revenge and permissible public retribution "rather too fine for our optics," and for that reason denied retribution any role. But this was an unusual view before the Civil War. Most antebellum abolitionists were more comfortable arguing that the death penalty was not a legitimate *method* of exacting retribution. Capital punishment was "sanguinary"; it was "barbarism"; it was a form of "retaliation." Proper punishment required some attention to penitence and rehabilitation.[9]

Their opponents were equally confident of the opposite. "Beyond all question the murderer deserves to die," one proclaimed. "His crime is the greatest that man can commit against his fellow man." It was no coincidence that "for more than four thousand years, the laws of all civilized communities have affixed to the crime of murder the penalty of death." There was something in human nature that required a life for a life. If the state refused to fill that need, private groups would fill it instead. In 1843, when a divided committee of the Pennsylvania General Assembly recommended against eliminating the death penalty, the majority explained that capital punishment "is so clearly a law of nature" that it would be futile to try to amend it. "The mob finding the law impotent, would take its execution in their own hands. This cannot be looked upon as the feeling of revenge, but the voice of nature within us." When a convict was lynched in Janesville, Wisconsin, two years after Wisconsin abolished the death penalty, one Chicago newspaper took the incident as proof of the same natural principle: it found "the unwritten law of the human heart infinitely stronger than any mere theory."[10]

Retentionists' confidence in the death penalty's fitness for retribution was reinforced by the conviction that God was on their side. The Bible still played an important role in public life. Scriptural arguments in support of capital punishment received much wider circulation than they do today, and they were taken much more seriously. If "we would not reject our Bibles we must not abolish the penalty of death for murder," admonished the Reverend Samuel Lee. "Opposition to capital punishment for wilful murder *asserts* that men may *modify* the law of God to suit themselves," the minister Nathaniel West cautioned. "This is opposition to the government of God. This is making a grave mistake." The primary piece of evidence that God favored capital punishment was Genesis 9:6, his statement to Noah that "whoso sheddeth man's blood, by man shall his blood be shed." The passage "is the citadel of our argument, commanding and sweeping the whole subject," declared the minister George Cheever, one of the most visible public spokesmen in support of the death penalty in the 1840s. "All else is mere guerilla warfare, if you cannot carry this entrenchment." Judges often quoted the passage when condemning criminals to the gallows. It was constantly being cited as "an *imperative* law," as "a divine enactment, which men are attempting to repeal at the hazard of offending God."[11]

Abolitionists in the first half of the nineteenth century could not have persuaded many without denying that they sought to defy God's command. Some used the argument first popularized by Benjamin Rush in the late 1780s, that Genesis 9:6 was more accurately interpreted as a *prediction* than as a command. Some contended that the passage was meant to govern only Noah and his immediate family and cited as proof examples of uncapitally punished murders elsewhere in the Old Testament, most obviously the one committed by Cain. Perhaps most common was the argument that Genesis 9:6 stated a law God intended to enforce *himself*, not a law that was supposed to be enforced by human governments. Whatever the response, abolitionists were impatient with the claim that the passage outweighed all rational considerations. "It seems, on the face of it, to belong with other Theocratical hypotheses that have had their day," complained the editors of one Universalist magazine; "such as the divine right of kings, . . . the divine obligation of God's people, in all times, to exterminate obstinate heathens, the universal obligation to put witches to death, &c."[12]

Other aspects of the scriptural case for capital punishment were weaker, and abolitionists were quick to attack them. The death penalty pervaded the laws of Moses, but to a degree that discomforted even the most ardent retentionists. "If Moses is our lawgiver at this time," smirked John Edwards, "let us obey him, not in part only, but wholly, and put every sabbath breaker, blasphemer, and adulterer, to death." In any event, added a Philadelphia committee formed in the early 1840s to advocate the abolition of capital punishment, "the Jews when Moses wrote were a semi-barbarous people" quite unlike nineteenth-century Americans. Retentionists recognized that the laws of Moses punished too many offenses with death for contemporary tastes, and that the death penalty's supporters were accordingly obliged to select among them.[13] As a result, arguments from Mosaic law never carried the same force as arguments from Genesis.

Retentionists liked the words of Genesis; abolitionists preferred the spirit of the New Testament, with its emphasis on forgiveness. "The very pretence, that we 'love them that hate us,' and 'do good to them that despitefully use us,' while at the same moment, we hang them up by the neck," wrote one minister to the governor of Massachusetts, "is the most barefaced and impudent of all pretences. What if Jesus Christ had loved his enemies after that sort?" Another wondered: "How can its infliction be reconciled with the gospel of Christ?" This was an understanding of the Bible that might be expected to have had some appeal for condemned prisoners themselves, so it is perhaps not surprising that Enos Dudley, hanged for murder in 1849, left behind a note in which he argued along these lines.[14]

The abolitionists were on the defensive when they talked about the Bible, but they took the initiative in attacking the retributive value of capital punishment on other fronts. Foremost among these was the argument that death was too severe a punishment because crime was a product of the criminal's environment rather than his free will. "Crime indicates a diseased mind in the same manner that sickness and pain do a diseased body," the Iowa Supreme Court's chief justice told the Iowa Anti-Capital Punishment and Prison Discipline Society. "And as in the one case we provide hospitals for the treatment of severe and contagious diseases, so in the other, prisons and asylums should be provided for similar reasons." The conception of crime as disease was a common one. "They argue, that crime is the result of diseased or perverted mind," complained one supporter of the death penalty about the abolitionists; "that it can no more be charged upon any one than sickness or insanity; that where there is blame, it rests upon society for suffering the infection that corrupts the innocence." President John Quincy Adams pardoned the condemned burglar Betsey Ware after receiving a petition suggesting that because

Ware "is one of that miserable class of society whose minds are seldom il-
lumined by education, . . . she deserves more the commiseration, than
the denunciation of Society."[15] If crime was a social disease, contracted
through no fault of the criminal, then retribution of *any* kind, not just
capital punishment, ought to have been considered inappropriate. This
was a step many would make in the later nineteenth century. In the first
half of the century, however, most reformers stopped at opposition to the
death penalty and a preference for prison.

The spread in the understanding of crime as a disease was facilitated by
the attention a particular kind of disease—insanity—was beginning to receive. Strange behavior of all sorts, once thought to have supernatural
causes, was coming to be widely understood as due to natural causes that
could be treated by medical techniques. Crime seemed to many to fit
within this broader classification of insanity. The murderer "is a *moral* lunatic," affirmed one opponent of the death penalty. "He is as infatuated as
a maniac." Some criminals were evidently insane, and even supporters of
capital punishment agreed that they ought not to be executed. There was
no dispute that the basis of punishment "is the power to distinguish between right and wrong," as one Delaware judge instructed a jury, and that
"no just public example can be made by the execution of an irresponsible
being."[16] For retentionists the insane were a tiny subset of the class of
criminals, but for some of the abolitionists they were the entire class.
"There are many different degrees of irrationality found to exist, between
that extreme of it which is usually called insanity, and that mild degree of
mental infirmity which requires a very attentive and skillful examination," James Richmond assured the governor of New York in his petition
to abolish the death penalty. Expanded so broadly, insanity ceased to be a
useful category, and arguments like Richmond's soon became objects of
ridicule. At the 1844 murder trial of Abner Rogers, who truly was insane
(and who would soon afterward jump to his death from his room in the
Massachusetts State Lunatic Hospital), his lawyer recognized that he had
to battle the common opinion that insanity "is little else, in fact, than a
general pretext for the worst crimes."[17] But while the most extreme versions of the argument lost their plausibility, the milder variants did not.
Crime might not *be* insanity, but it was at least *like* insanity, in that it was
the criminal's affliction, not his choice.

The conception of crime as disease was further advanced by Americans' intense interest in phrenology, the ostensibly scientific effort to at-

tribute personal characteristics to the relative sizes of different parts of the brain. Today phrenology is classed with palmistry, astrology, and the like, but in the first half of the nineteenth century it was a respected discipline widely believed to offer scientific insight into human behavior. All over the country phrenologists studied the heads of condemned criminals and found ample confirmation of their theories. Some did their work while the subject was still alive, as in the case of the Connecticut murderer Caesar Reynolds, pronounced to be "a very remarkable negro" by the "distinguished phrenologist, who examined his head." Some waited until later. Sarah Reed was hanged in Illinois in 1845 after poisoning her husband with some arsenic in the buttermilk. Years later the jailer's daughter recalled that "as Phrenology was one of the leading Sciences of the Period they secured her head in toto for an examination by the Experts of Crawford Co[unty]. So they had her head on exhibition for many months."[18]

The lesson of phrenology, a lesson that would long outlive belief in phrenological doctrine itself, was that mentality had a physical basis. "All the manifestations of the mind, including the feelings and the passions, are dependent upon the conformation and state of health of its material instrument, the brain," declared M. B. Sampson, one of the many writers who sought to link brain structure with crime. If the decision to commit crime could be traced to a physical defect in the criminal's brain, crime began to look much more like disease than like sin. The appropriate response became treatment, not retribution. "The infliction of punishment for disorders of the brain is no more reconcileable to our ideas of justice than would be the infliction of punishment for disorders of any other organ of our physical frame," Sampson concluded.[19] If criminals were victims of brain defects that invisibly propelled them to commit crimes, they lacked the free will that all agreed was a moral prerequisite for the infliction of capital punishment.

Many phrenologists believed that the relative sizes of the parts of the brain were influenced by the individual's environment. Once crime was attributed to physiological causes, however, it was not a big leap to the conclusion that at least some criminals were *born* with defective brains. The reform minister Theodore Parker was one of the first to divide criminals into two classes, the "born-criminals, who have a bad nature," and the "made-criminals," who "become criminals not so much from strength of Evil in their Soul, or evil propensities in their organization, as from strength of Evil in their circumstances." Theories of biological causation would gain influence in the latter part of the century, when they would be reinforced by the popular interest provoked by Darwin in heredity and evolution. But even in its embryonic form, so to speak, the concept of the born criminal had powerful implications for capital punishment. "I would not kill them more than madmen," Parker concluded. There was no point in executing a criminal who had been "born with a defective organization."[20]

The idea of free will, that evildoers had chosen to commit evil, thus came under increasing attack in the first half of the nineteenth century, and in corresponding measure so too did the retributive justification for capital punishment. Supporters of the death penalty fought back by insisting on the criminal's power to choose alternatives to crime. "The Committee talk as if law were against disease, against innocence and not against crime," one complained about an 1850 New York legislative report recommending abolition. "Why are we told nothing of the many cold-blooded murders where malice, with intent to kill, took the place of every other disease?" Another retentionist despaired at "the wide spread habit of referring sin and crime, not to the immediate actor of the sin and the perpetrator of the crime, but to temptation, as an efficient cause." The criminal "is a moral agent," one minister affirmed, "and having acted according to the freedom of his own will, he must fall by the righteous law of the state." Lawyers and judges feared that a justice system based on individual responsibility for criminal action would break down under a broader conception of the origins of crime. Supreme Court Justice Joseph Story refused to allow William Cornell's lawyer to introduce evidence of Cornell's poor education in mitigation of his murder. "If a bad or low education would in point of law justify or excuse crimes," Story lectured from the bench, "it would be the most facile mode of avoiding punishment that could be devised."[21] But evil was coming to be understood as produced by something other than free will, as the consequence of the criminal's brain or his circumstances. The new understanding weakened many Americans' faith in the death penalty.

Abolitionists were meanwhile formulating a new way of attacking the death penalty's retributive justification. They began to argue that innocent people were often executed by mistake. Individual condemned men and women had long claimed their own innocence, of course. What was new was the broader assertion that government ought to abandon capital punishment in general because so many innocent people were going to their deaths on the gallows. The era saw the first nationally known American cases of apparently innocent people executed or condemned. Charles Boyington was hanged in Alabama in 1835, protesting his innocence all the while, for murdering a man in a tavern. A few months later the tavernkeeper confessed to the crime on his deathbed. Even more spectacularly, the Boorn brothers of Vermont were about to be executed in 1819 for murdering Russell Colvin, when Colvin himself (or someone who looked very much like him) turned up at the hanging. Abolitionists got a lot of mileage out of these and similar cases. Not everyone was convinced that executing innocent people undercut some of the death penalty's justification. "The innocent have sometimes been imprisoned," the minister Joseph Berg pointed out; "shall we, therefore, tear down our penitentiaries, and abolish imprisonment in every case?"[22] But to abolitionists the prospect that some of the hanged were innocent, and that nothing could be done to right that wrong, was further evidence that capital punishment failed to serve a retributive purpose.

In light of the emphasis late twentieth-century abolitionists would place on the inequality with which capital punishment was administered, it is worth noting that inequality played almost no role in the antebellum debate. To the extent that inequality was complained of at all, it was economic, not racial. "This is a d—d cold blooded selfish world," swore the murderer Amos Miner, awaiting his execution in Rhode Island in 1833. "If I but possessed some five hundred dollars I could find friends enough; but as it is, I suppose I must be abandoned!" After Wisconsin abolished capital punishment, a local prosecutor told a jury that the "death penalty hangs poor, penniless men, guilty or innocent; and it sets free and turns at large the wealthy and the influential, whether they be guilty or innocent; and every good citizen should abhor and deprecate a law that works so alarmingly unequal." But even this kind of commentary was unusual. The prevailing view may have been accurately summed up by an anonymous Massachusetts writer:

> To the honour of this state be it said, that most of the felons, who have here died on the scaffold, have been vagrant foreigners—fugitives from jails and gibbets—the refuse and dregs of society, thrown off in the effervescence of that morbid mass which lies at the bottom of old and dense communities, and

cleaves like leprosy to decaying governments. Such wretches we yield to the executioner without much more regret, than when we witness the extermination of a beast of prey.[23]

In the first half of the century it appears to have been simply taken for granted, as an inescapable fact of life, that the poor were more likely to hang than the rich. Few—or rather few with the liberty to complain—commented on whether blacks were more likely to hang than whites.

REFORMATION

Capital punishment continued to be defended in the early nineteenth century as a means of facilitating the criminal's repentance. "May we not fairly reason from what we know of the nature of the mind, and the deceitfulness of sin," asked the New York minister John McLeod, "that the criminal will be more likely to give all the energies of his mind to the work of preparation for meeting his God, when he knows that his days are numbered, than when they appear to him to be lengthened out indefinitely?" Judges continued to advise condemned prisoners at sentencing to use their remaining time in "preparation for the great change that awaits you," as Massachusetts Chief Justice Lemuel Shaw put it. "The day is far spent," thundered a Maine judge at the just-convicted murderer Seth Elliot, "the night is at hand—the eleventh hour is come—a voice proclaims, *behold the bridegroom cometh.*"[24] Many still viewed an impending execution as a uniquely powerful tool for concentrating the mind.

But this function came under increasing attack in the first half of the nineteenth century, from two different angles. Some critics began to question whether the weeks between conviction and execution were long enough. For a hardened criminal, true penitence could take years to attain, one reformer asserted; "that he should thus in a few months, nay, perhaps only weeks, attain to such a state of readiness is to me very extraordinary." As the *United States Magazine* suggested, reviewing some pro–capital punishment poetry recently published by William Wordsworth, "He who is unfit to live is far more unfit to die." Others began to question whether repentance was the proper goal in the first place. The new penitentiaries opening up throughout the nation promised instead to serve the goal of *reformation,* of saving the soul *without* killing the body. With proper instruction during a lengthy term of imprisonment, the criminal could be converted into a law-abiding and industrious citizen. The point was a controversial one. Many retentionists were convinced that prison was even less likely to work reformation than the prospect of death, but would instead degrade criminals' characters even further.[25] But as more and more states constructed penitentiaries that offered the hope of turning bad people into good, the death penalty lost much of its attraction as a method of saving souls.

Characters and Feelings

If all the arguments for and against abolition were stock debating points with standard responses, what made people choose one side or the other? As early as 1817 one perceptive commentator suggested that opinions on capital punishment were produced not by the evaluation of empirical evidence but by the "characters and feelings" of the people on either side:

> In every society, there are multitudes, who defend capital punishments, just as they favour a severe mode of education, from violence of passion, from a propensity to harsh and expeditious measures, and from an impatience which cannot stop to employ the milder methods of persuasion and reformation. Their indignation is more operative than their compassion. When they think of a criminal, they think only of his crime, and forget that he is a man. They have too little humanity to inquire, whether his fate may not be mitigated; and regard the advocates of a milder system, as a set of visionaries, who would sacrifice the peace of society to a sickly and childish tenderness of heart.

But if the supporters of capital punishment could see only one side of the issue, the advocates of abolition were just as bad:

> There is another class, who are accustomed to feel rather than to reason; whose imagination, quickened by sensibility, represents to them, with vividness and power, the unhappy criminal, immured in his dark and lonely cell, his limbs fettered, his countenance fallen, his conscience harrowed with guilt, his mind abandoned to despair, his feverish sleep haunted by past crimes, and by horrid images of approaching death and judgment; and who forget, during this quick and tumultuous sympathy, the claims of the community, the necessity of restraining

crime by terrour, and the difficulty of deciding, what modes and degrees of punishment are necessary to balance the temptations of the present state of society.[26]

In short, one's views on capital punishment were determined by what would much later be called one's "personality." On one side were those whose sympathy for the criminal precluded an ability to see the larger picture; on the other were those who saw the larger picture but not the human beings who made it up. One side was too forgiving, the other too severe. Abolitionists were too person-oriented, retentionists too rule-oriented. This was how the participants in the debate would understand one another over the next four decades.

The abolitionists of the early nineteenth century, like those of the late eighteenth, were optimists. They believed in progress. "This is an age of inquiry—of excitement growing out of the spirit of investigation," exulted one abolitionist reviewer of the debate. "The human mind has been throwing off shackle after shackle," and capital punishment would be just one more. The Universalist pastor Abel Thomas retold the old joke about "the traveller who thanked God for the evidence afforded him, by the appearance of a gallows, that he had reached the territory of a civilized, a Christian people!" His point was that the gallows was anything but a sign of civilization or Christianity. As one poet suggested in Rochester's black newspaper:

> Still in this Christian land of hope,
> of Bibles and of hallowed time,
> The gibbet and the hangman's rope
> Fit relics of a barb'rous clime.

The editors of a black newspaper in New York City were even more concise. *The Colored American*'s account of a bill pending in the Connecticut legislature to abolish capital punishment was headlined simply "PROGRESS."[27]

And as in the late eighteenth century, retentionists were people skeptical of the possibility of such dramatic progress. "We detest the new lights of the age—and they who stand in high places would do well to reflect before they advocate these new-fangled notions which tend to render our property and lives insecure," complained one Bostonian. "It needs no gift of prophecy to foresee that by abolishing capital punishments, every kind of evil would environ us." In 1849, when a bill to abolish the death penalty was pending in the New York State Senate, one senator decried "this Spirit of the Age, of which we hear so much." Just a year earlier the same spirit of reform had moved the state legislature to adopt a simplified mode of court procedure and to allow married women to own property. The former had thrown the courts into chaos, in the senator's view; the latter threatened to rip apart the family. Now reformers wanted to get rid of capital punishment. "In view of these things," the senator asked, "whither is the Spirit of the Age leading us?"[28] Capital punishment had always been necessary for the prevention of crime. Human nature could hardly have changed so quickly.

The problem with the abolitionists, as retentionists saw it, was that they were so confident in the march of progress that they ignored the actual circumstances in which people lived. Christian benevolence was fine as a general principle, but, said one retentionist, "were society invariably to act on general principles, there would follow social ruin." People who interpreted the New Testament to disallow capital punishment "may be suitable legislators for a community of infants, or angels," William Dwight suggested, "but they are mere dreamers in a world of living men." When Joseph Story was asked to write an entry called "Punishment of Death" in the new *Encyclopedia Americana,* he took the opportunity to diagnose the cause of opposition. Some people doubted the right of the state to execute criminals, he conceded, but "the doubt is often the accompaniment of a highly cultivated mind, inclined to the indulgence of a romantic sensibility, and believing in human perfectibility."[29] The retentionists saw themselves as hard-headed realists, battling the abolitionists' reveries of progress.

Why would abolitionists let themselves be carried away with such a "shabby and deplorable looseness of feeling," as one newspaper put it? It was because they had lost their firmness in all aspects of life. "Those insane men . . . do not punish their children for filial disobedience; nor allow their schoolmasters to use the rod," a New Englander complained about the abolitionists. "Nothing can surpass the soft sentimentality" of some opponents of the death penalty, admitted one of their own number. An antebellum zoologist was sure that the fact that strong storks kill weak storks "will no doubt greatly horrify the sickly word-heroes of the anti–capital punishment" movement. To be soft and sickly in the early nineteenth century was to be feminine, so it is no surprise that one retentionist referred to abolitionists as "mostly females of very tender feelings, and men of a similar spirit."[30] To favor capital punishment, by contrast, was to be hard, firm, disciplined—in short, to be masculine.

As evidence of the abolitionists' softness, retentionists had only to point to their constant professions of humanity, which often included implicit assertions of a superior capacity for sympathizing with the distressed. When Nathaniel Hawthorne's "new Adam and Eve," virtuous innocents set down in the fallen America of the 1840s, encountered their first gallows, they exhibited a reaction that Hawthorne and his fellow abolitionists would have proudly called their own:

> "Eve, Eve!" cries Adam, shuddering with a nameless horror. "What can this thing be?"
>
> "I know not," answers Eve; "but, Adam, my heart is sick! There seems to be no more sky!—no more sunshine!"[31]

This kind of sensibility, a pride in one's own sympathy for others and an implicit claim of superiority to those who did not share it, was becoming common in the early nineteenth century. It only exasperated the retentionists. "When the awful sentence of death is pronounced, then a sentiment of compassion begins to operate in favour of the unfortunate convict," complained the Connecticut judge Zephaniah Swift; "the sense of justice is drowned in the feelings of compassion; and false humanity begins to run riot." A New York execution broadside agreed that "the indulgence of false sympathy is the most dangerous feeling that can pervade a community." *True* humanity or *true* sympathy was an understanding of what was best for the community as a whole, which might well be the execution of a single member. Partisans of the condemned were losing the forest for a single tree. "The question becomes one of simple computation," explained one writer; "shall the interests of one individual, or those of the nation conflicting with his own, turn the scale." The more the abolitionists professed their sympathy for criminals, the more they opened themselves to this kind of criticism. The New Yorker John Pintard scoffed in 1824, with reference to what he called the "mistaken philanthropy" of those who took up the cause of condemned prisoners, "It is a great distinction to be hung in this quarter."[32]

Reformers were criticized for false humanity in a second sense as well. Their vaunted humanity was insincere, their opponents charged, because they were less interested in the welfare of criminals than in smugly reveling in their own sensitivity. "As for the humanitarian pretexts, they are a little shaky," the New York magazine *Vanity Fair* suggested when a bill to abolish the death penalty was pending in the state legislature. "The framers of this bill are not so celebrated for their gushing love of their species." The charge had some truth to it. During the Mexican War, as one critic pointed out, "these same tender-hearted people" who emphasize the sacredness of human life "advocate the doctrine that it is right to call out innocent men from their families, and butcher them by the thousands to vindicate the honor of our national flag."[33] Few of the abolitionists had any actual contact with the men whose lives they sought to save. Few exhibited much concern for the conditions of the penitentiaries in which those men would spend their lives if not executed, conditions that worsened almost from the moment the penitentiaries were built.

Retentionists savored a basic inconsistency in the abolitionist argument: reformers simultaneously asserted that the death penalty was too severe a sentence and that prison would be a superior deterrent. Abolitionists have "discovered a punishment which is far preferable to that of death," mocked the *Methodist Quarterly Review*, "first, because it is more severe, and, therefore, more efficacious; secondly, because it is less severe, and therefore more humane." The tension can be traced back to Beccaria, but that did not make it any easier to explain away. "Hanging is either more severe than imprisonment for life or less so," another opponent of reform argued. "If more severe, it deters more; if less so, what right have we to imprison! Have we a right to do a thing more cruel than hanging?" The only possible conclusion was that "opponents of a death penalty are at variance with themselves." If prison were to replace hanging, the abolitionists might come back to claim that *prison* was too severe. "The popular sympathy for the *poor sufferers* will fill thousands of streaming eyes with tears," one minister predicted; "and most *probably*, the doctrine will *then* prevail, that a state-prison punishment for life, *is a thousand times more cruel* than hanging, which might probably lead to the abolition of all laws against murder whatsoever."[34] Retentionists interpreted the inconsistency as evidence that abolitionists cared more for their own tender feelings than for the fate of condemned criminals.

Abolitionists, meanwhile, attributed support for capital punishment to the character of *their* opponents. Retentionists were people afraid of all change, the sort who had defended every evil practice from the slave trade to the divine right of kings, for no reason other than a terror of the new. "The class of thinkers to which they belong," one abolitionist complained, "suppose it is only necessary to cry bug-a-boo! to terrify the whole of us out of our wits." Abolitionists were confident they could overcome this pathological fear of change, because after each step along the path of progress in the past, conservatives had learned to welcome the reform. "Most of those who have regarded with favor existing death penalties," noted Robert Rantoul, the leading abolitionist in the Massachusetts legislature, "have united in the chorus of condemnation of those which have been repealed; so that no sooner is any one item stricken from the bloody catalogue, than the voices of its former defenders are silenced."[35] On this view, the complete abandonment of capital punishment was just a matter of time.

No group of retentionists angered reformers more than the clergy. In speaking out in support of capital punishment, they contended, men who purported to be followers of Jesus were acting most un-Christlike. "My soul is filled with amazement, indignation and horror, utterly uncontrollable," reported a young New York poet who in 1845 still called himself Walter Whitman. He was shocked that "clergymen call for sanguinary punishments in the name of the Gospel . . . instead of Christian mildness and love, they demand that our laws shall be pervaded by vindictiveness and violence." With the exception of some members of some of the more liberal denominations, the clergy tended to favor the death penalty, a position reformers saw as the "obstinate dogmatism and resistance to progress . . . of a piece with the history of priestcraft throughout the world."[36]

The abolitionists' criticism of pro–death penalty ministers bristled with resentment at a group they believed ought to have been their allies and who they feared were pulling their congregations along with them. Such ministers were no better than "benighted and blood-thirsty pagans." They seemed "ambitious to assume the function of the very Body-Guard of the Hangman." The clergy were "mad for the gallows." John Greenleaf Whittier's anti–capital punishment poem "The Human Sacrifice" reserved its greatest venom for the minister who attended the condemned prisoner:

> And near him, with the cold, calm look
> And tone of one whose formal part,
> Unwarmed, unsoftened of the heart,

Is measured out by rule and book,
With placid lip and tranquil blood,
The hangman's ghostly ally stood,
Blessing with solemn text and word
The gallows-drop and strangling cord;
Lending the sacred Gospel's awe
And sanction to the crime of Law.

The abolitionists' disgust could hardly have been made any clearer. They occasionally tried to turn the ministers' views to their own public relations advantage. In 1843 the Massachusetts legislature received a petition praying for the abolition of capital punishment and, in case that request should not be granted, asking that pro–death penalty ministers be appointed as hangmen. "This has caused much fluttering among the clergy," chortled William Lloyd Garrison. "It certainly places them in a ludicrous dilemma; for it cannot be degrading to do what God requires."[37] The ministers embodied all that abolitionists hated about retentionists — their blind adherence to the status quo, and their quickness to cite scripture as a bar to change of any kind.

Participants in the battles over capital punishment that took place throughout the North thus understood themselves to be divided more according to character type than anything else. Opinions about the death penalty do not appear to have been related to political party or to economic interest. The only factor that correlates with the division was religious denomination, a characteristic that was itself closely related to one's views about progress and the possibilities of reform. In Rhode Island, for example, the most influential abolitionists tended to be Unitarians, Universalists, and Quakers, the most liberal denominations, whose theology emphasized salvation and reformation, while the vocal retentionists tended to be Calvinists, who emphasized retribution and innate depravity and were inclined to take the commands of the Old Testament more literally. A similar split can be found in Massachusetts, between the Unitarians and the Universalists on one side and the more orthodox Congregationalists on the other. The leading retentionists in New York were members of the Calvinist clergy. Outside the Northeast the denominational breakdown was not so clear. When the Michigan legislature voted in 1846 to abolish capital punishment, the vote did not track the religious affiliation of the legislators, most of whom were in any event not affiliated with *any* denomination.[38] The debate over capital punishment was in part a sectarian struggle, but a struggle caused less by theological doctrine than by the divergence in the temperaments of the members of the various sects. The death penalty was a battleground in a larger war between two fundamentally different ways of understanding human nature and the world.

Northern Reform

The practical results of all this debate were minimal before the 1820s. After the wave of statutes enacted in the 1790s, there was little legislative activity for the next three decades. In 1801 Connecticut decapitalized arson, but only where no victim's life had been placed in danger. In 1805 Massachusetts removed the death penalty from arson and burglary except of dwellings during the night, and from robbery except on the highway. Indiana decapitalized robbery and armed burglary in 1807. In 1812 New Hampshire became the sixth state to limit capital punishment to murder and treason (after the five that had done so between 1794 and 1798). Ohio became the seventh two years later. But northern legislation proceeded in the opposite direction at the same time. Connecticut's new 1796 criminal code retained capital punishment for murder, rape, bestiality, sodomy, certain arson, and various kinds of maiming. Indiana capitalized rape, arson, and horse-stealing in 1807, and then the following year capitalized receiving a stolen horse. New York, which had limited the death penalty to murder and treason in 1796, brought it back in 1808 for residential arson and in 1817, after a prison riot, for arson in a prison. In 1809 and 1811, when Governor Simon Snyder of Pennsylvania asked the state legislature to abolish the death penalty completely, the suggestion went nowhere.[39] The movement for reform had stalled after its initial successes in the 1780s and 1790s.

From the 1820s through the 1850s, however, legislation in the northern states was all in the direction of abolition. As opposition to capital punishment spread, state after state removed the death penalty from the lesser felonies like rape, robbery, burglary, and arson, while no state added to its list of capital crimes. Rape, for instance, ceased to be a capital crime in Maine in 1829, in Illinois in 1832, and in Massachusetts in 1852. By 1860 no northern state punished with death any offense other than murder and treason. Many of the northern states followed Pennsylvania in dividing murder into degrees, with capital punishment only for the first. The pace of executions for each of the lesser felonies dwindled close to zero well before capital punishment was formally abolished for that crime. The last person executed for rape in the North appears to have been Horace Carter, a white man hanged in Massachusetts in 1825. The last northern arsonist executed may have been Horace Conklin, hanged in 1851 after burning down several buildings in Utica, New York. But Conklin's execution was an aberration, apparently the first for arson in any northern state since Simeon Crockett and Stephen Russell were hanged in Massachusetts in 1836,[40] and apparently the first in New York for any crime other than murder since the 1826 hanging of a black arsonist known only as Will. If one leaves out executions for the federal crime of mail robbery, the last robbers hanged in the North seem to have been Gilbert Close and Samuel Clisby, in Massachusetts in 1822. And no northern state appears to have hanged anyone for burglary in the nineteenth century. After the 1820s capital punishment in the North was in practice imposed almost exclusively for murder.

Northern legislatures meanwhile found themselves, beginning in the 1830s, devoting much of their attention to the issue of whether to eliminate capital punishment completely. A committee of the New York Assembly recommended abolition in 1832, but the Assembly as a whole did not agree. Legislative committees recommended against abolition in 1838 and 1839. In 1841 the issue was referred to a committee chaired by the young progressive lawyer John O'Sullivan, the editor of the *United States Magazine* and a leader of the New York abolitionists. O'Sullivan produced a 165-page report that summed up all the arguments for abolition and that, after being printed and widely sold as a book, became one of the best-known statements of the abolitionist position. "I have never read a more convincing document," one reviewer concluded. The Assembly nevertheless rejected abolition by a close margin. O'Sullivan ended his political career at the age of twenty-nine by declining to seek reelection in 1842. But reformers did not give up. In 1844 they formed the American Society for the Collection and Diffusion of Information in Relation to the Punishment of Death, an organization based in New York City that soon changed its name to the more accurate New York State Society for the Abolition of Capital Punishment. The society circulated petitions, sponsored speeches and meetings, and briefly even published its own magazine.[41]

In and around Albany, James Richmond and other abolitionists also repeatedly petitioned the state legislature. As a result, the issue would not go away. Assembly committees recommended abolition in 1845, 1846, and 1847. None of these bills passed. In 1848, when yet another Assembly committee took up the issue, the arguments on both sides were so stale that the majority (which rejected abolition) simply reprinted the minority report from 1846, and the minority likewise reprinted the 1846 majority report. Assembly committees again recommended abolition in 1851, 1859, and 1860.[42] But these bills all failed too. In three decades of effort the abolitionists several times came tantalizingly close to persuading the New York legislature to abandon capital punishment, but they never succeeded.

Similar events took place in legislatures throughout the North. Massachusetts House committees chaired by Robert Rantoul recommended abolition in 1835, 1836, and 1837, to no avail. As one of Rantoul's critics put it, "I should say that he was as fit for the Insane Hospital in Charlestown, as he is for the legislative hall in Boston." Reformers pressed on, by organizing public meetings and circulating petitions. A House committee rejected abolition in 1848. Special joint committees of both houses voted in favor of abolition in 1851 and 1854, but no legislation passed. In Massachusetts, as in New York, the abolitionists never quite achieved their goal. Abolitionists were well organized in Pennsylvania too—in 1847 a committee of 30 women managed to get 11,777 women to sign a petition asking the state legislature to abolish the death penalty. Bills were before the legislature almost every year from the late 1820s through the early 1850s. All were rejected. The governor of Connecticut recommended abolition in 1842, and a joint committee of the state legislature agreed, but no bill passed. When another joint committee recommended abolition ten years later, again no bill passed.[43]

Abolitionists came close to success in several other northern states. A series of New Hampshire governors proposed abolition almost every year beginning in the mid-1830s, and in 1842 the state House of Representatives came within a few votes of it, but the measure lost 109–104. In 1844 the issue was given to the voters, in a referendum appearing on that year's presidential ballot. Prisoners awaiting execution were reprieved, to see what the voters would say. They rejected abolition by a margin of nearly two to one. In Vermont the state House of Representatives passed an abolition bill in 1838, but the Senate rejected it. A New Jersey assembly committee reported in favor of abolition in 1847, to no avail. The issue was before the Ohio legislature every year from 1836 to 1838 and 1844 to 1850, and was even considered at the 1850–51 Ohio Constitutional Convention, but no action was ever taken. The governors of Illinois and Indiana urged their legislatures to abolish capital punishment, but the legislatures refused.[44]

The abolitionists did register some accomplishments. In Maine, after a bill abolishing the death penalty completely was rejected, the legislature enacted a measure that would prove to have an identical effect. A statute of 1837 required a one-year waiting period between conviction and execution. At the expiration of the year, the governor would have to sign a warrant before the execution could go forward. The intent of the measure was to delay hangings until the passions aroused by the crime and the trial had subsided, and then to require the governor to take a very visible (and perhaps politically costly) step to set the process of execution in motion. It worked. Maine did not execute a single person between 1837 and 1863. In later years so-called Maine laws swept through the Northeast, enacted by Vermont, New Hampshire, Massachusetts, and New York.[45]

Finally, in 1846, Michigan became the first state to abolish the death penalty for murder.[46] The debate in Michigan was no different from that anywhere else. If the state had any relevant distinguishing features, they were a relatively small political and economic elite and a correspondingly egalitarian distribution of wealth and power, and a relatively small number of citizens who were members of the more conservative religious denominations, which may have created conditions conducive to reform of all kinds by virtue of the absence of powerful interests favoring the status quo. The state's small population allowed a determined minority pushing reform to have a greater impact.

Michigan was followed by Rhode Island in 1852 and Wisconsin in 1853. Like Michigan, these were relatively egalitarian states in which the conservative Protestant denominations were not very large, and states with populations small enough to permit focused abolitionist groups to have some influence.[47] Michigan, Rhode Island, and Wisconsin would be the only three states to abolish capital punishment before the Civil War.

The movement to abolish the death penalty tailed off in the late 1850s, as sectional controversy and slavery crowded out other issues, and then the movement virtually ceased during the Civil War. Abolitionists could look back on a mixed record. They had persuaded the legislatures of three small states to abolish the death penalty. Five other states had established a one-year waiting period between conviction and execution. The abolitionists' biggest success was in abolishing capital punishment for crimes other than murder. In 1800 capital punishment had been common throughout the North for rape, robbery, burglary, and arson; by 1860 it was gone. But along with these achievements had come a consistent string of failures. Year after year, in state after state, they had been unable to convince legislatures to repeal the death penalty completely.

Abolishing capital punishment for murder was probably never as popular as its proponents believed. They could see considerable opposition to the death penalty in individual cases, but opposition to the death penalty in the abstract was much less pervasive. The era was thick with reform movements, and like many of them, from the establishment of utopian communities to the adoption of strange new diets, abolition may have been a cause favored primarily by educated elites. In the one instance when abolition was put up to a popular vote, New Hampshire's 1844 referendum, it lost resoundingly. Legislators, who had to answer to a widening electorate, were almost certainly more closely attuned to public opinion on the subject than were the reformers. The abolitionists' limited successes were most likely due more to their own persistence, organization, and access to legislative agendas than to any groundswell of popular support for their cause. It was a movement heavy at the top, full of energetic leaders like John O'Sullivan and Robert Rantoul, but too light at the bottom.

The abolitionists hurt themselves by the breadth of their own interests. They needed to stay tightly focused on capital punishment to have any chance of prevailing, but many were too interested in other reform issues to devote more than a fraction of their time to the death penalty. In 1821, when Elisha Bates of Ohio founded an anti–capital punishment magazine called *The Moral Advocate*, the death penalty was only part of its charter, which encompassed "war, duelling, capital punishments, and prison discipline." That range of issues was compact compared with *The Daily and Weekly Chronotype*, founded in Boston, which advertised that it advocated

> equality of human rights, and the abolition of slavery, thorough land reform, cheap postage, abstinence from intoxicating drinks, exemption of temperance men from taxes to repair the damages of drinking, a reform in writing and spelling the Eng-

lish language, the abolition of capital punishment, universal
and kindly toleration in religion, life and health insurance,
water-cure, working men's protective unions, and all other
practical forms of association for mutual aid—and generally,
Progress.[48]

When the death penalty was tucked into such a long list of proposed reforms, real legislative change was unlikely.

Such a scattering of interests weakened even the most successful of
the antebellum anti–capital punishment periodicals, *The Hangman*,
founded by Charles Spear in Boston in 1845. When it began, the weekly
journal was devoted to nothing but showing "the entire inutility of the
gallows." A year later, however, *The Hangman* changed its name to *The
Prisoners' Friend*. As Spear explained, "We intend to enter on a still wider,
though not a more important question, that of the Proper Treatment of
the Criminal," and "to point out also the Causes, Effects and Prevention
of Crime." By 1851, when Spear listed the sixteen "main topics" of his
journal, abolition of the death penalty was number sixteen. It had been
pushed aside by such issues as the "comparison of the advantages and dis-
advantages of the separate and congregate systems of prison government"
and the "best means of securing a uniform method of reporting prison
sentences." And in 1855, when Spear again listed the purposes of *The Prisoners' Friend*, their number had shrunk to fourteen and abolishing capital
punishment was not one of them. A journal devoted to abolition had
slowly transformed into one devoted to prison conditions. Spear's own
handbills soliciting subscriptions suggest that a magazine about capital
punishment could not make ends meet.[49] He had to broaden his subject
to find a readership, a market made up largely of people interested in
many other reforms that had little to do with the death penalty.

Opposition to the death penalty tended to go along with a cluster of reform positions on other issues. "It holds capital punishment cruel, barbarous and unnecessary, the diffusion of useful information a panacea for
all social evils, and so forth," remarked the New York lawyer George
Templeton Strong in 1848 about a book he was reading—"anybody can
gulp its doctrines on all other subjects from these specimens." Nearly all
the leading abolitionists had other issues they considered more important. Lydia Child proposed circulating anti–capital punishment petitions
along with anti-slavery petitions, because she knew that the same people

would be willing to sign both. Arguments against capital punishment were sometimes made in temperance broadsides. Some of the movement's leaders were better known for other causes. An anti–death penalty meeting in Rochester, New York, was led by Susan B. Anthony and Frederick Douglass.[50] Many of the abolitionists simply had too many balls in the air to be effective lobbyists against capital punishment. With public opinion in most northern states still running in favor of death as a punishment for murder, part-time leadership was not enough.

Southern Retention

The institution of slavery caused events in the South to take a very different course for both whites and blacks. Much of the debate that took place in the North simply did not occur in the South because of the perceived need to discipline a captive workforce. By the Civil War there was a wide gulf between the northern and southern states in their use of capital punishment.

The South did move somewhat in the direction of the reforms that swept through the North. In South Carolina, one resident complained in 1805, "mercy is reserved for the murderer, and applause for the assassin." The South Carolina lawyer William Grayson recalled that in the early nineteenth century, when the ringleaders of an incipient slave conspiracy were convicted and decapitated and their heads placed on poles along the highway, the "sight was so disgusting that some of the younger people refused to bear it. They so far disregarded the majesty of the law as to take down the hideous butcher's work and bury it where it stood." An aggravated punishment for slaves that had been routine in the eighteenth century was becoming unbearable in the nineteenth. Grayson considered that new sensibility an improvement over "the barbarity of judicial proceedings in the good old time." Some southerners engaged in the same kind of utilitarian calculation as northerners concerning the efficacy of a punishment jurors were reluctant to impose. Matthew Brandon, a member of the North Carolina state legislature, complained of a deficiency "in our criminal laws, as far as they respect slaves; for if I am not much mistaken, there is not amongst us, one capital punishment, for ten crimes that are committed." The problem was the law's severity. Brandon accordingly proposed "to abolish capital punishments except it be for 3 or 4 crimes of the deepest dye, for crimes committed by slaves; and substitute in their room, some-thing more lenient, and consequently more certain."[51] From comments like these, one can infer the existence of at least some sentiment among southerners to reduce the use of capital punishment.

Petitions for clemency in the antebellum South often included arguments in favor of partial abolition. The impending execution of a slave named Jesse for attempted rape in 1837 caused one petitioner to explain to North Carolina Governor Edward Dudley that the state's law "is generally regarded, as one of terrible severity, if not of harsh cruelty." Ervin Robinson's death sentence for stealing fifty pounds of seed cotton, and those of Calvin Lyttle and James Adcock for minor burglaries, all drew complaints from North Carolinians that capital punishment was disproportionate to the offenses. Similar claims of disproportion came from residents of Baltimore and Alexandria on behalf of the pirate Israel Denny and the burglar Richard Hull, each sentenced to death for stealing a few dollars.[52] Again, such comments suggest a broad if often unarticulated belief that the southern states ought to punish fewer crimes with death.

The South did not have a visible corps of penal reformers as the North did, but it had a few prominent individuals who took an interest in abolishing capital punishment. The best known was Edward Livingston of Louisiana, who joined the state assembly in 1820 and was soon after appointed to draft the state's new criminal code. Livingston took the opportunity to press for the abolition of capital punishment in reports he submitted to the legislature in 1822 and 1824. Neither of his proposals was adopted, in part because Livingston was elected to the U.S. House of Representatives in 1822 and so was away from Louisiana for long periods. In Washington Livingston again took up the cause of abolition. He joined the Senate in 1828, and in 1831 he introduced legislation that would have abolished the death penalty for federal crimes. By the time the bill was before the Senate, however, Livingston had become Secretary of State, and so once again his rising career prevented him from being an effective promoter of his own cause. None of his proposed measures on capital punishment was ever enacted.[53]

Livingston was not the only prominent southern advocate of abolition. In South Carolina Francis Lieber advised the governor to limit capital punishment to murder, and the Charleston lawyer and judge Thomas Grimké advocated complete abolition. Governor John Sevier of Tennessee asked his state legislature to abolish the death penalty in 1807. Legislators in Kentucky and Alabama urged their states to do the same. "Were I supreme Legislator there should be no capital punishment," affirmed one correspondent to North Carolina Governor William Graham.[54] These lesser-known southern reformers had no more success than Livingston, if measured by the fact that no southern state abolished capital punishment completely.

If measured by partial abolition, however, reformers did accomplish something. All the southern states abolished the death penalty for certain crimes committed by whites. In 1809 Maryland decapitalized burglary, robbery, counterfeiting, and horse-stealing. Louisiana abolished the death penalty for arson in 1817 and for certain burglaries in 1818. In 1826 Florida decapitalized manslaughter, robbery, burglary, and slave-stealing. Delaware decapitalized manslaughter in 1829 and burglary and kidnapping in 1841, and then divided murder into degrees in 1852. As most of the southern states began building penitentiaries, some cut back drastically on their use of capital punishment for whites. Tennessee restricted capital punishment to first-degree murder when it revised its penal code and began building a penitentiary in 1829, and in 1838 it became the first state in the country to give juries discretion, in cases of first-degree murder, to sentence defendants to prison instead of death. When Alabama constructed its penitentiary in 1841, it limited capital punishment to treason, first-degree murder, and participation in slave rebellion. Even in South Carolina, which lacked a penitentiary and may have had the most severe criminal law of any southern state, the number of capital crimes in the penal code steadily decreased.[55] By the Civil War every southern state punished whites with something other than death for at least some crimes that had been capital in 1790.

The southern states moved nearly as far as the North in ceasing to execute whites for crimes other than murder. No white rapists are known to have been hanged in the antebellum South. Between 1800 and 1860 the southern states are known to have executed only seven white burglars (including four in North Carolina, the last in 1859), six white horse thieves (including three in South Carolina, the last in 1824), and four white robbers (two each in North and South Carolina, the last in 1835). By the Civil War capital punishment for whites was, with a few exceptions, in practice reserved for murder throughout the South nearly as much as in the North.

But most of the northern debate over eliminating capital punishment completely was absent from the South. No committee of any antebellum southern state legislature recommended complete abolition. The issue was never part of any legislative agenda. Public debates on the subject were not held; societies devoted to abolishing the death penalty were not formed; the pages of magazines and newspapers were not filled with articles taking one side or the other. Many of the laws and practices abandoned by the northern states in the first half of the nineteenth century were retained in the South.

While few whites were actually executed for crimes other than murder in the antebellum South, many of the lesser felonies remained capital on the books. In 1860 rape was still a capital crime for whites in Arkansas, Delaware, Florida, Louisiana, Maryland, North Carolina, and South Carolina. Burglary was still capital in Delaware, Louisiana, and the Carolinas. Arson was capital in Florida, Louisiana, Maryland, Mississippi, North Carolina, South Carolina, and Virginia. A few southern states, including Georgia and Texas, punished horse-stealing with death. Many retained capital punishment for the crime of "slave-stealing," or aiding runaway slaves. Many used it for conspiring in a slave revolt. Scattered other crimes remained capital in individual states—buggery and sodomy in Florida, forgery in Georgia and the Carolinas, and "wilfully and maliciously depriv[ing] any person of any one or more of the genital members" in Delaware. A man in Guilford, North Carolina, was even sentenced to death for bigamy, although the sentence was apparently never carried out.[56]

The even North-South distribution of power in Congress ensured that federal criminal law embodied a hybrid of northern and southern policies toward capital punishment. By the middle of the century the federal criminal code included more capital crimes than any northern state, but fewer than most southern states. Rape, arson, piracy, and aggravated mail robbery remained federal capital crimes, along with murder and treason. Throughout the North, the same act could be a noncapital crime if prosecuted by the state but a capital crime if prosecuted by the federal government. George Wilson was sentenced to death in federal court in Pennsylvania for robbing the mail, but as his mother argued in her successful plea for mercy to President Andrew Jackson (in a passage most likely written by a lawyer), "the state of public feeling" in Pennsylvania was against the death penalty for mere robbery.[57]

If the list of capital crimes for whites in the antebellum South was much longer than in the North, it was far shorter than the corresponding list for southern blacks. In Texas slaves but not whites were subject to capital punishment for insurrection, arson, and—if the victim was white—attempted murder, rape, attempted rape, robbery, attempted robbery, and assault with a deadly weapon. Free blacks were subject to capital punishment for all these offenses plus that of kidnapping a white woman. In Virginia slaves were liable to be executed for any offense for which free people would get a prison term of three years or more. Free blacks, but not whites, could get the death penalty for rape, attempted rape, kidnapping a woman, and aggravated assault if the victim was white. Attempted rape of a white woman was a capital crime for blacks in these two states as well as Florida, Louisiana, Mississippi, South Carolina, and Tennessee. In his 1856 treatise summarizing the slave laws of the southern states, George Stroud counted sixty-six capital crimes for slaves in Virginia against only one (murder) for whites. In Mississippi he found thirty-eight crimes capital for slaves but not for whites. The ratios in the other southern states were less skewed but all had a similar imbalance.[58]

The black-white divergence in southern criminal codes was reflected in actual practice. Blacks were hanged in numbers far out of proportion to their percentage of the population. When the Reverend Preston Turley was executed in Charleston, Virginia, in 1858, observers noted that while it was unusual to hang a minister, the real interest in the event arose "from the strange spectacle of the execution of a white man in this region. It was the first occurrence of the kind ever known to have taken place within the county."[59] Blacks were executed for many more crimes than whites were. All of the whites known to have been hanged in Virginia between 1800 and 1860 were hanged for murder. But of the hundreds of blacks hanged in Virginia in the same period, only about half were murderers. The other crimes for which blacks were commonly hanged included rape, slave revolt, attempted murder, burglary, and arson. In Louisiana nearly all the whites executed were murderers, but the blacks hanged for murder appear to have been outnumbered by those executed for planning slave revolts, and several others were hanged for arson and attempted murder. Kentucky hanged whites only for murder but hanged blacks for attempted murder, rape, attempted rape, arson, and slave revolt. The Carolinas were the states most likely to hang whites for crimes other than murder, but even they executed many more black nonmurderers than white.

Even if it were possible to count the official antebellum executions, the figure would underestimate the intensity with which capital punishment was used for black criminals in the South, for two reasons. First, it would not include the growing number of lynchings—that is, unofficial executions. These often had the approval, and sometimes the actual participation, of government authorities. Blacks were the primary victims. They were often lynched because they were believed to have committed crimes, so we can assume that many would have been executed officially had they lived a bit longer. Second, to the official count one would also have to add the many slaves who were spared execution only to be sold abroad. In Virginia (and perhaps in other southern states as well) condemned slaves were often sold to contractors who agreed to convey them out of the United States. Between 1801, when Virginia established the program, and 1858, when it was abandoned, nearly nine hundred condemned slaves were transported out of the country.[60] Because the state had to compensate the slaves' owners—a rule that prevailed in almost all the southern states, to ensure that owners would not attempt to protect their property from the criminal justice system—selling slaves rather than hanging them represented a substantial saving for the public treasury. If these slaves had been executed, the proportion of blacks hanged in the antebellum South would have been significantly higher.

The South's retention of capital punishment for blacks was surely a direct result of slavery. In the middle of the nineteenth century whites formed a minority of the population in South Carolina, Mississippi, and Louisiana. Blacks made up more than a third of the residents of Virginia, North Carolina, Georgia, Florida, and Alabama. From the perspective of slaveowners, harsh punishments were necessary to manage such large captive populations. The institution of slavery prevented southern states from developing alternatives to the death penalty for blacks. Incarceration or forced labor would not have been much worse than slavery itself, so these would not have been effective deterrents. Most white southerners had little interest in the reformation of black criminals—many would have dismissed the goal as impossible—so the ideal of prison as a penitentiary would not have held any appeal. With two million captives on their hands, southern state governments saw no solution other than capital punishment.

Slavery was also responsible, although less directly, for the South's retention of capital punishment for whites. In the North the most outspoken supporters of abolishing capital punishment were also in favor of abolishing slavery and a host of other reforms. Northern reformers such as Robert Rantoul or John O'Sullivan operated within networks of like-minded people who had similar positions on a wide range of issues. The social and economic importance of slavery in the South prevented this culture of reform from emerging there.[61] The South had always been a more violent place than the North, and one may suppose that the contin-ued employment of violent punishments for slaves acclimated white southerners to violent punishments generally, further reducing the oppor-tunity for any significant anti–capital punishment movement to take hold. Hangings remained public in most southern states long after they had moved into the jail yard in most of the North, which also suggests that antebellum white southerners were simply more comfortable with public violence than white northerners. Finally, the idea that crime was caused by environmental or biological influences appears not to have been as widespread in the South as in the North, perhaps because such a belief would have entailed difficult moral questions about the propriety of punishing slaves. The loss of confidence in the criminal's blameworthi-ness had contributed to the North's movement away from capital punish-ment. The absence of comparable change in the South helped keep the death penalty relatively intact.

By the time of the Civil War the North had been through decades of debate over capital punishment. The South had not. Three northern states had abolished the death penalty completely, and the rest had confined it to murder and treason. In the South capital punishment still existed on paper for a wide range of crimes committed by whites and still existed in practice for an even wider range committed by blacks. Slavery had produced a wide cultural gap between the northern and southern states in attitudes toward capital punishment.

6

INTO THE JAIL YARD

DAVID MASON WAS HANGED for murder in Asheville, North Carolina, in 1852, before a crowd of approximately five thousand. Two spectators left very different accounts of the event.

Mary Gash, a farmer from Reems Creek in the western part of the state, described Mason's execution in a letter to her cousin Adda. The hanging was the first Gash had ever attended. "I don't think I ever in my life saw as many people congregated together at one time," she told Adda. "The streets were full, the Hotells were full, the Town and every other place was full." With the help of some male acquaintances, she pushed through the crowd to reach a spot from which she could watch Mason being taken out of the jail and placed in a cart. The crowd, including Gash and her party, then rushed to the gallows to stake out positions there. Gash was close enough to get a good view of Mason mounting the platform and to hear the minister's sermon. "After the sermon was over," she reported to Adda, "I pressed through the guard and sprung into the cart" just vacated by Mason, "where I could see and hear all that was going on." Mason called out to the witnesses who had testified against him, all of whom were present, and accused them of lying. Some of them shouted back to Mason. One of them even stepped up on the platform, Gash recalled, "and I think if the rope had not been around [Mason's] neck, he would have struck him." This witness and Mason kept up an argument at close quarters until the sheriff "told them the occasion was too solemn for any such altercation, the thing was then hushed, and the Sherriff proceeded to tie his arms, and legs, and then to knock the trap from under him, and left him suspended, between heaven and earth, by a rope." Gash held her watch, "to see how long till he be dead." Mason was left to hang for twenty-five minutes to ensure that he had died. Later Gash reflected on what she had seen and realized that "it did not have that effect upon me that I expected it would." She had watched a man die, and that was that.[1]

Zebulon Vance was in the crowd too. Vance was a young Asheville lawyer planning a political career. Ten years later, during the Civil War, he would become the governor of North Carolina. After the war he would serve again as governor, and he would then spend the last fifteen years of his life as a U.S. senator. Vance's account of Mason's execution was part of a letter to Harriet Espy, the woman he was courting and would eventually marry, so it is fair to assume that he was trying to make a good impression. Unlike Gash's matter-of-fact description, Vance's dripped with disapproval from the start: "There was a vast concourse of people from all parts of the country here, estimated about 5,000. One third of which at least was *women!*" Any doubt that Vance considered a hanging an inappropriate sight for women was dispelled in his next sarcastic sentence. "I followed the crowd out to the place of execution, heard the religious exercises usual on such occasions, and then not being of such a tender heart as most of the women there, I left and came back to keep from seeing him hung." This was a barely implicit assertion of moral superiority to the women and the men in the crowd. A refined man, a civilized man, a man who truly had a tender heart, would stay for the sermon but not for the hanging itself. Hearing a sermon was a form of self-improvement; watching a hanging was a barbaric entertainment. "I suppose such details are not pleasant to you by any means," he added, "and I therefore forbear." By not saying more, Vance was according Espy the same superiority he had just claimed for himself. Ordinary people might enjoy a hanging, but someone as sensitive as Espy would be "filled with horror of the scene." The lesson of a public execution was normally that one ought not to commit crimes, but the horror experienced by Vance seems to have been less of violent death than of too much contact with the kind of people who turned up to watch executions. Vance concluded with an ambiguous prayer, to be "safe from the ebulitions of passion!"—ambiguous because the passion from which he sought protection might as easily have been that of the spectators as that of the criminal.[2]

Mary Gash was watching an execution; Zebulon Vance was watching himself watch an execution. Gash closely inspected the physical details of the hanging; Vance inspected his own response to it. Gash saw the crowd from the inside and considered its members as her equals; Vance saw it from the outside and thought of himself as better than Gash and her companions. Gash found nothing shameful about watching Mason die; Vance considered the sight beneath him and professed shock that so many women like Gash did not feel the same way.

Such differences were not expressed in the eighteenth century, if they existed at all. Americans of all kinds—men, women, and children—watched executions and believed that the experience was a wholesome one. In the nineteenth century, however, the public representation of capital punishment became embroiled in issues of class and taste. For members of a self-conscious elite, particularly in the North, sights that had been thought educational in 1800 were too shocking for display by 1850. As elites stopped going to hangings, they came to view the crowd as a rabble out for a good time, too caught up in a carnival spirit to appreciate the moral lessons that were being imparted. Between 1830 and 1860 every northern state moved hangings from the public square into the jail yard, a much smaller space within the control of government officials. Some southern states did so as well, but most kept the ceremony open to the public until the later nineteenth and early twentieth centuries.

The change in location had significant implications for the justifications underlying capital punishment itself. Public hanging had been the paradigmatic deterrent, broadcasting a message of terror as widely as possible, but once executions moved into the jail yard their deterrent influence had to work at second hand. The sort of people most likely to need deterring were those least likely to be invited to an execution. The ceremony had once brought the community together, in an emphatic and participatory statement of retribution, but now that community was dispersed. One could sit at home and read about an execution in the newspaper, or sign a petition to the governor asking that a death sentence not be commuted, but the visceral sense of collective condemnation was gone. Changes in attitudes toward the dramaturgy of capital punishment thus subtly undermined part of its very purpose.

Gentility and Display

"Thousands of both sexes and of every age assemble at the appointed hour. It is then, while their hearts are throbbing wildly with dismay and anxiety, that a breathless multitude witness the awful spectacle." That was how one Pennsylvanian described public executions in 1809. But he was no critic. "Could any scene be imagined," he asked, "more extensively and more permanently beneficial than this?" He was writing in *The Gleaner*, a Lancaster magazine that was in the midst of a series of three essays on the death penalty. The magazine's pseudonymous writers all took different points of view, but the one point on which they agreed was that a public hanging was the best possible opportunity to remind the public of the consequences of crime. "Where the whole is ceremoniously conducted and accompanied with decorous solemnity the effect must be in the highest degree awful and impressive," said a second writer, like the first using the word *awful* in its sense of awe-inspiring. "It is impossible but the stoutest resolution must shudder at such a sight," concluded the third. "Impressions are here made which time can never eradicate from the minds of the spectators."[3] As the nineteenth century began, much of the death penalty's deterrent value was still understood to reside in the way it was presented to spectators. It was almost unthinkable to execute criminals anywhere but in the open, where everyone could watch and learn.

As in the eighteenth century, executions were normally not raucous affairs. Eyewitness accounts of public hangings in the first few decades of the nineteenth century include very few instances of unruly behavior. Twenty thousand people saw the Thayer brothers hanged in Buffalo in 1825, but "every individual performed the part assigned him, whether as actor, or a spectator, with a kind of melancholy calmness that precluded the possibility of disturbance." Peter Lung was hanged in Connecticut in 1816, before a crowd that observed "the strictest discipline and decorum." The lawyer Allen Davidson attended a double hanging in Asheville, North Carolina, in 1835, along with several thousand others, many of whom had spent the previous night camping in the public square. Although Davidson saw some "toughs rushing about, drunken men," they were greatly outnumbered by the "thoughtful and sober people," including "women and children in their country finery." Four or five thousand spectators, the most people ever assembled in tiny Edgefield, South Carolina, gathered in 1850 to see Martin Posey hanged. "The only events to disturb the calmness and melancholy of the day," the local newspaper reported, "were a few drunken broils in the afternoon, which ended in several *fisticuffs*, that produced no more serious results, we believe, than a few scratches and bloody noses."[4] Incidents of violence or undue frivolity were noteworthy, and were accordingly included in accounts of executions when they occurred, precisely because they were so rare. At most hangings the behavior of the crowd gave rise to nothing worth reporting. Spectators were usually orderly.

They were also inclined to sympathize with the condemned prisoners. It had long been noticed that the execution ceremony, by focusing attention on the qualities of the person being hanged, produced as much pity as condemnation. An 1829 broadside poem commemorating the execution of Moses Lyon emphasized the affinity spectators came to feel for the condemned prisoner, who was publicly presented as a sort of victim himself:

> See! yonder the gibbet doth stand,
> on which he must shortly expire;
> While thousands all over the land
> Stand gazing in mournful desire.

Lyon was a sixty-year-old drunkard who had beaten his wife to a pulp, but the dramaturgy of a public hanging had a way of evoking sympathy even for the most unattractive people. The last verse of the popular ballad "Amasa Fuller," about a man hanged in Indiana in 1820, went:

> The time at length arrived when Fuller was to die,
> He smiled and bade the audience adieu;
> Like an angel he did stand, for he was a handsome man,
> On his breast he wore a ribbon of blue.[5]

The staging of public hangings could turn criminals into heroes.

In the eighteenth century sympathy had been accepted as an unfortunate but unavoidable aspect of capital punishment, but in the early nineteenth century people began to complain about it and to suggest that it provided a reason for abolishing public executions. A hanging creates in spectators "emotions of pity, humanity and sympathy, which incline them to take the part of the sufferer, and to blame those who inflict those sufferings upon him," one Philadelphian argued in 1811. "These emotions are excited in the breasts of the best part of the spectators: and cause, even in them, a temporary disaffection to the government." Such complaints became more and more common as time went on. "What can more effectually defeat the ends of justice," a magazine wondered, "than to present malefactors before the public, in their prisons, or on the scaffold, as if they were martyrs, dying joyfully in Jesus, and ascending from the gallows to glory?" Such had been a *goal* of public execution a century earlier;

now it was a consequence to be avoided. In John Neal's 1822 novel *Logan*, the character Oscar, whom Neal intended to be the voice of wisdom, argues against public hanging. "I have seen ten thousand people in tears because a handsome boy was to be executed," Oscar declares. "They have made up their minds to be sentimental."[6] By the 1820s the dramaturgy of hanging day was increasingly viewed as counterproductive because it made spectators side with the criminal against the state.

Meanwhile, an older critique of public executions—that by habituating spectators to violence they increased the incidence of violent crime—was gaining currency. The argument had been made by Cesare Beccaria in the 1760s and repeated by Benjamin Rush in the 1780s. Many more writers turned to it in the early nineteenth century. After the hanging of Jason Fairbanks in 1801, the Massachusetts minister Thomas Thacher concluded that "such exhibitions naturally harden the heart, and render it callous to those mild and delicate sensations which are the out guards of virtue." "The exhibition, of extreme punishment," an Ohioan argued, "seems to have a natural tendency to destroy the moral sensibility, and produce a shocking depravity of the human character." Stories began to circulate of crimes committed during and shortly after executions, by men presumably spurred on by what they had seen. One reform magazine gleefully recounted a murder recently committed in New Haven by Vinson Gunn, who not long before had been part of a team that constructed the town's gallows. Executing a criminal in public "is only exalting the profession of murder and making life cheap," concluded one midcentury observer.[7]

Critics never specified exactly how watching a hanging made a person more prone to violence. The argument had its skeptics, most memorably Ambrose Bierce, whose remarks remained as apt in the early twentieth century as they would have been in the early nineteenth: "Obviously, the thing is absurd; one might as reasonably say that contemplation of a pitted face will make a man go and catch smallpox, or the spectacle of an amputated limb on the scrap-heap of a hospital tempt him to cut off his arm."[8] But just as today's claims about violence on television and in films tend to attract supporters in the aftermath of a well-publicized murder, so too did arguments about public executions whenever it was discovered that a criminal had once been a member of the crowd.

The idea that public hanging promoted crime and the belief that it created undue sympathy for the criminal were already familiar in the eighteenth century. They gained added currency in the early nineteenth, however, because they were reinforced by a new conception of the crowd. Eighteenth-century Americans saw nothing unseemly about attending an execution. People from all walks of life watched hangings and described them without any hint of embarrassment about having been present. The experience was understood to be spiritually instructive, like attending a sermon, and for that reason parents took their children. In the first few decades of the nineteenth century, however, elite perceptions of mass gatherings shifted. The crowd came to be seen as an unruly, threatening mob. Spectators at an execution had once been perceived as a cross-section of the community, but now elites began to see the crowd as composed of the community's lesser members. Spectators showed up only to "witness the struggles of a dying man—to view the soldiery—to view the parade," and to consume "*food* and *spirituous liquors*," complained one early critic in 1811. By the 1820s and 1830s the spectators at hangings were widely understood to constitute an "ignorant mob" propelled toward the gallows by "the love of death like that which demons feel." They were "grossly vulgar" people who were there to enjoy "this scene of dissipation and confusion" around the scaffold.[9]

After one hanging in western Massachusetts in 1826, a local magazine published an account that is representative of this disdainful view of the crowd:

> The demoralizing effect of *public executions* was very fully exemplified in this county last week. Never, as we are informed, was there so great a debauch. Cattle shows, musters, sleigh-rides, all the public gatherings and drunken bouts put together, could not equal it . . .
>
> An hundred persons are made worse, where one is made better by a public execution. Rioting, drunkenness, and every species of disorderly conduct, prevail on such an occasion to an extent never witnessed from any other cause in this land of steady habits. There is on most occasions, that draw persons together in large bodies, some attention to decorum, some regard to character, some appearance of feeling; but all these are banished, for the time, by the thousands who flock together to witness a *public execution*.[10]

The theme of this 1812 broadside, that an execution provided an occasion for spectators to reflect on their own lives, was typical of the speeches given by ministers and by the condemned prisoners themselves. In the drawing at the top, a horse pulls the cart away from the gallows, causing the prisoner to drop. Courtesy of the Library of Congress.

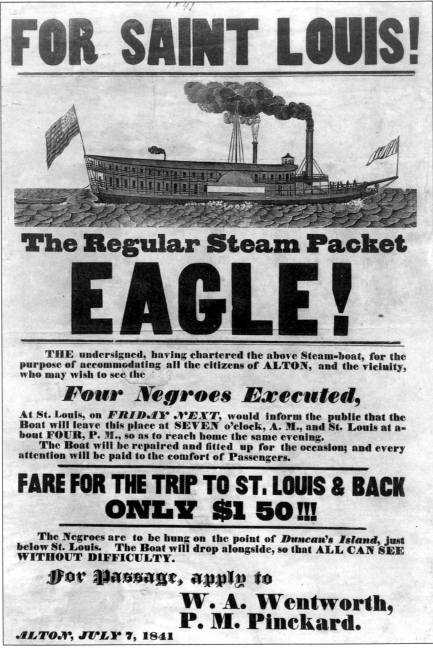

Most states still conducted hangings in public in 1841, when two entrepreneurs chartered this steamboat to take residents of Alton, Illinois, across the Mississippi to St. Louis to see the execution of four men. The crowd was estimated at between twenty and thirty-five thousand. Courtesy of the Missouri Historical Society, St. Louis.

The hanging of John Presswood Jr. in Smithville, Tennessee, in 1872. Atop the gallows, in the upper right-hand quadrant of the photograph, between the two trees, Presswood wears a white robe and a white hood. Courtesy of the Library of Congress.

The "upright jerker" was adopted in many places between the 1830s and 1870s in an effort to make hanging less painful. When the man holding the ax at left cut the rope, the weight at the upper left would drop, yanking the condemned person into the air. The failure of this and other refinements in gallows design led to the invention of the electric chair and the gas chamber. Back cover of *Hunter-Armstrong Tragedy: The Great Trial* (Philadelphia: Barclay and Company, 1878).

Top: The 1893 hanging of Weldon Gordon, Paris Strickland, Hiram Jacobs, Lucien Manuel, and Hiram Brewington in Mount Vernon, Georgia, was one of the state's last to be conducted in public. By the late nineteenth century public hanging survived only in a few southern states, and was sharply criticized in the North. Georgia had abolished public hanging in 1859 but reinstated it briefly around the turn of the century at the discretion of local officials. Courtesy of the Georgia Department of Archives and History.

Bottom: A large crowd gathered on a rainy day in Nash County, North Carolina, for the hanging of the murderers John Taylor and Robert Fortune in 1900. This was the county's last public hanging; North Carolina adopted the electric chair in 1909. Courtesy of the North Carolina Division of Archives and History.

The electric chair in New York's Auburn Prison, where in 1890 William Kemmler was the first person executed by electricity. This photograph was taken by Lew Collings for the Syracuse *Post-Standard* in 1908, by which time electrocution had proven, despite some gruesome exceptions, to be on average less painful and less repulsive to watch than hanging. Courtesy of the Library of Congress.

This cartoon, by William A. Rogers, appeared in the *New York Herald* in 1911. The sign plays on the old tradition of electrical medicine, suggesting that New York's electric chair at Sing Sing Prison would be a cure for crime, represented here by a man with a time bomb. Courtesy of the Library of Congress.

Cook County Jail officials inspect Illinois's newly installed electric chair in 1927. By that time nearly half the states used the chair as their means of execution. Courtesy of the Chicago Historical Society. *Chicago Daily News*, DN-083971.

One of only two known photographs of the electric chair in operation, this picture of Ruth Snyder's electrocution was taken by Thomas Howard of the *Daily News*, who strapped a miniature camera to his ankle and ran the shutter release wire up his pants to a bulb in his pocket. Snyder, executed by New York in 1928 for murdering her husband, was the object of so much public sympathy that her execution kept the death penalty in the newspapers for months. Copyright New York Daily News, L.P. Reproduced with permission.

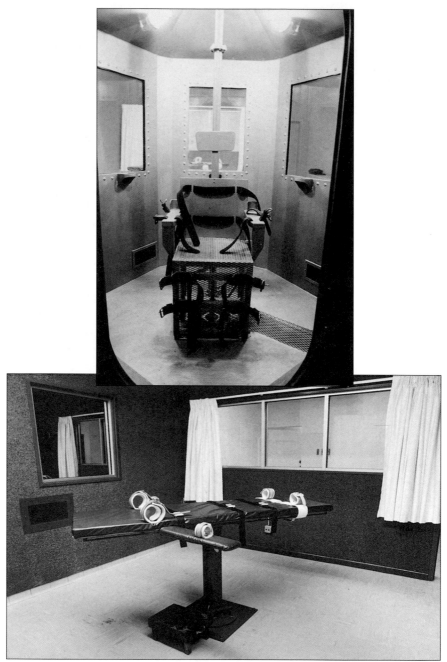

Top: By 1955, when Maryland's gas chamber was installed, most states had abandoned hanging in favor of either the electric chair or the gas chamber. After the Supreme Court reinstated capital punishment in *Gregg v. Georgia* (1976), Maryland, like most states, switched to lethal injection, in time for its first post-*Gregg* execution in 1994. Courtesy of the Maryland State Archives, Special Collections (Death Chamber Photograph Collection), MSA SC 4407–12.

Bottom: Maryland conducts executions in this room—three between 1994 and 2000. While the condemned person lies strapped to this table, a series of three chemicals is injected into his arm. The long window at the right provides a view for a small number of spectators. Courtesy of the Maryland State Archives, Special Collections (Death Chamber Photograph Collection), MSA SC 4407–7.

There had been an enormous change in opinion over the past two decades. Elites had become less comfortable in the presence of large numbers of those they perceived as their inferiors. Respectable people had once been proud to go to an execution. Now they were embarrassed and more than a little apprehensive.

Attitudes toward the public staging of violent death had already begun to change in the late eighteenth century, when the colonies/states replaced the public forms of aggravated capital punishment—burning, dismemberment, and the gibbet—with dissection, a punishment seen by a relatively small number of people. In the early nineteenth century that change in sensibility was brought to bear on ordinary hangings. The protest spread and intensified throughout the rest of the century.

Critics were quick to contrast the vulgarity of the execution crowd with the superior taste they found in themselves. "Persons of refined feeling and just sentiment are not disposed to be present" at hangings, asserted Thomas Upham, professor of mental and moral philosophy at Bowdoin College, in 1836; "it is a sight, however criminal the victim may be, which they find to be strongly repugnant to something within them." The reformer Lydia Child contrasted "the dense crowd . . . swelling with revenge, and eager for blood" with people like herself—"the innocent, the humane, and the wise-hearted"—who would never go to a hanging.[11]

In 1824, when a committee of the Pennsylvania House of Representatives became the first American legislative body to recommend abolishing public executions, this was the primary reason. "That the serious and well disposed on witnessing such a scene, should be deeply and solemnly impressed with a sense of the awful demerit of crime," was no doubt true, the committee observed. The problem was that "few, very few of such characters attend an execution from choice, and while they approve of the sentence of the law, they avoid being spectators of its execution." The drama was played to an audience "composed chiefly of those among whom moral feeling is extremely low." The crowd was made up of "the thoughtless; the profligate; the idle; the intemperate; the profane; and the abandoned," who were there not to profit from the moral lesson being presented but "to be amused; to enjoy a day and season of mirth and indulgence." These were people "in pursuit of *pleasure*, and the closing scenes of the day are evidently indicative of their success. They retire from the execution evidently delighted."[12] Pennsylvania kept its hangings public for a few years longer, but it was already clear that a transformation in polite taste had driven a wedge between those who would attend an execution and those who would not.

Refinement in the early nineteenth century was intimately connected with gender. As men and women came to be understood to occupy separate spheres of life, as the hustle and bustle of public space became a male domain, people contemptuous of execution crowds were shocked above all at the number and the behavior of the women present. "When the drop fell, shrieks were heard from females, and it was said some fainted," a Worcester minister lectured from the pulpit the Sunday after the rapist Horace Carter was hanged. "It is a matter of surprise and regret, that female curiosity should so far get the better of female delicacy, as to induce their presence at such spectacles." In 1835, after William Enoch was executed on Long Island in one of the last public hangings in New York, *Niles' Weekly Register* remarked on the "great number of *females*" present, and used the developing convention of femininity to joke that "the dear creatures have but few occasions to shew their *sensibility* at hanging parties." An enormous crowd, estimated at between twenty and thirty-five thousand, gathered in St. Louis in 1841 for the hanging of four men convicted of a double murder. "We were surprised to see the number of women attending the execution," the local newspaper reported. "The place and occasion seemed to us to be one at which no female should have appeared. Nevertheless, judging from the equipages and dress which we saw, we supposed that some who rank high in fashion were present." That respectable women should watch an execution was too much to bear. "We, however, trust they really were not of that class." Despite the outward appearances of refinement, these must have been the kind of women with tastes low enough to enjoy a hanging.[13]

To what extent were these changing perceptions of the crowd based on real changes in the crowd's behavior? The vast majority of eyewitness accounts of executions from this period include no mention of any untoward activity on the part of spectators, and some explicitly compliment the crowd on its deportment. But the few incidents that did occur were widely known. When Joel Clough was hanged in New Jersey in 1833, for example, a committee of the Pennsylvania House of Representatives was so troubled by reports of drinking and gambling in the crowd that it once again recommended abolishing public executions.[14] These seem to have been unusual occurrences, but they provided critics with some empirical confirmation of their views of the crowd.

But the transformation in the polite understanding of the execution crowd was almost certainly due less to actual changes in the crowd than to changes in perception. In the early nineteenth-century United States, the people we would today call the middle class began to see great differences in the realm of taste and manners between themselves and those they considered to be less refined. Respectable people placed a new emphasis on etiquette and gentility, matters that had once been the province of the rich. The respectable took an intensified interest in proper behavior in public spaces. Public gatherings and entertainments had once appealed to a wide range of people, but now they were dividing along class lines into the highbrow and the lowbrow, with different codes of spectator conduct. One aspect of this developing genteel sensibility was an aversion to the sight of death. Disease and dying moved away from the home and into hospitals. Cemeteries moved away from urban areas to garden-like spots far from living people. The genteel no longer wished to see death, and they began to feel contemptuous of those who did. Once they had viewed the spectators at executions as fellow citizens; now the crowd became a vulgar mob. Reformers, drawn from the middle class, were humane and sensitive to the suffering of others; the crowd was callous to the sight of violence and enjoyed watching the infliction of pain. This change in perception was an international phenomenon that took place across Europe at the same time.[15]

There *were* intelligent, literate supporters of public hanging in the nineteenth century, who recognized that critics were less concerned with the fate of the condemned prisoners than with the delicacy of their own feelings. Whether or not to conduct hangings in public "is a purely sentimental consideration," argued *The Nation*. Life in prison was not a pretty sight either, and yet few seemed to be complaining about that because it was not on public display. George Cheever lashed out at the "revolting hypocrisy" of moralistic writers who deplored public hangings but showed up at each one, to compose "high-wrought pictures of public executions, detailed in all their minutiae," all the while criticizing their fellow spectators as vulgar thrill-seekers. (As if to confirm the view of Cheever and others that critics were more interested in publicizing their own sensitivity than in the welfare of criminals, the reformer Margaret

Fuller began her review of Cheever's book in the *New York Tribune* with the claim: "We have had this book before us for several weeks, but the task of reading it has been so repulsive that we have been obliged to get through it by short stages, with long intervals of rest and refreshment between.")[16] The supporters of public hanging recognized that they were witnessing a change in polite taste rather than in actual behavior.

If the crowd was a mob oblivious to the moral lesson a hanging was supposed to impart, it followed that public executions had ceased to serve their original purposes of deterrence and retribution. "To the ignorant and unenlightened" who watched hangings, death was exciting, not frightening.[17] Worse, spectators like these were precisely the ones inclined to sympathize unduly with criminals and the ones most likely to commit crimes themselves after watching a public display of violence. Delivering a message of retribution required that the spectators at a hanging acknowledge the legitimacy of the state and the justice of the criminal law, but a rowdy crowd of drunkards appeared to respect neither. The new perception of the crowd reinforced older critiques of public punishment to create a wave of opposition to public hanging in the first half of the nineteenth century.

In some places, such as New York and St. Louis, local officials moved individual executions into the jail yard, apparently on their own initiative. But it became far more common for state legislatures to require *all* hangings to be conducted out of the public eye, either inside the jail itself or within the jail's high walls. The first state to abolish public executions was Connecticut, in 1830. By 1836 six other northeastern states had done the same—Rhode Island, Pennsylvania, New Jersey, New York, Massachusetts, and New Hampshire. In 1838 Iowa gave its judges discretion to order hangings in public or in jail. Soon after, Mississippi and Alabama became the first southern states to move hangings into the jail yard. By 1860 public hanging had been abolished throughout the North and in Delaware and Georgia. As the Georgia legislature explained, the practice "is believed by many to be demoralizing in its tendency and disgraceful to the character of our people for refinement and good taste." In later years, as the West gained population, the western states did the same.[18]

Public execution held on longer in parts of the South, where the mounting frequency of lynchings prevented whites from becoming too sensitive to the public display of violence. There it was still possible to argue, as one Virginian did in 1849, that "a criminal, dangling from the gallows, is well calculated to excite a train of sober thought. He is a fresh promulgation of the law." The notion of hiding punishment from public view would have seemed vaguely tyrannical in the late eighteenth century, and as late as 1859 a member of the Georgia legislature could declare that he "wanted no Bastille in Georgia—he wanted the trials in public and so ought to be the executions." Many, and perhaps a large majority, of the public hangings in the late nineteenth-century South were of blacks, often before largely black crowds.[19] Genteel contempt for the crowd was most likely tempered by the feeling among whites that nothing short of a vivid display of force could deter such an audience, and that in any event little better could be expected from them.

But sensibilities were changing in the South as well. By the end of the nineteenth century public hangings had been abolished in Virginia, Kentucky, Maryland, Louisiana, Missouri, South Carolina, and Tennessee. In 1901, giving a clear signal that government officials had differing expectations for the two races, Arkansas abolished public hanging except for rape, a crime for which capital punishment was in practice largely limited to blacks. Arkansas moved even rapists' hangings out of the public eye five years later. Kentucky, which had abolished public hanging in 1880, brought it back for rape and attempted rape in 1920, at the discretion of local officials. Legislators explained that electrocution inside the state penitentiary, the execution method for other capital crimes, would not be adequate to deter rapists. Georgia and Mississippi each briefly reauthorized local officials to conduct public hangings around the turn of the century. Soon, however, the handful of states that still hanged criminals in public began switching to the electric chair, a method of punishment that for technical reasons had to be inflicted indoors. As the electric chair was adopted in North Carolina, Oklahoma, Florida, and Texas between 1909 and 1923, these states by necessity stopped executing their criminals in public.[20] The only state where public hanging remained was Kentucky.

The later public executions were attacked in the northern press, which saw them as evidence of southern backwardness. Northern reports emphasized the availability of food and liquor, sold by vendors on the grounds. "There were 50 fakirs doing business with exhibitions which bordered on the side-show variety," noted one Massachusetts newspaper about a 1901 hanging in Arkansas. In 1915, when the hanging of two men in Starkville, Mississippi, before a crowd of five thousand was accompanied by picnic lunches, free lemonade, and political speeches from the candidates in the approaching primaries, the *New York Globe* called the affair a "carnival of brutality."[21] By that point there had been no public hanging in the Northeast for nearly a century. It seemed a throwback to a less civilized era.

The execution that drew the greatest attention, and the one that ended the practice of public hanging in the United States, was that of Rainey Bethea, hanged for rape in Owensboro, Kentucky, in the summer of 1936. Estimates of the crowd ran between ten and twenty thousand. The town's hotels were so full that thousands had to camp out overnight at the execution site. Hot dog and drink vendors set up near the gallows. Spectators jeered throughout, even while Bethea prayed. As soon as the trap was sprung, before Bethea had been pronounced dead, souvenir hunters tore off pieces of the hood that covered his face. The event gave rise to a whirlwind of criticism in the national press. The headline in the *Philadelphia Record* read "They Ate Hot Dogs While a Man Died on the Gallows." The *Boston Daily Record* decried the "callous, carnival spirit" exhibited by spectators. "The revolting spectacle at Owensboro was not the hanging of Rainey Bethea," cried the *Cincinnati Enquirer*. "It was the crowd which found in a hanging grand entertainment." Indignant editorials from all over the country were reprinted in the local newspapers. A few days later officials in Covington, Kentucky, who had an imminent execution of their own, announced that it would be conducted in jail, and that journalists would be barred from attending. Bethea's was the last public hanging in Kentucky. The state legislature abolished the practice in 1938.[22] There have been no public executions in the United States since then.

Some of the death penalty's later opponents looked back with mixed feelings at what they came to see as a bad bargain, in which supporters of capital punishment had bought off much of the opposition by agreeing to remove executions from public view. Many of the opponents of public hanging were indeed the very same people who argued against the death penalty generally. "When men begin to weary of capital punishment," the reformer Wendell Phillips concluded, "they banish the gallows inside the jail-yard, and let nobody see it without a special card of invitation from the sheriff."[23] But the timing of the move suggests this view is too cynical. The initial wave of statutes abolishing public hanging came in the early 1830s, but the movement to eliminate capital punishment generally did not peak until the 1840s and early 1850s. By 1846, when Michigan became the first state to abolish the death penalty, virtually all the northern states had long been conducting their hangings in jail. If the move into the jail yard had been a compromise with those who wished to do away with the death penalty outright, the move would have come *after*, not before, the peak of opposition to capital punishment itself.

Two Audiences

As hangings moved into the jail yard, local officials gained the power to control access to them. They tended to use that power, not to ban spectators altogether, but rather to divide the audience for executions into two groups. Inside the yard's walls, a few hundred well-connected observers packed into a small space for an intimate view of the execution. Outside, a much larger crowd milled about, hoping for a glimpse of the action. The division in polite taste that ended old-fashioned public hangings was reproduced in the physical division of the public. The genteel had taken the whole show for themselves.

A jail-yard hanging was open to a much smaller number of spectators than could attend a public hanging. In some states the number was set by statute. In others it was a function of how many people could fit in the jail yard or in the indoor space where the gallows had been set up. Attendance was by invitation. Many localities printed up formal invitations, with blanks for the sheriff to fill in the name of the invitee. Sheriffs were besieged with applications for invitations. Thousands pestered the New York sheriff to watch the hanging of Jeremiah O'Brien in 1867, including one well-dressed individual who, after his application was denied, showed up in the Police Court and asked to be committed to jail for ten days as a drunkard, in the hope that his cell would afford a view of the execution. Crowds often numbered in the hundreds. Three hundred fifty watched the hanging of George Pemberton in Boston. Over five hundred saw the execution in southern Illinois of the outlaw Charlie Birger. A thousand jammed into the Harrisburg jail for the execution of Weston Keiper and Henry Rowe.[24]

When there were more would-be spectators than could fit into the jail yard, political realities forced sheriffs to allocate the limited number of spaces to those with connections to power. In Brooklyn the hanging of Henry Rogers was witnessed by "over a hundred low beer-house politicians" and "between twenty and thirty lager-beer saloon-keepers" who were friends of the sheriff's.[25] "Every man whose uncle was a second cousin to the Sheriff's step-brother by marriage was on hand" to see a multiple execution in Pennsylvania. It took some clout to get an invitation, so the crowd often included large contingents of politicians, lawyers, and doctors. Spaces were normally reserved for journalists as well. In states where the number of spectators was limited by statute, sheriffs routinely gave the surplus temporary appointments as deputies. New York allowed only twelve spectators, but the sheriff of Utica appointed four hundred deputies for the hanging of William Henry Carswell in 1869. In Manhattan the special deputies numbered approximately one hundred fifty for James Eager in 1845 and Matthew Wood in 1849 and nearly six hundred for Aaron Stookey in 1851. Minnesota law limited attendance to six spectators, but there were over four hundred special deputies at one 1898 hanging.[26] Admission tickets and commissions as deputies often sold in an active market outside the yard's walls.

Jail-yard hangings were thus still conducted before a crowd, but a smaller and more elite crowd than before. The crowd's behavior was often not particularly somber. Jacob Harden was hanged in New Jersey before hundreds of men, including reporters from all the New York, New Jersey, and Philadelphia newspapers. As they waited, the spectators compared the autographs many had obtained from Harden. Some examined the gallows, trying out the pulleys and playing with the spring. Everyone smoked, some whittled. An old man sold photographs of Harden. Another showed off his collection of obscene pictures. The well-connected audience at one 1878 hanging scrambled immediately afterward for pieces of the rope as souvenirs. A similar rush took place in Pottsville, Pennsylvania, in 1908, among hundreds of invited spectators who apparently shared a local belief that a piece of rope used in a hanging was a cure for rheumatism. Henry Wadsworth Longfellow summed up the atmosphere in the yard in 1854:

> Then within a prison-yard,
> Faces fixed, and stern, and hard,
>   Laughter and indecent mirth;
> Ah! it is the gallows-tree!

The most sober among the spectators may have been the prisoners, who could often see the events of the day from the windows of their cells.[27] But crowd behavior inside the jail yard never came in for the same kind of criticism as comparable behavior on the part of the wider public. It mattered a great deal precisely whose conduct was at issue.

As room for spectators dwindled, the percentage of women in the crowd decreased. The trend was in part a matter of power—men were more likely than women to have access to the informal mechanisms for allocating tickets—and in part a continuation of the gender-based demarcation of space that began in the early nineteenth century. Women had once been as welcome at hangings as men, but no longer. By the early twentieth century it was national news when an actress dressed up in a man's overcoat and hat and managed to sneak into a Chicago hanging.[28] Capital punishment had become a male domain.

Because the event was still staged before a crowd, most of the rituals of hanging day survived the move into the jail yard. There was still a procession, though now much shorter, from the cell to the gallows. Ministers no longer gave sermons, but they still led prayers. The condemned person still had an opportunity to address the spectators. In New Jersey James Donnelly spent two hours asserting his innocence. In Ohio John Hughes rambled on so long, in a transparent attempt to prolong his life by filibustering, that the sheriff had to intervene. The audience was much smaller, but it was still large enough that many condemned prisoners tried their best to keep up appearances. John Ward of Vermont told the chaplain that he was reluctant to pray on the scaffold because "he desired to keep quiet, and to exclude all that would excite and unman him, and that he wanted a face of brass before the guard and others who might see him." James McMahon of Newark declared that he "was going to die like a soldier," William Delaney of Long Island that he would go to the gallows "like a man, and not like a nigger with his mouth open."[29] Had executions been conducted in jail from the start, the ceremony would doubtless have looked quite different, but much of the ritual retained vestiges of the old public hangings.

Another kind of vestige—the public itself—often waited just outside the gates. Hangings could draw thousands of people who had no expectation of being allowed inside. Fifteen thousand streamed into Fonda, New York, in 1878 to stand outside the jail during the execution of Samuel Steenburgh. The roads outside the Troy, New York, jail were impassable for three blocks around for the 1867 hanging of Hiram Coon. At the execution of Walter Goodwin in rural northern Pennsylvania, a large crowd stirred outside, many screaming "hang 'im." Executions were rare enough in any given place to attract huge crowds, even when there was nothing to see. In New York, the biggest city in the country, there were only thirty hangings between 1830 and 1880. In more sparsely populated areas a hanging could come once in a lifetime. The crowd outside the gates became the object of the same contempt among polite society that had once been turned on those watching the execution itself. These vicarious spectators were "men and women, summoned by the smell of blood, attracted to the gallows by the instincts of their ferocious natures," people with "savage faces and hands uplifted in drunken frenzy," argued George Lippard in *The Empire City*, his midcentury novel of New York life.[30] When hangings moved out of public space, all that remained was the excitement of being part of a crowd near a big event—precisely the experience the genteel believed one was *not* supposed to savor.

At some hangings sympathetic sheriffs gave the public a chance to inspect the gallows before clearing the yard of the uninvited. At others the public was let inside after the hanging was over, to get a good look at the dangling corpse. Five thousand people from surrounding farms and villages, including many women with babies on their shoulders, rushed in to see the body of Harry Butler, hanged in Delaware in 1926. Sometimes there were less formal opportunities for inspection. The body of the Mississippi outlaw James Copeland was stolen and put on display in a drug store in Hattiesburg.[31]

At most hangings, however, the best chance to see anything was to find a spot on a nearby roof or in a tree. "The roofs of the neighboring houses and barns and the limbs of trees were black with people," reported a member of the crowd outside Jacob Harden's hanging in New Jersey. The roof of one barn collapsed. The limb of a cherry tree broke off, bringing a dozen people down with it. The commotion was so great that spectators inside the yard rushed onto the scaffold to get a view over the walls to see what had happened. At Charles Eacker's execution, someone constructed viewing stands outside the walls and charged two dollars per place, until the sheriff noticed and sent officers outside to kick everyone off. Homeowners around the jail in Pottsville, Pennsylvania, rented out their rooftops for the hanging of Joseph Brown. Sheriffs in New York and Buffalo fought back by constructing awnings above the scaffold to prevent people from watching from atop houses and trees. In Philadelphia the sheriff moved the gallows into a corridor inside the jail, where it could not be seen from the outside.[32] But efforts to exclude the crowd outside

were limited by the need to cater to the crowd inside, which normally required space and sight lines for a few hundred people.

Officials feared that tension over access to executions would erupt into
violence, and sometimes it did. At the execution of Peter Robinson in
New Jersey in 1841, when the mayor mounted the top of the wall to announce that the hanging was over, the crowd pushed through the gates
and swarmed into the yard. Robinson's body had been removed, but the
rope was still there, so it was cut into pieces and distributed. In 1878 a
crowd of ten thousand awaiting the hanging of Edward Webb in
Mansfield, Ohio, overran an armed guard and demolished the jail's
fence. A nervous sheriff telegraphed the governor, who telegraphed back
to go ahead with the execution in public. A similar incident occurred the
following year in Nebraska.[33] The public's desire to attend hangings was
so strong that people were still turning out, decades after they had been
barred from the grounds.

The chance to watch a hanging clearly meant something to a great
many people. They applied in large numbers for tickets, they traveled
long distances to hangings they had no realistic hope of seeing, they
risked their safety to sit in tree branches and on rooftops for hours at a
time, and on occasion they overpowered local officials to gain a spot inside the walls. Why? One suspects that the motivation for attending an
execution was the same as it had been for centuries. Part of it was the
need to express retribution for crimes against the community. Part was
the thrill of watching violent death. Part was the excitement of being in a
big crowd. Part was the chance to see celebrities, especially famous criminals. Whatever the intent of the individual spectators, the effect of their
collective presence in the days of public hanging had been the creation
of a meaningful community ritual, in which they made manifest their
condemnation of crime in the most visceral way possible, by being present at the law's execution. But not any longer.

A Different Kind of Public

The public lost direct access to executions between the 1830s and the
1930s, but other changes in the process of capital punishment were taking
place at the same time, changes that redefined the nature of the "public"
with respect to the death penalty. Three were particularly important: the
growth of the press, an intensification of the attention paid to celebrated
trials, and the widening of participation in clemency decisions. The pub-

lic was still closely involved in capital cases, but it was involved in a very different way. It was transformed from an actual crowd into a collection of readers and writers, a crowd that never physically assembled.

The first step in the decline of public hanging—the spate of statutes in the North and part of the South between the 1830s and the 1850s—coincided with the development of the newspaper as a mass medium. The new "penny press" included lavish descriptions of crimes and executions, which allowed readers a vicarious experience in place of the real one that was now being denied. Journalists were always allowed a place at jail-yard hangings. Front-page stories included descriptions of the same stock elements that had once transfixed spectators—the condemned person's behavior, his last words, and a vivid account of the physical details of death. Contemporaries recognized that the newspaper was serving as a substitute for public hanging. "Privacy, by means of the modern newspaper, no longer exists," claimed one midcentury observer; "a criminal to-day is hanged with even greater publicity than when swung off at Tyburn, to the delectation of a mob—for to every person in the land comes the elaborate description, the minute particularization of every incident." Newspaper accounts were "so far detailed as virtually to bring even the unimaginative reader into the death chamber and make him an eye-witness of what went on," one paper complained; "how much has really been gained against publicity over the old method of execution in the public square or on the hilltop?" But the same flood of information could be viewed more happily, as providing all the deterrence of a public hanging without the unseemly aspects of public spectacle. "The example lives and is multiplied by the newspaper," crowed *Harper's Weekly* in 1857; "jurists of all countries may well arrive at the conclusion, that the example pondered upon by millions of readers is more powerful than the one gloated over by a few curious thousands of spectators."[34]

The changing nature of the public was not missed by condemned prisoners themselves. When Holly Vann was hanged in a jail yard in Dallas in 1905, he could look out over the ticket-holders wedged into the small space beneath him, but he knew where his real audience could be found. "If anything comes out in the newspapers about me going to the scaffold and dying nervous," Vann instructed the sheriff while his cap was being adjusted, "please have it corrected for me."[35] Vann was dying game in the old tradition, but he was performing for a new public of readers.

Newspaper accounts of executions could be so sensational, and so contrary to polite sensibilities, that in the late nineteenth and early twentieth centuries several states banned the press from reporting the details of executions. New York enacted the first of these laws in 1888. The following year Colorado and Minnesota barred journalists from describing hangings. Similar laws were later enacted in Virginia, Washington, and Arkansas. These bans were widely flouted. In 1891, after a quadruple execution was lavishly recounted in the New York press, the city's district attorney obtained indictments against the editors of several papers, but the resulting criticism of the ban was so strong that the legislature repealed it soon after. Although newspaper editors in the affected states claimed to be confident that such censorship was inconsistent with freedom of the press, the newspapers lost their primary constitutional challenge when the Minnesota Supreme Court upheld the state's statute.[36] (At the turn of the twentieth century the First Amendment and its state constitutional analogues were very rarely invoked and were interpreted more narrowly than they are today.) The statutes nevertheless remained largely unenforced, and the press continued to report the details of executions.

The newspapers covered sensational trials too. By running daily accounts of the proceedings, often in copious detail, the press helped the trial replace the execution as the primary forum at which spectators could participate in the criminal justice system. People had always been attracted to the drama of litigation, but not on the scale that developed in the middle of the nineteenth century. Trials became national events. Famous defendants became celebrities to an unprecedented degree. "Where throughout the United States has not his criminal history been the subject of conversation?" asked one tourist about the Harvard professor John Webster, convicted of murder in 1850. "In Charleston and Savannah, as well as in Boston and New York, the public has universally given the closest attention to the trial."[37] The earliest of the celebrated trials took place at the same time states were moving their hangings into the jail yard. The infamous Lucretia Chapman was tried for murder in Philadelphia in 1832, the year before Pennsylvania abolished public hanging. The equally well-known Richard Robinson was tried for murder in New York in 1836, the year after New York began conducting its hangings in jail. By devoting so much space to trials like these, newspapers were responding to a preexisting demand among their readers, but they were simultaneously stimulating that demand by defining the criminal trial as an event deserving intense public attention.

Barred from executions, the public turned up at trials instead. Spectators packed into courtrooms so tightly that it could become difficult to move the defendant in and out. Women were now normally unable to watch hangings, but they could see trials, and they did in large numbers. During closing arguments at the Cincinnati trial of William Arrison in 1854, there were so many women present that they occupied the area normally reserved for the judge, including the judge's own seat.[38] The biggest criminal trials were often handled, even for the state, by private lawyers celebrated in their own right for eloquence, so closing arguments attracted big crowds. So did the announcement of the jury's verdict.

But the phase of the trial that seems to have been the most popular was sentencing, the part most similar to the old public hanging. Sentencing involved no suspense. The jury had already returned a verdict requiring a death sentence. As in a hanging, everyone knew how it would come out in the end. The drama resided in the emotion of the moment, in the words chosen by the judge and in the reaction of the condemned person. The sentencing of John Hanlon in Pennsylvania in 1870 was watched by a huge crowd including dignitaries and several professional actors studying the performances. At the 1881 sentencing of Albert and Charles Talbott in Missouri for killing their father, "the Judge broke down, covered his face with his hands, and quivered with emotion; strong men wept, women shrieked. The vast multitude present were shaken as if by a tempest."[39] Spectators at hangings had inspected the demeanor of the condemned prisoner, who, aware he was being scrutinized, had tried his best to remain stoic. Now the scrutiny came at the end of the trial, often accompanied by the same affected unconcern on the part of the defendant. A sentencing had many of the aspects of a hanging but none of the violence. Like a hanging, it was a moment of dramatic community condemnation, but it was an event the respectable could still feel good about attending.

Trials had to be conducted in courtrooms, however, and courtrooms were never large enough to accommodate crowds even a tenth of the size of those that had attended executions. The public that followed celebrated trials was primarily a reading public, not an actual assembly of people. As with jail-yard executions, a small number could be physically present, but a much larger number experienced trials at one remove.

The same wider public was meanwhile becoming more involved in the process of clemency. In the eighteenth century letters to governors concerning pardons and commutations had tended to come only from prominent individuals or from small groups of local leaders. But the country was becoming more democratic in general, and clemency was no exception. By the middle of the nineteenth century governors were frequently receiving petitions signed by hundreds or thousands of ordinary citizens. Petitions in favor of Washington Goode, who was ultimately hanged in Massachusetts in 1849, were said to have been signed by twenty-four thousand people. Hundreds of residents of Rock Island County, Illinois, petitioned Governor Thomas Ford to pardon William McKinney in 1845. Nearly a thousand asked Missouri Governor Silas Woodson to commute Joseph Hamilton's death sentence in 1874. Petitions were often printed and attached to blank pages, allowing as many people as possible to sign. Condemned prisoners and their supporters clearly believed that numbers mattered. "They have got the biggest number they can git," one victim's brother angrily reported to the governor of Illinois in 1854. By falsely claiming that the victim's family had forgiven him, the friends of the condemned Andrew Nash "got a grate many of there signers." In North Carolina one opponent of a pardon for John Medlin complained about "how very easy it is to get signers" for clemency petitions. Hundreds of people "usually sign such things as a matter of courtesy," admitted the lawyers filing a pardon application for Maria Eaddy in South Carolina in 1880.[40] A clemency campaign now normally required mobilizing a show of mass support.

Opponents of clemency fought back with mass petitions of their own. In Missouri nearly a hundred people threatened mob violence in the event of any clemency for John Skaggs. Hundreds of South Carolinians, observing that "the people are much exercised on this subject," asked "that Pompey Easterling . . . be not pardoned." Over a hundred of William Cole's Missouri neighbors pleaded with the governor in 1869 not to believe Cole's claim of insanity. They "never heard of sutch a thing until after he had Committed this horid murder," they argued, "not Even men that new him from a Boy." Clemency decisions turned into battles of petitions, between groups each claiming to represent the true wishes of the community, and each depicting the other as unrepresentative. The petitioners against commutation are "a small but noisy party of fanatics," their opponents assured the governor in one Illinois case.[41]

The point was to bring electoral pressure to bear on the governor by implicitly threatening that a wrong decision would alienate large numbers of voters. "Will the Governor dare to pardon him?" an anonymous New

York writer asked, referring to the recently convicted murderer John Colt. "We think not. The verdict seems to give general satisfaction." In 1878 a black employee named Friday Castles was convicted in South Carolina of murder after protecting his white employer's property by shooting and killing a thief, in a case that gave rise to considerable controversy over the justice of the sentence. "We would not for a moment, be understood, as bringing this to the attention of your Excellency, for whatever influence it may be thought to exercise on the State ticket, in the coming campaign," one group of petitioners assured the governor disingenuously. "Yet, we are free to say, that we believe a change of the death penalty to imprisonment in the Penitentiary for life in this case, would be acceptable to our people."[42]

So far as one can tell today, elected officials feared the consequences of a decision contrary to the popular mood. James Clements, sentenced to death in New York's federal court for murder on the high seas, was pardoned in 1851 by President Millard Fillmore because of doubts as to his guilt. Shortly before the pardon, Fillmore's treasury secretary received a note from A. Oakey Hall, the state district attorney in New York City, explaining that although the state's governor wished to advise granting a pardon, "he can do nothing publicly because of the example: having 3 respited scoundrels on our hands."[43] As participation in the clemency process broadened, whether to grant a pardon or commute a sentence could become a difficult political decision.

One must be careful not to overstate the degree to which clemency became a matter of public opinion. The views of the trial judge, the public official who knew most about the case, were still very important. The recommendations of the jurors, who also knew a great deal more than the average person, still meant a lot. As insanity became a common basis for clemency petitions, the expertise of medical professionals became correspondingly important.[44] Clemency was never just a matter of counting votes. But the public was more involved in clemency decisions in the nineteenth century than it had been in the eighteenth.

By the early twentieth century the death penalty's public had been redefined. People had once gone to hangings, but that privilege was now reserved for a select few. Instead they read about executions in newspapers, they watched or read about trials, and they signed petitions for clemency. The public had once been made up of spectators who came together and stared death in the face; now it was made up of individuals reading and writing about death in their own homes.

Consequences

"How do we have to get to be hung—sit or stand up?" asked Samuel Steenburgh in his cell a week before his 1878 execution.

"You will be pinioned at the ankles and at your knees, and your arms pinioned and stand up, and the sheriff will read his warrant; then you will be asked what you have to say, and will make your farewell speech," replied the reporter who had been taking down Steenburgh's confession. "Will you make a speech, Sam?"

"I am going to tell them something, yes; and if I could talk like that little minister, I would give them a good long speech," Steenburgh replied. Then he thought of another question. "Is hanging a hard death?"

"No, Sam, I think it is instantaneous, and all the punishment about it is the awful suspense before the execution." If the reporter knew what he was talking about, he was being kind. "Your heart ache is the punishment, and the hanging is only for a warning to others not to take a life."

"Well," Steenburgh concluded, "I'll take it like a man."[45]

Steenburgh was forty-five years old when he was hanged, which meant he had been only two when New York abolished public hangings. Steenburgh had never seen an execution before his own. He lacked the education necessary to read about executions in the press. He had little idea of what his own would be like.

Capital punishment had long been justified as the most obvious way to deter crime. By vividly demonstrating the consequences of wrongdoing, the state was displaying a message that everyone could understand. But once executions moved into the jail yard, their deterrent value was increasingly called into question. Advocates of jail-yard hangings "give up the whole ground that Capital Punishments do good as an example," the abolitionist Charles Spear argued. "If such spectacles are calculated to strike the mind favorably, or to have a moral influence, why not have them in the squares of our crowded cities?" Soon after Alabama abolished public hangings in 1841, a southern magazine complained that "the lawmakers of Alabama, have abandoned . . . the last remaining ground in favor of capital punishments." What kind of deterrent was kept hidden? The people allowed inside the yard to watch executions were not the ones likely to commit serious crimes. Officials were careful to exclude the very spectators for whom the sight of a hanging would be most beneficial. "We are accustomed to justify the death penalty as a deterrent example," observed the pardon attorney to the governor of Missouri, "but we take pains to render the example as inconspicuous as possible by dispatching the victim with the utmost privacy."[46]

By excluding the crowd, moreover, the move into the jail yard changed the character of capital punishment. Executions lost much of their symbolic meaning. The community no longer gathered to make its statement of condemnation. There was no more ritual to reinforce communal norms proscribing crime, no more ceremony at which to display one's participation in a collective moral order. Would-be spectators did not give up that ritual easily. They continued to gather outside the walls and to clamor for entry into the yard, and they developed alternative rituals— they eagerly read about hangings in the press, they flocked to trials, and they signed petitions and counter-petitions in the period between conviction and execution. But with executions conducted behind closed doors, before a small group of the well connected, out of the public eye, the *people* were no longer punishing the criminal. Now the government was doing the punishing, and the people were reading about it later.

Changing tastes in the nineteenth century about how death should be displayed thus began changing capital punishment itself. Form and substance were not easily separated. Without all the theater, the death penalty was not the same.

7

TECHNOLOGICAL CURES

A NEW WORD ENTERED the American vocabulary in 1889. Formed by combining *electricity* and *execution,* the word filled a need that had not been felt until the year before, when New York became the first state to abandon hanging for another method of putting criminals to death. Sticklers pointed out that *electrocution* made no linguistic sense—the second half derived from the Latin for "to carry out" or "to follow," so the compound referred literally to the following of electricity—but common usage quickly pushed aside early competitors like *electrocide,* even for accidental deaths by electricity.[1]

Between 1888 and 1913 fifteen states adopted the electric chair as their means of execution. By 1950 eleven more states plus the District of Columbia had followed. Another new device, the gas chamber, was first adopted by Nevada in 1921 and then by ten other states by 1955. Hanging had been the universal American method of execution in the late nineteenth century, but by the middle of the twentieth only a handful of states retained the gallows.

The cause of the transformation was an intensified public focus on the suffering of those who were executed. Aspects of hanging that had once been viewed as inevitable came to be perceived as barbaric and unnecessarily cruel. The result was the development of the new execution technologies, which were expected to be more humane on two fronts—painless to the condemned prisoner and less visually troubling to the spectators. But the search for a clean, clinical, undisturbing method of execution had some unexpected consequences. Hangings had once been public events, conducted by local sheriffs with little more expertise than the average spectator. By the middle of the twentieth century executions were being conducted not by ordinary representatives of the community acting on its behalf but by specialists running expensive, complex, and dangerous machinery. The new devices further centralized and privatized the ritual of execution. Capital punishment now had to be administered indoors, before a very small group of people, none of whom would be the sort of person the execution's message was intended to reach.

Perceptions of Pain

Ever since the establishment of the North American colonies, hanging had been the traditional means of execution. Many and perhaps most hangings were evidently painful for the condemned person because they caused death slowly. Hanging was not *intended* to be painful. The ideal for most spectators, and for the officials who conducted the executions, was a sudden jerk that severed the condemned criminal's spinal cord and brought an instant and painless death. But while real hangings were often very different from the ideal, the use of hanging as a method of carrying out a death sentence was virtually never questioned. Pain was accepted as an unfortunate but inevitable accompaniment to an execution.

Science, however, was producing new ways of treating biological conditions that had once seemed irremediable. With the invention of anesthesia in the nineteenth century it became possible to think of pain as something other than an inescapable part of nature. The desire to minimize the condemned person's pain had been present for centuries, but now technological change allowed that desire to be acted upon. For the first time, critics began to argue that something should be done to make hanging less painful. "The object should be to make it not only death, but death abhorred and despicable," the *American Review* noted in 1848. "But must it be made more painful than is absolutely necessary?" The *Review* accordingly concluded that the condemned prisoner should be given enough chloroform to render him unconscious during the execution. Many agreed that the government ought to "kill kindly," as one critic put it. "Even this extreme penalty should be executed, not with any adjuncts of needless ignominy or cruelty," a reformer urged, "but in as mild a form as possible, and with every token of reluctance, of sympathy and humane regard."[2]

The problem was that hanging was extraordinarily variable. The difference between a painless and a painful death, it was thought, could depend on a wide range of conditions—the height of the drop, the elasticity of the rope, the position of the knot, the weather, the tension in the condemned person's neck muscles, and not least the skills of the hangman. To reduce some of this variability, officials began tinkering with the design of the gallows as early as the 1830s. In a conventional hanging one end of the rope was tied to a crossbeam, and the condemned person was dropped through a trap door in the scaffold. The rope applied its force to the neck, a force proportional to the person's weight, at the bottom of his fall. In 1831, when the pirate Charles Gibbs was hanged on Ellis Island in New York harbor, federal officials tried something new. The end of the rope not around Gibbs's neck was tied to two other ropes, which were run through two pulleys, one on each end of the crossbeam. Each rope was then attached to five 56-pound weights, resulting in a total of 560 pounds, far exceeding Gibbs's own weight. At the appropriate time, officials let the weights drop, and Gibbs was jerked up into the air by the neck.[3]

There is apparently no surviving evidence of the purpose of this new design, but it is not hard to guess. By yanking the condemned prisoner up rather than dropping him down, officials could apply a force to the neck greater than could be supplied by the prisoner's own weight. Because the pull on the neck came in an instant, officials could also be more confident that they were applying the force suddenly rather than gradually, as could be the case if the trap door allowed the prisoner to fall slowly. Both reasons are indications that officials wanted a painless death and were willing to do some engineering to get it.

The "upright jerker," as it came to be called, soon spread from county to county, as local officials searching for a surer means of conducting painless hangings adopted the new design. In 1839 in Morrisville, New York, a 238-pound weight gave Lewis Wilber so much momentum that he soared four feet off the floor before dropping back down to an elevation of two feet. By 1845 the upright jerker had become the standard gallows used in New York City. Many other New York counties began using it in the next few decades. The upright jerker was used in several New Jersey counties in the 1850s and 1860s. It arrived in Pittsburgh by 1866, in Charleston, South Carolina, by 1872, in Chicago by 1874, and in Plymouth, Massachusetts, by 1875.[4] Wherever it went, we may suppose that local officials were uncomfortable with the thought that they might be inflicting pain on the people they were executing. The popularity of the upright jerker is a barometer of the growing concern with what it felt like to be hanged.

But the upright jerker never lived up to its promise. Whatever its technical advantages, it still had to be operated by men who were likely to be conducting the only hanging of their careers. At the 1860 execution of James Stephens, the deputy responsible for letting the weights drop failed to chop their supporting rope with an axe in the usual way, but instead let the rope run slowly off its cleat, which gradually raised Stephens four feet off the ground, where he died after eight minutes of gurgling and contortions. When the apparatus broke because of faulty preparation at the hanging of Benjamin Hunter, one spectator reported, "a chill ran through the witnesses present. It was awful." Even when the upright jerker was operated correctly it failed to sever the spinal cords of a significant number of people, who were left to die painfully by asphyxiation, presenting sights that were all the more distressing because they were unexpected. Successive failures made spectators nostalgic for the old-fashioned drop. After the hanging of William Foster, one critic complained of "the hideous and torturing process of putting criminals to death by the brutal process of elevating or 'jerking' them up, instead of precipitating them down by the more certain and humane method of the 'drop.'" The *New-York Daily Tribune* reported in 1875 that many people "object to this method of hanging because the neck is seldom broken."[5] Hanging, no matter how it was engineered, continued to be painful in many cases.

As time went on, the pain associated with hanging became more and more disturbing. Before the last third of the nineteenth century, accounts of bungled or obviously painful executions contain no indication that spectators found them too troubling to bear. But that began to change. In 1868, when Thomas Welsh died in Newark after five minutes of writhing, the press reported that "the cry of 'shame!' if not spoken, was written on fifty faces. The Sheriff, much too gentle for his work, rested his head against the wall, in suppressed emotion." The slow painful death of Charles Sterling in Ohio in 1877 was described by a local paper as a "scene of horror, . . . sickening in the extreme." There was nothing new about painful hangings; what *was* new was the shock that they produced in spectators. When Stephen Ballew struggled for fifteen minutes in Texas, when spectators in Albany watched the convulsive movements of Emil Lowenstein's arms and legs, when it took Joshua Griffin ten minutes of struggle to die in Maryland, when the rope holding James Murphy of Dayton snapped and tumbled a near-dead Murphy to the ground — witnesses in the 1870s were horrified at events that would not have horrified them as much in the 1840s or even the 1860s. "Execution by hanging is as much a relic of barbarism as slavery or polygamy," complained the *Cincinnati Commercial* after William Bergen's noose slipped and Bergen fell half-strangled to the floor.[6] Hangings were as variable as they had ever been, but now spectators were upset at the sight of suffering.

In the 1870s, in an effort to make a painless death more likely, local officials in several places that still used the old downward method of hanging began trying longer drops. The longer the fall, they reasoned, the greater the velocity the condemned criminal would achieve before he reached the end of the rope, and thus the greater the force on his neck and the greater chance his spinal cord would be severed. But longer drops also brought a new danger, that the force on the neck would be too great. In Potosi, Missouri, in 1871 Charles Jolly's throat was torn open and his head half ripped off his body. In Baltimore in 1873 blood flowed out of James West's nose and mouth, slowly saturating the white hood covering his head. "BEASTLY," read the headline in St. Louis when Henry Hollenscheid's head was nearly torn from his shoulders. In Worcester, Massachusetts, only a few ligaments at the back of the neck connected Samuel Frost's head with his body, while a fountain of blood spurted all over the gallows and the floor. In the Ohio Penitentiary Patrick Hartnett's head was ripped completely off his body. In the District of Columbia James Stone's severed head clung to the noose for a moment before landing several feet from the rest of his corpse.[7] These were accidents that did not happen before the move to longer drops. They resulted from the best of intentions.

Sheriffs and their employees had always been local amateurs without much skill or experience, and the new concern about pain only made them more likely to be apprehensive. "The Sheriff and his deputies, unused to such work, were nervous and greatly excited," read one account of an 1877 hanging in Virginia. At the 1886 execution of Allen Adams in Northampton, Massachusetts, the first in the county since 1814, the sheriff was so visibly nervous that Adams kept jokingly offering him a drink. When Aurelio Pompa strangled slowly in San Quentin Prison, kicking and lunging, one of the guards fainted.[8] Rightly or wrongly, spectators often blamed officials for painful hangings, so the men charged with conducting executions felt more pressure than their predecessors had felt earlier in the century.

To ease their discomfort, some local officials sought methods of removing their own agency from the process of hanging. In 1892 a deputy warden in Colorado built a gallows that the condemned prisoner could operate himself. The prisoner stepped onto a platform raised a few inches off the floor. The platform was attached to a cord, the other end of which was connected to the plug in a large cask of water. The cask was in another room, hanging from one side of a beam like that of a balancing scale. Hanging from the other side, in perfect balance, was a heavy iron weight. A rope ran from the weight up over a pulley, across into the next room, down over another pulley, and around the prisoner's neck. When the prisoner stepped on the platform, his weight dropped the platform down to the level of the floor, which pulled the plug out of the cask of water, which caused the water to run out of the cask, which caused the weight on the opposite side of the beam to drop, which jerked the prisoner up into the air. As improbable as the device may sound, T. Thatcher Graves was executed in this manner in Denver in 1892.[9]

A gallows in which the flow of water released a trap door, dropping the condemned person downward in the traditional way, was later used in Idaho. In 1894 a Connecticut prisoner with experience as a machinist invented a gallows in which the weight of the prisoner on a platform released a sliding valve that opened the bottom of a cylinder containing fifty pounds of shot. The shot running out caused the weight to which the prisoner's neck was tied to be released, and the prisoner was jerked up into the air. That year John Cronin became the first person hanged this way. A Nebraska prisoner named Francis Barker invented, for his own 1905 execution, an electrical device that allowed him to release the trap door himself by pressing a button strapped to his thigh.[10]

All these gadgets allowed condemned criminals to hang themselves. Once everything had been set up, there was nothing left for officials to do. That these methods were used at all is further evidence that the government employees who carried out hangings, like the spectators, were becoming more and more uneasy about the prospect of inflicting pain. Barker's push-button trap door, exulted *Popular Mechanics*, "would be most welcome to sheriffs and wardens generally." The tension between support for capital punishment in the abstract and revulsion from the acts necessary to effect it in specific cases had always been present, but that tension intensified as the condemned person's pain became more troubling to his executioners.

Joining this heightened concern about pain was another worry about the variability of hanging. In some cases, it was feared, hanging did not kill. Like the knowledge that hanging could be painful, the belief in the possibility of life after hanging was not new. Stories had always circulated of people revived after having been hanged. All through the century it was common for physicians to carry out so-called galvanic experiments on the corpses of recently hanged men, running electrical currents through various parts of their bodies and watching arms and legs move, fists clench, and facial features distort, to the delight of spectators. The ostensible purpose of these experiments was to see if electricity might reanimate the dead. (The hypothesis is perhaps remembered today only as the basis for the early nineteenth-century novel *Frankenstein*.) After John Skaggs was hanged in rural Missouri in 1870, for example, doctors hooked him up to a battery and produced a gasp from Skaggs's mouth and twitching in his fingers. "Take him back and hang him again," called several of the spectators. The sheriff, worried that he might have to perform a second hanging, was caught trying to pocket the wires to prevent further reanimation. With more electricity, Skaggs appeared to begin breathing. His legs and his lower jaw moved violently. An hour later, after rubbing Skaggs's skin with cayenne pepper and whisky, the doctors detected a pulse. Signs of life did not abate for several hours.[11]

People had long worried that the hanged might not be irrevocably dead. But the worry seemed more intense in the later nineteenth century. From the late 1870s on, every year or two brought another celebrated case of a hanged person believed to be still alive. In Arkansas Joe Bogard revived and went into hiding. In North Carolina Jack Lambert was reported to have been seen walking around on the Sunday after his hanging, and was rumored to have been revived with an electric battery, brandy, and aromatic spirits of ammonia. Locals demanded that Lambert's grave be opened and his body exhibited. As Coleman Blackburn's relatives took him to the cemetery to be buried after his hanging in Mississippi, they heard scratching on the inside of the coffin lid and discovered that Blackburn was still breathing. He was revived and hanged a second time. Episodes like these were troubling enough by 1880 to cause the *New York Times* to suggest replacing the gallows with the guillotine, which "makes no failures, but is an absolutely certain and rapid agent of death."[12]

Bungled hangings often caused intense pain and on occasion failed to kill. This had been true for centuries, but in the second half of the nineteenth century it upset many more people than ever before. Hanging, one of the oldest parts of the Anglo-American criminal justice system, began for the first time to be perceived as a problem.

One possible solution was to establish a group of expert hangmen, following the European model, to replace the local amateurs. "Under the present practice, by which each county hangs its own criminals," complained one critic, "an entirely inexperienced Sheriff is often called upon to superintend the execution, and the risk of failure is increased if the duty is revolting as well as novel to him." Some states accordingly transferred authority over hangings from county sheriffs to the state penitentiary, where officials could be more easily supervised and could gain expertise by conducting all of the state's executions. In many places where hangings remained under local authority, sheriffs began hiring private-sector experts. By 1882 James Van Heise of Newark, a carpenter, had conducted thirteen hangings in six different New Jersey counties. "He is an expert hangman," noted one approving newspaper, "and is not credited with a single blunder." By the 1930s G. Phil Hanna of Epworth, Illinois, was traveling all over the country to run hangings. But hanging was variable enough to be often painful even when handled by professionals. And even experts made mistakes. At one 1875 hanging on Long Island, when the rope frayed and the condemned man had to be manually hauled up with a new rope, to suffocate slowly, the press blamed the professional hangman, who had committed a similar error the year before.[13] One could never be sure that hanging would produce the desired kind of death.

So it was that after hundreds of years of hanging Americans began to look for alternative methods of executing criminals. "Let some less revolting plan than hanging be fixed upon," the *New York Times* had urged as early as 1852. "The bullet, the guillotine, the garrote, are incomparably better in the eye of the connoisseur, than the gallows." Such proposals were common in the 1870s. "Whenever an executioner has done his work clumsily," reported one correspondent, "there is a cry for some new and surer and more humane way of putting the capitally convicted to death." After recounting a series of botched hangings under the headline "Torture by the Law's Executioners," the *Pittsburgh Legal Journal* called for the development of a new method of execution. In 1884 the *New-York Daily Tribune* published an editorial that summarized this school of thought. "It is indeed a little surprising," the *Tribune* argued, that there has not been more effort to substitute for the gallows some less savage and rude form of execution. Science has abundant means of killing in the most swift and painless manner, yet we cling to a method which is often neither one nor the other. If human life is to be taken at all in the interest and for the protection of society, it certainly ought to be taken as mercifully as possible. Anything that suggests torture is unworthy [of] modern civilization. The punishment—the most severe that can be conceived—consists in forcing the criminal out of this world. To insist that the manner of death also should be harsh is a refinement of cruelty.[14]

The gallows had been taken for granted for centuries, but not any longer. Changing perceptions of pain, driven by a new faith in the power of science to ameliorate what had once seemed to be inevitable aspects of the human condition, had caused too many people to view hanging as an inhumane method of execution.

Electricity

In April 1881 Lucretia Garfield visited some friends in New York. The wife of the recently elected President of the United States wanted to see a device that was being touted as a remedy for lame limbs, stiff necks, and rheumatism, because she was thinking of having one installed in the White House for her husband. The new sensation was an "electric bath," a zinc-lined tub filled with water, through which ran wires connected to a battery. The electric current would cause the bather's muscles to twitch. The electric bath was just the latest innovation in a tradition of electrical medicine that dated back to the mid-eighteenth century. James Garfield never had the chance to take an electric bath—he was assassinated not long after his wife returned from New York—but if he had, he would have participated in a practice too widespread and too long-lasting to be called a fad. For Americans in the late nineteenth century, electricity was therapeutic.[15]

Meanwhile, as city after city began to construct networks of wires to carry electricity into homes and workplaces, the newspapers were reporting frightening new kinds of accidents. "Killed by Electricity," ran the headline when a Pittsburgh iron mill worker unknowingly leaned on a fence over which a live wire had been draped. The first known death from commercial electricity in the United States did not occur until 1881, but by 1888 there had been approximately two hundred in the preceding five years.[16] If electricity was therapeutic, it was also dangerous.

And at the Ohio State Penitentiary the guards found a new way to discipline prisoners. The prisoner was stripped, blindfolded, handcuffed, and placed in three inches of water. One pole of a battery was in the water, the other fastened to a sponge. When the sponge was placed on the prisoner's skin, the completed circuit was enough to make him scream. Prison officials reported that their prisoners were much better behaved since the battery had been substituted for the ducking-tub. From England, meanwhile, came reports of a new electrical apparatus for slaughtering animals. It was not any faster than the traditional method, but it was painless for the animal and less revolting for the sympathetic observer. "Slaughtering mercifully" was how one newspaper described it.[17] Electricity was both therapeutic and dangerous at the same time, and that could make it extraordinarily useful. There were times when electricity's destructive force would be welcome, provided it could be confined to certain narrow objectives.

Electricity in the late nineteenth century was something like the computer in the late twentieth. It was newly ubiquitous yet still a bit mysterious. It offered the promise of new conveniences but also the nightmare of unpredictable peril. Everyone who could afford it had to have it, but most were only slightly familiar with how it worked. Like the computer, electricity was within the province of a brand-new class of experts. The new electrical systems and appliances were designed and managed by people who possessed an esoteric knowledge that had scarcely existed a generation before.

Electricity was in the air, so to speak, when in 1886 the New York legislature became the first to respond to the growing dissatisfaction with hanging by appointing a commission "to investigate and report at an early date the most humane and practical method known to modern science of carrying into effect the sentence of death." The commission promptly consulted with several of the new electrical experts, including Thomas Edison, who despite his avowed opposition to capital punishment advised that of all the means of causing death, electricity would be the fastest and would inflict the least suffering. One of the commission's three members, the Buffalo dentist Alfred Southwick, witnessed a series of experiments on stray dogs conducted in 1887 by the Society for the Prevention of Cruelty to Animals, which seemed to prove that dogs at least could be killed instantly by the application of electric current. Of the two hundred responses the commission received to its survey of judges, sheriffs, district attorneys, and physicians, eighty favored retaining hanging, but eighty-seven preferred electricity, far more than the closest competitors, poison (eight) and the guillotine (five).[18]

Unsolicited support for electricity poured in, especially from doctors. Electricity is "absolutely painless," one supporter urged. "The electric current passes through the body of the criminal, and even before the bystanders have consciousness of the act of pressing the button all is over." Unlike other methods of putting a person to death, another supporter of electricity argued, the act of originating a current required no skill, and thus it could be performed competently even by untrained prison employees. Not all doctors favored electricity—at meetings of the New York Society of Medical Jurisprudence there were passionate arguments in favor of the guillotine and improved techniques of hanging—but the weight of medical opinion was on electricity's side. Death by electricity would be fast, painless, and humane.[19]

No one knew for sure why electricity killed. Some believed that electric current forced too much blood to the head. Others claimed that electricity deprived the blood of important magnetic properties, or constricted the arteries and blocked blood flow, or stopped the lungs from operating. Not until 1899 would two groups of scientists, working independently, establish that the usual cause of electrical death is ventricular fibrillation, in which the uncoordinated contractions of heart muscle prevent the heart from pumping blood.[20] But if the precise mechanism of death was uncertain, the simple fact that electricity caused death was not. Once New York began looking for alternatives to hanging, electricity was by a wide margin the most popular.

The commission issued its report in January 1888. In ninety-five thorough pages it raised and rejected thirty-four conceivable methods of execution. These were considered alphabetically, from "auto da fé" to "suffocation," with brief but learned coverage of each. The report included more elaborate discussion of the techniques that were serious contenders. The guillotine, then in use in several European countries, was rejected because of "the profuse effusion of blood which it involves," a display that "must be needlessly shocking to the necessary witnesses." The guillotine was also associated in the public mind "with the bloody scenes of the French Revolution" and would accordingly "be found totally repugnant to American ideas." Spain used the garrote, a metal collar around the neck tightened with a screw that pierced the spinal column, a device that avoided the blood associated with the guillotine and usually caused death instantly. The garrote, however, killed by two means simultaneously— strangling and severing the spinal cord—and that was enough for the commission to reject it. "Surely an apparatus can be arranged such that one, single, simple cause of death can be put in operation quickly, certainly and humanely," the commissioners averred. "To multiply the causes savors of barbarity." Shooting was quick, as military executions had long demonstrated, but it "would be objectionable as requiring the attendance of a number of executioners, and, further, demoralizing particularly because of its tendency to encourage the untaught populace to think lightly of the fatal use of fire-arms." The commission considered hanging as well, but its very purpose had been to replace hanging with something better. Hanging, it unsurprisingly concluded, was "harrowing to the feelings of the sensitive" and "demoralizing to the brutal." The commission recounted a long series of bungled hangings, from Britain and the United States, to support its conclusion that "the time has come when a radical change should be effected."

After finding fault with all the alternatives, the commission turned to electricity. An electrical death was painless, it reported, because "the velocity of the electric current is so great that the brain is paralyzed; is indeed dead before the nerves can communicate any shock." An electrical death would be certain, unlike death by hanging, because it would be a simple matter to apply a current so powerful that death would result. Electricity would not mutilate the body, again unlike hanging in many cases. A fast, painless, certain, and clean execution would be more humane for the condemned person and less troubling for spectators and officials than hanging. Electrical execution, moreover, would not require any expensive equipment: "All that would be essential would be a chair, with a head and foot-rest . . . one electrode would be connected with the head-rest, and the other with the foot-rest, which would consist of a metal plate." The prisons already had electric light, so the chair could draw its power from the same source. Even if a prison was supplied with its own generator, a complete apparatus could be built for under $1,000, after which each execution would be practically costless. Measured by any criterion, electricity was the best method of execution. "It is the duty of society to utilize for its benefit the advantages and facilities which science has uncovered to its view," the report concluded. Electricity had provided cleaner light; now it would provide cleaner death. The state of New York officially switched from hanging to electricity a few months later.[21]

Prison officials now faced the task of acquiring machinery that had not yet been designed. There was no name for the device yet. Elbridge Gerry, one of the three commissioners, called it an *electrolethe*.[22] Nor was there any agreement as to how the device would be constructed, except on one point. Everyone seems to have accepted that it would be a chair of some sort. One of the commissioners was a dentist, a man presumably accustomed to working with mechanical chairs, so his influence may have been responsible for the commission's assumption that the prisoner would be executed while seated. More likely, the long tradition of visual display associated with hangings ensured that all concerned took for granted that the condemned criminal had to be visible to spectators at the moment of death. He could not be executed standing up, because unless propped up in an undignified manner he would crumple to the ground once the electricity had passed through his body, and the sight would be displeasing to spectators. He could not be executed lying down, because spectators would have to come uncomfortably close to get a good view. Many would doubtless have perceived something unmanly or undignified about being executed in any position—lying down, kneeling, and so on—that so dramatically signified submission to the state. Electrocution in a chair was the most visually acceptable alternative.

But how would the chair work? On this question state prison officials found themselves in the middle of what contemporaries called the "battle of the currents." The incipient commercial electricity market was dominated by two firms, one owned by Thomas Edison, which sold systems that used direct current, and the other by George Westinghouse, which sold systems that used alternating current. Edison had implemented his system first, but Westinghouse's was less expensive, so by the late 1880s Edison was grasping for ways to hold on to his share of the rapidly expanding market. One way was to disparage the safety of alternating current.

In the summer of 1888 a little-known New York engineer named Harold P. Brown conducted public experiments demonstrating that dogs died when subjected to lower voltages of alternating than direct current, a result from which Brown concluded that direct current would be safer for home use. Brown's experiments received extensive press coverage at precisely the moment New York's legislature instructed state prison officials to acquire a machine that would execute criminals by electricity. It was only natural that prison officials would turn to Brown, suddenly the most famous electrical engineer in the state, for advice. As Brown explained, his work with animals "gave me expert knowledge of death-currents, and brought to me a request from the New York State authorities to select and purchase for them the apparatus for electrical executions."[23] Edison immediately recognized the possibility of a marketing coup. He invited Brown to use his Menlo Park laboratory and financed Brown's continued work, including the development of an electric chair using alternating current. There could be no better demonstration of the danger to life posed by alternating current than the fact that the state used it to kill criminals.

Hiring Brown was not Edison's first attempt to turn the electric chair to his advantage, nor would it be his last. When the commission that recommended electricity as a replacement for hanging had sought Edison's guidance in 1887, Edison had been careful to specify that the most effective execution technology would be the "'alternating machines,' manufactured principally in this country by Mr. Geo. Westinghouse." One of Edison's associates would later suggest *westinghouse* as an appropriate noun for the device and handy verb to describe the process in which it would be employed. Just as French criminals were *guillotined*, he reasoned, American criminals could be *westinghoused*. But alternating current had neither been suggested by the commission nor mandated by the legislature. Edison accordingly met with state officials in late 1888 to persuade them that alternating current would be the most effective means of execution. "Beyond a doubt the alternating current will be adopted for execution purposes," Brown assured one of Edison's employees in December, "which will make my fight against its use for house lighting a much easier one."[24]

In the end Westinghouse would win. Despite the unfavorable publicity associated with the electric chair and the fact that at equal voltages direct current really is less likely to cause death, the cost advantages of alternating current were enough for it to prevail. But because the electric chair was invented during the brief period when the battle of the currents was at its peak, it was designed in Thomas Edison's laboratory, using the current Edison was trying to drive from the market.

Through late 1888 and early 1889 Brown conducted a series of experiments on animals in Edison's laboratory for the purpose of determining the optimal amount of alternating current. Too little, and the result would be not death but intense pain. Too much, and the corpse would burn—"something extremely undesirable," Brown explained to reporters. If killing with electricity was easy, killing cleanly was not. Brown soon discovered that the voltage necessary to cause death could vary drastically even among animals of the same weight, because there were wide variations in the animals' resistance. The dogs alone varied in resistance from 3,600 to 200,000 ohms, depending on the thickness of the skin and hair and on the amount of moisture between the skin and the electrodes. It was only after electrocuting forty to fifty dogs, six to ten calves, and two horses that Brown concluded that at least 1,500 to 2,000 volts would be necessary to ensure the death of a human being. The state prisons at Auburn, Clinton, and Sing Sing each purchased the necessary equipment, including Westinghouse generators, to use for executions. Westinghouse had refused to sell generators for that purpose, so Brown arranged the purchase of used machines.[25]

The impending switch from hanging to electrocution was not welcomed by all. Critics argued that the change would undermine both the deterrent and retributive justifications for capital punishment. "Menlo Park wizards and electricians . . . would wantonly rob society of whatever deterring influence may repose" in the death penalty, one critic complained, by staging a clinical, sanitized death. Electrocution "certainly seems to be more in keeping with the scientific spirit of the age in which we live, and it has an air of respectability about it that hanging has not," another conceded, but in fact the chair would be a "device that rivals in horror the worst tortures of the worst ages in the world." The horror of electricity was not that it would be painful but rather that it was puffed up to be something other than punishment, an ostensibly humane treatment inflicted by fatuous men who denied their true identity as executioners. "This new system of judicial murder seems to me worse than the roastings of the savages," the second critic concluded, "worse than those if for no other reason than that it is to be practised by those who claim to be enlightened, civilized beings." A punishment that pretended to be something else entirely undercut the retributive rationale for punishment itself.[26] But the critics were in a small minority. The electric chair represented science, progress, and modernity, in the service of making executions more uniform and less painful. Technology would make the death penalty more humane by making it less human.

A Buffalo man named William Kemmler, convicted of murdering his girlfriend, became the first New Yorker sentenced to death after January 1, 1889, the date the new statute took effect. The world's first electrical execution was scheduled for June 1889 in Auburn Prison. It did not actually take place, however, until after nearly a year of litigation. Two weeks before the scheduled execution date, Kemmler's lawyers filed a petition for a writ of habeas corpus in state court, seeking to prevent the execution on the ground that the use of the electric chair would constitute cruel and unusual punishment, in violation of the state constitution. Because the electric chair was conceded to be unusual, the only issue on which there was any litigation was whether it was cruel—that is, whether it was more painful than hanging. On this subject the court took the testimony of several witnesses, the most important of whom were Thomas Edison and Harold P. Brown, who described in some detail the experiments on animals. The Cayuga County Court held in October that Kemmler had failed to prove that death in the electric chair would be any more cruel than death on the gallows. That conclusion was then affirmed by two state appellate courts. Finally, in May 1890, the United States Supreme Court held that electrical execution would not infringe any of the rights guaranteed to Kemmler by the relatively new Fourteenth Amendment to the Constitution.[27]

Kemmler had no money. In the late nineteenth century governments did not pay lawyers to conduct this kind of litigation for the indigent. Yet Kemmler had some prominent New York lawyers, including Roger Sherman and W. Bourke Cockran, a former member of Congress. These men had not built their reputations or their fortunes representing indigent criminals. The press had little trouble figuring out that they were being paid, not by Kemmler, but by Westinghouse. Westinghouse had more to gain than did Kemmler from a successful outcome to the litigation. Had Kemmler won, he would simply have been executed by hanging instead. The motive for the lawsuit "is not a desire to save Kemmler," the *New York Times* complained, "but the objection of the Westinghouse Company to having its alternating current employed for the purpose, lest people using its apparatus for other purposes should get the impression that the current is dangerous." That Kemmler was nominally a litigant was only "a convenient legal fiction for getting the electricians a standing in court." George Westinghouse angrily denied that he or anyone associated with his company was financing Kemmler's litigation, and rather unpersuasively implied that Edison was the real backer.[28]

A century later there appears to be no solid proof that Westinghouse paid for the year-long litigation, but bits of circumstantial evidence point in that direction. Sherman admitted being paid by someone other than Kemmler, but refused to say by whom. Westinghouse Electric's regular corporate lawyer, Paul Cravath, often retained Bourke Cockran to conduct litigation on behalf of Cravath's clients. During a respite in the litigation in April 1890, when it appeared as if Kemmler's execution might proceed, a clerk with Cravath's firm was spotted at Auburn Prison. When asked by a reporter why he was there, the clerk declined to respond. Cravath himself denied that Westinghouse was involved, but when pressed about who might be paying Kemmler's lawyers, Cravath could only provide the unlikely theory that "somebody has started this proceeding because it involves an interesting point of law, and simply for the fun of it."[29] If Westinghouse was not paying the lawyers, it is hard to imagine who was.

By the time the litigation was over, prison officials were more than ready for the electrocution. The chair was placed in a dimly lit room. On one wall were a voltmeter for measuring the force of the current and a switch for sending the current to the two wires leading to the chair. The generator was a thousand feet away, in a different wing of the prison.[30] Early in the morning of August 6, 1890, Warden Charles Durston led Kemmler into the death chamber. The twenty-five invited witnesses included several physicians, several state officials, a representative of the Associated Press, and Alfred Southwick, a member of the commission that had recommended the adoption of the electric chair. "Gentlemen, I wish you all good luck," Kemmler announced. "I believe I am going to a good place, and I am ready to go." As he settled into the electric chair, he told the warden to "take your time and do it all right." Durston attached one electrode to the base of Kemmler's spine, where a triangular hole had been cut in his trousers with a pocket knife. The other was attached to a metal cap, which was tied onto Kemmler's head with leather straps that crossed his forehead and chin, partially concealing his face. Durston stepped to the door and said "Good-bye, William," a prearranged signal to the prison employee standing by the switch. Spectators heard the click of the switch as the current was sent to the chair.

What followed was more gruesome than anyone present could have imagined. "FAR WORSE THAN HANGING," screamed the next day's headline in the *New York Times*. "KEMMLER'S DEATH PROVES AN AWFUL SPECTACLE." At the moment the current ran through his body, Kemmler's muscles drew taut and then relaxed. For seventeen seconds Kemmler remained perfectly still. "He is dead," announced E. C. Spitzka, the attending physician. Durston pressed a button that sent a signal to the generator room indicating that the generator should be stopped. The spectators sighed with relief. Durston began loosening the electrode on Kemmler's head. One spectator suddenly shouted "Great God! He is alive!" Kemmler indeed appeared to be still living. His chest was rising and falling, and the sound of breathing could be heard by all. "Turn on the current!" shouted another spectator. "For God's sake kill him and have it over!" urged a third. Durston hastily screwed the electrode back into place and then ran to the door and sounded two bells, which informed the men in the generator room to turn the generator back on.

The generator was being operated by Charles Barnes, the Rochester City Electrician, who was having problems of his own. The generator had been placed on an ordinary wooden floor. While it was running it made the floor vibrate, which caused the generator's belt to begin to slip off its pulley. One of Barnes's assistants had to hold a board against the moving belt to keep it on, but despite that effort more than half the belt was off the pulley by the time Durston signaled to turn off the generator. Had the belt come completely off, the electricity would have been cut off midway through the execution. When the signal came to resume, two men had to press against the belt to keep it from flying off the pulley.

Terrified that the first seventeen-second dose of electricity had failed to kill Kemmler, Durston kept the second dose on for over a minute. The capillaries in Kemmler's face ruptured, and beads of blood appeared like sweat on his face. The overpowering smell of burnt flesh permeated the room. The hair around the electrode on Kemmler's head started to singe, apparently because in all the commotion Durston had failed to reattach the electrode completely. Kemmler's body was left limp in its chair to cool, and then transferred to the autopsy table. The nauseated spectators filed out. "I would rather see ten hangings than one such execution as this," exclaimed New York's deputy coroner.

The Kemmler execution was subjected to sharp criticism that day and the next. Paul Cravath, Westinghouse's attorney, announced that "it has now been proven that killing a man by electricity is the height of cruelty." Opponents of capital punishment seized the occasion to proclaim that the goal of executing cleanly and painlessly had been proved impossible. But most of the criticism placed the blame not on electrocution generally but on the mistakes made by Durston. The current was supposed to be at approximately 1,700 volts, but because Durston had neglected to turn off twenty lamps that were on the circuit for testing purposes to indicate the presence of current, the actual voltage that reached Kemmler was closer to 700. The voltmeter was not working, so there was no way to know for sure. The physicians agreed that Kemmler had almost certainly been dead after the first seventeen-second bout of electricity, that his apparent breathing afterward was not breathing at all but merely muscular contractions, and that Durston should not have panicked and turned the electricity back on.[31]

But even if Kemmler had not experienced pain, there was no dispute that the first electrocution had been bungled. Electricity had been expected to create an atmosphere more dignified than that at a hanging, but the chaos accompanying Kemmler's death had been far from dignified. Electricity had been expected to provide a cleaner death than hanging, but the spectators at Kemmler's execution had been treated to a grotesque display. "No form of death which draws blood or dissevers the body would be tolerated in America," affirmed the *New-York Daily Tribune* the following day. New York's first experiment with electricity "was not a complete success. The current was not steady, and neither were the nerves of those who supplied it."[32] The purpose of the electric chair had been to remove the possibility of human error from the process of execution. Judged by that standard, the first electrocution had been a failure.

New York's prison officials had several chances to practice in the next few years. They steadied both the current and their nerves. Within a year after Kemmler's execution four more murderers, convicted of unrelated crimes, were ready for the electric chair. All four—James Slocum, Harris Smiler, Joseph Wood, and Shibaya Jugiro—were electrocuted on the same day in Sing Sing Prison. (In his unsuccessful effort to obtain a writ of habeas corpus, Jugiro was represented by Roger Sherman, Kemmler's lawyer, who once again refused to admit he was being paid by Westinghouse.)[33] The quadruple execution was a model of efficiency. Slocum entered the chamber at 4:31 A.M., was given two contacts of twenty-six seconds each which were completed by 4:39, and was removed from the chair at 5:00, once his body had cooled and the attending physicians were certain he was dead. By 5:05 Smiler was in the chair. After two bouts of current and a brief waiting period his corpse was wheeled out. It was only 5:23. "The whole procedure was regular, methodical and dignified," noted the Albany physician Samuel Ward, who was in attendance, "and every action positive and sure and carried on in orderly sequence." Wood walked in at 5:29; his body was taken out at 5:53. Jugiro was in at 5:59 and out by 6:22. None of the four evidenced any pain. All appeared to have died instantly. The four corpses bore no external signs of physical damage. This second experience with the electric chair fulfilled all the hopes that had been placed on electrocution. New York had finally found a clean and painless technique of killing.

Part of the improvement was a result of technical changes. The electricians operating the equipment had been able to produce a consistent current that did not drop below 1,450 volts. The electrodes, one applied to the forehead and the other to the calf, had been kept wet with saline solution. But some of the improvement was attributable simply to prison officials' confidence that the initial jolts of electricity would kill. They were able to keep the duration of the charge to a minimum, which prevented a recurrence of the troubling aspects of the Kemmler execution. Although the water near the electrodes rose close to the boiling point and blistered the skin, that was the extent of the visible damage. As Ward proudly observed, "there was absolutely nowhere any smoking, or charring, or burning."[34]

The success of the second electrocution put to rest any lingering doubts as to the efficacy of the electric chair. In early 1892, after another electrocution had gone off without incident, the *Brooklyn Daily Eagle* found it difficult "to see how any intelligent person can hesitate to believe that the new method is the more decent, orderly, swift, certain and humane." By the end of 1893 New York had electrocuted twenty-one people, and the electric chair had ceased to be a subject of public interest. Accounts of electrocutions, if reported at all in the local press, were no longer on the front page. Even a second botched electrocution at Auburn in the summer of 1893 failed to arouse much concern. The initial jolt of over 1,700 volts failed to kill William Taylor, who gasped spasmodically for breath. When the machine was turned on a second time, no current came. The generator had burned out. Taylor was carried on a cot into an adjoining room. He was groaning aloud and trying to rise. Guards held his arms and legs down to prevent him from standing. He was given a shot of morphine to ease his pain. The electricians quickly strung wires from the city's electric plant through the windows of the prison and connected them with the switchboard that operated the chair. An hour after the first jolt, Taylor finally received a second, this one lethal. Despite a scene in some respects even more distressing to spectators and officials than the Kemmler execution, Taylor's electrocution drew considerably less attention.[35] New York had already successfully electrocuted several of its criminals. The electric chair had been proven to satisfy, at least most of the time, the hopes placed on it.

With success came emulation. In 1896 Ohio became the second state to switch to the electric chair, followed by Massachusetts (1898), New Jersey (1906), Virginia (1908), North Carolina (1909), Kentucky (1910), and South Carolina (1912). "It is a swift, sure, solemn and awe-inspiring mode of punishment," proudly reported the Virginia State Penitentiary's surgeon when his prison acquired one. He found it "infinitely more humane than hanging." In some of these states the chair was challenged in court as cruel and unusual punishment, but all such challenges were easily rejected on the ground that the chair was simply a more humane means toward a traditional end. Seven more states adopted the electric chair in 1913—Arkansas, Indiana, Nebraska, Oklahoma, Pennsylvania, Tennessee, and Vermont. The chair was equally popular in the North and the South; the West was the only region in which few states switched to electrocution in the early part of the century. Wherever change occurred it was motivated by the same faults found in hanging—the pain suffered by the condemned person and the distaste felt by the spectators. As the Texas legislature explained when it made the switch in 1923, hanging "is antiquated and has been supplanted in many states by the more modern and humane system of electrocution." By 1950 the electric chair was also in operation in Alabama, Florida, Georgia, the District of Columbia, Illinois, New Mexico, Connecticut, South Dakota, Louisiana, Mississippi, and West Virginia. In 1937 the federal government ceased hanging criminals convicted of federal crimes and began instead to follow the execution method of the state in which the death sentence was imposed, after Attorney General Homer Cummings pointed out that many states had "adopted more humane methods, such as electrocution."[36]

Scarcely a year passed without a small item in the press observing that a particular defendant was the last person to be hanged in his state, or the first person to be electrocuted. Prison officials from the later states to adopt the chair traveled to the earlier states to learn how to construct and operate the necessary equipment. Employees of the Indiana Department of Corrections, for example, visited New York and Ohio in 1913 to make sketches of electric chairs. On their return, in an act both efficient and symbolic, they had Indiana prisoners use the components of the state prison's defunct gallows to build the electric chair. The back and the legs of the chair were formed from the braces and uprights of the gallows, while the seat and arms were cut from the platform beneath.[37]

As it spread around the country, the electric chair encountered only sporadic opposition. The last conceivable legal obstacle to electrocution was removed by the United States Supreme Court, which held in 1915 that the switch from hanging to electrocution was not an increase in punishment, and so it was not inconsistent with the Constitution's Ex Post Facto Clause for a state to use the electric chair for a criminal who committed his crime at a time when hanging was still the state's method of execution. There were occasional protests such as the one soon after the District of Columbia adopted the chair, when twelve men, including one physician, offered to take the place of the first condemned murderer in the District's new chair in an effort to prove that electrocution was painful. They wanted to invite the President and the governors of all the states to see them die. Their request was refused.[38] Such opposition was unusual. Wherever it was adopted, the electric chair was widely understood to represent progress.

Electrocution's only significant setbacks came early in its history, in the form of a recurring scientific controversy, raging through learned journals and the popular press, over whether the electric chair actually killed its occupants. Before the chair was invented it had been noticed that people electrocuted by touching live wires sometimes revived after a period of unconsciousness, even when the wires were carrying very large amounts of electricity. A respectable minority of the medical profession thought it possible that electricity itself might not cause death but only unconsciousness, and that people apparently dead as a result of contact with electricity might be revived if they were given proper medical attention soon enough after the injury. In 1894 Dr. Peter J. Gibbons of Syracuse requested permission to attempt to revive Charles Wilson, who was about to be executed in Auburn Prison. The request was refused, but it set off several months of debate in the New York newspapers over the efficacy of the electric chair. Many argued that the state's condemned criminals were killed not in the electric chair but on the autopsy table afterward. Edison and others assured the press that electrocution was fatal, but among the skeptics were some with undisputed electrical expertise, including the inventor Nikola Tesla. (Tesla's patents were the basis of Westinghouse's electrical systems, and Tesla earned a royalty on Westinghouse's sales, so he had reasons of his own for his opinion.)[39]

A decade later, in 1905, the issue emerged once more when the physician Louise Robinovitch, editor of the *Journal of Mental Pathology*, published the results of experiments in which she electrocuted and revived several rabbits. Her findings, Robinovitch argued, "show how crude and horrible is the method of electrocution now applied in capital punishment in the State of New York." That same year one Frederick Hendershot of East Orange, New Jersey, tried to turn on the current at the local power house with his bare hand, received 13,500 volts, and was knocked unconscious, but was revived and treated in the hospital. As Robinovitch's *Journal* noted with some understatement, "survival after receiving a shock from the passage of 13,500 volts through the human body is of great interest in itself."[40] If people did not necessarily die when they were electrocuted, the logic of the electric chair was undermined. Electricity would be *less* uniform, *less* humane, than hanging.

The debate returned to the public stage every few years. In 1908 the county physician in Essex County, New Jersey, where the state prison and the state's new electric chair were located, announced that he would attempt to revive John Mantasanna, whose execution was scheduled in two weeks' time. The purpose of the experiment would be to prove once and for all that the chair caused irrevocable death. The prison's warden, who by statute was required to electrocute the condemned until they were dead and was not eager to make the job any harder, barred the county physician from attending any executions. Again, however, the controversy lasted long enough to elicit strong opinions on both sides from many electricians and doctors. In 1912 the sheriff of New York City made headlines when he traveled to Sing Sing to attend the execution of Philip Mangano for the purpose of determining whether electric shock really caused death. "Among medical men of the highest reputation," the sheriff explained, "it has been a question, ever since the invention of the electric chair, whether the shock, or the subsequent autopsy, caused death." A close look at the electrocution satisfied him that the chair was lethal.[41]

The debate faded away slowly. Amos Squire, the physician at Sing Sing Prison, explained in 1923 to the annual convention of the American Prison Association that he had tried unsuccessfully to revive more than twenty executed people. In 1927, by which time twenty states and the District of Columbia had substituted electricity for hanging, Sing Sing's warden was still considering attaching an apparatus to the condemned person's chest to record heart action during and after the flow of the current, to dispel the belief that life persisted after electrocution. Even as late as 1938 *Popular Science Monthly* reported "serious scientific skepticism" about the chair and noted that recent research at Harvard Medical School suggested that the electrocuted person "may only be shocked into a semblance of death and that the final spark of life is extinguished unwittingly in the autopsy room."[42]

But apart from these occasional episodes, the electric chair spread uncontroversially throughout the country. It had proven itself to be normally faster, less painful for the condemned person, and less disturbing to spectators than hanging.

The chair was far from perfect. Electrocutions could be unsettling to watch. Even if the doctors were sure that the prisoner felt no pain, an electrocution *looked* painful. When the electricity hit George Winyard, executed in South Carolina in 1939, his body tensed and banged into the back of the chair. His fingernails pierced his flesh, causing blood to run down his leg. Flames flickered on his skin. As the current was turned on and off three times, Winyard stiffened and buckled each time. Guards carried away his corpse, frozen into a seated position. At Sing Sing the chair normally crackled, whined, and buzzed while the current ran through it. The prisoner's face typically turned crimson. His limbs and eyes contorted. Sometimes smoke rose from the top of his head. Sometimes spectators were overwhelmed by a smell resembling that of roast pork. Charles Monroe, a Massachusetts mail clerk, got to watch an execution at Sing Sing in the 1930s because his brother-in-law worked in the prison. "It was an ugly business," Monroe recalled. "One witness fainted and another vomited, and it was a big relief to get out of there." At the 1936 electrocution of Bruno Hauptmann several of the witnesses had to be helped from the room. Even when executions by electric chair went according to plan, they could be "appalling and disgusting," as the novelist William Dean Howells complained.[43] But if electrocutions were sometimes painful for the condemned person and often gruesome to watch, on balance they were less painful and less gruesome than hangings had been.

With the new method of execution necessarily came new dramaturgy. The technical requirements of the electric chair brought important changes to the ceremony of execution.

Unlike a hanging, an electrocution had to be held indoors, where the chair, the generator, and the rest of the apparatus could safely be housed. Hangings in the jail yard could accommodate several hundred and sometimes over a thousand spectators, but only a much smaller number could fit in the interior space available for watching an electrocution. As states switched from the gallows to the electric chair, execution crowds accordingly shrank dramatically.

Unlike gallows, which could be quickly and cheaply built wherever they were needed and then easily dismantled afterwards, the machinery required for an electrocution was expensive and permanent. When Georgia adopted electrocution, the legislature appropriated nearly $5,000 for the equipment. South Dakota and Tennessee each appropriated $5,000. Congress appropriated $10,000 for the District of Columbia's electric chair. Hangings were traditionally conducted in the county where the crime had been committed, because it was not difficult for each county to have its own gallows, but it would have been prohibitively expensive for every county to have its own electric chair. As a result, every state but Mississippi that adopted electrocution moved all its executions to a single state prison. (Mississippi used a portable chair that could be moved around the state. Louisiana briefly experimented with a portable chair, but then transferred all executions to the state prison at Angola. New York began with chairs in three prisons but soon required all electrocutions to take place in Sing Sing.)[44] No longer was the death penalty carried out in the locality where the people most directly affected by the crime lived, in a public space accessible to all or in a jail yard accessible to hundreds. Now it was inflicted in a single well-fortified location that might be hundreds of miles from the crime, a place convenient for those officiating but not for those most likely to want to watch, and not for those for whom the deterrent effects of the punishment were intended.

Most important of all, hangings had always been conducted by local amateurs, sheriffs and their employees. Almost anyone could operate a gallows. An electric chair was a very different matter. One needed to know a great deal about electrical equipment, but there was more to it than that. To provide enough current to ensure death without causing too much damage to the body, the operator of an electric chair needed to carefully modulate the voltage and the amperage of the current, in ways that were learned from experience. Even the early electrocutions involved some modulation. Leon Czolgosz, President McKinley's assassin, was executed in New York in 1901 with a current of 1,800 volts for seven seconds, then 300 volts for twenty-three seconds, then 1,800 volts for four seconds, and then 300 volts for twenty-six seconds. Within a couple of decades the pattern became far more complex. Sing Sing's warden explained in 1928 that condemned prisoners were given 2,000 volts for three seconds at eight to ten amperes, then 500 volts for fifty-seven seconds at three to four amperes, then another three-second bout of 2,000 volts at the higher amperage. The current would then be gradually reduced to 500 volts at the lower amperage for another fifty-seven seconds, and then rapidly increased to 2,000 volts again. The short periods of higher voltages and amperages were meant to cause instantaneous unconsciousness and death; the longer periods of lower voltages and amperages were intended to keep the heart, brain, and lungs paralyzed without burning the body.[45] One had to possess a substantial amount of learning in order to operate an electric chair correctly. Contrary to the expectations of electrocution's early proponents, one could not simply throw a switch.

As states turned to electrocution, they had to take the responsibility for conducting executions out of the hands of local sheriffs, who lacked the necessary expertise. Executions came to be managed by a small number of trained specialists. Gallows had been constructed by carpenters, but only electricians were qualified to build electric chairs and the associated apparatus. They tended to be state employees, who learned their craft by visiting their counterparts in states that already used electrocution. Expertise, to be sure, varied widely from state to state. Jimmy Thompson, the ex-convict who traveled around Mississippi with the state's electric chair in the back of his pickup truck, insisted that rapists needed more voltage than murderers because of their greater strength and sexual drive.[46] But if Thompson knew little about human anatomy, he had more experience with electrocution than any county sheriff, because in every county in Mississippi Thompson was the man who operated the chair.

Electrocutions were supervised by a very small number of people. Within a few years after the first electrocution New York turned over all its executions to Edwin F. Davis, the electrician at Auburn and the man who had built the original electric chair in 1890. Davis executed 240 people before he retired in 1914. His position was taken by John Hulbert, another state prison electrician, who had been trained by Davis himself. Hulbert executed 120 more. Hulbert's successor was Robert Elliott, who also became the official executioner in five other states that used the electric chair—New Jersey, Pennsylvania, Massachusetts, Vermont, and Connecticut. He was so famous that he often figured as prominently in the headlines as the people he executed. One contemporary account marveled that "Elliott is now the principal figure at all executions at which he presides." The need for specialized expertise was underscored toward the end of Elliott's career, when his poor health prevented him from attending an electrocution in Boston. The result was disaster—the untrained substitute needed five separate shocks, lasting twenty minutes, to do the work. As electrocution grew more common, the states with electric chairs came to depend on the services of a tiny cadre of executioners.[47]

The managers of electrocutions were professionals, and so were many of the spectators. Considerations of space typically limited attendance to no more than twenty or thirty people. A few, the friends and family of the condemned prisoner, were attending their first electrocution. But the rest were often old-timers. A few spots were reserved for representatives of the media, at first just newspapers and later radio and television as well. The death house became a regular beat. Reporters like Leo Sheridan in the Northeast or Don Reid in Texas witnessed hundreds of electrocutions and became as knowledgeable about the process as the executioners themselves. The remaining spectators tended to be state officials, many of whom were in regular attendance. The prisons housing electric chairs were flooded with letters from ordinary citizens seeking to be witnesses, but virtually all these applications were denied.[48]

Because photography was forbidden, the outside world rarely even saw pictures of an electrocution. There have been only two known photographs of the electric chair in use. The first was taken by Thomas Howard of the *New York Daily News*, who captured Ruth Snyder's 1928 electrocution on film by strapping a miniature camera to his ankle and running a shutter release wire up his pants to a bulb in his pocket. The blurry photograph, run on the front page of the next day's *Daily News*, caused a sensation. New York officials were so angry that they threatened to exclude members of the press from future executions, and then replaced the frosted lamps in Sing Sing's execution chamber with glaring light intended to make photography impossible. In 1949 Joe Migon of the *Chicago Herald-American* hid a miniature camera in his shoe to get a front-page shot of the electrocution of James "Mad Dog" Morelli.[49] But apart from these two incidents the public could not see an electrocution even in the press. In the audience and backstage, capital punishment became a small world, shut off from the public, where the same handful of people encountered one another again and again. The understanding of an execution as a community ritual had utterly disappeared.

Gas

In the late nineteenth century, as Americans began searching for more humane alternatives to hanging, one of the methods sometimes suggested involved placing the condemned person in an airtight chamber and releasing into the chamber a poisonous gas. Unwanted dogs were sometimes put to death in this fashion in the 1870s, so it took no great imagination to envision the same technique being used for humans. Gas was not an attractive option compared to the electric chair, however, because it was believed that gas would take several minutes to kill, in contrast to the chair, which was assumed to kill instantly.[50] The New York commission that recommended adoption of the electric chair in 1888 considered gas, but not very seriously.

When some of the early electrocutions produced unsettling results, gas began to look better. The Medical Society of Allegheny County, Pennsylvania, received a great deal of attention in the winter of 1896–97 when it concluded that gas would be more humane than electricity. If a prison cell could be made airtight, poisonous gas could be introduced while the prisoner was asleep. The benefits to the prisoner would be twofold: he would die without experiencing pain, and he would be spared the anxiety of attending a ceremony devoted to his own death.[51] But as electrocutions came to run more smoothly, the interest in gas waned. Few perceived a need to improve on the electric chair. Over the next two decades there was little advocacy of lethal gas.

All that changed in 1921, when Frank Kern, Nevada's deputy attorney general, persuaded two members of the state assembly that lethal gas would be more humane than hanging or the firing squad, Nevada's existing methods of execution. Within a week, apparently without any debate in either house of the legislature, both houses passed a bill providing for execution by lethal gas.[52]

The statute left all the details to prison officials, but the law's proponents made it clear that they expected condemned prisoners to be killed while asleep in their cells, without ceremony, in the sight of a small number of spectators. They reasoned that death while sleeping would be more humane than even the electric chair. Not everyone was convinced. The statute required the death sentence to be scheduled for a particular week. It was silent as to whether the condemned prisoner would know when the week began, but everyone seems to have assumed that he would. Was the suspense of knowing that any night's sleep could be one's last any easier to bear than the certainty that one would die at an appointed hour? In such circumstances would a condemned person be able to sleep at all?[53]

The idea of executing the condemned prisoner in his sleep proved impractical. To satisfy the twin goals of humanity and visual display would have required an airtight cell large enough to live in for several days, with thick glass windows along one wall, and with two systems of valves, one for ventilation during the prisoner's last days and the other for releasing the gas.[54] Prison officials settled for a small airtight chamber, just large enough to hold a wooden chair, with a window through which spectators could see the prisoner's head. As for the precise gas, a matter not addressed by the legislature, the state's food and drug commissioner recommended hydrocyanic acid, a chemical used extensively in southern California to kill parasites on orange trees. The gas would kill people equally well, by blocking the ability of the body's cells to receive oxygen.

The closest manufacturer of liquid hydrocyanic acid was in Los Angeles, but the firm refused to ship the acid to Carson City because liquid hydrocyanic acid begins to gasify, posing the danger of explosion, at 22 degrees Fahrenheit. Warden Denver S. Dickerson had to send an employee to Los Angeles to drive several tanks of liquid hydrocyanic acid back to Carson City in a truck. He arrived without incident. In early 1924, in preparation for the chamber's first use, prison officials tested the acid on several bedbugs and two kittens. The animals died just as hoped. The difficulty of transporting hydrocyanic acid was soon surmounted by the adoption of a different technique of producing the gas. In a compartment adjoining the chamber would be placed pellets of sodium cyanide suspended by strings above a container of liquid sulfuric acid. When all was ready, the strings would be cut, the sodium cyanide would drop into the sulfuric acid, and the mixture would generate hydrocyanic acid gas, which could then be blown into the chamber.[55]

The first person put to death in Nevada's new gas chamber was a Chinese immigrant named Gee Jon. Four pounds of hydrocyanic acid were sprayed into the chamber with a pump. Warden Dickerson had hoped to heat the chamber to 75 degrees to ensure that the acid would quickly gasify, but the electric heater failed to work, leaving the chamber at a chilly 52 degrees. A liquid pool of hydrocyanic acid formed on the floor. Dickerson's employees had to wait nearly three hours for the pool to evaporate before they could enter the chamber to clean up. With that one exception, the execution proceeded smoothly. "Gee Jon nodded and went to sleep," reported the local press. "It was as simple and humane as that. Those who witnessed the execution are agreed that never was man put to death as painlessly." Gee Jon's head moved up and down for six minutes after the gas had been released, but the doctors unanimously attributed the motion to involuntary muscular movements, and assured spectators that Gee Jon was already unconscious or dead.[56]

The national reaction to the gas chamber was mixed. The apparent absence of suffering on the part of the condemned person no doubt made the gas chamber an improvement over hanging, and perhaps over the electric chair as well, in a purely technical sense. But some perceived something sinister, something creepy, about the gas chamber. "There is a terror in this thing that even Edgar Allan Poe could not equal," observed the Philadelphia *Public Ledger*. "There is a hissing from the walls, like the Satan's hiss of the hooded cobra . . . The Invisible Thing strikes." In trying to make capital punishment more humane, Nevada had "stumbled into new refinements and depths of cruelty." The *New York Times* complained: "There is something peculiarly dreadful in the voluntary, cold-blooded killing of a man, by putting him in a tightly closed room and letting in on him a poisonous gas." Editorials in several papers around the country expressed the hope that other states would not follow Nevada's lead.[57]

What was so sinister about the gas chamber? Its creepiness was in part a product of its being a *chamber*, a small enclosed space occupied only by the condemned prisoner. With every other method of execution known to Americans, the killing took place in a much larger space, and in that space the prisoner was hardly alone. Even the electric chair was located in a large room into which several officials and spectators could fit. But if lethal gas was to be kept away from officials and spectators, the condemned person had to be shut in a tiny space of his own, a room from which there could be no contact with the world outside. The gas chamber must have summoned up half-remembered stories of dark European dungeons, of prisoners left to die alone at the hands of an oppressive state. The sinister impression was no doubt reinforced by the invisibility of the gas rising slowly to the prisoner's nose and mouth. Even the few spectators present could not see the agent of death. Electricity had been an invisible killer too, but at least the machinery that produced the electricity and the wires and electrodes that carried it to the prisoner were in plain sight. Gas lacked even a visible pathway. And Americans had just finished fighting World War I, in which lethal gas had caused a great many slow, painful deaths. "The average person looks upon the use of gas with horror, because of the experiences incident to the late war" the Nevada Supreme Court had to concede in the course of rejecting Gee Jon's claim that the gas chamber amounted to cruel and unusual punishment.[58] The gas chamber was intended to be more humane than hanging, but many concluded that painlessness had come at too high a price.

For a decade Nevada was the only state with a gas chamber, but after Nevada conducted several more apparently painless executions other states began switching to gas as well. There were eleven in all, all western or southern states, and with only three exceptions they were states that had not yet adopted the electric chair. The first were Colorado and Arizona in 1933. Next came North Carolina, which had become one of the early electric chair states in 1909 but which switched to gas in 1935. The rest were Wyoming (1935), California, Missouri, and Oregon (1937), Mississippi (which switched from the electric chair in 1954), Maryland (1955), and New Mexico (which switched from the electric chair in 1955).[59] The electric chair had been slower to reach the West and parts of the South. When most of these states abandoned hanging they jumped straight to the latest technology, the gas chamber. As a result, the gas chamber was entirely a western and southern phenomenon.

As with the electric chair, claims that the new gas chambers amounted to cruel and unusual punishment were easily dismissed, on the ground that the state was simply adopting a kinder means toward a traditional end. "The fact that it is less painful and more humane than hanging is all that is required to refute completely the charge that it constitutes cruel and unusual punishment," held the Arizona Supreme Court. If the gas chamber was "modern and scientific," one commentator concluded, that was enough to satisfy the Constitution.[60]

In some states the initial use of the gas chamber proceeded as smoothly as it had in Nevada. The death of William Cody Kelley, executed in Colorado's gas chamber in 1934, was described in the local press as "far quicker and much more humane than any of the hangings which have preceded it." Prison officials called it "the most humane and probably the speediest in Colorado's history." In Missouri William Wright and John Brown both died apparently without pain. Oregon's execution of Leroy McCarthy went off without a hitch.[61]

But in other states things went horribly wrong. In Arizona, at the execution of Fred and Manuel Hernandez, the witnesses noticed a strange smell and a metallic taste in their mouths. "Stand back!" shouted a prison official. "It isn't working—it isn't safe!" A few seconds later came the command to clear the room. It turned out that no lethal gas had escaped the chamber; the smell and taste were those of some ammonia standing ready to neutralize any lingering gas when prison workers removed the bodies from the chamber. But the experience left a vivid reminder that the gas chamber was the only method of execution that posed a significant risk to spectators. When North Carolina executed John Redfern, the mechanism that released the cyanide pellets jammed. The executioner had to drop the pellets into the acid by hand and then run for his life as the warden slammed the door behind him. Some executions by gas were evidently very painful for the condemned prisoners. In North Carolina Allen Foster gasped and retched convulsively for more than three minutes before he lost consciousness. "That's just hell," remarked one witness afterward. The warden admitted he had been sickened. "Never again for me," said the coroner. "It's slow torture—that's what it is, and I cannot see anything humane about it." The gasping and choking displayed by Albert Kessel and Robert Lee Cannon, the first two men executed in California's gas chamber, were enough to nauseate even the hardened prison employees who had seen hundreds of hangings.[62] The earliest gas chamber executions proved to be just as variable as the early electrocutions. Like the electric chair, the gas chamber sometimes inflicted pain, and when it did, the results were just as troubling to watch.

Those shortcomings gave rise to a sporadic debate over the gas chamber similar to that which had taken place in the early years of the electric chair. The debate was primarily centered on the experience of the condemned prisoners. Was death by the inhalation of lethal gas painful? Some physicians said it was, some said it was not. The few who witnessed gas chamber executions were likewise divided. In 1937, at the peak of a brief period when the gas chamber was much in the news—six states had adopted it within the previous four years—the issue had grown so prominent that the *Reader's Digest* recapitulated it in a stylized debate between "Mr. Pro" and "Mr. Con." "Gas is practically foolproof," asserted Mr. Pro, unlike hanging and electrocution, which could be painful because of human error. "No black hood to hide a hanged man's fantastic grimaces. No sickening among witnesses as an electrocuted man's hair stands straight on end, burning smokily. No chance of some horrible miscue to make the headlines scream." In rebuttal, Mr. Con denied that gas was painless or easy to watch. Some of the condemned prisoners seemed to lapse into unconsciousness instantly, he conceded. "But, if he has an unluckily resistant physique, it may take thirty seconds before unconsciousness liberates him from this panting struggle against internal asphyxiation. And, whether he is conscious or not, his tortured body suddenly protests with clutching, writhing convulsions."[63]

In an effort to resolve the debate, prison officials in Nevada and Colorado monitored the heart rates of two condemned men (from a safe distance). The results merely replicated the debate. In Nevada Bob White's heart stopped upon inhaling the gas, but ten seconds later it resumed beating, and it continued beating for more than seven minutes. In Colorado Pete Catalina's heart stopped for good when the fumes reached him.[64] White and Catalina at least appeared to have become unconscious quickly. The more troubling cases were those in which the condemned person remained conscious long enough to struggle for breath. As with the electric chair, there were enough individual cases of apparently painful death to call the humanity of the gas chamber into question every few years.

Part of the sporadic debate over the gas chamber involved the safety of participants other than the condemned prisoner. Mr. Con pointed out that "hydrocyanic gas is the only form of capital punishment which imperils the witnesses." No one other than the condemned prisoners had been killed yet, but tragedy lurked around the corner, "some time when a long unused gasket round the door blows out under the pressure of the generating gas."[65] Mr. Pro would prove to have the better of this argument in the end, as there would be no fatal gas chamber leaks, but there was of course no way to be certain of this at the start. It is likely that a single mishap would have ended the use of lethal gas in the United States.

As with the electric chair, time smoothed out some of the difficulties associated with the gas chamber. Execution by lethal gas became a matter of routine, conducted by prison employees who gained experience with each new person they executed. In Missouri the prison physician had a form to fill out, in which he noted the time each step in the execution had been reached. The steps were so standard that they were printed on the form, with blanks for the times. George Bell, for instance, was executed in 1949 on the following schedule:

Prisoner Entered Chamber	12:01 A.M.
Doors Closed	12:06
Pellets Released	12:07
Gas Strikes Face	12:07:05
Head Falls Forward	12:07:30
Head Falls Backwards	12:07:35
Apparently Unconscious	12:08:10
Muscular Movement Apparently Stopped	12:10
Respiration Apparently Stopped	12:12
Head Falls Forward	12:08
Blower Started	12:25
Chamber Doors Opened	12:44
Body Removed	12:45:10
Pronounced Dead	12:46

Every person executed in Missouri's gas chamber proceeded through each of these steps, at times duly recorded and filed. Prison officials knew for certain that the head would fall forward, then backward, and then forward again. Even electrocution was not this predictable, not this clinical.[66]

Techniques other than electrocution and lethal gas were occasionally considered as alternatives. In 1911, long before Nevada adopted the gas chamber, the state legislature rejected a bill that would have given condemned criminals the choice of drinking poison or being hanged. A year later the warden of Maryland's state penitentiary asked his state's legislature to permit execution by the administration of large quantities of chloroform. People occasionally proposed using convicted murderers as subjects in extremely risky scientific experiments. In 1930, for instance, the attorney general of New Mexico discussed with a group of scientists the possibility of allowing Woo Dak San, scheduled for execution, the alternative of offering his body for a series of experiments aimed at curing trachoma.[67] But none of these suggestions was ever adopted.

Apart from the electric chair and the gas chamber, the only alternative to hanging ever actually used by any state before the late twentieth century was shooting, and that option was present only in Utah and Nevada. The use of a firing squad in those states was originally a consequence of the Mormon doctrine of blood atonement, the concept that some sins are so heinous that the offender can atone only by literally shedding his blood. Hanging in most cases shed no blood, so the Utah Territory's earliest laws gave condemned prisoners the choice of being hanged, shot, or beheaded. The option of beheading was dropped in 1878. Nevada, another state with a substantial Mormon population, adopted a similar statute in 1912. The firing squad was located in a tent to hide the sharpshooters' identity from the spectators. A target was placed over the condemned person's heart. Some of the guns were loaded with bullets and others with blanks, in a pattern not known to the shooters, so that none would know whether he was actually an executioner. The several shootings conducted in the two states appear to have caused instant and thus painless death, but the press in other parts of the country was nevertheless quite critical of the practice because of its lack of dignity and the damage it caused to the prisoner's body.[68] Shooting never spread beyond Utah and Nevada. Nevada abandoned it when the state switched to the gas chamber in 1921. In Utah shooting is still an option today.

Like the electric chair, the gas chamber brought about a transformation in the dramaturgy of capital punishment. An execution by lethal gas could only be conducted indoors. A gas chamber was an expensive and stationary piece of machinery. It made no economic sense to put one in each county. Every state that adopted the gas chamber built but one and placed it in a state prison. Gas, like electricity, moved executions away from the people most affected by the crime and placed them behind prison walls in a remote part of the state.

For reasons of economy gas chambers were constructed within existing rooms of the prison, not in specially built wings, so space constraints left room for only a very small number of spectators. Most of the spots were taken by state officials and representatives of the media, leaving very few for anyone else. Lloyd Anderson was put to death in Missouri in 1965 before fourteen people, a group including three state representatives, the chaplain of the state legislature, three prison officials, a member of the state Public Service Commission, an assistant attorney general, an assistant circuit attorney, a reporter from the *Kansas City Star*, and a reporter from a local radio station. There were only two witnesses unaffiliated with the state government or the media. Without such an affiliation it was not easy to get a place in front of the gas chamber. Ben Abelson, a druggist in St. Louis who had raised a considerable sum of money to offer as a reward for catching Anderson, asked to be allowed to watch. He was turned down. But when requests came from a highway patrolman or a sheriff they were immediately granted.[69]

Like the electric chair, the gas chamber made the small world of capital punishment even more exclusively male. In earlier times whole families—men, women, and children—had gathered to watch hangings. When hangings moved into the jail yard, very few women and children attended. The electric chair and the gas chamber completed the trajectory. When Dorothy Turner, a nurse in Columbia, Missouri, requested permission for her husband and herself to watch the execution of Kenneth Boyd in 1953, she was tersely informed that "it is against the rules of this institution to permit women to attend an execution." Her husband was invited to submit his own application.[70] Except for the condemned person's family members, capital punishment had become a strictly masculine domain.

Gas chambers were a bit simpler to operate than electric chairs, but they were much more dangerous. They could not be handled by amateurs. Capital punishment thus became even more a matter for specialists, men who worked within the state prison system. The routine nature of the work, combined with the lack of any direct personal contact with the men they were killing, made it easier for prison employees to take on the repeated role of executioners. Clinton Duffy, the warden at San Quentin during many of its gas chamber executions, surveyed the officers under his command and discovered that all of them preferred the gas chamber to the gallows. The men felt less "directly responsible for the death of the condemned," he explained. Technology served as a buffer between the condemned prisoner and his executioners, reducing the distaste experienced by the latter. "Death by lethal gas was more mechanical, which made it less personal."[71] But it was less personal in another sense as well. Hangings had been carried out by ordinary people, who could more easily be perceived as representatives of all the people. The prison employees who ran the gas chamber were not ordinary people at all. It was harder to think of them as the public's representatives. Like the electric chair, the gas chamber was the tool not of the local community but of a distant state. Capital punishment had been removed from public sight.

One remarkable example of the distance between state and people created by the new technologies of capital punishment took place after the execution of Lloyd Anderson. The *Kansas City Star* reporter who had been present wrote to the warden, noting that during the execution he had seen a prison official jotting down a minute-by-minute account on a standard form just like the one quoted above for George Bell. He said he was considering writing a series of articles on capital punishment, and he asked whether the warden would send him a copy of the form. The warden responded with a flat lie: he denied that such records were ever made or kept.[72] As prison officials viewed it, the details of the death penalty were their business, not the public's. Employees of the state could know how the state killed, but others could not. There could be no stronger indication of the disjuncture between the government that performed capital punishment and the public in whose name that punishment was carried out.

The voters of Kentucky acknowledged this widening gulf between the state and the people in 1920. Kentucky had adopted the electric chair ten years earlier, but in 1920 the legislature brought back local public hanging for two crimes—rape and attempted rape.[73] In the South rape was in practice a capital crime only when the defendant was black and the victim white. This was the offense that provoked the most community outrage. Murderers could be electrocuted in secrecy by employees of the state prison, but when black men raped white women, the community preferred to take matters into its own hands. Kentucky's return to hanging was a clear indication that capital punishment's audience believed that the location of the execution and the identity of the executioner made a difference. The difference lay not in punishment's efficacy but in its public representation. A century earlier executions had been occasions for the public to gather in condemnation of crime and criminals, but now they no longer gathered or condemned. Behind closed doors, the state did the condemning for them.

Such had not been the purpose of the electric chair and the gas chamber when they were first dreamed of in the late nineteenth century. The motor driving the change had been called "humanity"—a revulsion from the thought that the condemned person would experience pain during his execution. Solicitude for the condemned prisoners had prompted the development of new machinery, which was widely adopted for its superior ability to kill painlessly. But once the machinery was in place it became a motor of change in its own right. The machinery had needs of its own, needs that changed the meaning of capital punishment in two ways.

One change involved the goal of deterrence. For executions to deter crime, information about the executions had to reach potential criminals. The old public hangings had transmitted that information directly, through immediate visual experience. But because the electric chair and the gas chamber had to be in small indoor spaces, because those spaces had to be located in remote state prisons, and because political realities required allocating the small number of witness positions to the well connected, there was virtually no chance that one of the new technological executions would be conducted in the presence of the kind of person it was supposed to deter. The audience for the message of deterrence heard about the execution at second or third hand through the media. It was a story of death in a distant place, at the hands of a mysterious machine most would never see except in movies. The eighteenth-century exponents of capital punishment, who placed great emphasis on the deterrent value of visual display, would have been astonished had they known what was coming.

The second change involved the intuitive sense of justice that required the community to punish crime. The new execution technology needed trained specialists, and it needed to be inaccessible to all but a tiny number of people. The drama of a hanging had ensured that all would perceive the execution as a collective act of the community, but the very different ceremony surrounding the electric chair and the gas chamber focused attention on a very different actor. It was the state, not the people, that was doing the killing.

In the long run, the changes brought about by the electric chair and the gas chamber were just one more episode in the continual centralization and professionalization of punishment, a process that had been under way since the birth of the prison a century earlier. Had the states retained hanging as their sole method of execution, perhaps the dramaturgy of execution would eventually have changed in any event. Maybe hangings would have eventually been conducted indoors, deep within remote state prisons, by specialists, before tiny hand-picked audiences. But there can be no doubt that this process was accelerated by the technical demands of the electric chair and gas chamber. A distaste for inflicting pain had been assuaged by technology, and technology had transformed the meaning of an execution.

8

DECLINE

IN THE FIRST HALF of the twentieth century capital punishment went into decline. The annual number of executions in the United States reached what was probably its all-time peak in 1935, at 199. It then began to drop sharply. Nineteen forty-seven was the last year with more than 150 executions. Nineteen fifty-one was the last with more than 100. In 1961 the death penalty was carried out only 42 times; in 1963, only 21. Finally, in 1968, for the first year in the history of the United States, not a single person was executed. Measured per capita, the death penalty's decline stretched back even longer: the execution rate had been dropping since the 1880s.

The consistency of the decline masks a change in its location that took place around 1950. Before 1950 it was primarily a northern phenomenon. As more northerners came to doubt whether crime was a product of the criminal's free will, and as critics weakened the conventional wisdom about the death penalty's deterrent value, northern support for capital punishment diminished.

Involuntary Criminals

"To inflict the death penalty for crime was perfectly logical in the days when nobody doubted that criminality was voluntary," the *New York Times* reflected in 1912. But times had changed. "Something of dubiety on that point is now at present in every mind that has been at all exposed to the influences of discussion on the effects of heredity and environment."[1] Capital punishment had a retributive basis only so long as capital crime was seen to be freely chosen. In the late nineteenth and early twentieth centuries, however, as crime came increasingly to be viewed as a consequence of biological or social forces beyond the criminal's control, as certain people came to be understood as genetically or environmentally predisposed to commit crimes, the death penalty correspondingly ceased to be seen as a just punishment.

In the 1870s many began to argue that crime was caused by inherited physical defects in the brain. The idea had been in circulation in the United States since the 1790s, but as interest in evolution intensified and as immigrants from southern and eastern Europe crowded into American cities, biological theories of crime spread more widely than ever before. What was popularly called the *mind*, the physician John Stolz noted in 1873, was only the outward manifestation of the brain. If a so-called evil mind was attributable to a flaw in the physical brain, a flaw that the criminal had not chosen to acquire, there could be no such thing as "voluntary" crime. Writers began to emphasize the extent to which crime ran in families, as a way of demonstrating that it was caused by inherited rather than freely chosen qualities. Robert Dugdale's *The Jukes*, for instance, first published in 1877, traced a single family back 150 years to show the prevalence of criminal behavior in each generation. The influential Italian criminologist Cesare Lombroso spoke of the "born criminal," a person with biological abnormalities that led him to crime.[2]

"Everything now-a-days is made to depend upon the state and structure of the human brain," complained the minister Charles Wiley as early as 1871. "Crimes, instead of being traced, as they formerly were, to the obvious and old-fashioned principle of human depravity, are now attributed, under scientific authority, too, of a certain sort, to some original maladjustments, or to some unfortunate disturbance of the particles of the brain." Wiley recognized that this new mode of explanation carried implications for the death penalty. "Just in proportion as such sentiments as these are entertained," he despaired, "the conviction of human accountability will be greatly weakened and impaired, and the ground taken away on which capital punishment, and indeed all punishment, must be legitimately based."[3] The new interest in criminals' brains was slowly but surely beginning to undermine the retributive justification for capital punishment.

As belief in the biological causation of crime continued to spread, so did the belief that crime was caused by environmental influences. This too was a view with a long history, but one that attained unprecedented levels of acceptance in the late nineteenth and early twentieth centuries. "It is generally admitted," asserted one correspondent in 1912, "that it is environment, social conditions, rather than individual depravity, that creates crime." The capital criminal was coming to be widely understood "as an unfortunate person whom society has wronged by early depriving him of the legitimate opportunities for self betterment." Crime was often described as a disease brought on by poverty and deprivation, a phenomenon deserving treatment rather than punishment. The analogy between crime and disease was such a cliché by 1899 that one legal newspaper could have a laugh at its expense:

> Science, the final authority, has long since decreed crime to be a disease.
>
> Accordingly, when the man killed his wife and children his friends were very apprehensive for his health. In no small anxiety they awaited the progress of the malady.
>
> But the next day the man killed only his grandmother and one of the servants; it was plain that he was mending.
>
> The attending physician issued hopeful bulletins, predicting that within a week or so the man wouldn't be killing anybody to speak of.[4]

But the consequences of understanding crime as disease were no joke. If crime came upon the criminal involuntarily, capital punishment lost its retributive justification.

In the first few decades of the twentieth century models of biological and environmental causation merged into a single attack on the idea that crime was a product of the criminal's free will. In a widely publicized 1924 debate on capital punishment, Clarence Darrow ridiculed the New York judge Alfred J. Talley's assertion that criminals possessed the capacity to choose whether or not to commit crimes. "My friend doesn't believe in heredity," Darrow scoffed, before an audience that laughed along with him at Talley's ignorance, in what proved to be a dress rehearsal for Darrow's similar performance in the Scopes trial a year later. "Am I to enter into a discussion about the A-B-C's of science? There isn't a scientist on earth who doesn't believe and say that man is the product of heredity and environment alone." The sociologist Harry Elmer Barnes made the case against capital punishment with a thundering confidence in recent scientific progress. "Modern physiological chemistry, dynamic psychology and sociology have proved the free moral agent theory of human conduct preposterous alike in its assumptions and its implications," Barnes

announced. "The human animal has his conduct and his thoughts absolutely determined by the combined influences of his biological heredity
and his social surroundings. There is not the slightest iota of choice allowed to any individual from birth to the grave." But one did not need to
possess the certainty of Darrow or Barnes to believe that the new social
scientists were in the midst of making great discoveries about human behavior. Modern criminology, the Quaker Clifford Kirkpatrick believed,
was making apparent "that conduct was not determined by an unknowable something called free will but by personality traits built up through
the interaction of heredity and the environment."[5] Whether crime was
the product of brain chemistry or bad neighborhoods, the important
thing was that it was not freely chosen by the criminal.

To deny the criminal's free will was to remove the retributive basis for
capital punishment, because it could hardly be just to execute a person
for a crime he had not chosen to commit. The Reverend Philip Burkett
was a supporter of the death penalty, but he recognized that "as long as
crime is held to be the symptom of an abnormal mental condition or of a
disease contracted by the patient without any guilt whatever, so long will
it be considered immoral to put that patient to death." New York State As-
semblyman John J. Ryan made a similar point while introducing a 1915
bill to abolish the death penalty. Because "many famous criminologists
teach that heredity [and] environment" are the primary causes of crime,
Ryan argued, "we cannot help but conclude that capital punishment
seals a life that often the culprit could not change if he wanted to." The
point was sometimes made even more sharply, by critics who shifted responsibility for crime from the criminal to the society that produced the
conditions in which the criminal lived. "No state has the right to kill men
when it contributes to their downfall," concluded lobbyists for a 1913 bill
that would have abolished capital punishment in Tennessee.[6]

Determinism tended to undermine the death penalty, and determinism was on the ascendant in the several decades surrounding the turn of
the century, advanced by a new kind of expert—the university-based social scientist. Many of the early opponents of retribution as a ground for
punishment were members of this new elite. Whether they called themselves sociologists, criminologists, or law professors, they were a kind of
expert that had not existed in significant numbers in the United States before the growth of universities in the later nineteenth century. Speaking at
gatherings of new professional organizations like the American Social

Science Association, or writing in new academic journals like the *Journal of the American Institute of Criminal Law and Criminology*, they understood themselves to be approaching the death penalty from a newly scientific point of view. But the new social scientists had no monopoly on the idea that there was more to crime than free will. Even the novels of the period, such as those of Frank Norris and Theodore Dreiser, reflected this changing conception of the roots of crime by depicting characters unable to avoid the slide into criminality.[7]

As deterministic models of criminality pushed aside traditional concepts of individual responsibility, retribution increasingly came to be perceived as an outmoded notion. "The retributive defense of capital punishment is . . . so out of date," declared one critic. "Those who use it are as much anachronisms, morally, culturally and scientifically, it has been recently insisted, as if they were to champion magic, blood-letting or crusades against witches." The law professor and criminologist George Kirchwey, opposing the death penalty before the 1922 meeting of the American Prison Association, explained that while "the vindictive sentiment is latent in all our legal system, it is no longer respectable to avow it or admit its existence." The philosopher W. J. Roberts, writing in 1905, saw capital punishment as "the one definite and practically unmitigated survival in our criminal law of the old traditions of vengeance and retaliation."[8] It became common in the first few decades of the twentieth century to reject retribution altogether as a ground for punishment of any kind, and especially for capital punishment.

Believers in retribution found themselves on the defensive. "Anyone in our day who takes up the defence of capital punishment should stand ready to be branded as a conservative and as a defender of the so-called 'dark ages,'" complained one writer in 1925. The lawyer John Whitman feared that to "admit the negation of responsibility is to destroy the very foundation of all morality." But they knew they were bucking the tide of elite opinion. Some angrily contrasted "the wire-drawn theories of the super-academic," under which "faddists would treat murderers by scholastic theories of psychology," with the superior common sense of ordinary people, which held criminals responsible for their crimes. H. L. Mencken castigated penologists who forgot "that retribution is still a motive in punishment, despite all the fine talk about reforming the criminal."[9] But to speak up in favor of retribution as a ground for punishment was, in the early twentieth century, to brand oneself unscientific.

If crime had biological roots, capital punishment might be favored for eugenic reasons, and indeed there were a few proponents of the death penalty on the ground that it would prevent the worst criminals from reproducing. W. Duncan McKim's eugenic treatise *Heredity and Human Progress* advocated capital punishment for all criminals "found to be idiots, imbeciles, epileptics, habitual drunkards, [or] insane." But the idea never attracted many adherents, because, as its critics (who were often sympathetic to eugenics) pointed out, capital punishment was a patently inefficient eugenic program. Most so-called "defectives" never committed a crime serious enough to invoke the death penalty, and even those who did so were likely to have fathered children already. "A much better plan" than capital punishment, affirmed the sociologist Edwin Sutherland in his criminology textbook, "would be to make a search in the schools and elsewhere for all who are defective and then get rid of them by a policy of segregation or sterilization or both."[10] The early twentieth century was the heyday of eugenics in the United States, but the death penalty was never widely perceived to have a eugenic basis. Biological theories of crime tended to undermine, not support, capital punishment.

The death penalty's retributive justification was meanwhile being further eroded by the declining role of religion in public life. For centuries Americans advocating capital punishment had looked to the Bible for support, because the Bible was saturated with the death penalty. But biblical arguments for particular public policies began to lose intellectual respectability toward the end of the nineteenth century, and capital punishment was no exception. Samuel Hand was a supporter of the death penalty, but when he was invited to state his position in a short essay in the *North American Review* in 1881, Hand omitted what had once been the standard quotation from God's instructions to Noah, because he knew his audience was "inclined to look with scant credulity upon the book of Genesis, its deluge, its ark, and its Noah." A few years later C. H. Eaton, an opponent of capital punishment, found it unnecessary to rebut the stock scriptural arguments, as he presumed that "the authority of the Bible has become somewhat impaired."[11] Believers in the biblical warrant for the death penalty had hardly disappeared, but in public intellectual circles they were on the defensive.

Deterministic models of the causation of crime, if followed to their logical conclusion, would have radically transformed the entire criminal justice system, a system based on assigning guilt to individuals for their acts.

That kind of transformation of course never occurred. But the associated decline in the belief in capital punishment's retributive appropriateness—the weakening of a sense that execution was the only just punishment for murder—began to make itself felt in a variety of ways as early as the 1870s. Long before any decline in the frequency of executions, the death penalty was exhibiting signs of strain.

One sign was the frequent complaint that jurors were refusing to return guilty verdicts in capital cases because they feared sending defendants to their deaths. The death penalty "will become a dead letter upon our statute book," asserted James T. Rice of Marshfield, Missouri, in 1872, "for it is now difficult, in many counties, to find 12 men who have not conscientious scruples in pronouncing the sentence of death even if they find the party guilty as charged." Similar observations became commonplace in the first two decades of the twentieth century. "The reluctance of men to enforce it," one Chicagoan predicted of the death penalty in 1907, "will strengthen as they come to have better conceptions of the real causes of crime." By 1926 the *New Republic* concluded that "capital punishment is a failure because juries refuse to convict when to do so means the taking of life on their responsibility."[12]

The same biological model of crime that made jurors reluctant to convict afforded them a legal vehicle—the insanity defense—for avoiding the death penalty without acquitting the defendant outright. The defense had long roots, but in the late nineteenth century complaints abounded among lawyers and doctors that it was being overused in capital cases. Insanity was a "very common defence now-a-days," a skeptical Massachusetts prosecutor observed in 1886. It was a defense "too often witnessed" and "too frequently applied," another agreed.[13] The increasing use of the insanity defense, like the spreading complaints of jurors' reluctance to convict, was a sign that capital punishment was losing some of its retributive justification.

The fear that juries, facing a mandatory death penalty for first-degree murder, would not convict defendants clearly guilty of that crime caused every state to abandon the mandatory death penalty and to give juries the discretion to sentence the defendant to life in prison instead. The idea was not entirely new. In the early part of the nineteenth century many states had divided murder into degrees for the same purpose—to allow jurors to convict a defendant of murder without having to cause his death. In the 1830s and 1840s Tennessee, Alabama, and Louisiana had gone even further, granting juries discretion to sentence *all* murderers to something short of death. The purpose of these early discretion statutes was almost certainly to allow jurors, who were all white, to take race into account in setting the penalty. In the years immediately following the Civil War, most of the South adopted the same strategy with respect to some crimes.[14] In the first half of the century the southern states punished many crimes with death only if committed by blacks; in the second half of the century they accomplished the same result by delegating to all-white juries the discretion to choose capital or noncapital punishment.

But in 1867, when Illinois became the first northern state to authorize its juries to provide a sentence short of death for first-degree murder, an important change was under way. Illinois was followed soon after by Minnesota and Nebraska, and then in the 1870s and 1880s several more states abandoned the mandatory death penalty. By 1939, when New Mexico gave its juries the same discretion, only four states and the District of Columbia were left with a mandatory death penalty for first-degree murder. In 1963 New York became the last to abandon it.[15] The trend was a gradual one, encompassing no more than eight states and no fewer than two in any decade between the 1860s and the 1930s. In each case the driving force was the concern that many juries would not convict guilty defendants for fear of sending them to their deaths. The change followed no regional pattern. In North and South, East and West, every state enacted similar legislation. This slow but unmistakable movement may be the best barometer of the decline in capital punishment's retributive justification in the late nineteenth and early twentieth centuries.

Juries thus became legally empowered to decide, on a case-by-case basis, whether life or death was the appropriate sentence. They had possessed this discretion all along, in an informal sense, in their ability to acquit obviously guilty defendants or to convict them of an offense less grave than first-degree murder, but now, for the first time, the American legal system explicitly authorized juries to make life-or-death decisions. None of the statutes offered jurors any guidance as to how those decisions should be made. None listed any criteria jurors might use to divide murderers into two classes, those who would be executed and those who would be sent to prison. Judges did not instruct juries as to how they should carry out this new responsibility, and they did not sit in review of the sentencing decisions jurors reached. This broad discretion vested in the jury did not, so far as one can tell today, cause anyone any concern until the late 1940s.[16] By the late 1960s, however, the unguided power of juries to decide between life and death would prove to be of major importance.

As faith in retribution declined, the delay between sentencing and execution lengthened, to allow for more appellate review of alleged trial errors and closer examination of the facts on applications for executive clemency. The Pennsylvania judge Robert Ralston complained in 1911, in an address to the state bar association, that with the six months allowed for condemned persons to appeal, plus the time taken by the appellate courts to reach a decision, plus the several months it normally took the Board of Pardons to decide about clemency, years could go by before a condemned criminal was executed. In California, by approximately the same time, there were already long delays before execution, in one case nearly five years from the time of the crime. Even in Texas, where the norm of a speedy execution was well entrenched, the mean time between arrival on death row and execution rose from one and one-half months in the 1930s to five months in the late 1950s. By 1959 delays between sentencing and execution throughout the nation ranged from sixty-five days to nine years, with most falling between seven and twenty-four months.[17] These were spans of time that would have been unimaginable in the first half of the nineteenth century. They provide further evidence of the rising ambivalence provoked by capital punishment. It could take so long to review the propriety of a death sentence only in a culture that had grown uncertain about the death penalty.

Juggling Figures

Americans had argued over whether death was a better deterrent than prison ever since the invention of the prison in the late eighteenth century. The arguments on the opposing sides had tended to be based on competing understandings of human nature. That debate continued all through the nineteenth century and into the twentieth. Those who believed capital punishment to have a greater deterrent effect than prison emphasized the near-universal fear of death. "Few cases of capital punishment occur without a strenuous effort in behalf of the criminal, to secure a commutation of his sentence for imprisonment," observed the philosopher James Fairchild. Those who questioned the deterrent value of capital punishment focused instead on the moment at which the criminal committed the crime. "Imagine a man who would like to kill another, sit-

ting down and balancing the relative gravity of hanging or imprisonment," scoffed the lawyer Jerome Turner, "and ending it all by giving up
the formation of the purpose because of capital punishment, or nursing
and maturing it because of imprisonment for life!" Sing Sing warden
Lewis Lawes, one of the most visible opponents of capital punishment in
the first half of the twentieth century, concluded from his long acquaintance with condemned prisoners that virtually all murders were committed impulsively, without any consideration of the possible penalty, and
accordingly that "thoughts of the chair do not even enter their heads."[18]
Arguments like these carried on a tradition dating back to the earliest
significant opposition to capital punishment.

But the late nineteenth and early twentieth centuries saw two developments that transformed the debate over deterrence. Taken together, these
developments effectively removed deterrence as a justification for capital
punishment by the middle of the twentieth century.

First, changing conceptions of the causes of crime had significant implications for the debate on deterrence. If particular people were genetically doomed to a life of crime, how could the death penalty, or indeed
any punishment, prevent crime from being committed? "The causes and
cures of crime, whatever they may be," despaired the attorney Thomas
Speed Mosby, "are far removed from anything within the power and
scope of the penal code." Capital punishment could not deter "the defective or unbalanced type of criminal," another early twentieth-century lawyer insisted, because such a person is "the most incapable of men to consider possible future consequences."[19] The ground of the debate shifted
from whether capital punishment actually *was* a deterrent to whether it
was even possible, given new understandings of human nature, that capital punishment could *ever* be a deterrent.

Second, the debate over deterrence became more sophisticated on
both sides. The new social scientists of the late nineteenth and early twentieth centuries had an empirical orientation that led them to seek statistics on comparative murder rates in jurisdictions with and without the
death penalty. More and more data became available as time went on,
because the few states that had abolished capital punishment at
midcentury offered points of comparison with the majority of states that
retained it. The empirical attitude quickly filtered out to non-academic
critics of the death penalty. One popular magazine invited "friends of
capital punishment . . . to make what they can of the fact that in a period

of eight years there were fewer murders in the State of Michigan, without the death-penalty, than occurred in the city of New York, under the death-penalty, in a single year of that period." The American League to Abolish Capital Punishment collected homicide data from the Census Bureau to demonstrate that the states with capital punishment had an average homicide rate more than twice as high as those without. By the middle of the twentieth century the abolitionist case was often made with a mass of statistics, to show that the absence of capital punishment did not produce crime.[20]

As some foreign countries abolished the death penalty, the same kinds of statistical lessons could be drawn. The penologist Maynard Shipley pointed out that the Belgian crime rate appeared not to be increasing despite the lack of any executions for nearly half a century. Abolitionists emphasized that there were many countries with less crime than the United States, and many of them had either abolished capital punishment or used it far less frequently than did Americans.[21] Whether the comparison was among states or among nations, those who argued that the death penalty was an ineffective deterrent had adopted the method of the new social sciences. Once the case against deterrence had been made with speculation as to human motivation, but now it was being made with data.

Supporters of capital punishment fought fire with fire. Some sought data suggesting that the death penalty *was* a more effective deterrent than prison. In some years Maine and Rhode Island had higher per capita murder rates than the neighboring states that retained capital punishment, a fact retentionists cited as evidence of deterrence. Others attempted to poke holes in the statistical case against deterrence. If the death penalty did not deter, they argued, that was because it was not used enough. "There really is no capital punishment nowadays in America," complained one correspondent in 1912. "If there were, and it were carried out strictly in every case of murder, I think you would see a large decrease in the annual wholesale crop of killings."[22]

The most telling criticism of the statistical case against deterrence, and a criticism often made, was that one could not adequately measure deterrence simply by comparing murder rates across states or countries. Jurisdictions differed in any number of respects—population density, wealth distribution, education level, religious adherence, and so on—and all of these factors were likely to have some influence on the crime rate. That there were fewer murders in Michigan than in New York, for instance, was surely attributable to a set of circumstances within which the penalty for murder played at most a very small part. It was a common observation by the 1920s that deterrence "can be proved and disproved—whichever way one cares to juggle figures." Clarence Darrow was one of the most prominent death penalty opponents of the decade, but when it came to measuring deterrence even Darrow conceded that "it is a hopeless, useless job."[23]

Such was the conclusion of the more careful of the early twentieth-century social scientists: that data on comparative homicide rates were incapable of proving or disproving the deterrent effect of the death penalty.[24] Measuring deterrence required holding all the other conceivable causes of crime constant while varying only the expected penalty. That was both a technical problem (how to adjust for the inevitable differences across jurisdictions?) and a sociological problem (what *are* all the other conceivable causes of crime?). The technical problem would later be solved, and modern econometric techniques would be applied to capital punishment beginning in the 1970s. The sociological problem, however, would last much longer. The social scientists of the early twentieth century never solved it, nor have we today. In the end, the debate over deterrence that raged through the late nineteenth and early twentieth centuries was fought to a standstill.

But that standstill was significant, because it undermined the proposition that capital punishment was a necessary deterrent. If the death penalty might or might not be a more effective deterrent than prison, one of the two primary arguments in favor of the death penalty lost most of its force. The abolitionists did not need to win this battle in order to advance their cause. All they needed was a draw.

Legislative Abolition

Rates of violent crime were declining in the late nineteenth century, so far as one can measure such things today, so the general fear of crime ordinarily underlying support for capital punishment was most likely at a low point. As the retributive and deterrent justifications for capital punishment began to weaken, therefore, the question of abolition emerged on the public agenda with new force. Opinion on the death penalty was "sharply and decisively divided," one observer reported in 1882. By 1907 the lawyer James Vahey reported that "no question, aside from economic ones, has received as much attention, or been so thoroughly discussed in

Massachusetts in the last twenty-five years or more as the abolition of the death penalty." One indication of the issue's prominence was the publication of a debater's handbook containing sketches of the primary arguments pro and con as well as relevant excerpts from books and magazine articles. The handbook went through five editions between 1909 and 1939. Another indication is the frequency with which short pairs of articles, one giving the case in favor of capital punishment and the other the case against, began appearing in popular magazines.[25] The less faith was placed in the old arguments based on retribution and deterrence, the more controversial the death penalty became.

The flame was fanned by an assortment of abolitionist organizations. Some were old hands, like the Quaker societies that had been opposed to capital punishment for centuries. Some were new opponents, like the theosophists, who believed that a criminal should not be executed because his "astral body is not ready to separate from his physical body, nor is the vital, nervous energy ready to leave." Members of the Housewives' Union of Palo Alto, California, wore black armbands on execution days to signify their opposition to the death penalty.[26] The most long-lived of the abolitionist organizations, and the one that had the greatest impact, was an association formed in New York in 1900. It went by different names at different times, but for a long period it was called the American League to Abolish Capital Punishment. The League lobbied state legislatures, published pamphlets, and organized speeches throughout the first half of the twentieth century.

The controversy soon reached the state legislatures. In 1872 Iowa became the fourth state to abolish capital punishment, and in 1876 Maine became the fifth. (They joined Michigan, Rhode Island, and Wisconsin, all of which had abolished the death penalty between 1846 and 1853.) In both Iowa and Maine public opinion had been divided for decades. The Iowa legislature voted on abolishing capital punishment sixteen times between 1851 and 1878, and the losing side never registered fewer than one-third of the votes. Executions in Maine had long been rare; indeed there were none at all from 1837 to 1863. In both states, well-publicized cases involving sympathetic defendants had the short-run effect of tipping a majority of the legislature toward abolition. And in both, high-profile crimes a few years later tipped opinion back in favor of the death penalty. Iowa became the first state ever to *restore* capital punishment in 1878, after only six years of abolition. Maine restored the death penalty in 1883 and then abolished it again in 1887. There would be no capital punishment in Maine for the rest of the nineteenth and twentieth centuries.[27]

The only other state to abolish the death penalty before the turn of the century was Colorado, which did so in 1897, only to bring it back in 1901. But the issue was repeatedly on state legislative agendas. "The annual crusade against capital punishment is proceeding in the New York legislature," one magazine reported in 1892. The legislatures of New Jersey, Connecticut, Massachusetts, and Minnesota all considered ending the death penalty. State constitutional conventions of the period included proposals to include abolition in the new constitutions. There was growing sentiment against capital punishment in North Carolina, a legal journal reported in 1881, and "if made a political issue it would be carried."[28] The record of actual abolition between 1870 and 1900 was meager, involving only three small states, two of which restored capital punishment within a few years. But actual abolition was only the tip of a large iceberg of unsuccessful legislative activity.

The pace of change accelerated in the first two decades of the twentieth century. By the 1910s the abolitionists included some prominent and outspoken people. The governors of New York, California, Oregon, Illinois, Arizona, and Oklahoma all made public announcements of their opposition to capital punishment between 1911 and 1915. Governor George Hunt of Arizona was so troubled by the death penalty that he even considered staging a mass execution of several prisoners as a publicity stunt, to draw attention to what he called "the barbaric practice of exacting one life in expiation of another." Abolitionists gained another highly visible leader in 1914, when the well-known prison reformer Thomas Mott Osborne was appointed warden at New York's Sing Sing Prison. Osborne used his position to advance the cause by giving speeches, participating in debates, providing testimony during the annual legislative hearings on abolition, and even walking out of Sing Sing the night before each execution as a form of protest.[29]

All this activity paid off. Between 1907 and 1917 nine more states abolished the death penalty. The first was Kansas, which by 1907 had conducted no executions for more than three decades. Minnesota came next in 1911, followed by Washington in 1913, Oregon in 1914, North and South Dakota in 1915, Arizona in 1916, and Missouri in 1917. Tennessee abolished capital punishment for murder in 1915 but retained it for rape, a crime for which in practice only black defendants were sentenced to death.[30]

In almost every case, however, the majorities in favor of abolition were small and temporary. Abolition had been accomplished by referendum in Oregon and Arizona. In Oregon the vote was 100,552–100,395; in Arizona it was 18,936–18,784; in both states similar referenda had failed a year or two earlier. Supporters of the death penalty quickly organized referenda of their own. Arizona readopted capital punishment in 1918 and Oregon in 1920, in votes not nearly as close. High-profile murders in Washington and Missouri aroused public support for capital punishment and caused the legislatures of both states to restore it in 1919. Tennessee also reinstated capital punishment for murder in 1919. Kansas would bring it back in 1935, South Dakota in 1939. Of the nine states to abolish the death penalty between 1907 and 1917, the change would be permanent in only two, Minnesota and North Dakota, and even in those the controversy hardly died down. In Minnesota it would be fourteen years before there would be a legislative session that did not include a bill to restore the death penalty.[31]

Again, even this much actual legislative change does not fully indicate the issue's prominence, because for every state that abolished capital punishment during the first two decades of the century there were two that came close. A bill ending capital punishment was passed by both houses of the Illinois legislature in 1918 but was vetoed by the governor. Similar bills were passed by the Vermont House of Representatives in 1902, the Illinois House of Representatives in 1909, the California Assembly in 1911, the New Hampshire Assembly and the New Jersey Senate in 1915, and the Pennsylvania Senate in 1917, but in each case the other house of the legislature rejected the bill. In Massachusetts bills to abolish capital punishment were before the legislature so regularly that by 1911 the local newspapers were referring to "capital punishment day," the day the legislature voted on that year's bill. The issue came before the New York legislature with the same regularity, and it received a great deal of attention at the state's 1915 constitutional convention. The Connecticut legislature rejected abolition bills in 1915, 1917, 1921, and 1923. Abolition came before the voters in the form of referenda in Ohio and California in 1912. At one time or another between 1903 and 1918 the legislatures of Nebraska, New Jersey, Indiana, Utah, Colorado, West Virginia, North Carolina, and Virginia considered abolition.[32] In the years before World War I, capital punishment was up for grabs. There was often little separating the states that abolished capital punishment from those that did not. A single well-publicized case could be enough to tip the balance.

As legislatures pondered abolition, the actual use of the death penalty began to decline. The nation conducted 161 executions in 1912, 133 in 1913, and only 99 in 1914. By 1919 the figure was down to 65, in absolute terms the lowest in half a century and per capita the lowest ever.

The flurry of legislative reform came to a stop between 1917 and 1919. Many of the states that had abolished the death penalty brought it back. Of the fifteen that had done away with capital punishment for murder at one time or another before 1917, by 1920 there were only eight left. In a wartime and postwar culture fearful of politically motivated crime, a few states even adopted capital punishment for crimes like sabotage and the commission of anarchist acts resulting in death.[33] The death penalty would remain a prominent issue for the rest of the century, but an era of legislative abolition—the most active the nation had ever seen—was over.

Administrative Abolition

No more states would abolish capital punishment until the 1950s. For the next thirty years there was not nearly the level of legislative activity, even unsuccessful, there had been in the ten years ending in 1917. What little movement there was pointed in the opposite direction. Fear of gangsters in the 1920s and 1930s caused many state legislatures to consider punishing armed robbery or burglary with death. The Lindbergh kidnapping in 1932, and two years later the arrest of Bruno Hauptmann for the crime, inspired a wave of statutes, state and federal, making kidnapping a capital offense in some circumstances.[34] Measured by both the statute books and actual use, the period between 1920 and 1935 saw a resurgence of capital punishment. The years 1917–1919 had been the first three-year span in decades in which the annual number of executions failed to top 100, but that figure was back in the 140s by 1921 and 1922. It reached the 150s in 1930 and 1931 and then hit its all-time peak of 199 in 1935.

But this was also a period of intense abolitionist activity directed as much at molding public opinion as at effecting legislative change. The American League to Abolish Capital Punishment and its local affiliates published pamphlets, sponsored speeches, and staged debates, all for the purpose of keeping the death penalty a visible issue. The message was amplified by the ever-increasing number of celebrities, and near-celebrities with a legitimate claim to expertise, joining the cause. In the former category were people like William Randolph Hearst, who in 1926 wrote an anti–death penalty editorial that appeared in twenty-three of his newspapers and as a pamphlet. Henry Ford declared his opposition to capital punishment in an article in the popular magazine *Collier's*. "I wouldn't mind giving a man a licking," Ford affirmed, "but I wouldn't want to kill him." Clarence Darrow spent much of the last two decades of his life speaking against the death penalty and writing against it in popular magazines. In the 1930s Darrow became president of the American League to Abolish Capital Punishment. Fame attracted press coverage. A speech by Darrow, reported in several local newspapers, was worth hundreds of speeches by ordinary lawyers.[35]

Abolitionists nearly achieved the greatest public relations coup of all when Franklin Roosevelt, toward the end of his first year as President, announced that he "would like to see capital punishment abolished throughout this country." He qualified his statement by observing that the issue "is, primarily, a legislative matter," but when his remarks were published in the press the abolitionists quickly sought to make use of this unexpected gift. The Massachusetts Council for the Abolition of the Death Penalty wrote to Roosevelt's secretary for a copy of the President's statement so the Council could print and circulate it.[36]

Equally important in spreading the word were figures who were less well known but who were involved professionally in administering the death penalty. Governors like Harry Davis of Ohio and J. C. Walton of Oklahoma had faced the responsibility of clemency decisions in several cases. Their statements of opposition to capital punishment carried a weight much greater than normal. Prison employees who knew many condemned prisoners very well, such as the Sing Sing chaplains Jacob Katz and John McCaffery, had a credibility other opponents of capital punishment lacked. Other prison officials, such as Hastings Hart, the president of the American Prison Association, and Amos Squire, for many years Sing Sing's physician, were known for their opposition to the death penalty. The League to Abolish Capital Punishment gathered and published the anti–capital punishment views of a large number of prison wardens. The involvement of people with a plausible claim to expertise was important because it deflected the old criticism of the abolitionists as impractical dreamers without an informed appreciation of the difficulty of fighting crime. "They are not mere sentimentalists," wrote one admirer in 1925. Such abolitionists "have first-hand knowledge of the criminal and a definite opinion as to the effectiveness of the death penalty as a preventive of crime."[37] The nineteenth-century movement to abolish the death penalty had been led by outsiders to the penal system, but in the twentieth century many of the leading voices were those of insiders.

The most visible of the insiders was Lewis Lawes, Thomas Mott Osborne's successor as warden at Sing Sing. Lawes wrote books and articles in the popular press criticizing capital punishment. He made himself available to journalists for interviews. He was constantly giving speeches on the subject, in person and on the radio. He repeatedly testified in favor of abolition before the New York state legislature. For a time he was chairman of the League to Abolish Capital Punishment. The incongruity of Lawes's public life—as simultaneously the country's leading anti–death penalty activist and the warden of a prison that may have conducted more executions than any other—did not escape notice. Critics called him a *poseur* and a hypocrite. His habit of averting his eyes at the moment of electrocution was condemned as the cheap theatrics of a publicity-seeker. Lawes nevertheless remained at the head of the abolitionist cause until his death in 1947, a conspicuous symbol of the fact that opposition to capital punishment could be consistent with a practical, hard-nosed attitude toward crime.

Church groups and religious leaders also began arguing for the abolition of the death penalty in increasing numbers in the late 1920s. Committees of the Universalist General Convention and the New Jersey Conference of the Methodist Episcopal Church published reports advocating abolition. Methodists, Congregationalists, Baptists, Unitarians, Episcopalians, Jews—all sermonized against capital punishment.[38] No matter where one looked, in churches, in speeches, in newspapers, on the radio, capital punishment was in the air.

Most important of all, a series of controversial capital cases kept the issue before the public all through the 1920s and 1930s. In 1924, when the wealthy teenage murderers Nathan Leopold and Richard Loeb received life sentences instead of death because of their youth, there was a wave of public commentary on the relationship between the death penalty and moral responsibility for crime, as well as considerable criticism of the differential treatment of rich and poor criminals. Contemporary accounts suggest that the case caused many to question the propriety of capital punishment generally. Two years later the execution of Gerald Chapman in Connecticut produced a similar result. Chapman, convicted of killing a police officer, was widely believed to be innocent. His death prompted many editorials and letters on both sides, which often included statements of support for or opposition to capital punishment in the abstract. That same year the California execution of Clarence "Tuffy" Reid provoked a similar outpouring of sentiment, including clemency petitions to the governor bearing more than 50,000 names.[39]

In 1927 the Massachusetts execution of Nicola Sacco and Bartolomeo Vanzetti, also widely thought to be innocent and the victims of politically motivated persecution, was believed at least by abolitionists to have caused many to doubt the wisdom of the death penalty. Membership in the League to Abolish Capital Punishment doubled within a year. Sacco and Vanzetti "have struck a death blow at capital punishment in America," declared the criminologist George Kirchwey at the League's annual meeting. An even greater media frenzy was produced by New York's 1928 electrocution of Ruth Snyder. A few weeks after Snyder's death the *New York Evening Post* kicked off a series of fourteen articles on capital punishment with the assertion: "Never in America's history has the controversy over capital punishment waged so hotly as today. The death penalty is the most debated subject in New York State at present." The death sentences imposed in Alabama on the "Scottsboro boys" in the early 1930s, and then a similar case a few years later in Mississippi, focused public attention on the extent to which racial prejudice infected the legal process in capital cases. The 1936 New Jersey execution of Bruno Hauptmann, whom many thought innocent of the Lindbergh murder, may have been the most controversial of all.[40]

Every year or two there seemed to be a case that placed capital punishment in doubt. "Hosts of American citizens hitherto largely indifferent to the issue must have had their minds deeply troubled concerning capital punishment," observed one magazine after the Hauptmann execution. "Time and time again there have been executions which, for varying reasons, have raised questions with regard to this form of punishment. The Sacco and Vanzetti execution did so; the Ruth Snyder execution did so; the failure to execute Loeb and Leopold did so." Just after Hauptmann was electrocuted, another magazine despaired: "This is the third time in ten years that the whole world has been horrified by the savagery of America. First, Sacco and Vanzetti, the innocent anarchists, guilty only of having Communist support; then the Scottsboro Negroes, also innocent, guilty only of being black; and lastly Hauptmann, who might have been either innocent or guilty, but whose punishment was more atrocious than his crime."[41] A run of high-profile capital cases between 1924 and 1936 had probably done more to plant doubts about capital punishment than anything the advocates of abolition could have accomplished on their own.

These doubts might have been ephemeral in another era, but by the 1930s the long-term decline in the retributive and deterrent justifications for capital punishment made them stick. Despite the absence of much legislative activity, the execution rate—the incidence of capital punishment in actual practice—began to drop. In the 1930s the United States embarked on an extended period of what might be called *administrative* abolition, the slow erosion of capital punishment not by legislation or court decision but through a gradual change in the output of the criminal justice system.

The decline in the execution rate began in a handful of populous northern states. Illinois electrocuted an average of 7.6 people per year between 1931 and 1935, 4.4 between 1936 and 1940, and 2 between 1941 and 1945. New Jersey executed 4 per year from 1931 to 1935, 2.2 from 1936 to 1940, and 1.6 from 1941 to 1945. From the decade of the 1930s to that of the 1940s, the annual average fell from 8.2 to 3.6 in Pennsylvania, from 8.3 to 5.1 in Ohio, from 3.3 to 0.7 in Indiana, from 1.8 to 0.9 in Massachusetts, and from 15.3 to 11.4 in New York. The rest of the North followed soon after. This was not just the usual trough in the execution rate in wartime, when the military absorbed some of the men who would otherwise have committed murder. This decline lasted even after the war was over. The northern states executed 84 people in 1938, but by the early 1950s the annual figure fluctuated around 30.[42]

This decline in the frequency of executions was driven by a sharp drop in the annual number of death sentences. American juries imposed 158 death sentences in 1935 but only 79 in 1950. The murder rate had dropped slightly, but not enough to make this big a difference. Northern juries were simply choosing prison over execution more often. In the North the frequency of capital punishment had been cut by more than half without any legislative or judicial intervention. Changing public attitudes, as filtered through juries, had done all the work.

The southern states experienced no similar decline until the late 1940s, or about a decade after decline began in the North. Capital punishment in the South occupied a very different social context.

The Negro Question

With the end of slavery, southern whites feared what a young Charleston woman called "the foulest demoniac passions of the negro, hitherto so peaceful & happy, roused into being & fierce activity by the devilish Yankees." The Virginia chemist and farmer Edmund Ruffin complained that the freed slaves were committing so many crimes that "burglary, robbery, & arson ought to be again punished by death." Southern whites turned toward alternative forms of racial subjugation, and one of those was the death penalty. That capital punishment was necessary to restrain a primitive, animalistic black population became an article of faith among white southerners that persisted well into the twentieth century. George W. Hays, a former governor of Arkansas, explained in 1927:

> One of the South's most serious problems is the negro question. The legal system is exactly the same for both white and black, although the latter race is still quite primitive, and in general culture and advancement in a childish state of progress.
>
> If the death penalty were to be removed from our statute-books, the tendency to commit deeds of violence would be heightened owing to this negro problem. The greater number of the race do not maintain the same ideals as the whites.[43]

In this intellectual climate there was little room to indulge in theories of determinism. White southerners perceived themselves to be in a constant state of crisis with respect to their former slaves. Experiments in penology were a luxury they could not afford.

As a result, most of the southern states' capital crimes on the eve of the Civil War were still capital nearly a century later. As of 1954 rape was punished with death in eighteen states, sixteen in the South—Alabama, Arkansas, Delaware, Florida, Georgia, Kentucky, Louisiana, Maryland, Mississippi, Missouri, North Carolina, Oklahoma, South Carolina, Tennessee, Texas, and Virginia—plus Nevada and West Virginia. Robbery was capital in nine, again all but Nevada in the South—Alabama, Georgia, Kentucky, Mississippi, Missouri, Oklahoma, Texas, and Virginia. Five states, all southern, still retained the death penalty for arson—Alabama, Arkansas, Georgia, North Carolina, and Virginia. Burglary was still capital in four—Alabama, Kentucky, North Carolina, and Virginia.[44] While northerners were vigorously debating whether to abolish capital punishment even for murder, most of the southern states barely changed their capital codes. Change in the North combined with stasis in the South made the gap between the two regions wider than ever.

The practice of lynching, which reached its peak in the South in the late nineteenth and early twentieth centuries, provided an additional barrier to change. Lynching was a form of unofficial capital punishment, adjudication of guilt and execution by groups lacking the formal authority for either. The victims were usually black, the executioners usually white. The line between a lynching and an official execution could be thin. The participants in lynchings often included the very same people who, in their official capacities, administered the criminal justice system. Official trials and executions in the South could take place astonishingly fast, so fast as to closely resemble lynchings, when a case carried racial implications. In Kentucky in 1906 a black man convicted of raping a white woman was hanged only fifty minutes from the time the jury was sworn. In Galveston, Texas, a black defendant was indicted, tried, and hanged in less than four hours. But if the line was thin, everyone knew it existed. Participants and victims alike could tell the difference between an official and an unofficial execution. At its peak, lynching was much more common than official capital punishment. In Kentucky, for instance, between 1865 and 1940 there were 229 executions and 353 lynchings. Lynchings outnumbered executions 82 to 6 in the 1870s and 92 to 40 in the 1890s.[45] A culture that carried out so much unofficial capital punishment could hardly be squeamish about the official variety.

The relationship between lynching and capital punishment was a subject of considerable controversy in the late nineteenth and early twentieth centuries. Some took the position that the frequency of lynching demonstrated the need for capital punishment in the South. Without an officially sanctioned outlet, they argued, southerners' strong desire to exact retribution for crime would result in even more lynching. Others replied that if lynching were a substitute for capital punishment one ought to see frequent lynchings in places like Michigan and Wisconsin that had abolished the death penalty long before. Lynching, they argued, was not a substitute for the death penalty; rather, lynchings and executions rose and fell in tandem. Recent students of the subject, armed with statistical techniques that were unknown in the early twentieth century, have generally concluded that both sides were wrong. Most of the time lynching rates and execution rates showed little or no correlation one way or the other.[46]

But the racial pattern of capital punishment in the South closely resembled that of lynching. Of the 771 people of identified race known to have been executed for rape between 1870 and 1950, 701 were black. For robbery, 31 of 35 were black; for burglary, 18 of 21. Racial disparities were smaller but still noticeable for murder. In Virginia blacks known to have been executed for murder during the same period outnumbered whites 217 to 57; in Texas, 301 to 135. Throughout the South, for all crimes, black defendants were executed in numbers far out of proportion to their population. The death penalty was a means of racial control.

The South accounted for fewer than half of the nation's executions in the 1920s, but as the frequency of execution began to drop in the North, the South's share grew, to around 60 percent in the 1930s and over 65 percent by the late 1940s. And then the execution rate began to drop even in the South. The southern states executed 105 people in 1947, 48 in 1957, and 13 in 1963. The dramatic decline in the frequency of executions through the 1950s and 1960s would be a nationwide phenomenon, affecting the South as much as the North. Unlike the northern decline between the 1930s and 1950s, however, this later and more widespread drop would not be a result of changing public attitudes toward capital punishment. It would be the work of the Supreme Court.

9

TO THE SUPREME COURT

"I WAS LYING ON MY BUNK," recalled the rapist Lucious Jackson, condemned to death in Georgia, "when I heard one of the fellows shout that they've knocked it out. I had just about given up hope." The ninety-nine inmates on Florida's death row had just finished watching the film *Dirty Harry* when a guard broke the news. "We laughed, we whooped, we hollered and shook the doors," Calvin Campbell remembered.[1] Jackson, Campbell, and more than six hundred other condemned prisoners had been released from their death sentences. On June 29, 1972, in a group of cases collectively called *Furman v. Georgia*, the Supreme Court declared the death penalty unconstitutional, as cruel and unusual punishment in violation of the Eighth Amendment.

If Jackson and Campbell were surprised, they were hardly alone. That the Court would abolish capital punishment was, as the *New Republic* put it, "one of the biggest surprises in its history."[2] Even the lawyers arguing against the death penalty had held little hope of winning. And if the decision was unexpected in the summer of 1972, it would have been unimaginable in 1872. Attitudes toward capital punishment had undergone enormous change. Just as important, so had the legal community's understanding of constitutional law.

Cruel and Unusual Punishments

By 1791, when the Eighth Amendment to the United States Constitution was ratified, the phrase *cruel and unusual punishments* was already a stock verbal formula. It originally appeared in the English Bill of Rights of 1689, which declared that "excessive bail ought not to be required, nor excessive fines imposed, nor cruel and unusual punishments inflicted." That sentence was copied into Virginia's Declaration of Rights of 1776, and versions of it were included in several more state constitutions in the next few years. The new federal government included a clause banning cruel and unusual punishments in the Northwest Ordinance of 1787. By the time the Constitution was up for ratification, the prohibition of cruel and unusual punishments was such a standard element in documents of the sort that its absence was a common source of complaint among the Constitution's opponents. There was accordingly almost no debate over the constitutional amendment that became number eight.[3]

Neither the Eighth Amendment's cruel and unusual punishments clause nor its state constitutional analogues were used much in the century that followed. The lack of much early litigation on the subject, combined with the virtual absence of recorded debate over the Eighth Amendment and its antecedents, has left little evidence of exactly what Americans of the late eighteenth century understood by the concept of cruel and unusual punishment. The phrase appears to have been used in three distinct but related senses.

By prohibiting cruel and unusual punishments, some may have believed themselves to be holding government to the principle of proportionality, the idea that the harshest sentences had to be reserved for the worst crimes. The notion that government ought not to impose disproportionately harsh punishment was already very old by the late eighteenth century. Leviticus required punishment to be proportioned to the gravity of the offense, "eye for eye, tooth for tooth." The Magna Carta and subsequent English legislation likewise commanded that penalties be imposed according to the severity of the crime. That the punishment should fit the crime was a truism of Enlightenment penology, repeated by Beccaria, Montesquieu, and virtually all eighteenth-century writers on the subject. The original appearance of the cruel and unusual punishments clause in the English Bill of Rights had been a response to judicial overreaching in the political trials of the 1670s and 1680s, during which several defendants had received sentences widely perceived to be disproportionate to their crimes.[4] This understanding of the phrase may have crossed the Atlantic, although the surviving evidence of its American use in this sense dates only to the nineteenth century, not the eighteenth.

A second meaning was more common. Some understood *cruel and unusual* to refer to punishment unauthorized by law and therefore outside the authority of a court to impose. Such had also been a standard complaint about the harsh sentences imposed after the English political trials

of the 1670s and 1680s—that the penalties had been not just disproportionate but illegal. Unlike the concern with disproportion, which could
apply to any branch of government, this was a definition that connoted re-
straints on executive and judicial authority only. The legislature could
provide any range of punishments it chose, without limit, but the other
branches of government would then be confined to that range. The future Supreme Court Justice James Iredell seems to have had this
definition in mind in 1788, when he referred to the cruel and unusual
punishments clause and related provisions of the English Bill of Rights as
limitations that "went to an abuse of power in the Crown only, but were
never intended to limit the authority of Parliament."[5]

The third meaning of *cruel and unusual* in circulation in the late eighteenth century referred only to *methods* of punishment. Regardless of the
gravity of the crime, that is, and regardless of the legislature's desires,
there were certain ways of punishing crime that were so painful or otherwise oppressive as to be out of bounds. This is the sense of the phrase for
which there is the greatest amount of surviving evidence, so it is probably
the one that was most widely held. Abraham Holmes worried at the Massachusetts ratifying convention that in the unamended Constitution
Congress was "nowhere restrained from inventing the most cruel and unheard-of punishments . . . *racks* and *gibbets* may be amongst the most
mild instruments of their discipline." At the Virginia convention, Patrick
Henry complained that without a ban on cruel and unusual punishments Congress might "introduce the practice of France, Spain, and
Germany—of torturing, to extort a confession of the crime." Anglo-
Americans had long been proud of a criminal justice system they believed to be far more humane than those of continental Europe. After
covering the full range of bodily mutilation available as punishment in
eighteenth-century England, from cutting off the hand to slitting the nos-
trils, William Blackstone marveled at the mildness of the English criminal law. "Disgusting as this catalogue may seem," Blackstone concluded,
"it will afford pleasure to an English reader, and do honour to the English
law, to compare it with that shocking apparatus of death and torment,
to be met with in the criminal codes of almost every other nation in
Europe."[6]

Under none of these definitions would capital punishment have been
considered cruel and unusual. Only a small fraction of the population
considered capital punishment disproportionately severe for the gravest

crimes; the death penalty was hardly unauthorized by statute; and a death by hanging was often not painful at all and was not intended to be painful. Other parts of the Constitution indicate that those who drafted and ratified it contemplated the continued existence of the death penalty. The Fifth Amendment requires indictment by a grand jury before trial "for a capital, or otherwise infamous crime," ensures that no defendant will "be subject for the same offence to be twice put in jeopardy of life," and forbids the government to deprive a person "of life, liberty, or property, without due process of law." Article II empowers the President to grant reprieves and pardons for federal offenses. While pardons would be relevant to any kind of sentence, reprieves were most likely to apply to executions. Article III prevents Congress from punishing treason with "Corruption of Blood"—disinheriting the defendant's heirs—but says nothing about the traditional death sentence imposed on the defendant himself. Capital punishment was practiced everywhere in the decades before and after the ratification of the Constitution. Few eighteenth-century Americans could have conceived the Eighth Amendment or its state analogues to have any bearing on the general issue of capital punishment.

Nor would the Eighth Amendment have been considered to put an end to the forms of aggravated capital punishment or the use of ordinary capital punishment for lesser crimes. Burning, gibbeting, and dismemberment were all replaced by dissection in the late eighteenth century, but not because of the Eighth Amendment or the corresponding provisions in state constitutions. Dissection continued well into the nineteenth century, unhampered by the ban on cruel and unusual punishment. So did the practice of executing robbers, rapists, and the like. The extensive debate over abolishing capital punishment in the nineteenth and early twentieth centuries was conducted without reference to the concept of cruel and unusual punishment.

The cruel and unusual punishments clauses of the federal and state constitutions were intended as precautions, just in case a future legislature should perceive a need to adopt barbarous European punishments, or perhaps even familiar serious punishments for trifling crimes, or perhaps in case a future court or executive should attempt to inflict a punishment greater than that provided by law. Because none of these events came to pass, the cruel and unusual punishments clauses were used very infrequently for a century. "The provision would seem to be wholly unnecessary in a free government," Justice Joseph Story declared in 1833, "since it is scarcely possible, that any department of such a government should authorize, or justify such atrocious conduct."[7] So long as the state limited itself to established forms of punishment, it was for the most part safe from constitutional challenge.

Lawyers began to attack aspects of capital punishment as cruel and unusual only when governments began to depart from tradition. When the Utah Territory in the late nineteenth century provided for execution by shooting instead of hanging, the method was challenged as inconsistent with the Eighth Amendment. In rejecting the claim, the United States Supreme Court emphasized that shooting was indeed a traditional means of execution, in the military. The new execution technologies of subsequent decades, the electric chair and the gas chamber, were also claimed to be unconstitutional, but these arguments were easily brushed aside. There could be nothing cruel and unusual about a device intended to produce a death less painful than hanging. These new techniques gave rise in the 1920s to the opposite kind of claim, that the states guilty of cruel and unusual punishment were the ones that *retained* hanging despite the availability of less painful alternatives. This argument was uniformly rejected as well, on the basis of tradition.[8]

As capital punishment for crimes other than murder faded from memory in the North in the early twentieth century, southern state courts began to face arguments that the death penalty was disproportionate for robbery, burglary, or assault. These challenges all failed. Capital punishment was held not to be cruel and unusual for either aggravated arson or kidnapping. By 1952 the lawyers for Julius and Ethel Rosenberg could not have reasonably entertained any hope of prevailing on their claim that the death sentence for peacetime espionage amounted to cruel and unusual punishment.[9] No such claim had ever succeeded with respect to capital punishment for *any* crime.

Meanwhile, however, the Supreme Court was deciding a handful of cases that were transforming the legal community's understanding of the Eighth Amendment. Most of these cases did not explicitly concern capital punishment, but they established principles broader than the particular crimes and punishments at issue. Brick by brick, they laid a foundation that lawyers would eventually use to challenge the constitutionality of the death penalty.

One brick was the principle that the Eighth Amendment prohibited disproportionately severe sentences, not just painful methods of punishment. *United States v. Weems* (1910) concerned an American official in the Philippine Islands, who had been convicted of falsifying a minor government record and sentenced to fifteen years imprisonment at hard labor plus lifetime disqualification from many civil rights, under a local statute apparently derived from Spanish colonial law. The punishments imposed on Weems were so severe by contemporary American standards that, as Justice Joseph McKenna put it, they "excite wonder in minds accustomed to a more considerate adaptation of punishment to the degree of crime." Imprisonment, labor, and the imposition of civil disabilities were all familiar punishments, and none was necessarily painful or oppressive, so under the then-dominant view of the Eighth Amendment Weems could not have prevailed. But the Court held that the sentence amounted to cruel and unusual punishment because it was so disproportionate to the crime.[10]

Weems was widely recognized as a novel interpretation of the Eighth Amendment. Most contemporary legal commentators found the decision both unsupported by evidence of the Framers' intent and likely to invest judges with extraordinary discretion to review sentences for severity. But over the next few decades lawyers made use of *Weems* to argue that various kinds of punishments, both capital and noncapital, were disproportionate. While all of the capital and nearly all of the noncapital claims failed, they testified to the effect of *Weems* in transforming lawyers' understanding of the concept of cruel and unusual punishment. By 1962, when the Court next considered a similar claim, the idea that the Eighth Amendment barred disproportionate sentences was so well accepted that it required little discussion. Lawrence Robinson had been sentenced to a ninety-day jail term for being addicted to narcotics. "To be sure, imprisonment for ninety days is not, in the abstract, a punishment which is either cruel or unusual," the Court noted. But the Eighth Amendment also prohibited punishments that were too severe for the crime to which they were attached, and the Court considered narcotics addiction an illness, not a crime at all. "Even one day in prison," Justice Potter Stewart's opinion concluded, "would be a cruel and unusual punishment for the 'crime' of having a common cold."[11]

A second brick in the foundation was the principle that interpretation of the Eighth Amendment should change over time to conform to changed circumstances. Implicit in the dominant view of the Eighth

Amendment through the nineteenth century had been a theory of constitutional interpretation—that the intent of the Constitution's framers controlled how the Eighth Amendment was to be understood. In *Weems*, however, the Supreme Court began to disconnect the Eighth Amendment's historical purpose from its contemporary interpretation. Even if the concept of cruel and unusual punishment had originally embraced only painful or barbaric methods, the Court held, the concept was capable of expansion over time. "Time works changes, brings into existence new conditions and purposes," Justice McKenna argued. "Therefore a principle, to be vital, must be capable of wider application than the mischief which gave it birth." The Court's language was abstract, but commentators did not miss the point.[12] The Court was employing a method of constitutional interpretation new to the Eighth Amendment.

In later years the Court became more willing to depart from the original understanding of constitutional provisions generally, particularly in the area of criminal procedure, and *Weems* came to seem less remarkable in this respect. By 1947, when the Court decided *Louisiana ex rel. Francis v. Resweber*, the Justices had no doubt that the Eighth Amendment ought to be understood with reference to current attitudes toward punishment. "A punishment which is considered fair today may be considered cruel tomorrow," Justice Frank Murphy reasoned. He was acutely aware that the Court was taking on the inevitably subjective task of assessing contemporary opinion. "More than any other provision in the Constitution," he continued, "the prohibition of cruel and unusual punishment depends largely, if not entirely, upon the humanitarian instincts of the judiciary. We have nothing to guide us in defining what is cruel and unusual apart from our own conscience."[13]

By 1958 the Court was explicit about its willingness to overlook the original meaning of the Eighth Amendment. Albert Trop had been deprived of American citizenship after being convicted of desertion during World War II. Had the case arisen a century earlier, denationalization might well have been found to be a cruel and unusual punishment because of its novelty. But in *Trop v. Dulles* the Court tested the sentence, not against historical precedent, but against contemporary sensibilities. "The words of the Amendment are not precise," the Court began, and "their scope is not static. The Amendment must draw its meaning from the evolving standards of decency that mark the progress of a maturing society." Cruel and unusual punishment included whatever Americans were prepared to call cruel and unusual at any given time, not just what Americans of the late eighteenth century would have thought cruel and unusual. Denationalization was unconstitutional because it exceeded "the limits of civilized standards" as of 1958. Four Justices dissented, but even they did not question the Court's method of constitutional interpretation so much as endorse it, by arguing that denationalization was in fact *not* contrary to contemporary standards of decency.[14] That the Eighth Amendment was a mirror to society, with a content constantly in flux, was no longer controversial.

The third brick was the notion that the Eighth Amendment limited the power of state legislatures as well as that of Congress. Like the rest of the Bill of Rights, the Eighth Amendment was originally understood to apply to the federal government only. Beginning in the late nineteenth century, however, the Court gradually found most of the Bill of Rights "incorporated" by the due process clause of the Fourteenth Amendment and thus applicable to the states as well. The Eighth Amendment was no exception. The Court addressed the issue for the first time in 1947, when it assumed, but expressly refrained from deciding, that the states were bound by the Eighth Amendment. In later years several lower courts reached holdings to the same effect. Eventually, in 1962, so did the Supreme Court.[15]

The significance of the Eighth Amendment's application to the states was not that it subjected state governments to any new restriction. Most of the state constitutions prohibited cruel and unusual punishments too. The importance of the incorporation of the Eighth Amendment was rather that it centralized and thus magnified the potential for change. The development of *state* constitutional law is necessarily gradual, because final interpretive authority is lodged with fifty state supreme courts, none of which is bound by the decisions of the others. Federal constitutional law, in contrast, can change radically with a single decision of the United States Supreme Court. By holding the Eighth Amendment applicable to the states, the Court empowered itself to set death penalty policy for the nation.

Lurking just below the surface was the belief shared by some, perhaps most, of the Justices that capital punishment was simply unwise. "If my will were law," Robert Jackson wrote in 1946, "it would never permit execution of any death sentence. This is not because I am sentimental about criminals, but I have doubts of the moral right of society to extinguish a human life, and even greater doubts about the wisdom of doing so." Tom Clark announced his opposition to capital punishment in a 1961 speech at Villanova Law School. Earl Warren disclosed, upon his retirement in 1968, that all his life he had found the death penalty "repulsive." Felix Frankfurter proclaimed his opposition to capital punishment in a dissenting opinion in 1948, and then testified against it in 1950 before the British Royal Commission on Capital Punishment.[16] Educated opinion had been turning against the death penalty for decades, and members of the Supreme Court could not avoid being affected.

There was no reason to suspect, however, that the Supreme Court would one day declare capital punishment unconstitutional. The death penalty was so familiar that commentators considered its constitutionality scarcely worth discussion. Alexander Bickel, one of the leading constitutional scholars of the era, found it "quite unthinkable" in 1962 that the Supreme Court would even address the constitutionality of capital punishment within the next generation.[17] There was not yet any hint of the litigation that would be the focus of the Court's and the public's attention only a few years later.

Open Season

By the middle of the twentieth century belief in retribution as a basis for punishment had sunk to a new low among academic and political elites. "Retribution is no longer the dominant objective of the criminal law," declared Justice Hugo Black for the Supreme Court in 1949. A few years later the New York Court of Appeals went even further. "There is no place in the scheme" of criminal justice, the court announced, "for punishment for its own sake, the product simply of vengeance or retribution." "The retributive position does not command much assent in intellectual circles," the law professor Herbert Packer reported in 1968. The Model Penal Code, a collective product of elite lawyers and law professors nearly a decade in the making when it was published in 1962, was based on the premise that "'desert' alone is not a sufficient justification for punishment. It is inhumane and morally unacceptable."[18]

The decline of retribution, already under way for nearly a century, continued to undermine support for capital punishment. "The death penalty has become an unacceptable and ineffective method of punishment," explained the sociologist Robert Caldwell in 1952, "and has been largely replaced with imprisonment, in which the emphasis is being put more and more upon a scientific program of rehabilitation." The social scientists' deterministic models of crime had in great measure replaced the older conception of free will. As Maryland's Governor Theodore McKeldin put it in 1958, in commuting the death sentence imposed on Charles Stansbury, "There are some people whose early training, or lack of training, sets a pattern which leads them inevitably into crime."[19] If the criminal did not choose to commit the crime, capital punishment lost any claim to justice.

The movement to abolish capital punishment grew correspondingly stronger. The earliest Gallup polls to inquire about attitudes toward the death penalty, conducted in 1936, 1937, and 1953, all found approximately twice as many supporters as opponents. The numbers then began to change. In 1957 only 47 percent of respondents favored capital punishment, while 34 percent opposed it and 18 percent had no opinion. By 1965 death penalty supporters outnumbered opponents by only 45 to 43 percent. Nineteen sixty-six was the first year, and also the last, in which opponents outnumbered supporters: 47 to 42 percent. For the rest of the decade the responses approximated 50 percent in favor and 40 percent against. Public opinion was remarkably consistent across the country. Even in the South, opponents outnumbered supporters in the mid-1960s. (In the 1966 poll the South and the Midwest came out slightly against the death penalty while the East and the West were slightly in favor of it.)[20] There was no public opinion polling on the subject before the twentieth century, but it is doubtful that abolition had ever been as popular on a national scale as it became in the 1960s.

A number of famous people spoke out against the death penalty in the 1950s and 1960s. Some were intellectuals, such as Arthur Koestler and Albert Camus. Camus's book *Reflections on the Guillotine* was translated and published in the United States when he was at the peak of his fame, soon after he won the Nobel Prize. Some were politicians, such as Michael DiSalle, the governor of Ohio from 1959 to 1963. While governor, DiSalle campaigned to abolish the death penalty, even making it a point to hire convicted murderers for his household staff to demonstrate the possibility of rehabilitation. Out of office, DiSalle kept up the fight in speeches and a book. Governor Terry Sanford of North Carolina made so many anti–death penalty statements in the early 1960s that his position was familiar to the state's condemned prisoners, who made a point of mentioning it in their clemency applications. Hubert Humphrey opposed capital punishment in his unsuccessful 1960 presidential campaign, and Edmund G. Brown opposed it in his successful 1962 campaign to be governor of California. In 1965 even the U.S. Department of Justice called for abolition. By the 1960s elected officials and their appointees perceived little political liability in opposing the death penalty. "The season is presently open upon death as a penal sanction of a civilized society," declared the law professor Walter Oberer in 1961. "The pattern of assault has been frontal."[21]

The most famous opponent of capital punishment in the 1950s was himself a condemned man. Caryl Chessman had been convicted of kidnapping in Los Angeles in 1948 and sentenced to death, but a series of appeals kept him alive in prison until 1960. During that time he gave several interviews and wrote four books. By reviving the ancient literary form of the criminal autobiography, he became an international celebrity—a literate, intelligent, white man widely believed to be innocent, who in any event had not killed anyone. His first book, an autobiography entitled *Cell 2455, Death Row,* was so popular when it appeared in 1954 that translations were published in Milan, Oslo, Buenos Aires, Mexico City, Tokyo, Taipei, and Athens. His eventual execution inspired poetry in Chile, theater in Montreal, and accounts of his life and death in England, France, Spain, and Uruguay. Chessman's case aroused considerable criticism of capital punishment in the United States and kept the issue of abolition in the front pages for years.

A wide range of religious organizations, responding to changing points of view within their memberships, issued official statements criticizing capital punishment in the 1950s and 1960s. Some were huge national denominations like the Methodist Church, with 10 million members, and the Lutheran Church, with 3.3 million. The American Baptist Convention, the Protestant Episcopal Church, and the United Presbyterian Church all issued anti–death penalty statements. Some were local interdenominational groups like the New York State Council of Churches and the Church Federation of Greater Chicago. Several smaller denominational organizations, including the Union of American Hebrew Congregations and the Mennonite Church, embarked on publication and education programs aimed at abolition. The Quakers kept up their work as well, now as one voice in a large choir.[22]

Perhaps the clearest indicator of the growing salience of capital punishment as a political issue in the early 1960s was the swarm of letters received by state governors from students required to write essays and participate in debates on the subject. "In the Senior Government classes at our school we are having a series of panel discussions," wrote Scott Larabee of Black River High School in Sullivan, Ohio. "The topic I have been assigned is: 'Capital Punishment.' I would be interested to know your feelings and the feelings of the people in your state." The addressee was Warren Hearnes, the governor of Missouri. Hearnes responded with a detailed explanation of his support for the death penalty—the very same one he sent to young Bob Douse of Skyomish, Washington; Mark Tierer, a student in Kalamazoo, Michigan; Keith Corner, from Grandview, Missouri; and George Virchick, a student at Susquehanna University in Pennsylvania. Within a few months the questions from students were coming so quickly that Hearnes had to delegate the task of responding to his press secretary. Overwhelmed by mail from children, Connecticut Governor John Dempsey had an assistant send a standard bland response that took no position. The *Clearing House*, a magazine for junior high school teachers, ran a five-page article setting out the main arguments for and against the death penalty for teachers to use in guiding class discussion.[23] Learning to have an opinion about capital punishment was becoming a part of public education.

Similar debates were taking place all over the world. In Great Britain capital punishment was a contentious issue all through the 1950s and 1960s. Britain abolished the death penalty temporarily in 1965 and then permanently in 1969. Canada conducted its last execution in 1962, and abolished the death penalty (except for the murder of prison guards and police officers) in 1967. Mexico executed no one after 1937. Germany, Austria, and Italy all abolished capital punishment in the years after World War II. New Zealand's last execution was in 1957, Australia's in 1967. Denmark and Belgium conducted their last executions in 1950, the Netherlands in 1952, and Ireland in 1954. They joined the handful of nations that had abolished the death penalty in the late nineteenth and early twentieth centuries.[24] By the late 1960s the United States was one of the very few nations in North America or western Europe that still practiced capital punishment.

As the death penalty dwindled away in other countries, high-profile American capital cases attracted more international attention than ever before, and the American legal system began to come under intense foreign criticism. The impending execution of Julius and Ethel Rosenberg in 1953 drew clemency petitions from the mayor of Rome, two former prime ministers of France, eight Danish judges, and ordinary people all over the world. Caryl Chessman's execution provoked an outpouring of foreign criticism in 1959 and 1960. Petitioners on Chessman's behalf collected 90,000 signatures in Stockholm, 50,000 in Oslo, and 9,000 in Geneva. Demonstrators marched outside the American consulate in Montreal. The Vatican's official newspaper called upon California Governor Edmund G. Brown to pardon Chessman. The State Department, expecting that President Eisenhower would encounter hostile pro-Chessman crowds on a trip to Latin America, persuaded Brown to delay Chessman's execution until Eisenhower returned home. Some of the countries that had already abolished capital punishment began to ask the United Nations to pressure the United States to do the same.[25] In the early nineteenth century Americans had boasted of penal codes milder than any in Europe, but by the middle of the twentieth century the tables were beginning to turn.

The harshest foreign criticism was reserved for the death sentences some of the southern states were still imposing on black defendants for lesser felonies. In 1958, when Jimmy Wilson was sentenced to death in Alabama for robbing a white woman of $1.95, the case was known around the world. At the height of the Cold War, newspapers in Prague published an account under the headline "This Is America." Belgrade's evening newspaper asked whether the value of human life had dropped to $1.95. The American embassy in Venezuela reported that the Wilson case was being discussed in the major Caracas newspapers. "It is known that the communists have been active in eastern Venezuela," the embassy explained. "The news stories have all the earmarks of the commie line." But criticism of the racial inequality inherent in capital punishment in the United States came from everywhere, regardless of political beliefs. The London *Sunday Express* headlined its foreign news page "Negro to die in U.S. for 14s. theft." Editorialists in Ghana, Ethiopia, and Jamaica protested against what the *Jamaica Daily Gleaner* called "a macabre anachronism." The American embassy in London reported receiving six hundred letters of protest per day; another four hundred per day poured into the American embassy in Dublin. In Perth, Australia, demonstrators hanged a black effigy from the American consulate's flagpole under a sign reading "Guilty of theft of fourteen shillings." Alabama Governor James Folsom called a press conference to announce that he was "snowed under" by more than three thousand letters he received in a single box from Toronto. The American ambassador in the Hague received death threats in the event Wilson was executed. Finally, after Secretary of State John Foster Dulles complained to Folsom of the "international hullaba-loo," Folsom commuted Wilson's sentence.[26]

This vociferous opposition to capital punishment, from within the United States and outside, brought about the greatest flurry of legislative activity since the years before World War I. The territories of Alaska and Hawaii abolished the death penalty in 1957. Delaware abolished it in 1958, only to bring it back in 1961. Oregon conducted a referendum in 1964 in which more than 60 percent of the electorate voted for abolition. New York, Iowa, Vermont, and West Virginia abolished it in 1965. When New Mexico abolished the death penalty in 1969, it became the four-teenth state to do so.[27] There had never been so many.

As in similar periods of abolition in the past, many other states came close. Both houses of the Indiana legislature voted to end the death pen-alty in 1965, but Governor Roger Branigin vetoed the bill. Abolition bills passed the Massachusetts Senate in 1963 and the Kentucky House in 1964. In 1957 the Illinois and California Assemblies voted in favor of six-year moratoria on executions, and the Illinois Assembly did so again in 1967. Legislative committees voted for abolition in Massachusetts, Cali-fornia, Pennsylvania, and Maryland. Perhaps the best indication of the level of activity is to take a single slice of time: in February 1965 twenty state legislatures were considering bills to abolish capital punishment.[28]

The execution rate, in decline since 1935, began to drop even faster. There were 105 executions in 1951. In 1960 there were only 56. In 1965 there were 7. And on June 2, 1967, Luis Monge died in Colorado's gas chamber in what would be the last execution in the United States for a decade.

The declining execution rate was only in part a product of the dimin-ishing popularity of capital punishment.[29] An average of 142 people were sentenced to death each year between 1935 and 1942. By the 1960s the av-erage annual number of death sentences was down to 113. The drop in death sentences could not have been a result of the abolition of capital punishment in certain states, because most of the drop took place before the legislative activity of the mid-1960s. The states that abolished capital punishment tended to be those in which it had already dwindled away in practice. The decline in the annual number of death sentences was instead caused by jurors in states that *retained* the death penalty, who, taking advantage of their discretion to choose prison or execution, were simply less willing to impose death sentences than they had once been. Opponents of the death penalty were excluded from jury service, so the number of death sentences could never fully reflect diminishing popular support for capital punishment. If the "death-qualification" of juries could have been performed perfectly, one might have seen the same number of death sentences imposed year after year, by the ever-smaller segment of the population eligible to serve on juries. But even this restricted group of death-qualified jurors was condemning criminals to death 20 percent less often than before.

Yet the behavior of juries accounts for only a small fraction of the declining execution rate. In the 1960s the annual number of death sentences regularly exceeded the number of executions by a hundred or more. In 1969, when the number of executions was zero, 143 people were sentenced to death. Clearly events *after* sentencing were more important than sentencing itself in causing the execution rate to decline.

One such event was clemency, but its role in the decline was a small one. Clemency was the post-sentencing decision most directly subject to political pressure, so if popular disenchantment with capital punishment was to have any effect on the number of people executed this is where it would be. The annual number of capital sentences commuted to prison terms, however, never grew very large. Only about 15 percent of the people sentenced to death in the 1960s had their sentences commuted. The Justice Department only began collecting nationwide data in 1960, so nothing certain can be said about how these figures compare with earlier periods, but state-specific data suggest that it is very likely that a 15 percent commutation rate represented a substantial *decrease*, not an increase, over previous decades. In North Carolina between 1909 and 1928, for example, of the 200 people sentenced to death, exactly half had their sentences commuted. In Florida between 1924 and 1964, 23 percent of the death sentences were commuted.[30] If these states are representative, the commutation rate in the 1960s was lower than before, despite the increasing opposition to capital punishment. The annual number of commutations accounted, in any event, for only a small part of the gap between the annual number of death sentences and the annual number of executions in the 1960s.

The drop in the execution rate was instead primarily the result of a new phenomenon: many more condemned criminals were appealing their cases to higher courts than ever before, and many of them were winning. Before the middle of the twentieth century criminal appeals were unusual.[31] In the 1960s, however, the appeals rate skyrocketed. (I am using the word "appeals" here in a nontechnical sense, to include all the methods by which courts can review criminal convictions and sentences. Strictly speaking, an appeal is just one of them.) Criminal cases represented 14–17 percent of the business of state supreme courts between 1945 and 1960, but 28 percent in 1965 and 1970. Appealed convictions of murder, the crime most likely to carry a death sentence, were 1.7 percent of the caseload in 1935–1940 but 6 percent by 1965. Annual petitions for a writ of habeas corpus, the vehicle by which state prisoners can ask federal courts to review their convictions, nearly quadrupled between 1952 and 1963.[32]

Part of the increase can be attributed to the increasing crime rate. There were simply more criminals than ever before, so even if the percentage of convictions appealed held constant there would have been a rise in the number of criminal appeals. But much of the increase in the volume of appeals was the result of Supreme Court decisions in the 1950s and early 1960s that made it procedurally easier to appeal. Another set of Supreme Court decisions gave convicted criminals additional constitutional grounds upon which to base an appeal. By 1965–1970 nearly half the criminal appeals before state supreme courts involved constitutional issues. Only a quarter of criminal appeals had involved claimed violations of the constitution in 1955–1960, and only 18.5 percent in the period between 1870 and 1950.[33] Constitutional claims were the basis of *all* the federal habeas corpus petitions. Between 1951, when there were 105 executions in the United States, and 1965, when there were 7, the criminal justice system underwent a procedural revolution.

It was this new opportunity to appeal that accounted for the lion's share of the decline in the execution rate. Many condemned prisoners who appealed got their convictions reversed—an average of 43 per year between 1961 and 1970, or more than a third of those who had been sentenced to death and more than twice as many as those whose sentences were commuted. Many more on death row were able to stay alive by continuing to litigate. The cumulative population of death rows around the country began to mount, as each freshly condemned prisoner joined those whose appeals were still in progress. The death row population doubled between 1955 and 1961 and doubled again between 1961 and 1969. Each passing year saw a lengthening of the time a person spent on death row before his conviction was reversed, from a median of 17 months in 1962 to 41 months in 1967. A condemned man did not need to win on appeal to survive. He could live longer just by keeping his case in court. Appeals, not public opinion, put a temporary end to capital punishment in the United States.

Constitutional Attacks

The idea of mounting a systemic constitutional challenge to the death penalty was an outgrowth of the civil rights movement. The National Association for the Advancement of Colored People had battled against the unequal treatment of black criminal defendants in the South in both capital and noncapital cases almost from its founding in 1909, normally by representing individual defendants in racially charged circumstances. In 1950 the NAACP tried something new. The lawyers associated with the organization and its legal affiliate, the NAACP Legal Defense and Educational Fund (LDF), were riding a wave of success. They had just persuaded the Supreme Court to outlaw restrictive covenants segregating neighborhoods by race. They were coming off two major victories in which the Court had required the integration of universities, and they had determined to try to do the same for all levels of education—a strategy that would bear fruit a few years later in *Brown v. Board of Education*. Into this optimistic climate arrived a case from Martinsville, Virginia, in which seven young black men had been sentenced to death for raping a white woman. Martin A. Martin, a Richmond lawyer who was vice-chair of the NAACP's Virginia branch, represented the defendants. Everyone knew that blacks in Virginia were far more likely than whites to receive the death sentence for rape. Martin and his colleagues decided to use that disparity as the basis of a claim that the imposition of capital punishment for rape violated the Constitution's Equal Protection Clause. Other discriminatory institutions had been the objects of successful constitutional challenges; perhaps capital punishment would be next.[34]

The argument did not prevail, for the same reason it has failed ever since. The Equal Protection Clause has long been interpreted to prohibit only *intentional* discrimination, and it could not be shown that the jurors in this particular case, much less any of the prior rape cases, had intended to discriminate against the individual defendants before them. The

Martinsville Seven were electrocuted. Similar challenges to the racial pattern of capital punishment for rape were rejected soon after in Florida, Texas, Arkansas, and Alabama.[35]

But all over the country defense lawyers grasping for strategies to save their clients from execution began formulating other kinds of constitutional attacks on capital punishment. Some argued that the unguided discretion vested in juries to choose between life and death amounted to a denial of due process, because it resulted in a pattern of verdicts that was at best arbitrary, in that identical defendants could be treated differently, and at worst rife with discrimination. The argument failed several times. Some argued that the 150-year-old practice of excluding opponents of capital punishment from capital juries denied due process by stacking juries with the people most likely to convict. This argument was unsuccessful as well. Gerald Gottlieb, a lawyer associated with the Los Angeles branch of the American Civil Liberties Union (ACLU), suggested in 1961 that the Supreme Court's Eighth Amendment jurisprudence might support an argument that the death penalty constituted cruel and unusual punishment. Before the trial of Charles Hamilton, a black man charged in Alabama with the capital crime of burglary with the intent to commit rape, LDF lawyers were preparing to appeal, in the event of a death sentence, on the ground that capital punishment for burglary amounted to cruel and unusual punishment because it was disproportionately severe. They never got the chance, because Hamilton received a life sentence.[36] The era was one in which the courts were being used to challenge aspects of all kinds of institutions, and capital punishment was no exception. But the record as of 1962 was one of uniform failure.

And then an astonishing event changed everything. Arthur Goldberg was the newest Supreme Court Justice, a distinguished labor lawyer with virtually no experience with criminal cases. Upon taking his seat in the fall of 1962, he was bothered by the capital appeals that came before the Court. "I found disturbing evidence that the imposition of the death penalty was arbitrary, haphazard, capricious and discriminatory," he reflected later. "The impact of the death penalty was demonstrably greatest among disadvantaged minorities." In the summer of 1963, after a term's worth of capital cases, he instructed his new law clerk to prepare a memorandum on the constitutional issues surrounding the death penalty, with an eye toward writing an opinion on the subject in a future case. That clerk was a recent law school graduate named Alan Dershowitz, who shared

Goldberg's doubts about capital punishment. "I turned to the books with a sense of mission," Dershowitz recalled. "Here was a real opportunity for the Supreme Court to save countless lives."[37] Within a few weeks Dershowitz produced a lengthy discussion of the possible constitutional attacks on the death penalty.

After some editing, Goldberg circulated the memorandum to the other eight Justices in October. "I propose to raise the following issue," Goldberg began: "Whether, and under what circumstances, the imposition of the death penalty is proscribed by the Eighth and Fourteenth Amendments to the United States Constitution." Goldberg reviewed the Court's prior Eighth Amendment cases, with an emphasis on the portions of *Weems* and *Trop* which held that the concept of cruel and unusual punishment incorporated "evolving standards of decency." Those evolving standards, Goldberg concluded, "now condemn as barbaric and inhuman the deliberate institutionalized taking of human life by the state." Capital punishment had been abolished by "many, if not most, of the civilized nations of the western world."

American public opinion was almost equally divided, but Goldberg found that division no obstacle to determining that contemporary standards of decency had turned against the death penalty. "In certain matters—especially those relating to fair procedures in criminal trials—this Court traditionally has guided rather than followed public opinion in the process of articulating and establishing progressively civilized standards of decency," Goldberg reasoned. "If only punishments already overwhelmingly condemned by public opinion came within the cruel and unusual punishment proscription, the Eighth Amendment would be a dead letter; for such punishments would presumably be abolished by the legislature." This argument muddied the waters considerably. After first relying on *Weems* and *Trop* for the proposition that the Eighth Amendment required the Court to read the national (or maybe international) mood with respect to a challenged punishment, Goldberg here seemed to be saying that the Justices' own standards of decency, not those of their fellow citizens, were the ones that mattered, because the Justices' standards were likely to be "evolving" faster. In any event, Goldberg then turned to the standard catalogue of arguments against capital punishment. It raised the specter of executing the innocent. It failed to deter, rehabilitate, or perform any of the other functions of punishment, except that of retribution, which for most intellectuals by that time was no longer a permissible goal. The death penalty was therefore cruel and unusual.[38]

Some of Goldberg's colleagues were aghast. Warren "was furious," Dershowitz recalled, because he feared that the memorandum, if published, would turn public opinion against the Court and thus indirectly encourage defiance of controversial decisions in other areas, especially desegregation. Justice John Harlan thought it "a very poor time to bring the matter up." Black announced that he was "unalterably opposed to Goldberg's ideas." But Justices William Douglas and William Brennan, who shared Goldberg's view of the death penalty and his conception of the Court's role as a leader of public opinion, were more sympathetic. A week later Goldberg, joined by Douglas and Brennan, published a sharply truncated version of the memorandum as a dissent from the Court's refusal to hear *Rudolph v. Alabama,* an appeal from a death sentence imposed for rape. The published version simply stated Goldberg's belief that an important constitutional question was raised by capital punishment for a crime, like rape, that did not involve the taking of human life.[39]

Goldberg's dissent rang like an alarm clock in the offices of civil rights lawyers. If three Justices of the Supreme Court cared enough about capital punishment to signal their views in a case in which the death penalty's constitutionality had not even been raised by the defendant's lawyer, perhaps there was a chance of convincing a majority of the Court that capital punishment was unconstitutional. The LDF and the ACLU began organized campaigns aimed at abolition. Constitutional challenges to the death penalty had originated with the institutional civil rights community back in 1950, but in the intervening thirteen years most had been brought by individual defense lawyers in individual cases, attorneys of widely varying skill and commitment to the cause of abolition, who had little sense of what the others were doing. The effect of Goldberg's dissent was to concentrate death penalty litigation in the hands of a few extremely intelligent and highly motivated lawyers with considerable experience in persuading courts to adopt novel legal positions. As Goldberg later told his wife, that had been his intent all along.[40]

The LDF and the ACLU had each been organized to pursue a particular mission, and those differing goals determined the initial course each pursued. The LDF existed to help black people. It was interested in capital punishment primarily because of the racial disparities in capital sentencing. Although Goldberg's *Rudolph* dissent had not mentioned race, the LDF's first move was to send law students into the South to compile information about rape cases, in an effort to prove that the racial pattern of executions for rape was not attributable to any factor other than race. The plan was to conduct the same kind of equal-protection litigation the NAACP had originated in 1950, but to do it better, by accounting for all the possible reasons some defendants might be treated more harshly than others. The data were hurriedly assembled by the University of Pennsylvania criminologist Marvin Wolfgang in 1965 and 1966, just as Arkansas was preparing to execute William Maxwell, a black man convicted of raping a white woman. Maxwell's appeal became the first showpiece of the LDF's litigation campaign.[41]

The ACLU, by contrast, had been founded to protect individual rights regardless of race. The organization focused its energies on lobbying state legislatures to abolish the death penalty. Most of the litigation was left to the better-funded LDF. "If resources comparable to those the LDF invested in litigation had been made available for a state legislative campaign," the executive director of the ACLU's New York branch later reflected, a bit wistfully, "a good many states might have been persuaded to repeal their death penalty laws."[42] But the LDF's status as a tax-exempt organization prohibited it from lobbying, and in any event the LDF's lawyers had achieved their greatest victories in the courtroom, not the legislature. The battle against the death penalty would be waged primarily through litigation.

Once they had taken up capital punishment, however, the LDF's lawyers were pulled into a litigation campaign far broader than the one they had initially conceived. The racial disparity argument was no more successful in the late 1960s, even with better data, than it had been in 1950. As the court of appeals explained in 1968, in an opinion by Judge Harry Blackmun, "We are not yet ready to condemn and upset the result reached in every case of a negro rape defendant in the State of Arkansas on the basis of broad theories of social and statistical injustice." Tony Amsterdam, the University of Pennsylvania law professor who took charge of the LDF's capital litigation, and Jack Greenberg and Michael Meltsner, the LDF attorneys who focused on the issue, now had clients facing execution. They found themselves ethically compelled to raise other constitutional challenges to the death penalty, challenges that bore no necessary relation to race. "We could no more let men die that we had the power to save," Amsterdam explained, "than we could have passed by a dying accident victim sprawled bloody and writhing on the road without stopping to render such aid as we could." The LDF abandoned its early concentration on racial disparity and adopted all the other constitutional theories already in circulation. Once that decision had been made, there was no longer any reason not to take on white clients too.[43]

The LDF's visibility, aided by a timely grant from the Ford Foundation, enabled it to have a hand in virtually every capital case in the country, either directly as lawyers or indirectly as purveyors of advice. Amsterdam circulated sets of legal briefs containing every conceivable argument against the death penalty to hundreds of lawyers representing condemned clients. These collections quickly became known as "Last Aid Kits," because even a lawyer who knew nothing about the death penalty could use one to present a plausible case for a condemned prisoner facing imminent execution. Within a few years, an organization founded to combat racial prejudice had become the leading edge of the movement to abolish capital punishment.

Historians of the movement, and indeed some of the participants themselves, often credit the LDF with successfully employing a "moratorium strategy." By raising every plausible constitutional claim in every possible case, the LDF hoped to force the machinery of execution to grind to a temporary halt for the claims to be resolved. As the population of death rows around the country mounted, the stakes would rise, because each constitutional challenge rebuffed would cause the execution of hundreds of people. "The politics of abolition boiled down to this," Meltsner observed afterward: "for each year the United States went without executions, the more hollow would ring claims that the American people could not do without them; the longer death-row inmates waited, the greater their numbers, the more difficult it would be for courts to permit the first execution. A successful moratorium strategy would create a death-row logjam. Regardless of political stripe, there were very few governors who wished to preside over mass executions."[44]

There was no doubt a death row logjam in the late 1960s, but to call it the work of the LDF is to give the LDF lawyers far too much credit. By 1967, when the moratorium strategy began, the death row population had been rising for over a decade. There were 125 condemned prisoners awaiting execution when the Justice Department counted them in 1955, a figure not far different from what it had been in the late nineteenth century. In 1967 there were 435. The death row population continued to grow in later years, reaching 620 in 1972, and much of that growth can be attributed to the LDF's efforts, but the greater part of the logjam predated the LDF's involvement in any significant degree of capital litigation. As we have seen, the annual number of executions had been dropping for decades before the LDF took up capital punishment. From its peak of 199 in 1935, it was down to 21 by 1963, the year of Goldberg's *Rudolph* dissent. It was down to 7 in 1965, when the LDF first got involved, and 2 in 1967, when the moratorium strategy began. The LDF's lawyers were riding the end of a wave.

The real achievement of Amsterdam and the LDF lawyers was to get the arguments against the constitutionality of the death penalty before the Supreme Court in a context in which they would be taken seriously. That such a thing could be done was unlikely in 1962 but inevitable by 1968, and for that the LDF deserves much of the credit. Even in this respect, however, the LDF was following on the heels of others.

The first constitutional challenge to reach the Supreme Court arrived in 1967. Steven Duke, a Yale law professor representing the accused kidnapper Charles "Batman" Jackson, noticed something disturbing about the wording of the federal Kidnapping Act. Like many of the state statutes giving juries discretion to choose between life and death, the Kidnapping Act provided for a death sentence "if the verdict of the jury shall so recommend," but otherwise required a term of imprisonment. Duke recognized that the Kidnapping Act omitted, probably inadvertently, to provide for the possibility of a death sentence in cases not tried before a jury—that is, cases in which the defendant either pleaded guilty or agreed to be tried solely before a judge. The Kidnapping Act and the similarly worded state laws in effect penalized defendants who exercised their constitutional right to a jury trial, because only those defendants took the risk of receiving a death sentence. In *United States v. Jackson* the Supreme Court agreed that the Kidnapping Act was unconstitutional for this reason, a holding that had the effect of invalidating several other federal death penalty provisions and the capital sentencing schemes of ten states, all of which shared the same flaw. The abolitionists had won their first big case.[45]

The next one came soon after. William Witherspoon had been convicted of murder and sentenced to death in Illinois by a jury from which opponents of capital punishment had been excluded—a jury just like every other capital jury in the United States for well over a century. Witherspoon was represented by the prominent Chicago lawyer Albert Jenner, who argued that the jurors who survived the winnowing process did not represent a fair cross-section of the community, as the Sixth Amendment requires, but were rather a set of people disproportionately inclined to find the defendant guilty. The strategy had been in circulation for some time; Jenner was the first to get it before the Supreme Court. Social scientists had begun to conduct empirical tests of the theory, and the early results were promising: jurors willing to impose the death penalty really *did* seem to be more likely to convict. But more empirical research was under way. The LDF lawyers were terrified that the issue was coming to the Supreme Court too soon, before the claim had sufficient empirical grounding. If the Court found Jenner's argument factually unsupported, it would be impossible as a practical matter to bring the issue back before the Court, even when better empirical results were in. The LDF accordingly pleaded with the Court *not* to rule on Witherspoon's claim. Jenner's associates were furious. The one organization they counted in their corner was undermining their attack on the death penalty.[46]

The Court followed the LDF's advice. "We simply cannot conclude," the Court explained, "either on the basis of the record now before us or as a matter of judicial notice, that the exclusion of jurors opposed to capital punishment results in an unrepresentative jury on the issue of guilt." The Court ruled instead on a narrower issue. Rather than reversing Witherspoon's *conviction*, it reversed only his death sentence. The state could not exclude potential jurors who merely had *doubts* about the propriety of capital punishment, the Court held. The state could exclude only those jurors who would *automatically* vote against a death sentence.[47] *Witherspoon v. Illinois* had the effect of vacating many existing death sentences, imposed by juries selected in the same manner as Witherspoon's, although many of these would be reimposed after new sentencing hearings.

Jackson and *Witherspoon* concerned details of trial procedure, not the constitutionality of capital punishment itself. That issue finally arrived before the Court in late 1968, in another non-LDF case. Edward Boykin had been sentenced to death in Alabama after pleading guilty to robbery. When the Supreme Court agreed to hear his case, Amsterdam produced a lengthy amicus brief on the LDF's behalf, arguing that the death penalty for robbery was a cruel and unusual punishment. The brief was a wide-ranging discussion of the death penalty's history and current use, concluding that "the lesson of Anglo-American history is clear beyond all mistaking that the advance of civilization has been marked precisely by the progressive abandonment of the death penalty." The "evolving standards of decency" that were the Court's stated criteria for evaluating Eighth Amendment claims thus disapproved of capital punishment, at least for robbery. But it turned out to be unclear whether Boykin had realized the consequences of pleading guilty, so the Court reversed his conviction on that ground without addressing the LDF's broader argument.[48] The first major battle at the Supreme Court had no winner.

The LDF lawyers finally got one of their own cases before the Supreme Court in late 1968. *Maxwell v. Bishop*, the challenge to William Maxwell's death sentence for rape on the ground of race discrimination, had been the first important case of the LDF's campaign. When the Supreme Court agreed to hear the case, however, it expressly refused to consider the race issue. It accepted the case only on the LDF's other two arguments: that the unguided discretion given to juries to choose between life and death was inconsistent with due process, and that Arkansas's single-verdict procedure was likewise unconstitutional. As in most states, capital trials in Arkansas ended in a single verdict, at which the jury would declare guilt or innocence and, if the defendant was guilty, simultaneously announce the sentence. The procedure put defense lawyers in a bind. The most promising way to avoid a death sentence in the event of conviction was to present the defendant to the jury as a full human being, who had battled all his life against difficult circumstances. But the defendant's life story was also likely to include facts suggestive of his guilt, especially a criminal record. This was the LDF's second argument in *Maxwell*—that the constitution required bifurcating the trial into two proceedings, one on guilt and the other on sentencing, to permit an effective defense on both issues.

No one outside the Supreme Court knew it at the time, but after oral argument in early 1969 the Justices voted eight to one to declare Arkansas's death penalty unconstitutional. There was no consensus, however, on exactly why. Justices Abe Fortas and Thurgood Marshall thought a bifurcated trial was a constitutional requirement. John Harlan was leaning that way. Warren, Douglas, and Brennan agreed, but they also concluded that the lack of standards to guide the jury's life-or-death decision was a denial of due process. Potter Stewart and Byron White wanted to vacate Maxwell's death sentence for a reason Stewart first suggested in oral argument: the jury had been selected by the same method the Court had just rejected in *Witherspoon*. Hugo Black was alone in voting against Maxwell. Had Harlan been more decisive, a five- or six-Justice majority would have invalidated most capital sentencing schemes in the country on the bifurcated trial issue in the spring of 1969. But that never happened. Douglas circulated a draft majority opinion that declared Arkansas's scheme unconstitutional for the lack of a bifurcated trial. The opinion was quickly joined by Warren, Brennan, Marshall, and Fortas, to form a majority. Brennan wrote a concurring opinion also requiring standards, an opinion joined by Warren. Black circulated a dissent. Stewart circulated a short opinion reversing on the *Witherspoon* issue, and White joined it. Only Harlan's final vote remained.[49]

Before Harlan could make up his mind, Fortas resigned from the Court, forced out by the disclosure in the press of a series of unseemly financial arrangements. Harlan refused to replace Fortas as the fifth vote for declaring Arkansas's death penalty procedure unconstitutional. Without a majority for any course of action, the Justices set the case for reargument the following term. By then Earl Warren had retired as Chief Justice and had been replaced by Warren Burger, who found no constitutional violation in the absence of either standards or bifurcation. Fortas's seat had not yet been filled, so there were only eight Justices on the Court the second time around. Harlan had finally decided that a bifurcated trial was a constitutional requirement, but it was too late. Without Warren or Fortas, there were only four votes for that position, even including Harlan. In the end the Court took the easiest way out, vacating Maxwell's death sentence on the *Witherspoon* ground originally suggested by Stewart.[50] Although they did not know it at the time, the LDF lawyers had come within a whisker of a major victory.

On the day the *Maxwell* decision was announced, the Court agreed to hear two new cases, *McGautha v. California* and *Crampton v. Ohio*, both of which raised the issues the Court had failed to address in *Maxwell*. The LDF repeated the arguments it had made in *Maxwell*, but with Warren replaced by Burger, and with Fortas's seat now occupied by Harry Blackmun, the audience was less receptive than it had been a year earlier. A "bifurcated trial is a ludicrous thing," Burger argued at the Justices' conference immediately after the cases were argued. "This is an oblique attack on capital punishment . . . [the] abolition of capital punishment is what the case is all about." Harlan changed his mind and now agreed that the single-verdict procedure was consistent with due process. Of the six Justices who had once interpreted the constitution to require a bifurcated trial, only three were left—Douglas, Brennan, and Marshall. The same three were the only Justices who concluded that due process required standards to guide the jury's decision.[51]

Harlan's exhaustive opinion for the Court revealed none of his earlier vacillation. Bifurcation could not be part of due process, he explained, because criminal defendants had traditionally been subject to all the risks of cross-examination as a price for testifying in their own defense. Standards to guide the jury could not be part of due process for the same historical reason. Juries had never been guided by standards, dating back to the earliest statutes giving them sentencing discretion in capital cases. In any event, Harlan concluded, formulating standards would be an impossible task. "To identify before the fact those characteristics of criminal homicides and their perpetrators which call for the death penalty," Harlan explained, "and to express these characteristics in language which can be fairly understood and applied by the sentencing authority, appear to be tasks which are beyond present human ability."[52]

The movement to use the courts to abolish capital punishment seemed to have come to an end. A month after deciding *McGautha* and *Crampton*, the Court agreed to hear a group of cases raising the question of whether the death penalty constituted cruel and unusual punishment, but with six Justices squarely against them, the LDF lawyers and their allies could not have been optimistic. The issue was different in a technical sense from those decided in *McGautha* and *Crampton*, in that it involved the Eighth Amendment rather than the due process clause of the Fourteenth. As a practical matter, however, the Court was hardly likely to look favorably on a challenge to capital punishment dressed up in different legal language. The Justices had just approved of the procedures by which the death penalty was administered. There seemed to be little chance that they would disapprove of the penalty itself.

Struck by Lightning

The view from inside the Court was at first not very different. Black wanted to decide the Eighth Amendment cases as soon as possible, so the issue "may be disposed of once and for all . . . to make it clear to the nation that the death penalty and all of its aspects pass constitutional muster." Brennan was convinced that he was the only one who would find capital punishment unconstitutional, after hearing from Marshall and Douglas that neither believed the death penalty amounted to cruel and unusual punishment. "For the life of me," Douglas remarked to his colleagues in June 1971, just before the Court agreed to hear the cases, "I do not see from listening to any member of the Court, how anyone would entertain the thought that as a matter of constitutional law the death penalty was prohibited." Even as late as January 1972, when the newest Justices, Lewis Powell and William Rehnquist, took their seats just in time for oral argument, Powell was sure the Court would hold the death penalty constitutional.[53]

After combing through its nearly two hundred pending capital cases, the Court had agreed to hear four. Two were rape cases—*Jackson v. Georgia*, chosen because Lucious Jackson was represented by the LDF, so the Court could be sure the Eighth Amendment attack would be well presented, and *Branch v. Texas*, picked because, as Brennan's and White's recommendation put it, "it seems pretty clear that the victim suffered no special injury." If there was ever to be a case in which the death penalty was disproportionately severe for rape, in other words, Elmer Branch's was the one. The other two were murder cases—*Aikens v. California*, chosen because Ernest Aikens was represented not just by the LDF but also by Jerome Falk, one of Justice Douglas's former law clerks, and *Furman v. Georgia*, another LDF case. By hearing appeals from death sentences for both crimes, the Court was leaving itself the intermediate option of finding capital punishment cruel and unusual for rape but not for murder.[54]

Once again the LDF lawyers and their allies prepared a brief surveying the history of capital punishment to demonstrate that "evolving standards of decency" had rendered the death penalty cruel and unusual. The LDF's brief conceded that capital punishment could not have been found unconstitutional in an earlier era. But by the 1970s, the brief argued, "capital punishment has largely gone the way of flogging and banishment, progressively excluded by this Nation and by the civilized nations of men from the register of legitimate penal sanctions." The death penalty, to be sure, lingered on in the criminal codes of most states, but the LDF believed that time was on its side. "Like flogging and banishment, capital punishment is condemned by history," the brief maintained, "and will sooner or later be condemned by this Court under the Constitution. The question is whether that condemnation should come sooner or later." The brief emphasized that capital punishment was being abandoned by countries around the world, including the United States, where no executions had been conducted since 1967. The LDF admitted that current public opinion polls regularly found half the American people in favor of the death penalty, but discounted such findings as "notoriously fickle and particularly unreliable after several years without an execution." The proper measure of American attitudes, according to the LDF, was not what people say but what they do, as evidenced by the decline in the annual number of executions, a phenomenon reflecting "an overwhelming national repulsion against actual use of the penalty of death."

Toward the end of the brief the LDF devoted only a few pages to the issue that had brought it into the issue of capital punishment in the first place: the racial disparity in capital sentencing. Coming off *Maxwell v. Bishop*, in which the LDF had lost on the discrimination issue in the Court of Appeals (in an opinion written by Harry Blackmun, now a member of the Supreme Court), and in which the Supreme Court had specifically refused to address the issue, it was a prudent decision to downplay discrimination. For lawyers racial disparity was a matter addressed under the equal protection clause of the Fourteenth Amendment, but the Court had agreed to decide only the Eighth Amendment question of cruel and unusual punishment, which again counseled against a strategy that emphasized discrimination.

The LDF nevertheless found a clever way to connect the two issues. It was the very unusualness of capital punishment, the brief argued, that permitted discrimination. A "State can discriminate racially and not get caught at it," the LDF pointed out, "if it kills men only sporadically, not too often, by being arbitrary in selecting the victims of discrimination." Whether or not the argument made sense as a matter of mathematics, lawyers could recognize that it was right as a practical matter. A conscious government policy of wholesale discrimination in sentencing would leave a paper trail demonstrating intentional racism on the part of individual officials. But a death sentence imposed only in rare cases, without any rational mechanism for choosing those cases, permitted racially discriminatory results that could not be traced to anyone's intent to discriminate and thus could not be redressed under the Fourteenth Amendment.

The LDF lawyers recognized that discrimination could be made troubling to the Justices even where it was not legally cognizable in its own right. Subsuming a discrimination argument within the broader Eighth Amendment attack on the death penalty would prove to be a brilliant strategic decision.[55]

The Justices sat down on January 21, 1972, after oral argument, for their only formal face-to-face discussion of the cases. Speaking in the customary order of seniority, Burger went first. "All of us have reservations about the death penalty," he began. But the infrequency of executions did not make them "unusual" under the Eighth Amendment, because the constitution itself so clearly contemplated the existence of capital punishment. Douglas spoke next, and he had a surprise. Amsterdam and the LDF had persuaded him that the problem of race discrimination could be addressed under the Eighth Amendment. Douglas had been bothered in *Maxwell* and *McGautha* by the lack of standards to guide the jury, and now he saw a way to tie all his concerns together. The "lack of standards makes the system discriminatory," he explained, and if the system was "discriminatory in practice, it's unusual under the Eighth Amendment." The LDF had made one convert.

Brennan's expected vote against the death penalty gave that side a 2–1 lead, and then came an even greater surprise. The next in order of seniority was Stewart, who, although the author of *Witherspoon*, had not supported any of the more sweeping challenges to capital punishment. But Stewart was growing more troubled by the randomness with which the death penalty was imposed. That two identical crimes could be punished so differently, one with prison and the other with death, was weighing on his mind. Stewart announced his tentative view that capital punishment was unconstitutional. His vote was the third against the death penalty, with five Justices still to speak. The three recent Nixon appointees, Blackmun, Powell, and Rehnquist, would speak last, and everyone expected them to vote to uphold capital punishment. All would depend on White and Marshall.

Byron White was a gruff man with little sympathy for criminals. He had dissented at virtually every opportunity in the Warren Court's famous cases expanding the constitutional rights of criminal defendants, from *Miranda* through *Witherspoon*. He did not share Brennan's expansive view of the Court's role as a motor for social change. Like Stewart, however, White was in the process of changing his mind. "The nub of the case is that only a small proportion are put to death," he told his colleagues, and he could not believe that small proportion was chosen rationally. White may not have cared much about criminal defendants, but he had an instinctive dislike of arbitrariness. He found it intolerable that "one jury will put a person to death while on the same facts another is not." Like Douglas and Stewart, White was persuaded by Amsterdam and the LDF that the irrational pattern of death sentences made capital punishment cruel and unusual under the Eighth Amendment. He accordingly cast the fourth vote. When Marshall quickly cast the fifth, a majority of the Court had found the death penalty unconstitutional. Blackmun, Powell, and Rehnquist voted as expected, but their votes no longer mattered. To the Justices' own astonishment, they were on the verge of one of the most significant decisions in the history of the Court.[56]

Because the five Justices in the majority had expressed differing reasons for declaring the death penalty unconstitutional, and because two of them, Stewart and White, had been hesitant, an unusual step was taken: all nine set to writing opinions of their own. The five Justices who formed the majority were well aware that they were making new law. In the absence of the judge's conventional raw material—precedent, explicit text, and the like—and given the intensely moral nature of the issue at hand, each of the five produced an idiosyncratic opinion. None of the five joined any part of anyone else's opinion. There were few points on which more than two or three Justices agreed.

Douglas's opinion put discrimination front and center. He began with what he called the "incontestable" proposition that "the death penalty inflicted on one defendant is 'unusual' if it discriminates against him by reason of his race, religion, wealth, social position, or class, or if it is imposed under a procedure that gives room for the play of such prejudices." So defined, the Eighth Amendment clearly outlawed capital punishment as it had been practiced for all of American history, because of the race and class biases that had always played a part in determining who lived or died. But Douglas's opening premise was far from incontestable. No court, certainly not the Supreme Court, had ever said it before.

Brennan paid little overt attention to discrimination, focusing instead on the declining rate of executions. His opinion hinged on the assertion that Americans had demonstrated their rejection of the death penalty by their gradually mounting refusal to put it into practice. The argument's sticky point was the failure of most states to pass statutes abolishing capital punishment and the consistent polling results showing that half the population or more favored retaining the death penalty. Brennan adopted the LDF's response, that popular attitudes are best measured by watching what people do, not listening to what they say. "When an unusually severe punishment is authorized for wide-scale application but not, because of society's refusal, inflicted save in a few instances," Brennan concluded, "the inference is compelling that there is a deep-seated reluctance to inflict it. Indeed, the likelihood is great that the punishment is tolerated only because of its disuse." This was not an accurate reading of public opinion. Juries were still quite willing to sentence criminals to death. The decline in the execution rate was much less a result of popular disapproval of capital punishment than of procedural changes in the criminal justice system, changes largely created by the Court itself. The inaccuracy of Brennan's assessment of popular attitudes would be demonstrated very clearly in succeeding years.

Marshall's main point was that capital punishment served no legitimate purpose. He reviewed the recent literature on deterrence, which tended not to find any reduction in the murder rate caused by the death penalty. He noted that the death penalty was no more effective than prison at preventing recidivism. So far he was on firm ground, but there were two more necessary steps to the argument, and neither was easy. First, Marshall had to argue that retribution was not a legitimate penological goal. He cited Beccaria for the proposition that "punishment as retribution has been condemned by scholars for centuries." Beccaria, however, was a reformer, who was primarily interested in *criticizing* existing practices, not describing them. Marshall then turned to the even shakier argument that the Eighth Amendment itself had been intended to outlaw retribution as an end of punishment, a notion that would have seemed absurd in the eighteenth century, even to opponents of the death penalty like Benjamin Rush or William Bradford. One could certainly argue that retribution was not regarded as a legitimate goal in 1972, or that retribution had been on the decline among intellectuals for a century, but it was wrong to claim that retribution had been illegitimate for two hundred years. Second, Marshall had to make the leap from a *policy* argument, that capital punishment served no legitimate penological goal, to a *constitutional* argument, that it was therefore cruel and unusual. To hold capital punishment a violation of the Eighth Amendment, Marshall had to find that the Eighth Amendment implicitly incorporated the latest criminological learning at any given time.

The opinions of Stewart and White were far narrower. They found no need to address the constitutionality of the death penalty "in the abstract," because the legislative schemes at issue inflicted death on such a minuscule proportion of those who were convicted. That actual executions were so rare was evidence, in Stewart's view, of a determination by state legislatures that capital punishment served no purpose. Stewart then discussed his real concern. "These death sentences are cruel and unusual," he declared—in what became the best-known sentence from any of the nine opinions—"in the same way that being struck by lightning is cruel and unusual." The problem with capital punishment in practice was that it was imposed only on "a capriciously selected random handful" of criminals. Left unstated by Stewart or White was the obvious implication— that if a state could devise a sentencing scheme that rationally distinguished between who would live and who would die, the death penalty would once again be permissible.

The four newest Justices, all Nixon appointees, wrote dissenting opinions. Nixon had campaigned on a promise to appoint judges who would put a stop to the Warren Court's expansion of the rights of criminal defendants. In *Furman* he got what he wanted. Burger, Powell, and Rehnquist all began strategically by pointing out, in case anyone had failed to notice, that only Brennan and Marshall had unambiguously declared capital punishment unconstitutional. Stewart, White, and perhaps Douglas had found fault only with the way the states *administered* capital punishment. As Burger explained, in an unconcealed suggestion to state officials, "legislative bodies may seek to bring their laws into compliance with the Court's ruling by providing standards for juries and judges to follow in determining the sentence in capital cases or by more narrowly defining the crimes for which the penalty is to be imposed." Burger, Blackmun, and Powell all took issue with the notion that American public opinion had turned against the death penalty. What death penalty opponents called "public opinion," Powell concluded, was really the opinion of a narrow elite. In his working notes Powell observed that the abolitionist movement "has been singularly successful in the law reviews, the scholarly journals & some of the press. But if the standard is the public—not just an elitist segment—the crusade has not attained notable success."[57] The content of public opinion was, unlike some of the other issues involved in the cases, an empirical question. It would be put to the test in succeeding years.

The nine opinions in *Furman v. Georgia* occupied 233 pages of the official reports, the most for any case in the history of the Court to that time.[58] The Justices divided along philosophical lines that would have been familiar to participants in the earlier death penalty debates going all the way back to the late eighteenth century. The Justices willing to use the constitution to strike down capital punishment, especially Douglas, Brennan, and Marshall, were believers in progress, in the capacity of the legal system to reflect and even promote cultural change. This was a trait these constitutional abolitionists shared with the political abolitionists of earlier eras. The dissenting Justices tended to be more skeptical of the possibility of progress, just like the retentionists of earlier periods. But the constitutional abolitionists had to work against a double skepticism: they had to overcome not just doubts about progress but doubts about whether the courts were the proper governmental institutions for promoting progress. The LDF was able to leap both hurdles in *Furman*, but the second hurdle would in later years prove insurmountable. The nervousness about judicial power at the core of the American constitutional tradition would limit what abolitionists could attain in court.

In retrospect, *Furman* stands at the confluence of three broader, interrelated trends in constitutional law, all of which were at their high point in the late 1960s and early 1970s. Most important was the idea that constitutional law should be a vehicle for social change, and that the Court ought to promote change through innovative interpretations of the constitution. *Roe v. Wade,* to pick the most famous example, was decided a year after *Furman.* None of the five Justices in the *Furman* majority went as far as to argue explicitly, as Goldberg had argued in his 1963 internal memorandum in *Rudolph,* that the Court should lead rather than follow public opinion, but Brennan and Marshall were quick to reject the most obvious manifestations of public opinion—polls and the output of state legislatures—as inadequate. Marshall suggested that "American citizens know almost nothing about capital punishment" and was sure that if they only knew as much as he did "the great mass of citizens would conclude . . . that the death penalty is immoral and therefore unconstitutional." The assertion was not as arrogant as it may sound, in that Marshall was the only member of the Court with any significant experience as a lawyer in capital cases. He genuinely *did* know more about the death penalty than most people. One may fairly wonder, however, whether the causal connection between empirical knowledge and moral belief is as direct as Marshall believed. (When his prediction was tested in a survey three years later, information about the death penalty did cause many people to change their minds, but not in quantities approaching a "great mass." Even after respondents were told how capital punishment actually worked in practice, the death penalty still attracted as many supporters as opponents.[59])

Furman was also at the high-water mark of a second trend in constitutional law, the Court's gradual standardization of criminal procedure. In case after case the Court had removed official discretion from various aspects of the criminal justice system, because of the frequency with which that discretion was abused, and replaced it with sets of rules. The most famous of these cases was *Miranda v. Arizona*, establishing the circumstances under which the police could question suspects, but a host of other cases had set forth constitutional requirements for everything from obtaining search warrants to identifying suspects to conducting trials.[60] Capital sentencing was one more pocket of easily abusable discretion. By the early 1970s it was a glaring exception to a criminal procedure the Court had gradually bureaucratized. The opinions of Douglas, Stewart, and White reveal a high level of discomfort with a decisionmaking process completely ungoverned by rules.

Finally, *Furman* was decided near the peak of the Court's confidence in its ability to minimize the effects of racism. The year before *Furman* the Court approved of inter-district school busing; a few years later it would permit affirmative action.[61] Race discrimination was not formally part of *Furman*, and Douglas was the only Justice who emphasized it. But everyone knew it was lurking not far beneath the surface. The "randomness" that bothered the other Justices in the majority was not a true randomness. (Stewart's lightning analogy would have been accurate only if lightning chose its victims by race.) Randomness became in effect a code word for discrimination.

The genius of Amsterdam and the LDF attorneys was to find a way to put racism in the case within the confines of preexisting Eighth Amendment doctrine, a move that allowed White and Stewart to fight racism while claiming to fight only case-by-case inconsistency. The lawyers' superior advocacy seems to be the only answer to a puzzle. A year before, in

McGautha, White and Stewart had refused to hold that the Fourteenth Amendment's due process clause, a provision specifically about court procedures, required some means of guiding the jury's discretion to impose the death penalty. But in *Furman* they agreed that such standards were a constitutional requirement and were even willing to locate the requirement in the Eighth Amendment, a provision that says nothing about procedure. The most likely explanation is the simplest: that Amsterdam persuaded them to change their minds.

Five Justices had voted to invalidate the capital sentencing statutes of every state. The six hundred inmates on death rows around the country would all have their sentences vacated, because all had been sentenced according to a procedure that had now been declared unconstitutional. Capital punishment no longer existed anywhere in the United States. In Arkansas the electric chair would be unplugged and used for giving inmates haircuts. In Pennsylvania the room in which executions were held would be partitioned into offices. In New Hampshire the execution chamber would be used to store vegetables. In Idaho it would hold medical equipment.[62]

As the news hit the wire services, the LDF lawyers rejoiced. "General disbelief," Michael Meltsner recalled. "Numbness. Tears in people's eyes. Slowly smiles replaced gaping jaws; laughter and embraces filled the halls." Seven years of often frustrating work had paid off. At a quickly arranged party that night in the LDF office, lawyers danced to a rock band renamed "The Eighth Amendment."[63]

The celebration would not last long.

10

RESURRECTION

B Y THE END OF THE TWENTIETH century capital punishment would be back with a vengeance. The annual number of death sentences would be close to three hundred, a figure higher than at any time since the Justice Department began keeping count in the 1930s. The annual number of executions would be nearly one hundred, the most since the early 1950s. Death rows around the country would house more than thirty-five hundred condemned prisoners, easily the most in American history. After nearly a century of declining popularity and waning per capita use from the late nineteenth century through the early 1970s, capital punishment experienced a sudden resurrection.

But the death penalty looked very different in the late twentieth century. It took on a new political resonance, as a shorthand way for elected officials to signify to voters a cluster of positions on other issues. It was now administered within a complex structure of constitutional law that shaped the conduct of trials and the tactics of abolitionists. The old combination of the death penalty's popularity in the abstract and the human reluctance to apply it in specific cases—a hesitancy now expressed in the language of constitutional law—created a cumbersome, expensive, and ultimately pointless mode of litigation, as well as a new method of execution. Meanwhile, the death penalty placed the United States in an increasingly uncomfortable international role, as one of the very few wealthy democracies that executed its criminals.

Evolving Standards of Decency

The Supreme Court's 1972 decision in *Furman v. Georgia*, declaring existing death penalty laws unconstitutional, touched off the biggest flurry of capital punishment legislation the nation had ever seen. The day after the Court announced its judgment, legislators in five states professed their intention to introduce bills to resurrect capital punishment. President Richard Nixon asked the FBI to supply him with incidents in which convicted killers had committed a second murder after being released from prison. In California, where the state Supreme Court had found capital punishment banned by the state constitution, support for the death penalty was strong enough to put the issue on the ballot in November 1972. By a margin of two to one the voters amended the state constitution to permit the death penalty explicitly. By 1976, four years after *Furman*, thirty-five states plus the federal government had enacted new capital punishment statutes.[1]

Public opinion on capital punishment, as measured by the Gallup Poll, shifted dramatically. In March 1972, a few months before *Furman*, supporters outnumbered opponents 50 to 42 percent. The figures had barely changed in the previous few years. In November 1972, however, a few months after *Furman*, support beat opposition 57 to 32 percent. An eight-point margin had grown into a twenty-five-point margin in seven months. By 1976 supporters outnumbered opponents 65 to 28 percent, the widest gap since the early 1950s. The shift was uniform across all regions of the country.[2] The belief that Americans had repudiated the death penalty—the linchpin of the Legal Defense Fund's constitutional argument and of Justice Brennan's *Furman* opinion—had been decisively disproven. The "evolving standards of decency" that calibrated the constitutionality of the death penalty had once been progressing toward abolition, but now they were evolving the other way.

Neither the polling data nor the number of states with statutes authorizing capital punishment would change much for the rest of the century. This suggests that the swing back to the death penalty would have taken place eventually, with or without *Furman*. In the history of the death penalty, periods of abolition have always been followed by periods of sharp diminution in the strength of the abolitionist movement. The last three decades of the twentieth century, a period of mostly rising crime rates in which concern for law and order loomed large, would probably have been an era of restoration even without *Furman*. But if *Furman* did not influence the *direction* of change, it almost certainly influenced the *speed* of change. *Furman* suddenly made capital punishment a more salient issue than it had been in decades, perhaps ever. People who previously had had little occasion to think about the death penalty now saw it on the front page of the newspaper. *Furman,* like other landmark cases, had the effect of calling its opponents to action.

The new death penalty statutes, drafted to conform to the opinions of Justices Stewart and White, looked very different from those in force before 1972. What troubled Stewart and White in *Furman* was randomness. When juries were given complete discretion to choose between life and death, the two Justices concluded, the resulting pattern of verdicts had no rhyme or reason. There were two ways to correct the problem, and some states tried each.

One solution was to take discretion away from the jury by returning to the old practice of defining a class of crimes for which the penalty would always be death. In North Carolina, for instance, death became the mandatory sentence for first-degree murder and aggravated rape. In Louisiana the legislature made death the mandatory sentence for first-degree murder, aggravated rape, and aggravated kidnapping. If randomness was a product of discretion, it could be eradicated by the establishment of a clear rule.

The other solution was to legislate standards that would narrow the jury's discretion in determining who would live and die. The states that took this route were guided by the Model Penal Code, drafted a decade earlier by a group of eminent lawyers, judges, and law professors. Under the Model Penal Code, once a defendant had been convicted of first-degree murder, sentencing would take place at a separate proceeding, at which each side would be allowed to introduce evidence. The Code listed eight "aggravating circumstances," factors that tended to make a death sentence more appropriate, such as the fact that the defendant had previously been convicted of another violent felony. In order to sentence the defendant to death, the jury would have to find at least one aggravating circumstance present. The Code also listed eight "mitigating circumstances," factors that tended to make a death sentence less appropriate, such as the defendant's youth or lack of significant prior criminal history. If an aggravating circumstance was present, the jury was then to determine whether the presence of any mitigating circumstances called for leniency. The point was to specify precisely what the jury was to consider in choosing the appropriate sentence.[3]

After *Furman,* the Model Penal Code lived up to its name. Many states adopted the Code's general approach, with a separate sentencing proceeding after a jury verdict, but with considerable variation in the details of what the jury would be asked to do. Florida created eight aggravating circumstances and only seven mitigating circumstances. Georgia enacted a statute including ten aggravating circumstances but no mitigating circumstances. Once the jury had found one aggravating circumstance, it was simply to weigh all the aggravating and mitigating evidence, without reference to specified statutory circumstances, in settling on the appropriate sentence. In Texas the possibility of capital punishment was reserved for certain classes of murder, including murder of a police officer, murder committed during the course of specified felonies, and murder committed for financial gain. Once a defendant had been convicted of one of those types of murder, the jury was to impose death only if the murder had been deliberate and if the defendant was likely to commit violent criminal acts in the future. These new death penalty statutes were different in their particulars, but they all had a common structure, designed to rationalize the process of capital sentencing and thereby satisfy the concerns of Justices Stewart and White.

The new sentencing schemes were immediately put to use. Only 42 people were sentenced to death in 1973, but there were 149 death sentences in 1974, probably more than in any year since 1942. (The Justice Department did not count death sentences from 1951 to 1959.) In 1975, 298 people were sentenced to death—far more than in any previous year for which data exist.[4] The lawyers who had battled for years to persuade the Supreme Court to abolish the death penalty had inadvertently created a monster. Within three years of their victory, more death sentences were being imposed than ever.

No executions could be held, however, until the Supreme Court had ruled on the constitutionality of the new sentencing schemes. In October 1974 the Court agreed to hear the case of the murderer Jesse Fowler, another Legal Defense Fund client, sentenced to death under North Carolina's new mandatory death penalty. There were already approximately 150 condemned people in the country, and their number was growing nearly every week. Oral argument was scheduled for April 1975, during the last argument week of the Court's term, in the expectation that a decision could be published before the term ended in late June or early July.

In March, in a clear indication of the changing political climate, the federal government filed a lengthy amicus brief supporting the constitutionality of capital punishment. The federal government had stayed out of *Furman*, despite its obvious interest in defending the constitutionality of the federal capital statutes, which suggests some uncertainty within the Nixon administration in 1971 as to the possible political costs of taking a position. By 1975 supporting capital punishment entailed no political cost at all. Solicitor General Robert Bork, who viewed opposition to capital punishment as a symptom of moral decay, and who was motivated even more by a visceral disgust for the constitutional philosophy of Justices Brennan and Marshall, was given free rein to argue that the Court should overrule *Furman*. "If this Court were to hold that the death penalty violates evolving standards of decency," Bork asked, what was one to make of all the new capital sentencing statutes enacted in the past two years? Did they mean that Congress and the state legislatures "are unenlightened, that they are out of step with contemporary moral standards and the will and spirit of the people who elected them?"[5]

Just as in *Maxwell v. Bishop* a few years earlier, personnel changes on the Court delayed a decision. Justice Douglas had suffered a stroke during the winter, and with one brief exception had been in the hospital ever since. The death penalty was so important to him that he had himself wheeled to the bench for the argument in *Fowler*. But Douglas was too ill to attend the Justices' conference on the case later in the week. The Court deferred a decision on *Fowler* until the following year, when it would be at full strength.[6]

Capital cases continued to pile up at the Court in the meantime. By September 1975 the appeals of thirty-seven condemned prisoners had made their way to the Court, where they were all being held until the Court could rule on the constitutionality of the new sentencing schemes. It became clear that *Fowler* was not the best case to decide. Since Jesse Fowler's conviction, the North Carolina legislature had changed its statute. A decision in Fowler's case would have little bearing on any of the other cases. It would be far more efficient to decide cases involving inmates sentenced under the new statutes, because a decision in one would in effect be a decision in many.[7] But no action was taken until after Justice Douglas retired in November. His replacement, John Paul Stevens, was confirmed in December. Finally, in January 1976, the Court announced that it would hear five murder cases, one each from Georgia, Florida, Texas, North Carolina, and Louisiana. The sentencing schemes of those states encompassed the full range of variations in the post-*Furman* statutes, so the Court would be able to rule on the constitutionality of every new statute at a single time. To ensure a decision as quickly as possible, the Court set an expedited briefing schedule and ordered argument to take place in late March. The defendant in the Georgia case was Troy Gregg, who had been convicted of murder. The set of five cases would become collectively known as *Gregg v. Georgia*.

Tony Amsterdam and the LDF again took the lead in presenting the case to the Court. They represented Jerry Jurek (the condemned prisoner in the Texas case), James Woodson (North Carolina), and Stanislaus Roberts (Louisiana), and they filed amicus briefs on behalf of Charles Proffitt (Florida) and Troy Gregg. Each of the states had its own lawyer, but all five were overshadowed by Robert Bork, who filed another brief for the federal government seeking to overrule *Furman*, and who was given more time at oral argument than any of the states' lawyers. What were in principle five separate cases turned into a single contest between two of the foremost lawyers of the era—Amsterdam, by this time on the faculty at Stanford, who had devoted his career to abolishing the death penalty, and Bork, on leave from Yale to serve as Solicitor General, who had become the nation's leading advocate of the constitutionality of capital punishment.

Amsterdam and the LDF faced a strategic puzzle. They had advanced two kinds of arguments in *Furman* and the earlier cases: a *procedural* argument, that the means by which capital punishment was imposed (especially jury discretion and the single verdict) rendered it unconstitutional; and a *substantive* argument, that the death penalty was unconstitutional regardless of how it was administered. The substantive argument had commanded only two votes in *Furman*, and it was not likely to do any better four years later. The procedural argument had been the winner, but now the states had corrected the procedural flaws the LDF had identified. To have any hope of success, the LDF would have to find procedural problems in the new statutes. But making that argument opened the LDF lawyers to the charge that by their interpretation no death penalty procedure could *ever* satisfy the Constitution. And if that charge was justified, the procedural argument would have turned into the very substantive argument the LDF needed to avoid. Amsterdam and the LDF were boxed in by *Furman*. They had to find fault with the post-*Furman* methods of capital sentencing without seeming to find fault with the death penalty in general. Their argument had to leave room for the implicit possibility of a constitutional procedure for implementing capital punishment, but the argument could never specify what the possibility would be. For years the LDF had made procedural arguments to serve a substantive goal, the abolition of the death penalty, because the procedural arguments were the only ones with any chance of succeeding. In *Gregg* the mismatch between procedural means and substantive ends was staring the LDF square in the face.

The LDF's briefs all made the same point. The sentencing schemes of all five states purported to do away with discretion in the choice between life and death, but all they really did was shift that discretion to other parts of the process. "Prosecutorial charging and plea-bargaining discretion, jury discretion to convict of one or another amorphously distinguished 'capital' or non-capital crime, and gubernatorial discretion to grant or withhold clemency are all equally uncontrolled and uncontrollable," the LDF contended. "In its parts and as a whole, the process is inveterately capricious."[8]

There was nothing else the LDF could say, but the argument inevitably led Amsterdam into trouble at oral argument. Chief Justice Burger was the first to pounce. "Since there is always an initial discretion on the part of the prosecutor, and . . . at the far end a power of clemency by an executive," he pointed out, "then no statutes can meet [your] standards." Amsterdam was in a bind. If he agreed, he would be conceding that he was in fact arguing that capital punishment was unconstitutional under all circumstances, and he would lose. If he disagreed, he would be asked to identify the kind of statute that *would* meet constitutional requirements—that is, asked to identify the circumstances under which he would concede defeat. Amsterdam did the best anyone could do in the situation: he responded that he would "eventually take the position" Burger accused him of taking, but that "it is not a position that needs to be taken in this case" in order for the Court to rule in his favor. But the issue could not be avoided. "Suppose just one crime, say, air piracy, and nothing else," Justice Stevens posited. "Would your argument about total discretion render such a statute unconstitutional?" The question put Amsterdam back in the same bind. If he said no, he would be telling his adversaries how to bring back capital punishment. If he said yes, he would be confirming Stevens's suspicion that the LDF's argument would have the effect of invalidating every conceivable sentencing scheme. Amsterdam struggled to answer, but the dilemma was irresolvable. Either the states could draft constitutional statutes or they could not. There was no way to have both at once.[9]

At the Justices' conference two days later, most of the votes were unsurprising. Brennan and Marshall stuck with the positions they had taken in *Furman*, that capital punishment was unconstitutional regardless of the procedures by which it was imposed. Burger, Blackmun, and Rehnquist stuck with their positions too. If the statutes at issue in *Furman* were constitutional, the new ones were easily so. White found that all five states had satisfied the concern with arbitrariness he had expressed in *Furman*, so he joined the three Nixon appointees in voting to uphold all five statutes.

The surprising votes were those of Stewart, Powell, and Stevens. "In light of what 35 states have done since 1972," Stewart explained, one "can no longer argue that capital punishment is incompatible with evolving standards of decency." As for his view in *Furman* that uncontrolled jury discretion allowed for random or discriminatory verdicts, the states had responded with varying degrees of success. The Georgia, Florida, and Texas statutes, which set out aggravating circumstances to guide the jury, were constitutional in Stewart's view. The North Carolina and Louisiana statutes, which provided mandatory death sentences for certain crimes, were not. No sentence could ever really be mandatory, because the jury could always convict the defendant of a lesser, noncapital crime. The uncontrolled discretion that had been present before *Furman* was simply pushed back to an earlier time, when the jury had to choose the crime of which the defendant was guilty. Powell then joined Stewart in the middle. Powell had dissented in *Furman*, but now that *Furman* had been decided, Powell, alone among the dissenters, was willing to treat it as precedent. His acceptance of *Furman* was helped along by his belief that standards to guide the jury, even if not a constitutional requirement, were nevertheless a good idea. Taking the Stewart and White opinions as the law, Powell announced that he would approve the Georgia, Florida, and Texas statutes, because of the guidance they provided to juries, but not the other two.

The tally thus far was four to uphold all the statutes, two to strike them all down, and two to uphold some but not others. Stevens, the newest Justice, cast the deciding vote. Having never written on capital punishment before, Stevens was alone among the nine Justices in not feeling the pull of consistency with his own individual opinion. "*Furman* is law for me and that's my starting point," Stevens explained. By *Furman* he meant the pivotal opinions of Stewart and White, requiring some means of channeling the jury's discretion, and for that reason he joined Stewart and Powell in the middle. The final vote was four to three to two.[10]

The configuration of the voting meant that in each of the five cases Stewart, Powell, and Stevens were in the majority. Seven of the nine Justices—everyone but Brennan and Marshall—approved of the sentencing schemes that guided the jury with aggravating (or both aggravating and mitigating) circumstances. Five of the Justices—the three in the middle plus Brennan and Marshall—found the mandatory death penalty unconstitutional.[11] The opinions were published on July 2, 1976, almost exactly four years after the Court had declared the death penalty unconstitutional in *Furman*.

Capital punishment was back. The states that had enacted mandatory death sentences after *Furman* quickly switched to guided discretion schemes after *Gregg*. Constitutional challenges to specific aspects of the sentencing process would continue for the rest of the century, but the ultimate question of the death penalty's constitutionality had been laid to rest. Six and a half months later Gary Gilmore of Utah became the first person executed in the United States in a decade.

Why Don't Our Laws Protect Us?

Capital punishment's popularity held steady for the rest of the century. Between 1977 and 1998 the percentage of those polled who favored the death penalty for murder fluctuated between 66 and 76 percent. The percentage who opposed the death penalty fluctuated between 19 and 28 percent. (Some people report no opinion, so the percentages do not add to 100.) This was a degree of support consistently higher than at any time since the first polls on the issue were taken in the 1930s. After a long period of growing skepticism, public opinion had quickly and decisively swung back toward capital punishment.

Support for capital punishment in the 1980s and 1990s was remarkably consistent across regions and demographic groups. The only significant disparity in attitudes turned on race, unsurprisingly, but people of all races tended to favor the death penalty. White people just liked it more. Whites annually favored capital punishment by approximately a 4–1 margin, while the margin was much smaller for nonwhites. In 1996, for example, whites supported capital punishment 75 percent to 18 percent, while nonwhites supported it 54 to 35 percent. There were other demographic differences, but none was very large. Men favored the death penalty a bit more than women; Republicans a bit more than Democrats; the rich a bit more than the poor. Capital punishment was almost equally popular in all parts of the country—in some years a few percentage points more popular in the West and the South than in the Northeast and the Midwest, but never more than a few. There was no regional or demographic group of which a majority opposed capital punishment.[12]

If only a small minority of Americans considered themselves opponents of the death penalty in principle, a majority harbored reservations about putting it into practice when presented with alternatives. In the late 1980s and early 1990s, when polls were rephrased to ask whether murderers should be sentenced to death *or* to life in prison without parole, slightly fewer than half of respondents preferred the death penalty. When the alternative to death was life in prison without parole plus restitution to the victim's family (financed by the prisoner's labor), support for the death penalty dropped to around 30 percent. These results exhibited some regional variation, but not much. Many of those who reported that they supported or favored capital punishment in the abstract might more accurately be said to have considered it an acceptable second choice.[13]

It was nevertheless true that in the 1980s and 1990s the great majority of Americans, in all parts of the country, favored the death penalty at least as an option. For an elected official to disagree with that sentiment in public was often tantamount to giving up hope of continuing one's career. The most visible example took place during the 1988 presidential election, when Michael Dukakis was widely believed to have lost any chance of winning after he emphasized his opposition to capital punishment during a debate against George Bush. Four years later, in the midst of the 1992 campaign, Bill Clinton made it a point to return to Arkansas to sign the death warrant for Ricky Rector, a brain-damaged inmate so oblivious to his fate that he planned to save the dessert from his last meal to eat after his execution. The only national political figure to speak out against capital punishment was Mario Cuomo, the governor of New York, who each year vetoed legislation that would have restored the death penalty in the state. Cuomo was popular enough in other respects to survive three terms as governor, but he lost reelection in 1994, in part because his opponent George Pataki made capital punishment a major part of his campaign.

(And indeed a statute bringing back the death penalty was the first legislation of the Pataki administration.) In all parts of the country, politicians opposed capital punishment at their peril.

The new importance of the death penalty as a national political issue could be seen in the contortions Jimmy Carter and his staff went through in 1977 to avoid taking any public position. Carter was ambivalent about capital punishment and had argued during the 1976 campaign that it should be limited to a few aggravated crimes such as murder committed by an inmate already serving a life sentence. But he had the misfortune to take office shortly after *Gregg* was decided and Congress took up the issue of reauthorizing a federal death penalty. "We both agree that this subject should be kept low-key for the time being, and a public statement made only if pressed to testify," advised Griffin Bell, Carter's attorney general. "Public opinion polls show about two thirds of the population in favor of the death penalty. Such a statement would subject you to severe criticism." When Senator John McClellan, the proponent of the capital punishment bill, fell ill, Carter's staff was grateful for the respite. "Fortunately, we will not be required to take a position on the issue in the foreseeable future," noted a relieved Doug Huron from the White House Counsel's office. "Justice officials have indicated that certain factors, including Senator McClellan's illness, make it likely that we can dodge the question." Ronald Reagan's staff experienced no such unease. In a television program produced in 1987 by the United States Information Agency, for example, Donald Macdonald, the director of the White House Drug Abuse Policy Office, calmly declared that even drug trafficking ought to be punished with death.[14] The nationwide popularity of capital punishment was a basic fact of political life from the mid-1970s on.

The absence of significant regional variation in public opinion is quite striking when one considers the stark regional differences in actual practice. As of 1999 there were thirty-eight states with the death penalty, only three more than in 1976. Of the twelve without, nine were in New England or the northern Midwest—Maine, Massachusetts, Rhode Island, Vermont, Iowa, Michigan, Minnesota, North Dakota, and Wisconsin. (The other three were Alaska, Hawaii, and West Virginia.) New England and the northern Midwest were the only parts of the country where homicide rates were considerably below the national average.[15] It may be that in those regions capital punishment was popular but not particularly salient; that is, few citizens were opposed to the death penalty but most supporters simply did not consider the issue an important one. The list of non–death penalty states included most of those that were early abolishers: Michigan, Rhode Island, and Wisconsin from before the Civil War; Iowa and Maine from the late nineteenth century; and Minnesota and North Dakota from the years before World War I. The absence of legislative change in these states is just what one would expect if the issue was of low salience. Decisions, once taken, tended to stick, because elected officials had little to gain from disturbing the status quo.

There were also pronounced regional differences in the pattern of executions and death sentences. Of the 598 executions conducted between 1977 and 1999, all but a handful took place in the South. Texas was the leader, with 199, followed at some distance by Virginia (73), Florida (44), Missouri (41), Louisiana (25), South Carolina (24), Georgia (23), Arkansas (21), Alabama (19), Arizona (19), Oklahoma (19), and North Carolina (15). The leader among the northern states was Illinois, with only 12. The distribution of death sentences was less lopsided, but a regional bias was still apparent. Of the eighteen states with more than 100 death sentences between 1973 and 1998, 13 were in the South.[16]

These figures raise two questions. If capital punishment as a general policy was no more popular in the South than in the North, why did the southern states have so many more death sentences? And why was the distribution of executions so much more uneven than the distribution of death sentences? As we have seen, for centuries the South, because of slavery, had possessed a distinct tradition of capital punishment. But that tradition had been built on racial discrimination, and by the 1980s and 1990s black defendants were no more likely than white defendants to be executed in most states. So why were executions so much more frequent in the South?

Much of the regional pattern of death sentences was caused by the fact that the murder rate was much higher in the South than in the North. In most years between 1976 and 1998 the homicide rate in the region encompassing Texas, Louisiana, Arkansas, and Oklahoma was three to four times greater than in New England, for example, and two to three times greater than in the northern Midwest. The number of death sentences in a state in the decades after *Furman* was closely correlated with the number of homicides in that state. Southerners had more opportunities to impose the death sentence than northerners did, and the prevalence of murder may have made them more willing than northerners to impose the death sentence in any given case. But differences in murder rates were most likely too small to account for the North-South disparity in death sentences, and certainly too small to account for the much larger disparity in actual executions. By the end of the century the southern states were conducting as many executions as they had in the 1940s, but executions were still rare in the North. The South picked up where it had left off; the North did not.

The remainder of these regional differences was probably attributable primarily to disparities in the way states provided defense lawyers. Defendants charged with capital murder were almost always too poor to pay a lawyer. In most of the northern states with statutes authorizing the death penalty, capital trials were handled by experienced public defenders, often public defenders who specialized in capital cases. In most of the South, by contrast, capital defendants were represented by lawyers in private practice, who were appointed by trial judges to handle individual cases. Compensation was so low that it often attracted the least skilled segment of the bar. Many of these lawyers had little or no experience trying capital cases; many had no experience in criminal matters at all; some lacked any conception of what they were supposed to do. Many made no effort to gather evidence that might help their clients avoid a death sentence. Horror stories abounded of defense lawyers who slept through parts of the trial, or who were too drunk to do their jobs, or who used racial epithets to refer to their own clients before the jury.[17] The prevalence of such woefully poor defense counsel in many of the southern states produced large numbers of death sentences. Similarly inept appellate counsel ensured that death sentences were upheld on appeal. In these states someone accused of a capital crime might obtain a competent lawyer only once his execution date had been set. The South could thus conduct the lion's share of the nation's executions even if the death penalty was no more popular in the South than in the North.

Of all the aspects of capital punishment's popularity in the last three decades of the twentieth century, perhaps the most curious was the increasing irrelevance of what had once been a crucial question—whether capital punishment deters murder any more than prison does. That issue, a staple of the debate since the early nineteenth century, was taken over in the 1970s by economists. Rather than simply matching jurisdictions similar in most respects other than the use of the death penalty, as earlier participants in the debate had done, the economists constructed equations expressing the murder rate as the product of a host of different variables, one of which was the likelihood of being executed. They could then use the statistical technique called multiple regression to measure the effect on the murder rate of changes in that one variable, while holding all the other variables constant. The first to estimate the deterrent effect of capital punishment by this method was Isaac Ehrlich, who in 1975 calculated that each execution prevented approximately eight murders. Ehrlich's work received an enormous amount of public attention for a technical article in an economics journal because of its timing: it appeared just as the Supreme Court was considering the constitutionality of the new capital statutes in *Fowler*, and it was brought to the Court's attention by the Solicitor General.[18]

But Ehrlich's work was very quickly subjected to intense criticism. Any attempt to represent the murder rate as the product of an equation requires specifying the variables one intends to hold constant, the factors other than the expected punishment that might plausibly influence the frequency with which murder is committed. Ehrlich's list of factors had been a short one, including a few economic figures such as the unemployment rate and per capita income. Critics pointed out that surely more circumstances contributed to the murder rate than that—the availability of guns, the extent of migration from rural to urban areas, the rate of other violent crimes, and so on. A more complete list of independent variables could easily lead to the opposite result. Other critics demonstrated that Ehrlich's results were far too sensitive to tiny changes in the data used. Ehrlich had studied the period from 1933 to 1969, for example, but if the five most recent years were removed the deterrent effect disappeared. That was an artifact of the rise in the murder rate during the 1960s coupled with the scarcity of executions, but it was difficult as a logical matter to conclude that capital punishment was an effective deterrent between 1933 and 1969 but not between 1933 and 1964.[19] Some of this counter-research was prepared in time to be presented to the Supreme Court in *Gregg*. Neither Ehrlich nor his critics had much of an effect on the outcome of *Gregg*—it seems clear that a majority of the Court would have found the new capital statutes constitutional even if economists had been united in finding no deterrent effect—but the public visibility of the issue created by *Gregg* quickly attracted a swarm of social scientists to the attempt to measure deterrence.

The conclusions to be drawn from multiple regression all depended on the equation used to model the murder rate. The rest of the century saw repeated refinements in that equation—more variables, the use of state-level or even county-level data rather than national data, and of course the accumulation of more evidence as executions became more frequent in the 1980s and 1990s. By the end of the century there was an abundant literature in journals of academic law and economics. A few studies found a deterrent effect, but most did not. There was a raging methodological disagreement over how best to pick the variables, and a nagging suspicion that researchers' own attitudes toward capital punishment were subconsciously influencing the forms of equations. This diversity in academic opinion translated poorly into the public policy arena, where proponents of each side tended to ascribe validity only to those studies which supported their own view.[20]

Academic studies of deterrence had scarcely any impact, in any event, on the pervasive folk wisdom that the death penalty *had* to have a deterrent effect, simply because it was more severe than any other. "I have been a member of the bar for 51 years. I was a circuit judge for 8 years," noted Strom Thurmond, chair of the Senate Judiciary Committee, in 1981. "I am convinced the death penalty does deter crime." George Deukmejian, then the attorney general of California (and later the governor), found it "obvious that a major reason that murder and other violent crimes have reached intolerable levels" was the California Supreme Court's pattern of vacating death sentences.[21] The point was sometimes made more carefully. Whether or not the death penalty as actually practiced deterred murder any more than a prison sentence, one could plausibly argue that a death penalty administered differently—imposed more quickly or more frequently, for instance—*would* be a better deterrent than prison. The claim could not be tested empirically, so there was no way to know if it was true. Whether as a broad intuitive proposition about existing practice or as a narrower speculative claim about a hypothetical capital punishment scheme, the folk wisdom as to deterrence was hardy enough to survive criticism from economists.

It soon became apparent, moreover, that the popularity of capital punishment had little to do with deterring crime. Surveys conducted between 1983 and 1991 uniformly indicated that a large majority of supporters would still favor the death penalty even if it had no effect whatsoever on the murder rate.[22] Capital punishment was instead valued for two other purposes, ideals that were conceptually distinct but often intermingled in practice. Both were very old, and both had been in abeyance for some time.

First, the three decades after *Furman* saw the idea of retribution return to intellectual respectability. Long rejected as a legitimate goal of punishment in academic and policymaking circles, retribution made an astonishingly fast comeback. Part of its rise was a reaction to the widespread loss of faith in the power of prisons and similar institutions to rehabilitate criminals. Part grew out of the resurgence of causal models of crime that rested on the free will of the criminal rather than on social or biological forces beyond the criminal's control. In the 1970s and 1980s supporters of capital punishment turned more and more to retributive arguments. Speaking in favor of the death penalty before a committee of the New Jersey Senate in 1982, Edwin Stier, a representative of the state attorney general's office, made it clear that his opinion had little to do with deterrence.

> I think there is a more basic reason to support the enactment of the death penalty . . . For a generation now, we have been taught that the only valid purposes for punishing an offender are to seek his rehabilitation and to deter others from doing similar acts . . .
>
> We have been taught that the idea of retribution, the idea of seeking a method of punishment to satisfy a community's needs to see an offender punished is a primitive notion that no longer has a place in our society. I suggest to you, from my own experience, and in my own judgment, that that notion is wrong. The idea that the punishment must fit the crime is something more than the idea that we have to find a way to isolate the offender and to try to rehabilitate him, the idea that somehow we ought to try to discourage others from committing crimes by imposing prison sentences and other forms of punishment. But, that is not enough. Somehow society needs to feel that when a criminal act has been committed, its interests have been vindicated.[23]

The point was made again and again—capital punishment was a moral imperative, regardless of whether it reduced the murder rate or cut murderers off from the possibility of rehabilitation. Sometimes retribution was cited as an instrumental value, as in previous centuries. The intuitive anger felt toward criminals, disparagingly labeled "revenge" by the previous generation of criminologists, was in fact the glue that held society together, argued the political scientist Walter Berns. The criminal law "must remind us of the moral order by which alone we can live as *human beings*," Berns concluded, "and in our day the only punishment that can do this is capital punishment."[24] But it was probably more common to think of retribution as an end in itself, as an emotional need that only an execution could fulfill.

The second purpose that seemed to be served by the death penalty in the decades after *Furman* and *Gregg* was harder to defend intellectually but may have been more important. Back in the days of public hangings, an execution had been a vehicle for a collective condemnation of crime. Going to a hanging was a way of siding with the community against the criminal, a means of broadcasting the seriousness with which one took crime and its consequences. When the ceremony was moved indoors, the actual execution lost much of its purpose as a vehicle of denunciation. In the last three decades of the twentieth century, however, that symbolic function returned quite strongly, this time attached not to the ceremony of execution but to support of capital punishment as an abstract policy. To say that one was for capital punishment was often implicitly to announce that one wished to "get tough on crime" in order to reduce its frequency, that criminals ought to be held morally responsible for their actions, that crime was chosen by the criminal rather than forced upon him by his biology or his environment, and that the worst criminals were unlikely candidates for reintegration into society. These were the same symbolic statements that had once been made by spectators at a public execution. Now that they were barred from witnessing executions, Americans could only declare their support for capital punishment in the abstract.

What was unfortunate about the shift in symbol, from a concrete event to an abstract policy, is that it greatly muddied the debate by permitting support for capital punishment to be invoked in situations where the death penalty could not conceivably be applied. When the New Jersey legislature was considering a bill to reinstate the death penalty, one senator announced that he had received hundreds of letters and telephone calls pleading that the bill be enacted. "Many of the letters relate personal experiences of assaults received while walking alone at night, coming home from a bus stop or just leaving their home to mail a letter," he reported. "Almost all these letters ask the same questions: Why don't our laws protect us? . . . What has happened to justice in our country?"[25] Fear of crime was genuine and widespread, but the frequency of assaults and other common low-level crimes could hardly be affected by the presence of capital punishment for murder. Yet the symbolic role taken on by the death penalty in the 1970s made it a shorthand way of expressing one's concern about crime generally.

Elected officials were quick to capitalize on the social meaning of capital punishment by staking out positions that would allow them to claim support for the death penalty even in circumstances where few if any criminals would ever actually be sentenced to death. The best example may be the federal criminal law, which by 1998 included no fewer than forty-six capital crimes, virtually all of which were variations of murder defined so narrowly and yet with so much overlap among them that one suspects members of Congress were motivated primarily by the desire to claim credit for an inflated number of death penalties. The death penalty by the end of the twentieth century was less a method of punishing criminals than a terrain of cultural argument, within which one could declare one's allegiance either with the criminal or with the law-abiding majority.

This symbolic role provides the best explanation for what would otherwise be a puzzle—that an issue could be so politically important and yet touch the lives of so few people. Compared with abortion, say, or taxes, issues personally affecting large percentages of the population, capital punishment affected hardly anyone. The vast majority of Americans were neither murderers nor murder victims, nor even close acquaintances with either. But everyone had some experience with the fear of minor crime, and attitudes toward the death penalty had a lot to do with those fears, even if only murderers could be sentenced to death. To oppose the death penalty was to run the risk of being viewed as "soft on crime"—not just soft on murderers but soft on the kinds of criminals ordinary people believed themselves likely to encounter. It is this expressive quality that best accounts for the renewed popularity of capital punishment at the end of the twentieth century.

Aggravating Circumstances

Capital punishment after *Gregg* was not just a political issue. The Supreme Court's involvement turned it into a constitutional issue as well, one that returned to the Court year after year. Within a very short time the Court constructed an intricate Eighth Amendment jurisprudence on the foundation of *Furman* and *Gregg,* a body of cases distinguishing the practices that would or would not amount to cruel and unusual punishment. The result was a significant shift in decisionmaking authority among the three branches of government. The various issues involving the death penalty that had once been decided by legislatures, or by governors during the clemency process, now became constitutional questions to be decided by courts.

For instance, was capital punishment disproportionately severe for crimes less grave than murder? The question had been the subject of fierce political debate within legislatures since the late eighteenth century. Governors had always considered the gravity of the crime in deciding whether to grant clemency. But after *Furman* and *Gregg* the issue was recast as a constitutional question: Would it violate the Eighth Amendment to execute a criminal for committing a crime short of murder? In *Coker v. Georgia,* only a year after *Gregg,* the Court held that the death penalty was a cruel and unusual punishment for rape. Every death sentence imposed for the rest of the century would be for murder. But what about a defendant technically guilty of murder who was not the actual killer? The criminal law had always held accomplices guilty of the crime they helped another commit, but a defendant's minimal participation had always been a factor tending toward clemency. Now it became a constitutional question: Was it cruel and unusual to execute the accomplice? In 1982 the Court held that it was, by a 5–4 vote; in 1987, after Justice White switched sides, the Court held that it was not, also by a 5–4 vote.[26]

Just about every death penalty question that had once been decided by legislatures in enacting statutes or by governors in ruling on clemency petitions was addressed by the Supreme Court in the years after *Gregg.* What if the defendant was very young? The Court held that the Eighth Amendment permitted the execution of a defendant who was sixteen years old at the time he committed the crime. What if the defendant had become insane by the time of the execution? The Court held that the Eighth Amendment prohibited executing the insane. What if the defendant was mentally retarded? The Court held that the Eighth Amendment did not prohibit executing the retarded. These had been classic legislative or clemency issues for hundreds of years, but now they were novel constitutional questions. The ultimate issue on clemency was of course whether the defendant was in fact innocent, and it was only a matter of time before that too became a constitutional question. Was it cruel and unusual punishment to execute an innocent person? *Herrera v. Collins,* the 1993 case that posed the question, produced five separate opinions and no clear answer.[27] *Furman* and *Gregg* had the effect of moving some very old questions into a new forum.

The constitutionalization of capital punishment produced a host of *new* questions as well. Some of the states' aggravating circumstances turned out to be so vague as to raise doubts that they provided any guidance to the jury. Georgia, for instance, authorized the death penalty for every murder the jury found "outrageously or wantonly vile, horrible or inhuman," a category that might not have excluded any murders at all. The same could have been said about one of Oklahoma's aggravating circumstances, that the murder be "especially heinous, atrocious or cruel." The Court found both aggravating circumstances unconstitutional. A few years later, however, the Court approved an aggravating circumstance adopted by Idaho, that in committing the murder the defendant "exhibited utter disregard for human life." That too might easily be said about all murders, but because the Idaho courts interpreted "utter disregard" to refer only to what they called "the cold-blooded, pitiless slayer," the Court found that the aggravating circumstance adequately distinguished one category of murders from another.[28] It was in the interest of death penalty supporters to draft aggravating circumstances that pulled in as many murders as possible, so the Court found itself repeatedly examining whether particular circumstances sufficiently confined the jury's discretion to impose the death sentence.

Supporters of the death penalty had the opposite interest with respect to mitigating circumstances. There the incentive was to draft statutes narrowly, to *exclude* as many murders as possible. This practice also produced repeated constitutional challenges. In the end the Court held that the states could not restrict the jury's consideration of mitigating evidence—that the jury must be allowed to consider any kind of evidence that might point against a death sentence, not just the evidence relevant to one of the statutory mitigating circumstances.[29] That conclusion went halfway toward undermining the constitutional regime created by *Furman* and *Gregg,* under which state statutes were supposed to channel the jury's consideration of evidence at sentencing to prevent the random imposition of death sentences. If the constitution instead required juries to consider *any* mitigating evidence, half the decision was unguided.

Most of the other half of the decision, the identification of aggravating circumstances, was cut loose from statutory guidance not long after, when the Court allowed sentencing juries to consider nonstatutory aggravating evidence as well. By this point all that was left of the constitutional framework was the requirement that the jury find a single statutory aggravating circumstance before proceeding to what had become a virtually unguided exercise of discretion. And even that threshold requirement was generally acknowledged as something of a sham, because as time went on sentencing statutes were typically expanded to include aggravating circumstances phrased so broadly as to exclude very few murders. Missouri's statute, for example, included as aggravating circumstances that the murder evidenced "depravity of mind," that the murder was committed in the course of another felony or to conceal another felony, and that the murderer hoped he or a confederate would obtain some of the victim's property.[30] It was a rare murder for which an applicable aggravating circumstance could not be found, which meant that at sentencing just about any kind of evidence could be introduced for either side and considered by jurors any way they wanted.

For a time the Court did exclude one kind of evidence from sentencing, evidence of the effect of the murder on the victim's family and friends, but that was by a 5–4 vote. In 1991, after Brennan retired and was replaced by David Souter, the Court overruled its prior cases and let in such "victim impact evidence" as well.[31] After 1991 well-conducted capital sentencing hearings normally included emotional presentations by both sides, matching the defendant's weeping relatives against the victim's weeping relatives, in an effort to gain the sympathy of the jury. Any pretense that this was a rational process of distinguishing degrees of culpability was long gone.

In the twenty years after *Gregg* capital punishment occupied a significant percentage of the Court's time, resulting in scores of cases that made up a complex and ever-shifting body of law. Justice Antonin Scalia, among other critics, complained of "the fog of confusion that is our annually improvised Eighth Amendment, 'death is different' jurisprudence." Much of the fog was produced by the Court's constant effort to reconcile two irreconcilable goals—consistency across cases (a goal best reached by formal rules restricting jury discretion) and attention to the unique characteristics of each case (a goal best reached by allowing the jury unrestricted discretion). In 1994, a few months before he retired, Harry Blackmun finally gave up and decided the death penalty ought to be unconstitutional under all circumstances. "Over the past two decades, efforts to balance these competing constitutional commands have been to no avail," he despaired. "From this day forward, I no longer shall tinker with the machinery of death." Lewis Powell came to the same conclusion a few years after his retirement, when his opinion no longer made any difference.[32] But the rest of the Court tinkered on.

Many areas of the law are complex, but the tragedy of the Court's Eighth Amendment jurisprudence was that all the complexity served scarcely any purpose. Trials were long and expensive, lawyers had to master bodies of arcane doctrine, every case raised several issues that could be plausibly litigated on appeal, and yet, for all that, the process of distinguishing the murderers who would be executed from those who would be sent to prison seemed no less haphazard than it had been before the Supreme Court got involved. Lawyers and trial judges went through the motions, but in the end juries imposed death virtually for whatever reasons they chose. There was little dispute that the purpose behind *Furman* and *Gregg*, to use the Constitution to rationalize capital sentencing, had not been achieved. Critics on the right complained that the Court's Eighth Amendment jurisprudence forced state governments to spend time and money for no good purpose; critics on the left complained that the Court had watered *Furman* down to irrelevance. Both sides were right.

By the 1990s it was clear to lawyers practicing in the field that the major determinants of who lived and who died were not the statutory aggravating and mitigating circumstances. Whether a defendant was charged with capital or noncapital murder depended largely on whether the prosecutor was up for reelection, whether the county had enough left in the year's budget for an expensive capital trial, whether the local newspapers were publicizing the case, whether the victim's family members wanted the prosecutor to seek death (and, if so, how much influence they had), whether the defense lawyer was sophisticated enough to badger the prosecutor with pretrial motions, and a host of other factors that could be found in no statute. Whether a jury would return a death sentence depended in part on the awfulness of the crime and the criminal, but also on the relative skill of the lawyers, the social standing of the victim, the willingness of the victim's friends and family to testify, the unarticulated beliefs of the twelve people who had been selected for the jury, and a variety of circumstances that were likewise unexpressed in the written law.

This was precisely the unguided discretion that had prompted the Court to intervene in the first place.

There was one piece of good news. Before *Furman* it had been common knowledge that black defendants were sentenced to death at higher rates than white defendants. Econometric studies of capital sentencing conducted after *Gregg* revealed a less consistent pattern. In some states the race of a defendant was no longer a factor influencing the likelihood of a death sentence. In some states black defendants were still disadvantaged, but in others *white* defendants were now disadvantaged.[33] But this change almost certainly had little to do with the new sentencing schemes. It was instead most likely a product of two other developments. First was the Court's holding in *Coker v. Georgia* that the Eighth Amendment barred capital punishment for rape. Rape had always been the crime for which the race of the defendant made the biggest difference, so *Coker* instantly wiped away more discrimination than any reform of murder sentencing could have. Second was the fact that after the civil rights movement of the 1960s blacks gained better representation on juries, especially in the South, where most of the death sentences were imposed.

Capital sentencing was not free from racial disparities, however. In state after state econometric studies disclosed a pronounced bias based on the race not of the defendant but of the victim. The first and most extensive of the studies, conducted in Georgia, showed that when all other variables were held equal a death sentence was 4.3 times more likely when the victim was white.[34] Similar results were obtained in states all over the country. Here was a kind of discrimination, but not the kind that had been so troubling in the years before *Furman*. Abolitionists quickly adopted the race-of-victim disparity as a standard argument against the death penalty. Capital punishment, they contended, undervalued the lives of black victims. But the implications of the argument were not entirely clear. Would things be better, from the abolitionist point of view, if more killers of black victims were sentenced to death? Most murders involved criminals and victims of the same race, so equalizing the treatment of victims would cause more black defendants to be sentenced to death. From the point of view of one concerned with race discrimination, was that a desirable outcome? Before *Furman*, racial disparities had yielded clear moral positions; after *Furman*, the consequences of racial disparity were far murkier.

The race-of-victim disparity was the vehicle for the Legal Defense Fund's last serious effort to persuade the Supreme Court to declare capital punishment unconstitutional, in *McCleskey v. Kemp* (1987). Race discrimination had been the original reason for the LDF's involvement in death penalty litigation back in the 1960s. Race discrimination had been the silent specter that had prompted the Court to require statutory standards to guide the jury's discretion. The persistence of racial differences even under the new sentencing schemes, the LDF argued, demonstrated that the "post-*Furman* experiment has failed, and that [the] capital sentencing system continues to be haunted by widespread and substantial racial bias." But the argument fell one Justice short of a majority. Lewis Powell, who wrote the majority opinion, firmly believed that the pattern of results in thousands of cases should never upset the verdict in a single case. "My understanding of statistical analysis—particularly what is called 'regression analysis' ranges from limited to zero," he confessed to his law clerk. But he was well aware that allowing statistical attacks on criminal convictions promised to open a Pandora's box. What about other minority groups? What about gender disparities? Everyone knew that women were very rarely executed—did that violate the constitutional rights of men? What if there were racial or other disparities in the length of prison sentences? The LDF "is attacking the jury system," Powell noted to himself. There was "no limiting principle to judgments in criminal cases based solely on *statistics*."[35]

Suffusing the Court's opinion in *McCleskey* was a weariness, a pessimism about the possible. "Apparent disparities in sentencing are an inevitable part of our criminal justice system," Powell wrote. "The Constitution does not require that a State eliminate any demonstrable disparity." Fifteen years after *Furman* the Court had given up hope of eliminating the racism and the arbitrariness that had once been the motors of constitutional change. Scalia was even more frank, in a memorandum he circulated to his colleagues. "The unconscious operation of irrational sympathies and antipathies, including racial, upon jury decisions and (hence) prosecutorial decisions is real, acknowledged in the decisions of this court, and ineradicable," he concluded.[36] Racism and irrationality were facts of life, and that was that. There was nothing the law could do. This attitude lay beneath many of the Court's capital cases through the 1980s and 1990s. Skepticism about the possibility of progress steadily weakened the constitutional structure created in *Furman* and *Gregg*, just as it had weakened earlier cycles of political abolitionism.

The conservative Justices were tired; the liberal Justices were angry. For the rest of their careers, Brennan and Marshall dissented in every capital case reaching the Court in which the Court did not overturn the death sentence, even cases the Court decided not to hear. This was either a bold statement of principle or a flagrant disregard for precedent, depending on one's tastes. Their law clerks were even angrier. They began to conceive that their role was to save the lives of condemned prisoners. They demonized the conservative Justices as the executioner's accomplices. Within the Court, as in the world outside, one's attitude toward the death penalty became a symbolic self-defining statement.

But if the constitutionalization of capital punishment failed to impose any order on the task of distinguishing which criminals would live or die, it had a profound impact on the death penalty considered more broadly, in several different ways.

The most noticeable was the sudden decline of clemency. For centuries governors commuted death sentences in significant numbers. That pattern continued for the first two-thirds of the twentieth century. Florida commuted nearly a quarter of its death sentences between 1924 and 1966; North Carolina commuted more than a third between 1909 and 1954. Those figures dropped close to zero under the new sentencing schemes. In 1987, for example, there were 299 death sentences in the United States and only 5 commutations; in 1988 there were 296 death sentences and only 4 commutations.[37] Clemency was once a regular part of the capital sentencing process, but once the process was constitutionalized clemency became a freak occurrence.

Part of clemency's decline was attributable to the growing popularity and salience of the death penalty. A commutation could be political suicide for an elected official in the new climate, and so many of the post-*Gregg* commutations were granted by governors who did not intend to seek reelection. But of course the death penalty had also been very popular in earlier eras, when governors had nevertheless commuted death sentences in large numbers. The difference after *Gregg* was that many of the kinds of cases that had once been suitable for clemency were now being handled by the courts instead. Judges, not governors, now decided whether trials had been conducted fairly, so when considering applications for clemency governors tended to defer to the courts that resolved the defendant's constitutional claims. Such deference left a vacuum in cases where the death penalty seemed too severe, or where the defendant might have been innocent, because these were issues courts normally did not consider. Where the sentence had been affirmed as constitutional at all stages of judicial review, however, the assumption within governors' offices tended to be that the sentence ought not to be disturbed, an assumption very different from the one that had prevailed for the preceding several centuries, when the executive branch was supposed to exercise its independent judgment as to the propriety of an execution. When the courts moved in, the governors moved out.

A second striking result of the constitutionalization of capital punishment was the radical change in the nature of the abolitionist movement. From the late eighteenth century through the middle of the twentieth the movement had been *political*, aimed at persuading legislatures to replace the death penalty with prison. In the last three decades of the twentieth century the movement was largely *legal*—dominated by lawyers, who spent almost all their time litigating cases. The reason is not hard to find. Political success was impossible. The anti–death penalty message "is falling on stone ears," lamented the Illinois abolitionist Willard Lassers. "This is the day of law and order." In 1979 an organization called Floridians Against Executions announced that it would execute a dog in a specially designed electric chair in a public park. The announcement drew angry protests. Fifteen hundred people showed up to watch. After unstrapping the dog at the last moment, the group's president admitted that the whole event had been a hoax, staged to attract public attention the group could not attract by making straightforward arguments against capital punishment. With political activity unpromising, abolitionists turned their attention to constitutional arguments, which often did succeed in making executions more difficult for states to carry out. Even in the 1980s and 1990s, when Congress and the Supreme Court cut off some forms of judicial review in response to that success, an opponent of the death penalty could have more effect as a defense lawyer than in any other role.[38]

A lawyer for a condemned prisoner hoped above all to have the prisoner's death sentence invalidated, but the second choice was to make the litigation last as long as possible. Every day the case dragged on was another day the client stayed alive. Lawyers thus brought repeated claims of constitutional error before the courts, right up to the moment of execu-

tion. Knowing they could not win with a frontal attack, abolitionist lawyers fought a guerrilla war, seeking to sabotage the machinery of capital
punishment by tying it up in litigation. These efforts, combined with the
difficulty of finding lawyers for the growing number of condemned prisoners, caused the average length of time between sentencing and execution to increase. From 51 months in 1977–1983, the average delay grew to
95 months by 1990 and 134 months by 1995.[39] And even after all those
years, judges found themselves making hurried life-or-death decisions the
night before most scheduled executions, rulings on constitutional claims
in lengthy briefs faxed by lawyers hoping to have the execution put off to
another day. The defense lawyers could not be faulted. They were working within an adversary system in which their ethical obligation was to
do their best for their clients. It was the constitutionalization of capital
punishment that created the paradoxical twin problems of delay and last-
minute time pressure.

Those problems exasperated many, not least the judges. "In the most
recent case," Lewis Powell complained in 1984, "at least the equivalent of
two full days of my time was devoted to the repetitive petitions that clearly
were an abuse of habeas corpus. I know Byron [White] spent all night
here on one occasion." In another case, "there were perhaps a dozen people here until 1:30 A.M. prior to the morning hour set for execution." The
problem of last-minute filings only grew worse as scheduled executions
became more frequent. All through the 1980s and 1990s Congress debated limiting the scope of the writ of habeas corpus, the procedural vehicle that allowed state prisoners to ask federal courts to review the constitutionality of their convictions and sentences. Finally, in the Antiterrorism
and Effective Death Penalty Act of 1996, Congress set strict time limits for
condemned prisoners, much stricter than for other prisoners. By then a
Supreme Court impatient for congressional action had already done
much of the work itself in a series of opinions overruling precedent in order to make it harder for condemned prisoners to have their constitutional claims heard by a federal court.[40] The extraordinary amount of attention given to the normally obscure subject of habeas corpus in the
1980s and 1990s was a testament to the success of abolitionist lawyers.

A third result of the constitutionalization of capital punishment was the
creation of a unique legal proceeding, the post-*Gregg* capital trial. The
jockeying began well before a typical trial started, in the form of highly
technical legal argument over the aggravating and mitigating circum-

stances that would be alleged and the kinds of evidence that would or would not be introduced. Simply picking the jury could take months, devoted to questioning and counter-questioning on attitudes toward the death penalty. The sentencing phase of the trial could last weeks, as each side presented extensive biographical evidence about the defendant. From the prosecutor's perspective, sentencing was an opportunity to depict the defendant as an irredeemable villain who had consciously chosen to kill and who would kill again if given the chance, the sort of person unlikely to be rehabilitated by a lengthy period in prison. The defense tried to widen the social context to present the defendant as a victim of forces beyond his control, a human being who still had a kernel of goodness within him, a person deserving a second chance, capable of reform if placed under the proper care. Where the prosecutor introduced evidence of all the bad things the defendant had ever done, the defense introduced evidence of all the bad things that had ever happened to the defendant—bad neighborhoods, childhood beatings, mental illness, brain damage, and the like.

The sentencing phase of a capital trial, if conducted skillfully on both sides, was a battle of philosophies. The prosecutor told a story of free will, of a criminal with the opportunity to choose between good and evil. Defense counsel countered with a narrative of determinism, of social and biological forces that would have driven anyone to crime. This was a very old battle, dating back to the late eighteenth century, but it was a battle that had always been fought in the public, political arena, over whether capital punishment ought to exist at all. The sentencing scheme created by *Furman* and *Gregg* moved that battle into the capital trial itself, where it was replicated, in case after case, to be decided by juries rather than the public at large.

This was a legal proceeding with no parallel in the history of Anglo-American jurisprudence. A good death penalty lawyer had to be a technician, a detective, and a philosopher; she had to keep current with the latest Supreme Court cases on the Eighth Amendment, dig up a lifetime of character evidence, and persuade twelve citizens in the jury box of the validity of one or another theory of human nature. To do the job well required specialized training. Prosecutors' offices were staffed with experienced specialists. They attended seminars; they compiled manuals; they exchanged tips with their counterparts in other jurisdictions. In the states with specialized capital public defenders, the defense lawyers did the same, but many of the southern states lacked a corps of capital defense specialists. The Texas District and County Attorneys Association, for example, conducted seminars on capital litigation at a local resort, featuring lectures by some of the very judges before whom the attending prosecutors would soon be trying cases.[41] There was no such program for defense lawyers. The constitutionalized death penalty was a difficult and specialized practice area, but in many states the lawyers assigned to defendants had no training in the area whatsoever.

The length and complexity of a capital trial inevitably gave rise to difficult issues on appeal. Litigating a capital case through the courts normally took several years from start to finish. Because the defendant usually could not afford to pay a lawyer, everyone involved at every stage of the proceeding was being paid by the state—the prosecutors, the defense lawyers, the judges and other court employees, and even the expert witnesses needed by both sides to explain the psychological and sometimes neurological evidence presented at sentencing.

The constitutionalized death penalty was thus very expensive—much more expensive than sentencing murderers to prison, even accounting for all the costs of maintaining prisons and their residents. Of the several attempts to measure the cost of capital punishment to various states, the most neutral and thorough was conducted in the early 1990s at Duke University. It found that the cost of capital punishment to the taxpayers of North Carolina—that is, the amount by which sentencing murderers to death exceeded the cost of housing them in prison for their lives—was more than $250,000 per death sentence and more than $2 million per execution. The cost was similar in other states.[42]

The constitutionalization of capital punishment created an enormously complicated, expensive, and time-consuming apparatus that had little real effect on the outcomes of cases. Being executed was still, as Justice Stewart had put it in *Furman*, like being struck by lightning; the only difference was that it now took a decade and millions of dollars of public money for the lightning to strike.

Extremely Sanitary

When the Supreme Court permitted the resumption of capital punishment in 1976, the electric chair and the gas chamber were the most common tools of execution. By the end of the century, however, all but a few of the states with capital punishment executed their prisoners by lethal

injection. Of the ninety-eight inmates executed in 1999, three were electrocuted and one died in the gas chamber; the other ninety-four died
when poisonous chemicals were put into their veins. Never had a method
of execution swept the country so quickly.

The idea of executing criminals by poison is at least as old as Socrates.
It was briefly considered by the 1888 New York commission that recommended the electric chair. After some of the early botched electrocutions, the use of drugs was proposed as an alternative.[43] But lethal injection was never a serious option in any state before the 1970s. The
intravenous administration of medicine had long been familiar, as had
the use of lethal injection to kill unwanted animals, so the lack of attention to lethal injection as a means of executing *people* could not have
been a function of technology. There must rather have been something
abhorrent about the act of injection itself.

Two elements of lethal injection were particularly upsetting. First, an
injection of poison required an uncomfortable degree of closeness between the condemned person and the executioner. Even the hangman
had been farther away at the moment the trap was sprung, and with the
newer methods the executioner had been put at a progressively greater
distance. To stand inches away from the condemned person, perhaps to
be touching him with one hand while holding the syringe with the other,
was to cast oneself too conspicuously in the role of a killer. The ancient
tension between support for the death penalty in the abstract and revulsion from the actual act of causing death was as strong as ever, and it
made execution by injection difficult to contemplate long after lethal injection had become a simple technical procedure. Second, injecting
chemicals into the bloodstream was a task traditionally performed by physicians, many of whom found it troubling that one of their own might be
called upon to end life rather than prolong it. Physicians had long presided at executions, but their role had been limited to pronouncing
death, not causing it.

By the late 1970s, however, states had not used their electric chairs or
gas chambers in more than a decade. In Oklahoma the chair's electric
coils were rusted and its wood was rotting. Time had worn down the execution machinery in other states as well. To resume executions would require buying new equipment even if a state retained the method of execution it had used before *Furman*. The decade-long hiatus in capital
punishment created by the Supreme Court thus removed much of the or-

dinary financial disincentive to change. And from the perspective of the state, one great benefit of lethal injection was that it was cheap. Unlike gas or electrocution, it did not require any specialized equipment. All the chemicals, syringes, and intravenous tubing were readily available for purchase. The North Carolina Department of Correction calculated that the total cost of the equipment would be only $346.51 per execution.[44]

The other advantage of lethal injection was that it was ordinarily painless and clean. Americans had long sought a means of executing criminals that would minimize the condemned person's pain and the spectators' discomfort. The electric chair and the gas chamber had been the most recent steps in this process, but decades of occasionally gruesome electrocutions and gas chamber deaths, painful for the condemned prisoners and nauseating for the spectators, had eliminated the optimism associated with the two methods earlier in the century. Lethal injection promised to be cleaner. The benefits of cost and hygiene were enough to overcome the old obstacles to lethal injection.

In the spring of 1977 Oklahoma and Texas became the first states to adopt the new method. Not long after, most of the other states did too. In 1982 Charlie Brooks of Texas became the first person executed in this manner. Lying on a gurney, strapped down to prevent escape, Brooks was injected with three drugs. The first was sodium thiopental, a barbiturate that produced unconsciousness. Next came pancuronium bromide, a muscle relaxant that paralyzed Brooks's lungs. Last was potassium chloride, to stop his heart. The same chemicals, in the same order, were used in most succeeding lethal injections in other states. "It's extremely sanitary," marveled Missouri's prison chaplain. "The guy just goes to sleep. That's all there is to it. All of a sudden. And when it's said and done, he breathes a sigh, and he's gone."[45] The American Medical Association barred physicians from taking part in executions, so the tasks were usually performed by prison employees, with physicians providing a sedative ahead of time and an autopsy afterward.

Lethal injection encountered few obstacles on its way to becoming the primary means of execution in the United States. The lack of medical training among the prison officials conducting executions contributed to several mistakes. In Texas the syringe popped out of Raymond Landry's vein, spraying the fatal chemicals at the spectators. Often it took an embarrassingly long time for officials to find a vein. Some inmates had violent physical reactions to the chemicals, gasping and choking in their final minutes. All these incidents were publicized by abolitionists as proof that no method of execution was humane, but with no success. On average lethal injection was clearly less painful and gruesome than any of its predecessors. The only significant legal challenge to lethal injection was an ironic and ultimately unsuccessful lawsuit filed by the Legal Defense Fund, alleging that the chemicals could not be used because they had not been approved as safe by the Food and Drug Administration.[46] Lethal injection was in most cases easy, cheap, painless, and clean. It aroused no real controversy.

Some of capital punishment's opponents perceived a paradox in the shift to lethal injection, because they found concern for the condemned person's pain inconsistent with the renewed interest in retributive justice. But retribution had never required the infliction of pain. Death itself had always been the punishment most people felt to be intuitively just, not death preceded by torment. For centuries Americans had sought to make executions as painless as possible. As new technologies for doing so became available, they were put to use, as early as the trap-door scaffold in the seventeenth century, and as recently as the gas chamber in the 1920s. Lethal injection was just another step in the same direction.

The move to lethal injection continued the long-term trend away from visual display at executions. A public hanging had involved grand gestures, by a condemned person standing on a stage, before crowds numbering in the thousands. A hanging in the jail yard was a similar ceremony before a smaller audience. In an electric chair or a gas chamber the condemned prisoner was seated, not standing, and the audience was still smaller. Now, with lethal injection, the condemned person was lying down. The sense that death lying down was undignified had played a part in the design of the electric chair and gas chamber, but that sense had nearly vanished by the end of the century. Now few saw any significance in the posture of the condemned person.

Lethal injection was so simple and inexpensive that executions could have been returned to the community in which the crime had been committed, for local residents to manage and watch, as in the days of hanging. By the 1980s, however, executions had been centralized in remote state prisons and shut off from public view for nearly a century. The tradition of local community punishment had been almost completely forgotten. The dramaturgy associated with the electric chair and gas chamber was transposed to lethal injection. Death was inflicted by a small number of specialists. The number of witnesses was very small—in Missouri, twelve "state" witnesses (including members of the press) and up to five "inmate" witnesses (friends and family members). Everything took place in two small prison rooms, one for the condemned prisoner and the other, through a window, for the spectators. Small groups of protesters on one side or the other might show up outside the prison, to wave signs for the television cameras. Media organizations might go to court to claim, unsuccessfully, a First Amendment right to televise the proceedings. But despite capital punishment's popularity, there was no longer much public desire actually to see it.

Another old theme, the tension between support for capital punishment in the abstract and revulsion toward the acts necessary to carry it out in specific instances, showed through in the elaborate protocols the states adopted for conducting lethal injections. Amateur hangmen had turned to drink; professional lethal injection teams turned to carefully orchestrated procedures. The execution was broken down into several small tasks, each assigned to a different person, to minimize the sense of responsibility felt by each participant. Each prison employee could think of himself as a mere link in a long chain that led to the condemned person's death. The ultimate responsibility for killing a fellow human being always lay with someone else. Jim Willet, the warden in charge of Texas's executions, reassured his staff that each of their jobs "is just a fraction in this whole process." That thought, Willet explained, "helps you not to bear the whole burden of putting this guy to death."[47]

In several states the chemicals were injected into the condemned prisoner's bloodstream by a machine rather than a person. Fred Leuchter, the machine's inventor, included an ingenious feature: starting the machine required two people to push buttons simultaneously, so no individual could consider himself solely responsible even for that. The years of complex litigation that preceded most executions made it even easier for prison employees to avoid feeling responsible for causing death. For a death sentence to have survived review by so many courts, an employee could reason, it must be an appropriate sentence. "I've made peace with myself by knowing that the fellow that's being executed has had every chance of appeal," explained Bill Armontrout, who supervised executions as warden of the Missouri State Penitentiary. "When you know that the case has been scrutinized that closely, then it makes you feel much easier."[48]

International Criticism

As capital punishment became more common in the United States, it was being abolished in much of the rest of the world. As of 1995 no nation in western Europe practiced capital punishment. The countries of eastern Europe all had the death penalty under communism, but the advent of democracy caused most to abolish capital punishment. The non-European countries most culturally akin to the United States—Canada, Australia, and New Zealand—had abolished capital punishment. The death penalty was almost entirely absent from South and Central America: with the exception of Guyana, no nation in the region had conducted an execution in years. Capital punishment was abolished in parts of sub-Saharan Africa in the early 1990s.[49]

Apart from the United States, the death penalty flourished only in the Middle East, Asia, and the rest of sub-Saharan Africa, paradoxically the regions of the world with justice systems and economies most unlike those of the United States. In 1998, for example, China was the world leader in number of executions. Iraq was most likely second, followed by the Congo. The United States was fourth. The rest of the top ten were Iran, Egypt, Belarus, Taiwan, Saudi Arabia, and Singapore. This was not the company in which the United States normally found itself. For centuries Americans had been proud to possess a criminal justice system that made less use of the death penalty than just about any other place on the globe, including the countries of western Europe. At the end of the twentieth century the tables had been turned. Now the United States possessed one of the harshest criminal codes in the world.

What had happened? Over the long run, in the United States, nothing had happened. In the 1990s executions were about as frequent as they had been in the 1950s. The change had taken place in the rest of the world. Most of the countries that had abolished capital punishment had done so in the last few decades. The United States had participated in this international movement through the early 1970s, but had then in effect dropped out and returned to its older practice.

Why? Part of the answer, though by no means all of it, must have something to do with rates of violent crime. The American homicide rate rose dramatically in the 1960s and 1970s, to a level much higher than that of most similar nations. By 1990 the homicide rate was four and a half times higher in the United States than in Canada, nine times higher than in France or Germany, and thirteen times higher than in the United Kingdom. High rates of violent crime created a climate of fear, in which appeals for stiffer sentences, including the death penalty, attracted political support. The fear of crime lingered even after crime rates began to decline in the 1990s. But the crime rate is only part of the story. Homicide rates were even higher in several other countries that abolished capital punishment, including Mexico and Brazil, and much lower in some countries that retained capital punishment, such as Japan.[50]

Much of the answer has to do with differences among countries in the link between public opinion and the law. In most of the United States, popular support for capital punishment translated quickly into government policy. Many other countries, by contrast, abolished capital punishment *despite* considerable popular support for it. Britain abolished the death penalty in the 1960s, when only about 20 percent favored doing so, and did not restore it despite polls in the 1970s showing that over 80 percent supported restoration. A similar divergence between the results of polls and the output of legislation can be found in Canada, France, and Austria.[51] The difference between the United States and other wealthy democracies with respect to capital punishment may simply be that the United States is more democratic, in the sense that elected officials find it more necessary to implement policies supported by a majority of the voters.

Because of its anomalous status, the United States found itself the target of increasing international criticism toward the end of the twentieth century. Organizations like Amnesty International placed American capital punishment in the same category as South African apartheid and other human rights abuses. They organized international petition drives before high-profile executions. A 1996 mission of the International Commission of Jurists, a Geneva-based human rights organization, found the United States in violation of its international treaty obligations because of the way the death penalty was administered. Many American executions and death row inmates received more media attention abroad than at home. In 2000 French journalists and editorial writers debated the possible innocence of Odell Barnes, a name unfamiliar to Americans despite his scheduled execution in Texas. Benetton, a large Italian clothing manufacturer, based an international advertising campaign on photographs of death row inmates from seven American states.[52] The growth of the

Internet in the late 1990s only intensified international interest in pending American executions, as it became a simple matter for supporters and family members of condemned prisoners to set up worldwide clearinghouses for information and expressions of solidarity.

A more pressing source of concern than foreign individuals and nongovernmental organizations was the mounting criticism by foreign governments and the organized international political community. Courts around the world began objecting to aspects of American death penalty practice. In 1989 the European Court of Human Rights blocked the extradition from England of a German national to face a capital trial in Virginia, on the ground that the American norm of execution after a lengthy period in prison would violate the European Convention on Human Rights. One of the first acts of the new Constitutional Court of South Africa in 1995 was to declare the death penalty inconsistent with the nation's new constitution, after a lengthy review and explicit rejection of American practice. In 1998 a representative of the United Nations Commission on Human Rights was sharply critical of several aspects of capital punishment in the United States and urged a moratorium on executions until reforms could be carried out. The following year the Commission resolved that all nations should move toward abolishing the death penalty completely.[53]

Foreign condemnation took an even more troubling turn at the century's end. In 1998 Paraguay brought suit against the United States in the International Court of Justice in The Hague, just as Virginia was preparing to execute a Paraguayan national in blatant violation of an international treaty that required notification of the Paraguayan consulate before the defendant could be prosecuted. Germany brought an identical suit the following year, seeking to prevent the execution of a German national in Arizona. Both Paraguay and Germany also brought suit in the United States Supreme Court. In both courts, both nations presented the plausible argument that with help from the consulate the defendants might have retained better lawyers and avoided the death penalty. In both cases, the International Court of Justice ordered the United States government to do what it could to stay the executions, but the United States Supreme Court nevertheless allowed both executions to proceed. They went forward despite a storm of foreign criticism.[54]

By the end of the twentieth century capital punishment was an uncomfortable international issue for the United States. American efforts to remedy human rights abuses in other countries were weakened by the widespread perception, especially in western Europe, that the death penalty was one such abuse. Foreign criticism had little effect on actual practice, however. The state judges and prosecutors responsible for administering capital punishment were scarcely concerned that citizens of Germany or Paraguay might consider them a bloodthirsty lot. They were accountable to a local electorate that overwhelmingly favored the death penalty.

Fatal Errors

As the twenty-first century began, capital punishment was once again a firmly established part of American criminal justice. Americans conducted ninety-eight executions in 1999, more than in any year since 1951. Death sentences and executions had become so commonplace in some states that they were no longer news; they were given only brief mention on the inside pages of newspapers, if at all. And the execution rate looked poised to skyrocket. As of October 1, 2000, there were 3,703 residents of death row, more than at any time in American history. The death row population was still increasing, because the annual number of death sentences regularly exceeded the annual number of executions by a factor of three. As more and more of these inmates reached the end of their appeals, if all else stayed the same, the execution rate was likely to reach several hundred per year within the next decade. The abolitionist movement was so weak that it posed scarcely any political obstacle to this trend. The Supreme Court seemed quite unlikely to introduce any new constitutional limits to capital punishment. The death penalty looked as though it was back to stay.

If there was any hint of a possibility of change, it was the mounting number of innocent people turning up on death row. The risk of executing the innocent had haunted capital punishment for centuries, but until the post-*Furman* era it had been a problem handled by executive clemency. With the decline of clemency in the 1970s, there was no longer any routine mechanism for resolving post-trial claims of innocence. When an innocent person was sentenced to death, his only hope was that his cause would be taken up by an unpaid altruist with the time and the resources to conduct a thorough investigation. Such people were rare and not well organized, but they nevertheless produced some startling results. Between 1987 and 1999 sixty-one condemned inmates were released from prison because they were discovered to be innocent. A few were beneficiaries of DNA testing, a technology unavailable when they were convicted, but most were not. Most had instead been victims of dishonest witnesses, prosecutors, or police officers, whose lies were found out only years later. Twelve of the sixty-one had been convicted in Illinois, a state that probably conducted trials no more improperly than any other, but a state with a community of activists who took an interest in the death penalty. In January 2000 Illinois Governor George Ryan, a conservative Republican and a supporter of capital punishment, was so troubled by the number of innocent men released from death row that he declared a moratorium on further executions until an appointed commission could figure out what had gone wrong. Ryan's announcement prompted calls for similar moratoria in many of the other death penalty states.

Many supporters of capital punishment were unimpressed by the danger of executing the innocent. "I do not want to be overly simplistic," explained Senator Jeremiah Denton of Alabama,

> but saying that we should not have the death penalty because we may accidently execute an innocent man is like saying that we should not have automobiles because some innocent people might be accidentally killed in them. Or we should not have trucking or we should not have aircraft, or we should not have elevators because we are going to have accidents.
>
> There are going to be some mistakes committed. The question is, on balance, which way do we better promote the general welfare?

But not everyone was so rigorously utilitarian. The prospect of killing an innocent person seemed to be the one thing that could cause people to rethink their support for capital punishment. Some who were not troubled by statistical arguments against the death penalty—claims about deterrence or racial disparities—were deeply troubled that such an extreme injustice might occur in an individual case. A Gallup poll conducted in February 2000, while the Illinois moratorium was still a visible item in the news, found that support for the death penalty had dropped to 66 percent, the lowest level since 1981. Ninety-one percent of those polled believed that innocent people were sentenced to death, and when respondents were asked to estimate the percentage of people sentenced to death who were innocent, the average estimate was 10 percent.[55]

Capital punishment remained very popular despite the growing concern about innocence. Indeed, its supporters and opponents made virtually identical estimates of the frequency with which innocent people were sentenced to death, suggesting that a large majority of Americans still supported capital punishment even on the assumption that a tenth of those condemned had committed no crime. The execution of Timothy McVeigh in June 2001 demonstrated that when a criminal was clearly guilty, and when his crime was especially horrible, the death penalty was as popular as ever. But if any development had the potential to change that popularity, this was the one. If further investigation were to disclose even more innocent people, or if a highly sympathetic and apparently innocent person were to be executed, one could imagine support for the death penalty dwindling quickly. In the past, when the market for news was largely local, individual high-profile cases had quickly tipped public opinion in particular states one way or the other. In the early twenty-first century, with national media spreading information about a single crime or a single defendant to every part of the country, the right case might tip opinion across the nation.

EPILOGUE

A J. BANNISTER WAS EXECUTED in Missouri in October 1997. Fifteen years earlier Bannister had killed Darrell Ruestman in a trailer park, under circumstances that remained in dispute. Bannister contended that his gun had discharged accidentally during a fight. The prosecutors believed Bannister guilty of a contract killing. Whichever story was correct, the jury heard only the prosecutors' version. Bannister's court-appointed lawyer was so inept that he failed to perform any investigation or put up any defense. He scarcely spoke to Bannister before the trial. He did not even return telephone calls from Bannister's family and friends, who would have told him of witnesses and evidence to corroborate Bannister's account. In the absence of a defense, the jury unsurprisingly convicted Bannister of intentional murder after less than an hour of deliberation. At the penalty phase of the trial, Bannister's lawyer introduced no evidence in mitigation of punishment and did not even look into Bannister's background to find any. Belief in the individual criminal's responsibility for crime was at a high point. The death penalty was accordingly very popular. The jury, from which opponents of capital punishment had been excluded, had little trouble imposing it.

For the next decade and a half, claims of constitutional error in Bannister's conviction and sentence were presented to assorted state and federal courts. Most of the litigation, however, concerned not the merits of the claims but rather the antecedent and highly technical question of which claims Bannister would even be allowed to present. The answer was not many, because of the procedural hurdles interposed by the Supreme Court in its desperate effort to control the litigation machine it had created by constitutionalizing the death penalty in the 1970s. By October 1997, when the last request for a stay of execution was denied, Bannister's case had been before the Missouri Supreme Court twice, the Missouri Court of Appeals once, the United States District Court for the Western District of Missouri twice, the United States Court of Appeals for the Eighth Circuit three times, and the United States Supreme Court three times, but most of Bannister's claims of error had never been addressed on the merits.

Meanwhile, Bannister was changing. He had killed Ruestman as a twenty-four-year-old career criminal, but now he was in his late thirties, calmer, wiser, and an articulate satirist of the more absurd aspects of prison life. He was also a celebrity. Stephen Trombley, an English documentary filmmaker, had taken an interest in his case and had produced two films about him that had been televised in England and other countries. Bannister corresponded with people from all over the world who had seen the films, including Lindsay Graham, an English woman who moved to rural southeastern Missouri to be near Bannister's home, the Potosi Correctional Center. The two were later married. Bannister wrote a book of his own, *Shall Suffer Death*, an autobiography and critique of capital punishment. His impending execution was covered in the press as far away as New Zealand. He was interviewed live on Irish radio. The last stage of his litigation drew briefs from the Bar Association of Lyon, France, and human rights organizations in Sweden and the Netherlands. Among the Americans who sought clemency were the actors Ed Asner, Gregory Peck, and Sean Penn and the singer Harry Belafonte. Asner even flew to Jefferson City, Missouri, to meet with Governor Mel Carnahan. The proliferation of Internet sites telling Bannister's story created a loose network of supporters, which was later formalized as the International Bannister Foundation, run by a Scottish couple, with affiliates in eleven other countries, devoted to abolishing capital punishment in the United States.

Condemned people had always attracted sympathy from the local community, but as American support for capital punishment became increasingly anomalous, sympathy spread around the world to nations that lacked condemned prisoners of their own. Once sympathizers had stood physically close to condemned prisoners, but the combination of dramaturgical and technological change had minimized the significance of physical space. Supporters were as close to Bannister in Dublin or Auckland as in Potosi.

In an earlier era Bannister would have been an obvious candidate for executive clemency, but not in the late twentieth century. After his death sentence survived years of litigation there was little chance it would be commuted. Clemency had once been a vehicle allowing mercy, broadly conceived, to temper the rigor of the formal law, but Governor Carnahan made it clear that he understood his role as limited to the correction of legal errors. "I have determined that the verdict reached by the jury in the case of Alan J. Bannister and the subsequent rulings by the Missouri Court of Appeals–Southern District, the Missouri Supreme Court, the Federal District Court, the 8th Circuit Court of Appeals and the U.S. Supreme Court were correct," Carnahan announced. The legal issues raised in Bannister's appeals "are without merit and therefore, do not serve as a basis for overturning the jury verdict." Carnahan was hardly alone in this view. John Ashcroft, his predecessor as governor, had felt the same way, as did virtually all state governors. "My standard was this," Ashcroft reflected. "State law had given me powers as governor to step in and correct any mistaken sentence erroneously imposed by the people through our judicial system. It would have been arrogant and irresponsible of me to second-guess the people and the court system by arbitrarily reversing the decision of unmistaken juries and judges."[1]

The constitutionalization of capital punishment had yielded a narrower view of clemency in which the governor was in effect just another appellate court, a view that was politically expedient for governors newly fearful of the electoral consequences of commuting a death sentence. To say that in considering clemency the governor was limited to a review of legal claims, after those same claims had been reviewed and rejected by multiple courts, was to say that the governor lacked any clemency power at all. The ultimate authority over who lived and died had, in practice, shifted from state governors to federal judges.

Approximately sixty protesters stood outside the prison fence during Bannister's execution, a thin remnant of the thousands who had once gathered to watch hangings, indeed a remnant intentionally thinned by the remote location in which the state had chosen to build the Potosi Correctional Center and the standard midnight hour for conducting the execution. The last words of condemned prisoners had been published for centuries, so the media representatives were ready to hear Bannister's final statement, read by a spokesman for the corrections department. "The state of Missouri is committing as premeditated a murder as possible," Bannister declared, "far more heinous than my crime." Only a handful of witnesses saw the lethal chemicals injected into Bannister's arm. He was pronounced dead five minutes after midnight.

Some of Darrell Ruestman's relatives were at the prison too. "It is hard for me to understand how all these people around the world had such an interest in this," Ruestman's nephew told the press. "They tried to portray Alan Bannister as the victim, not my uncle. Ed Asner never met my uncle."

"We think it should have been a lot sooner than this," Ruestman's brother added. "We are glad that this is over, but you can't call us happy. There are too many victims here."[2]

As the twenty-first century began, capital punishment was an emotionally charged political issue administered within a legal framework so unworkable that it satisfied no one. Supporters and opponents of the death penalty had fought to a stalemate, in which most states had expansive capital statutes but only a fraction of those sentenced to death were executed, and then only after a decade or more of litigation over procedural issues. Mercy had been banished from the system, replaced by an arcane set of rules that haphazardly selected who would live and who would die. Americans were stuck with a compromise between adopting and abolishing the death penalty that embodied the worst of both options. Yet the issue was so important that neither side would budge.

There are two possible ways out, but neither seems likely in the short run. One would be for the Supreme Court to dismantle the constitutional structure it has built around the death penalty since 1972 and allow the states to return to older, simpler procedures for sentencing criminals to death. But those simpler procedures yielded the troubling pattern of verdicts that prompted the Supreme Court to intervene in the first place. Criminal procedure, meanwhile, has been so thoroughly constitutionalized in the past few decades that a return to the practices of the first half of the twentieth century is almost unthinkable.

The other would be for state legislatures to abolish capital punishment. The death penalty is so popular that abolition will be impossible without a significant shift in public opinion. Such shifts have occurred several times in the past 250 years, however, and may well occur again. In the past they have been caused by changing attitudes about the extent to which crime is a consequence of the criminal's free will, changes that at the time seemed to flow from better understandings of human behavior. We can expect similar developments in the future. Perhaps research on the physiology of the brain, for example, will yield new information about the ability to choose between good and evil. Perhaps deterministic explanations of crime will return to favor for some other reason. As of 2001 there was already a renewed debate over the justice of executing the mentally retarded, the least responsible for their actions of those eligible for the death penalty, which suggested that the retributive impulse so dominant in public discourse over the past two decades was beginning to weaken. Whatever the cause, the balance of Americans' beliefs about free will is not likely to remain static forever. When it changes, so too will opinion on capital punishment.

APPENDIX: COUNTING EXECUTIONS

The United States Department of Justice began counting executions only in 1930. Quantitative data from 1930 on are from the Department's annual *Sourcebook of Criminal Justice Statistics* and its annual pamphlets *National Prisoner Statistics* and *Capital Punishment*.

There is no reliable count of executions before 1930. Until relatively recently executions were conducted by units of local government and typically produced no official public record. Most executions we know about only because of a brief notice in a local newspaper. If there was no local newspaper, if the newspaper did not mention the execution, or if no copies of the newspaper have survived, an execution is likely to have left no record at all. The total number of executions in American history is unknown, and probably unknowable.

The closest estimate we have comes from the work of Watt Espy, who as of December 1998 had compiled information on 19,248 executions in the United States and its colonial predecessors, in the form of paper files in his house in Alabama. An earlier version of his database, containing the 14,634 executions then known to him, was coded and entered into a computer at the University of Alabama in the late 1980s and early 1990s. It is available on the Internet from the Inter-university Consortium for Political and Social Research, at www.icpsr.umich.edu. I have used this version cautiously for years before 1930, as a source of estimates rather than precise numbers, because many errors were introduced during coding and data entry, and because the database includes only about 75 percent of the executions known to Espy.

Because the Justice Department did not report information about methods of execution in some years, I have used Espy's data on execution method up through 1964. I have also used Espy's data on the race of the condemned through 1950, because the Justice Department did not break down its state-by-state data by race.

The relatively small number of executions conducted by the federal government I have allocated to the states in which they took place.

NOTES

Introduction

1 *Execution of Stephen Merrill Clark* ([Salem]: s.n., [1821]); *Account of the Short Life and Ignominious Death of Stephen Merrill Clark* (Salem: T. C. Cushing, 1821); *Lines Written on Reading an Account of the Execution of Stephen M. Clark* (s.l.: s.n., [1821]); *Salem Gazette*, 20 Feb. 1821, 3:2; 11 May 1821, 3:3; *Essex Register*, 17 Feb. 1821, 3:1; 12 May 1821, 3:2; *Essex Patriot*, 12 May 1821, 3:3; *Newburyport Herald*, 22 Aug. 1820, 3:3; 11 May 1821, 3:2.

2 Mass. House Doc. 32 (1836), 36; Charles Spear, *Essays on the Punishment of Death*, 5th ed. (Boston: Charles Spear, 1844), 46.

1. Terror, Blood, and Repentance

1 There is a sharp regional bias in the early American sources. We have much more evidence from the North than from the South. Within the North, New England sources dominate; within New England, there is much more from the Boston area than anywhere else. In the South, most of the surviving evidence is from Virginia. One obviously has to be careful about making national generalizations from regional data. But sometimes the circumstances giving rise to a particular belief or practice were identical in different regions, and in those cases I have felt justified in speculating that the belief or practice was likewise uniform, even in the absence of evidence from a given region. Sometimes we have evidence from a later period for a given region, and where reasonable I have guessed that beliefs or practices were similar in that region in an earlier period for which evidence is lacking. This problem recurs frequently throughout the first four chapters. I do not flag the issue at each recurrence, but it should be kept in mind.

2 J. Hammond Trumbull and Charles J. Hoadly, eds., *The Public Records of the Colony of Connecticut* (Hartford: Brown & Parsons, 1850–1890), 1:77; *The Colonial Laws of Massachusetts* (Boston: Rockwell & Churchill, 1889),

55; Nathaniel B. Shurtleff and David Pulsifer, eds., *Records of the Colony of New Plymouth* (Boston: William White, 1855–1861), 11:12; John D. Cushing, ed., *The Earliest Printed Laws of Pennsylvania* (Wilmington: Michael Glazier, 1978), 37–38, 40, 44; *The Colonial Laws of New York* (Albany: James B. Lyon, 1894), 1:20–21, 77; John D. Cushing, ed., *Acts and Laws of New Hampshire 1680–1726* (Wilmington: Michael Glazier, 1978), 207–208; John D. Cushing, ed., *The Earliest Laws of the New Haven and Connecticut Colonies* (Wilmington: Michael Glazier, 1977), 17.

3 Trumbull and Hoadly, eds., *Public Records of Connecticut*, 1:77; *Colonial Laws of Massachusetts*, 55; Cushing, ed., *Acts and Laws of New Hampshire*, 204; *Colonial Laws of New York*, 1:21; Mass. 1697, c. 20; 1694/5, c. 5; 1695/6, c. 2; N.H. 1718, c. 38; *Minutes of the Supreme Executive Council of Pennsylvania* (Harrisburg: Theo. Fenn & Co., 1851–1853), 14:588.

4 David Hackett Fischer, *Albion's Seed: Four British Folkways in America* (New York: Oxford University Press, 1989).

5 *Colonial Laws of Massachusetts*, 127; Mass. 1711/2, c. 3; 1761, c. 8; N.H. 1682, c. 4; 1718, c. 38; Cushing, ed., *Earliest Laws of the New Haven and Connecticut Colonies*, 83; *Colonial Laws of Massachusetts*, 152; Pa. 1718, c. 234; Edwin R. Keedy, "History of the Pennsylvania Statute Creating Degrees of Murder," *University of Pennsylvania Law Review* 97 (1949): 763; Pa. 1739, c. 353; 1768, c. 570; 1770, c. 612; *Colonial Laws of New York*, 1:389 (1699); 1:666–68 (1709); 5:418–21 (1772); Herbert William Keith Fitzroy, "The Punishment of Crime in Provincial Pennsylvania," *Pennsylvania Magazine of History and Biography* 60 (1936): 256.

6 Va. 1742, c. 1; 1748, c. 51; 1765, c. 18; 1705, c. 14; 1744, c. 16; 1762, c. 8; Del. 1741, c. 90; 1751, c. 120; S.C. 1712, no. 322.

7 *Colonial Laws of New York*, 1:761–67 (1712); S.C. 1740, no. 695; Va. 1748, c. 38; John D. Cushing, ed., *The Earliest Printed Laws of the Province of Georgia* (Wilmington: Michael Glazier, 1978), 19–23; Md. 1737, p. 8.

8 Philip J. Schwarz, *Twice Condemned: Slaves and the Criminal Laws of Virginia, 1705–1865* (Baton Rouge: Louisiana State University Press, 1988), 17–18, 25; Michael Stephen Hindus, *Prison and Plantation: Crime, Justice, and Authority in Massachusetts and South Carolina, 1767–1878* (Chapel Hill: University of North Carolina Press, 1980), 131–132; Donna J. Spindel, *Crime and Society in North Carolina, 1663–1776* (Baton Rouge: Louisiana State University Press, 1989), 135, 125.

9 William Hand Browne et al., eds., *Archives of Maryland* (Baltimore: Maryland Historical Society, 1883–1972), 24:11.

10 James Dana, *The Intent of Capital Punishment* (New-Haven: T. and S. Green, [1790]), 12; VG, 31 Jan. 1751, 1:1; *A Short Account of the Life and*

Character of John Campbell ([New York]: s.n., [1769]); Aaron Hutchinson, *Iniquity Purged by Mercy and Truth* (Boston: Thomas and John Fleet, 1769), 13.

11 Noah Hobart, *Excessive Wickedness, the Way to an Untimely Death* (New-Haven: Thomas and Samuel Green, [1768]), 29; Nathaniel Fisher, *A Sermon: Delivered at Salem, January 14, 1796* (Boston: S. Hall, 1796), 15; Nathan Strong, *The Reasons and Design of Public Punishments* (Hartford: Eben. Watson, 1777), 9.

12 William Williams, *The Serious Consideration, that God Will Visit and Judge Men for Sin* (Boston: Thomas Fleet, 1738), 20; Ezra Ripley, *Love to Our Neighbour Explained and Urged* (Boston: Samuel Hall, 1800), 31; *The Life, Last Words, and Dying Speech of Valentine Dukett* ([Boston]: s.n., [1774]); *The Dying Penitent; or, the Affecting Speech of Levi Ames* (Boston: s.n., 1773).

13 Dana, *Intent*, 8; VG, 14 Aug. 1752, 2:1.

14 *A Few Lines on Occasion of the Untimely End of Mark and Phillis* ([Boston]: s.n., [1755]); Abner Cheney Goodell Jr., *The Trial and Execution, for Petit Treason, of Mark and Phillis* (Cambridge, Mass.: John Wilson and Son, 1883), 30; *Collections of the Massachusetts Historical Society*, 1st ser., 5 (1798): 107–108.

15 VG, 3 Feb. 1774, 2:2; *Archives of Maryland*, 31:69; Victor Hugo Paltsits, ed., *Minutes of the Executive Council of the Province of New York* (Albany: State of New York, 1910), 1:157; PG, 2 Oct. 1729.

16 Aaron Bancroft, *The Importance of a Religious Education Illustrated and Enforced* (Worcester: Isaiah Thomas, 1793), 23; Chauncy Graham, *God Will Trouble the Troublers of His People* (New-York: H. Gaine, 1759), 12.

17 Daniel A. Cohen, *Pillars of Salt, Monuments of Grace: New England Crime Literature and the Origins of American Popular Culture, 1674–1860* (New York: Oxford University Press, 1993), 83–86; Increase Mather, *A Sermon (Preached at the Lecture in Boston . . .)* (Boston: J. Brunning, 1685), 24–25; *The Dying Criminal: A Poem by Robert Young, on His Own Execution* (New-London: s.n., [1779]).

18 Numbers 35:33; [Cotton Mather], *Tremenda: The Dreadful Sound With Which the Wicked Are to be Thunderstruck* (Boston: B. Green, 1721), 33; Samuel Danforth, *The Woful Effects of Drunkenness* (Boston: B. Green, 1710), 2; Enoch Huntington, *A Sermon Preached at Haddam, June 14, 1797* (Middletown, Conn.: Moses H. Woodward, 1797), 20.

19 *A Mournful Poem on the Death of John Ormsby and Matthew Cushing* (Boston: s.n., [1734]); *The Agonies of a Soul Departing Out of Time into Eternity* ([Boston]: s.n., [1757]).

20 A *Faithful Narrative of the Wicked Life and Remarkable Conversion of Patience Boston Alias Samson* (Boston: S. Kneeland and T. Green, 1738), 26.

21 H. R. McIlwaine, ed., *Minutes of the Council and General Court of Colonial Virginia* (Richmond: Colonial Press, 1924), 329; *Records of the Court of Assistants of the Colony of the Massachusetts Bay 1630–1692* (Boston: County of Suffolk, 1901), 1:36–39; *The Dying Speech and Confession of William Linsey* (Boston: s.n., 1770).

22 *Records of the Court of Assistants*, 1:50; H. Clay Reed and George J. Miller, eds., *The Burlington Court Book: A Record of Quaker Jurisprudence in West New Jersey 1680–1709* (Washington: American Historical Association, 1944), 142.

23 *The Wonders of Free-Grace: Or, A Compleat History of All the Remarkable Penitents That Have Been Executed at Tyburn* (London: John Dunton, 1690), intro.

24 George Birkbeck Hill, ed., *Boswell's Life of Johnson*, rev. ed., ed. L. F. Powell (Oxford: Clarendon Press, 1934), 3:167; Thomas Foxcroft, *Lessons of Caution to Young Sinners* (Boston: S. Kneeland and T. Green, 1733), i; *The Last Words and Dying Confession of the Three Pirates* (Philadelphia: Folwell's Press, [1800]).

25 Proclamation Book AAA, 1782–1823 (microfilm reel 40–41), 76, 121, 127, 202, 224, 263, 264, GAA; Connecticut Archives, Crimes and Misdemeanors, 1st ser., 5:393, CTA.

26 Massachusetts Archives, 44:514, MAA; Connecticut Archives, Crimes and Misdemeanors, 1st ser., 5:363c, 5:364, CTA.

27 Thomas Foxcroft, *Lessons of Caution to Young Sinners* (Boston: S. Kneeland and T. Green, 1733), i; (Newport, R.I.: Peter Edes, [1791]); *Reflections Occasioned by a Public Execution at Boston* ([Boston]: s.n., [1822]), 6.

28 Joshua Spalding, *The Prayer of a True Penitent for Mercy* (Salem, Mass.: Dabney and Cushing, 1787), 24; Moses Baldwin, *The Ungodly Condemned in Judgment* (Boston: Kneeland and Adams, 1771), 19.

29 Elhanan Winchester, *The Execution Hymn, Composed on Levi Ames* ([Boston]: E. Russell, [1773]); Christopher Flanagan, *The Conversation & Conduct, of the Late Unfortunate John Young* (New York: T. Kirk, 1797), 4; *An Authentic and Particular Account of the Life of Francis Burdett Personel* (New-York: s.n., 1773), 20; [Cotton Mather], *The Valley of Hinnom* (Boston: J. Allen, 1717), 1.

30 *An Account of the Robberies Committed by John Morrison* (Philadelphia: s.n., 1750–1751), 9; *Minutes of the Provincial Council of Pennsylvania* (Harrisburg: Theo. Fenn & Co., 1851–1853), 5:506.

31 Cotton Mather, *Speedy Repentance Urged* (Boston: Samuel Greene, 1690),

68; Dorothy Ripley, *An Account of Rose Butler* (New York: John C. Totten, 1819), 4; *The Diary of William Bentley* (Salem, Mass.: Essex Institute, 1905–1914), 1:48.

32 *The Last Words and Dying Speech of Thomas Goss* (s.l.: s.n., [1778]); *The Confession and Dying Words of Samuel Frost* (Keene, N.H.: Henry Blake, [1793]); Benjamin Colman, *It is a Fearful Thing to Fall Into the Hands of the Living God* (Boston: John Philip and Thomas Hancock, 1726), 29; John Williams, *Warnings to the Unclean* (Boston: B. Green and J. Allen, 1699), 6.

33 John Webb, *The Greatness of Sin Improv'd by the Penitent* (Boston: S. Kneeland & T. Green, 1734), 26–27; Increase Mather, *The Folly of Sinning, Opened & Applyed* (Boston: B. Green & J. Allen, 1699), 42–43.

34 Cotton Mather, *A Sorrowful Spectacle* (Boston: [ill.], 1715), 77–78.

35 Henry Channing, *God Admonishing His People of Their Duty* (New-London: T. Green, 1786), 30; *A Correct Journal of the Conduct of the Two Unfortunate Prisoners, Sinclair & Johnson* (New York: s.n., 1811), 11; Nathaniel Clap, *Sinners Directed to Hear & Fear* (Boston: J. Allen, 1715), vi; Webb, *The Greatness of Sin*, appendix.

36 Karen Halttunen, *Murder Most Foul: The Killer and the American Gothic Imagination* (Cambridge, Mass.: Harvard University Press, 1998).

2. Hanging Day

1 John Rogers, *Death the Certain Wages of Sin to the Impenitent* (Boston: B. Green and J. Allen, 1701), 153; *Diary of Joshua Hempstead of New London, Connecticut* (New London: New London County Historical Society, 1901), 619; *The Life and Confession of Daniel Wilson* ([Providence]: s.n., [1774]); *The Authentic Confession of Jesse Strang, as Made to the Rev. Mr. Lacy* (New-York: s.n., 1832), 10; *Trial and Sentence of John Johnson, for the Murder of James Murray* (New-York: Joseph Desnoues, 1824), 36.

2 Eliphalet Adams, *A Sermon Preached on the Occasion of the Execution of Katherine Garret* (New London: T. Green, 1738), 42.

3 William Shurtleff, *The Faith and Prayer of a Dying Malefactor* (Boston: J. Draper, 1740), i; Samuel Moodey, *Summary Account of the Life and Death of Joseph Quasson, Indian* (Boston: S. Gerrish, 1726), 25; Perry Miller and Thomas H. Johnson, eds., *The Puritans* (New York: American Book Co., 1938), 414; *Connecticut Courant*, 12 June 1797, 3:2.

4 *A Few Lines upon the Awful Execution of John Ormesby & Matth. Cushing* ([Boston]: s.n., [1734]); Olivia Robbins to Lucretia Miller, 8 June 1811, no. 9701, NYL.

5 *Minutes of the Common Council of the City of New York 1784–1831* (New York: City of New York, 1917–1930), 1:71, 6:473, 6:570, 13:647; *Execution of*

Richard Johnson and Catharine Cashiere ([New York]: s.n., [1829]), 9–11; *The Confession and Execution of George Brown* (New York: s.n., 1819), 10; *The Life, Trial, Confession and Execution of Albert W. Hicks* (New York: Robert M. DeWitt, 1860), 69–79; Elaine Forman Crane, ed., *The Diary of Elizabeth Drinker* (Boston: Northeastern University Press, 1991), 1298.

6 *A Solemn Farewell to Levi Ames* (Boston: Draper's Printing Office, [1773]); John Bryson Papers, P.C. 371.1, NCA; *Pennsylvania Herald*, 24 Mar. 1787, 3:1; *Pennsylvania Mercury*, 27 Nov. 1788, 2:1.

7 Steven E. Kagle, ed., *The Diary of Josiah Atkins* (New York: Arno Press, 1975), 20; *Diary of Joshua Hempstead*, 334; William G. McLoughlin, ed., *The Diary of Isaac Backus* (Providence: Brown University Press, 1979), 355.

8 Robert R. McCausland and Cynthia MacAlman McCausland, *The Diary of Martha Ballard 1785–1812* (Camden, Me.: Picton Press, 1992), 311, 225; Diary, III:81 (19 Mar. 1833), Henry Van Der Lyn Papers, NYHS; Thomas Foxcroft, *Lessons of Caution to Young Sinners* (Boston: S. Kneeland and T. Green, 1733), i.

9 *A Candid and Impartial Account of the Behaviour of Simon Lord Lovat* (Boston: J. Draper, 1747), 2.

10 Ephraim Clark, *Sovereign Grace Displayed in the Conversion and Salvation of a Penitent Sinner* (Boston: John Boyles, 1773), 17; Shurtleff, *Faith and Prayer*, ii; William Williams, *The Serious Consideration, that God Will Visit and Judge Men for Sin* (Boston: Thomas Fleet, 1738), 5.

11 *A Poem on Ebenezer Mason* ([Boston]: s.n., [1802]); Rogers, *Death the Certain Wages*, 153.

12 *A Poem Occasioned by the Untimely Death of Hugh Henderson* (Boston: s.n., 1737), 1; *A Few Lines Wrote Upon the Intended Execution of Levi Ames* ([Boston]: s.n., [1773]); "The Execution: A Pathetic Fragment," *New-York Weekly Magazine* 1 (1796): 307.

13 Thaddeus Maccarty, *The Power and Grace of Christ Display'd to a Dying Malefactor* (Boston: Kneeland and Adams, [1768]), 25.

14 *A Brief Relation of a Murder Committed by Elizabeth Shaw* (New-London: s.n., 1772); *Made on Ebenezer Ball* (s.l.: s.n., [1811]).

15 Jeffrey Goldstein, ed., *Why We Watch: The Attractions of Violent Entertainment* (New York: Oxford University Press, 1998).

16 Ronald A. Bosco, "Lectures at the Pillory: The Early American Execution Sermon," *American Quarterly* 30 (1978): 156–176; *Diary of Cotton Mather 1681–1708* (Boston: Massachusetts Historical Society, 1911), 1:30, 1:165; *The Life and Confession of George B. Jarman* (New-Brunswick, N.J.: Jacob Edmonds, William Packer, & Aaron Slack, [1828]), 5; Cotton Mather, *Speedy Repentance Urged* (Boston: Samuel Greene, 1690), 1.

17 Andrew Eliot, *Christ's Promise to the Penitent Thief* (Boston: John Boyle, 1773), 28.

18 Increase Mather, *A Sermon Occasioned by the Execution of a Man Found Guilty of Murder*, 2d ed. (Boston: R.P., 1687), 23; Aaron Bascom, *A Sermon, Preached at the Execution of Abiel Converse* (Northampton, Mass.: William Butler, 1788), 23; Timothy Langdon, *A Sermon, Preached at Danbury* (Danbury, Conn.: Douglas & Nichols, 1798), 18.

19 [Cotton Mather], *Fearful Warnings to Prevent Fearful Judgments* (Boston: Timothy Green, 1704), 30; Thaddeus Mason Harris, *A Sermon Preached in the First Parish in Dedham* (Dedham, Mass.: Herman Mann, 1801), 21; Hezekiah N. Woodruff, *A Sermon, Preached at Scipio, N.Y.* (Albany: Charles R. and George Webster, 1804), 20–21.

20 *An Address to the Spectator of the Awful Execution in Boston* (Cornhill: U. Crocker, 1819), 5; Dorothy Ripley, *An Account of Rose Butler* (New York: John C. Totten, 1819), 18.

21 Timothy Pitkin, *A Sermon, Delivered at Litchfield* (Hartford: Green & Watson, [1768]), 11–12; Parkman Family Papers, Box 1, Folder 7, no. 1932, AAS. I have spelled out several words that are abbreviated in Parkman's original manuscript.

22 George Webb, *The Office and Authority of a Justice of Peace* (Williamsburg: William Parks, 1736), 293, 303.

23 Nathaniel B. Shurtleff, ed., *Records of the Governor and Company of the Massachusetts Bay in New England* (Boston: William White, 1853–1854), 3:164; William Hand Browne et al., eds., *Archives of Maryland* (Baltimore: Maryland Historical Society, 1883–1972), 3:146, 49:545, 57:356, 51:214, 5:499; Massachusetts Archives, 40:279, MAA.

24 Joel Munsell, *The Annals of Albany* (Albany: J. Munsell, 1850–1859), 2:203.

25 Council Papers (A1894), 22:71, NYA; Negley K. Teeters, "Public Executions in Philadelphia," *Prison Journal* 38 (1958): 65–66.

26 *American Weekly Mercury*, 7 July 1737, 3:1; *The Confession of John Battus* ([Dedham, Mass.]: s.n., [1804]), 39; *Archives of Maryland*, 65:2–8.

27 PG, 15 July 1731; *The Letters and Papers of Cadwallader Colden* (New York: New-York Historical Society, 1918–1937), 6:120; *A Faithful Narrative of the Wicked Life and Remarkable Conversion of Patience Boston* (Boston: S. Kneeland and T. Green, 1738), 32.

28 *A Brief Narrative of the Life and Confession of Barnett Davenport* (s.l.: s.n., [1780]), 14; Samuel Stillman, *Two Sermons* (Boston: E. Russell, 1773), 28; John Shearman, *I Am Now to Finish a Life . . .* (Boston: Z. Fowle, 1764); VG, 14 Oct. 1773, 1:3; Timothy Hilliard, *Paradise Promised by a Dying Saviour* (Boston: E. Russell, 1785), 30; *Maryland Gazette*, 21 May 1752, 3:1.

29 [Cotton Mather,] *Instructions to the Living, from the Condition of the Dead* (Boston: John Allen, 1717), 37; Bartlett Burleigh James and J. Franklin Jameson, eds., *Journal of Jasper Danckaerts 1679–1680* (New York: Barnes & Noble, 1959), 136; *Narrative of the Life, Last Dying Speech & Confession of John Young* ([New York]: s.n., [1797]), 8.

30 Charles Biddle, *Autobiography of Charles Biddle* (Philadelphia: E. Claxton, 1883), 206; [Cotton Mather], *The Vial Poured Out Upon the Sea* (Boston: T. Fleet, 1726), 47. Jack Ketch was a seventeenth-century English executioner whose name came to denote hangmen in general.

31 *A Full and Particular Narrative of the Life, Character and Conduct of John Banks* (New York: s.n., 1807), 14; *PG*, 6 May 1742; Joseph B. Felt, *History of Ipswich, Essex, and Hamilton* (Cambridge, Mass.: Charles Folsom, 1834), 117. I have seen no other North American evidence of a hangman's right to keep the condemned person's clothes, but the tradition did exist in early eighteenth-century London; see Madame van Muyden, ed. and trans., *A Foreign View of England in 1725–1729: The Letters of Monsieur Cesar de Saussure to His Family* (London: Caliban Books, 1995), 78. It may have existed in parts of North America as well, or else Atwood may have erroneously assumed that it did.

32 Cotton Mather, *The Vial*, 48.

33 *A Narrative of the Life, Together with the Last Speech, Confession and Solemn Declaration, of John Lewis* (New-Haven: James Parker, 1762), 10; *The Last Speech and Dying Words of John Clarkewight* ([New York]: s.n., [1770]); *The Last Words, and Dying Speech of Elisha Thomas* (s.l.: s.n., [1788]); *The Dying Speech of John Ury* ([Philadelphia]: s.n., [1741]), 2; *The Last Speech, Confession and Dying Words of John Smith* (New-Haven: s.n., 1773), 4; *The Last Words, and Dying Speech of Joseph Lightly* (Boston: s.n., 1765).

34 *The Confession and Declaration of George Burns* (Charles-Town [Charleston, S.C.]: John Hugar Van Huerin, 1768); *PG*, 30 July 1752.

35 Lawrence W. Towner, "True Confessions and Dying Warnings in Colonial New England," in *Sibley's Heir: A Volume in Memory of Clifford Kenyon Shipton* (Boston: Colonial Society of Massachusetts, 1982), 525.

36 *The Declaration & Confession of Matthew Cushing* ([Boston]: s.n., [1734]); *The Confession and Dying Speech of Stephen Smith* ([Boston]: s.n., 1797); *The Last Speech & Dying Words of William Welch* ([Boston]: s.n., [1754]).

37 *An Exhortation to Young and Old to be Cautious of Small Crimes, Lest They Become Habitual* ([Boston]: s.n., [1773]); [William Gilpin], *The Life of William Baker* (Philadelphia: B. & J. Johnson, 1800), 31; *Last Words and Dying Speech of Samuel Smith* (Concord, Mass.: s.n., 1799).

38 *The Lives, Last Words, and Dying Speech of Ezra Ross, James Buchanan, and*

William Brooks (Worcester: s.n., 1778), 7; *The Declaration, Dying Warning and Advice of Rebekah Chamblit* (Boston: S. Kneeland and T. Green, [1733]).

39 *The Life, and Dying Speech of Arthur, a Negro Man* (Boston: s.n., 1768); *Life, Last Words and Dying Confession, of Rachel Wall* (Boston: s.n., 1789); *Letter from J[osep]h J[ohnso]n, One of the Mohegan Tribe of Indians, to his Countryman, Moses Paul* ([New London]: s.n., [1772]), 2; *Mr. Occom's Address to his Indian Brethren* (Boston: s.n., [1773]); *PG*, 16 Sept. 1772.

40 *The Life and Confession of Cato, a Slave of Elijah Mount* (Johnstown, N.Y.: Abraham Romyen, 1803), 3, 12; *The Address of Abraham Johnstone, a Black Man* (Philadelphia: s.n., 1797), 6–7.

41 Shurtleff, ed., *Records of the Governor*, 4(1):3; *A Short Account of the Life of John ********, Alias Owen Syllavan* (Boston: Green & Russell, 1756), 12; *The Wages of Sin; or, Robbery Justly Rewarded* (Boston: s.n., [1732]).

42 James Kendall Hosmer, ed., *Winthrop's Journal* (New York: Scribner's, 1908), 1:283; John Winthrop, *The History of New England from 1630 to 1649* (Boston: Little, Brown, 1853), 2:369–370; Cotton Mather, *Pillars of Salt* (Boston: Samuel Phillips, 1699), 62.

43 *VG*, 24 Nov. 1738, 4:1.

44 M. Halsey Thomas, ed., *The Diary of Samuel Sewall 1674–1729* (New York: Farrar, Straus and Giroux, 1973), 509; V. A. C. Gatrell, *The Hanging Tree: Execution and the English People 1770–1860* (Oxford: Oxford University Press, 1996), 52; *Life, Last Words and Dying Speech of Stephen Smith* ([Boston]: s.n., [1797]).

45 *The Last Words of Ebenezer Mason*, 2d ed. (Dedham, Mass.: Minerva-Office, 1802), 17; *The Last Dying Words, with a Particular Account of the Execution of James Hamilton* (New York: s.n., 1818), 11; *New-Haven Gazette*, 11 Jan. 1787, 1:363.

46 *PG*, 15 June 1738. The other suicides are reported in the issues of 27 Aug. 1730, 17 June 1731, 16 Mar. 1732, 18 May 1732, 12 Sept. 1734, 1 June 1738, 8 June 1738, and 26 Apr. 1739.

47 Ryk James and Rachel Nasmyth-Jones, "The Occurrence of Cervical Fractures in Victims of Judicial Hanging," *Forensic Science International* 54 (1992): 81–91; Alonzo Calkins, *Felonious Homicide: Its Penalty, and the Execution Thereof, Judicially* (New York: Russell Brothers, 1873), 17.

48 *The Life, Confession, and Atrocious Crimes of Antoine Probst, the Murderer of the Deering Family* (Philadelphia: Barclay, 1866), 103; Stuart C. Wade, *Lured to Death or the Minneapolis Murder* (Chicago: E. A. Weeks, 1895), 288.

49 Donald T. Reay et al., "Injuries Produced by Judicial Hanging: A Case Re-

port," *American Journal of Forensic Medicine and Pathology* 15 (1994): 185; James and Nasmyth-Jones, "Occurrence of Cervical Fractures," 91.

50 Lincoln B. Faller, *Turned to Account: The Forms and Functions of Criminal Biography in Late Seventeenth- and Early Eighteenth-Century England* (Cambridge: Cambridge University Press, 1987); J. A. Sharpe, "Last Dying Speeches": Religion, Ideology and Public Execution in Seventeenth-Century England," *Past and Present* 107 (1985): 144–167; Walter Lazenby, "Exhortation as Exorcism: Cotton Mather's Sermons to Murderers," *Quarterly Journal of Speech* 57 (1971): 51.

51 *Declaration & Confession of Matthew Cushing; The Narrative of Whiting Sweeting* (Lansingburgh, N.Y.: Silvester Tiffany, [1791]), advertisement; *Poor Julleyoun's Warnings to Children and Servants* (Boston: B. Gray and A. Butler, [1733]); *Advice From the Dead to the Living* (Boston: s.n., [1733]); *The Last Speech and Dying Advice of Poor Julian* (Boston: T. Fleet, [1733]).

52 *The Vain Prodigal Life, and Tragical Penitent Death of Thomas Hellier* (London: Sam. Crouch, 1680), 15; *Dying Confession of Pomp* ([Newburyport, Mass.]: Jonathan Plummer, [1795]).

53 *PG*, 12 Oct. 1752; *The Last Words and Dying Speech of Levi Ames* (Boston: s.n., [1773]); *A Journal of the Life and Travels of Joseph-Bill Packer* ([Albany]: s.n., [1773]), 10.

54 *A Short Account of the Life of Moses Paul* (New-Haven: s.n., 1772).

55 Erving Goffman, *Frame Analysis: An Essay on the Organization of Experience* (1974; Boston: Northeastern University Press, 1986), 264–265.

3. Degrees of Death

1 Council Papers (A1894), 26:56, NYA.

2 Douglas Greenberg, *Crime and Law Enforcement in the Colony of New York, 1691–1776* (Ithaca: Cornell University Press, 1976), 130; Arthur P. Scott, *Criminal Law in Colonial Virginia* (Chicago: University of Chicago Press, 1930), 119n232.

3 Colonial governors lacked the authority to pardon for murder and treason, a power that in principle resided in the crown. Julius Goebel Jr., and T. Raymond Naughton, *Law Enforcement in Colonial New York* (New York: Commonwealth Fund, 1944), 754; Hugh F. Rankin, *Criminal Trial Proceedings in the General Court of Colonial Virginia* (Charlottesville: University Press of Virginia, 1965), 204. But governors' recommendations regarding pardons in murder cases appear to have been virtually always followed, because of the imperial government's lack of first-hand knowledge of the cases.

4 *PG*, 15 Dec. 1763; William Hand Browne et al., eds., *Archives of Maryland* (Baltimore: Maryland Historical Society, 1883–1972), 31:32–33; Sandra Gioia

Treadway et al., eds., *Journals of the Council of the State of Virginia* (Richmond: Virginia State Library, 1931–1982), 5:218–219; Herbert A. Johnson et al., eds., *The Papers of John Marshall* (Chapel Hill: University of North Carolina Press, 1974–), 2:207–208; Connecticut Archives, Crimes and Misdemeanors, 1st ser., 4:80i, CTA; *Life and Confession of Charles O'Donnel* (Lancaster, Pa.: W. & R. Dickson, 1798), 14.

5 Jack P. Greene, ed., *The Diary of Colonel Landon Carter of Sabine Hall, 1752–1778* (Charlottesville: University Press of Virginia, 1965), 396–397; Treadway et al., eds., *Journals of the Council*, 5:294, 303; Council Papers (A1894), 42:72, 42:118, NYA; VG (PD), 22 Dec. 1768, 3:3.

6 Maryland State Papers (Series A), S1004, 6636–31–105/7, MDA; Colonial Papers (A1894), 82:38, NYA; *Archives of Maryland*, 32:315.

7 14 Jan. 1790, Edmund Randolph collection, CHS; Treadway et al., eds., *Journals of the Council*, 5:155–156; Connecticut Archives, Crimes and Misdemeanors, 1st ser., 4:118–119, 6:220, CTA.

8 E. B. O'Callaghan, ed., *Documents Relative to the Colonial History of the State of New-York* (Albany: Weed, Parsons, 1853–1857), 5:371; *Minutes of the Provincial Council of Pennsylvania* (Harrisburg: Theo. Fenn, 1851–1853), 8:336; Connecticut Archives, Crimes and Misdemeanors, 1st ser., 5:47–53, CTA.

9 *Archives of Maryland*, 31:33; Robert J. Cain, ed., *The Colonial Records of North Carolina*, 2d ser. (Raleigh: North Carolina Dept. of Cultural Resources, 1994), 9:210, 615–616; *Minutes of the Provincial Council of Pennsylvania*, 5:566, 6:136.

10 *Maryland Gazette*, 8 Aug. 1754, 2:3; *Minutes of the Provincial Council of Pennsylvania*, 5:506. Some suspected criminals were not prosecuted in exchange for their testimony against others. See, e.g., *The Last Speech, Confession and Dying Words, of John Wall Lovey* ([New York]: s.n., [1773]).

11 *A Narrative of the Treatment Coll. Bayard Received* ([New York]: s.n., [1702]), 3.

12 *The Last Words and Dying Speech of Robert Young* (New-London: s.n., [1779]); *The Lives and Dying Confessions of Richard Barrick, and John Sullivan, High-way Robbers* (Worcester: s.n., [1784]), 5–6; *Dying Speech of Cassumo Garcelli* ([Boston]: s.n., [1784]); *The Last Speech and Confession of John Ryer* ([New York]: s.n., [1793]).

13 *Dying Confession [of Three] Pirates* ([Boston]: s.n., 1794); *The Life, Last Words and Dying Speech of Dirick Grout* (s.l.: s.n., [1784]); Sylvanus Conant, *The Blood of Abel* (Boston: Edes and Gill, 1764), 34.

14 Connecticut Archives, Crimes and Misdemeanors, 1st ser., 5:363b, CTA.

15 *The Last Speech and Dying Advice of Poor Julian* (Boston: T. Fleet, [1733]);

Sketches of the Life of Joseph Mountain (New-Haven: T. & S. Green, [1790]), 17; *The Confession and Dying Words of John Jubeart* ([New York]: John Stewart, [1769]).

16 *The Last Speech and Dying Words of John Ormsby* (Boston: Thomas Fleet, 1734); Connecticut Archives, Crimes and Misdemeanors, 1st ser., 4:164, CTA.

17 VG (PD), 14 Oct. 1773, 1:3; Harry B. Weiss and Grace M. Weiss, *An Introduction to Crime and Punishment in Colonial New Jersey* (Trenton: Past Times Press, 1960), 43; *The Life and Confession of Herman Rosencrantz* (Philadelphia: James Chattin, [1770]), 11; Council Papers (A1894), 55:1, NYA; Connecticut Archives, Crimes and Misdemeanors, 1st ser., 4:119, CTA.

18 Leona C. Gabel, *Benefit of Clergy in England in the Later Middle Ages* (1928–1929; New York: Octagon Books, 1969).

19 George W. Dalzell, *Benefit of Clergy in America & Related Matters* (Winston-Salem: John F. Blair, 1955); Jeffrey K. Sawyer, "'Benefit of Clergy' in Maryland and Virginia," *American Journal of Legal History* 34 (1990): 49–68.

20 Md. 1720, c. 25; 1729, p. 3; 1737, p. 2.

21 Mass. 1784, c. 56; N.Y. 1788, c. 37; U.S. 1 Stat. 112, s. 31; Pa. 15 Stat. 174 (1794); Va. 1796, c. 2, s. 13; Md. 1809, c. 138, s. 11; S.C. 1868, no. 91.

22 *Archives of Maryland*, 49:545; *Boston Weekly Post-Boy*, 3 Sept. 1744; Connecticut Archives, Crimes and Misdemeanors, 1st ser., 5:392b–392c, CTA.

23 Mass. 1692/3, c. 18.

24 Mass. 1694/5, c. 5; 1695/6, c. 2; 1697, c. 20; 1728/9, c. 15; 1736/7, c. 18; 1784, c. 56.

25 Pieter Spierenburg, *The Spectacle of Suffering* (Cambridge: Cambridge University Press, 1984), 67; *Records of the Court of Assistants of the Colony of the Massachusetts Bay 1630–1692* (Boston: County of Suffolk, 1901), 1:29–30.

26 N.H. 1718, c. 38; R.I. 1749, p. 53; PG, 18 Mar. 1731, 19 Oct. 1752, 27 Feb. 1753, 17 Oct. 1754; Connecticut Archives, Crimes and Misdemeanors, 1st ser., 3:43, 6:83b, CTA.

27 PG, 30 Jan. 1753; Connecticut Archives, Crimes and Misdemeanors, 1st ser., 5:144a-146, CTA.

28 ([Boston]: s.n., [1773]).

29 PG, 20 Jan. 1730.

30 *Minutes of the Provincial Council of Pennsylvania*, 4:224, 15:31; Raphael Semmes, *Crime and Punishment in Early Maryland* (Baltimore: Johns Hopkins University Press, 1938), 169.

31 Dexter to Adams, 31 Oct. 1820, RG 59, 893/7/457, NA.

32 *A Brief Account of the Life, and Abominable Thefts, of the Notorious Isaac*

Frasier (New-London: Timothy Green, [1768]), 2; *Worcester Magazine* 4 (1788): 187.

33 George Ollyffe, *An Essay Humbly Offer'd, for an Act of Parliament to Prevent Capital Crimes* (London: J. Downing, 1731), 6–7.

34 Christopher Daniell, *Death and Burial in Medieval England 1066–1550* (London: Routledge, 1997), 106.

35 VG, 25 Feb. 1736, 4:1; William Nelson et al., eds., *Documents Relating to the Colonial History of the State of New Jersey* (Paterson, N.J.: Press Printing and Publishing Co., 1880–1931), 19:233; Daniel Horsmanden, *The New-York Conspiracy* (New York: Southwick & Pelsue, 1810), appendix; *PG*, 2 Sept. 1731, 23 Sept. 1731; William Blackstone, *Commentaries on the Laws of England* (1765–69), 9th ed. (London: W. Strahan et al., 1783), 4:75.

36 Cotton Mather, *Pillars of Salt* (Boston: Samuel Phillips, 1699), 71.

37 VG (P), 15 Sept. 1775, supp. 2:1; *Records of the Court of Assistants*, 1:199.

38 *PG*, 9 Jan. 1750, 4 June 1752; *Archives of Maryland*, 32:3; "Bradstreet's Journal," *New England Historical and Genealogical Register* 9 (1855): 46; *PG*, 9 May 1751; *Maryland Gazette*, 8 Aug. 1754, 2:3.

39 Benjamin Colman, *It is a Fearful Thing to Fall Into the Hands of the Living God* (Boston: John Philip and Thomas Hancock, 1726), 39; *A Narrative of Part of the Life and Adventures of Joseph Andrews* ([New York]: s.n., [1769]), 2; "Diary of Jeremiah Bumstead of Boston, 1722–1727," *New England Historical and Genealogical Register* 15 (1861): 202.

40 A. J. F. Van Laer, ed., *Minutes of the Court of Albany, Rensselaerswyck and Schenectady* (Albany: University of the State of New York, 1926–1932), 3:278; E. B. O'Callaghan, ed., *Calendar of Historical Manuscripts, in the Office of the Secretary of State, Albany, N.Y.* (Albany: Weed, Parsons, 1866), 2:135; Council Minutes (A1895), 7:227, NYA.

41 *The Reprobate's Reward, or, a Looking-Glass for Disobedient Children* (Philadelphia: s.n., 1793); *An Account of the Trial of Joseph Andrews for Piracy and Murder* ([New York]: s.n., 1769), 8; J. M. Beattie, *Crime and the Courts in England 1660–1800* (Princeton: Princeton University Press, 1986), 528.

42 Charles J. Hoadly, ed., *Records of the Colony and Plantation of New Haven, from 1638 to 1649* (Hartford: Case, Tiffany, 1857), 24; "Bradstreet's Journal," 46; Paul W. Keve, *The History of Corrections in Virginia* (Charlottesville: University Press of Virginia, 1986), 12, 13.

43 Md. 1729, p. 2.

44 Michael Kammen, *Colonial New York* (1975; New York: Oxford University Press, 1996), 126; *PG*, 18 July 1771; *Sentence of Death for High Treason* (Frederick, Md.: s.n., 1781); John Bellamy, *The Tudor Law of Treason* (London: Routledge & Kegan Paul, 1979), 202–205.

45 *Boston Evening-Post,* 11 Mar. 1765, 1:1.

46 Suzanne M. Shultz, *Body Snatching: The Robbing of Graves for the Education of Physicians in Early Nineteenth Century America* (Jefferson, N.C.: McFarland, 1992).

47 Jonathan Sawday, *The Body Emblazoned: Dissection and the Human Body in Renaissance Culture* (London: Routledge, 1995), 56; *The Colonial Laws of Massachusetts* (Boston: City Council of Boston, 1889), 43; Albert Matthews, "Notes on Early Autopsies and Anatomical Lectures," *Publications of the Colonial Society of Massachusetts* 19 (1918): 279; VG, 24 Nov. 1738, 4:1.

48 25 Geo. II, c. 37 (1752); Mass. 1784, c. 9; N.Y. 1789, c. 3; U.S. 1 Stat. 112, s. 4; N.J. 1796, c. 600; La. 1808, p. 304; Me. 1821, c. 2; Conn. 1824, c. 16; Ill. 1833, p. 208; Iowa 1838, p. 170; Neb. 1858, p. 77; Mass. 1904, c. 204.

49 *Life, Trial, and Confession of Thomas Jones* ([New York]: s.n., 1824), 10; *Trial and Confession of William Hill* (New-York: Christian Brown, 1826), 10; *Mutiny and Murder: Confession of Charles Gibbs, a Native of Rhode Island* (Providence: Israel Smith, 1831), 24; *Report of the Trials of the Murderers of Richard Jennings* (Newburgh, N.Y.: Benjamin F. Lewis, 1819), 132; Linda Grant De Pauw et al., eds., *Documentary History of the First Federal Congress of the United States of America* (Baltimore: Johns Hopkins University Press, 1972–), 13:970; Maeva Marcus et al., eds., *The Documentary History of the Supreme Court of the United States, 1789–1800* (New York: Columbia University Press, 1985–), 2:268.

50 *A Brief Account of the Trial of Winslow Russell* ([Troy, N.Y.]: s.n., [1811]), 5; *The Life and Confession of John Johnson, the Murderer of James Murray* (New York: Brown & Tyrell, 1824), 26; *A Brief Account of the Life, Trial, Sentence, Last Words and Dying Speech, of James Hamilton* (Albany: s.n., 1818), 6–7; *Report of the Trial of Dominic Daley and James Halligan, for the Murder of Marcus Lyon* (Northampton, Mass.: S. & E. Butler, [1806]), 87–88; *Particulars Relative to the Trials of Jesse Strang and Mrs. Whipple* (s.l.: s.n., [1827]), 25.

51 DePauw et al., eds., *Documentary History of the First Federal Congress,* 13:969; David C. Humphrey, "Dissection and Discrimination: The Social Origins of Cadavers in America, 1760–1915," *Bulletin of the New York Academy of Medicine* 49 (1973): 819–820; John Motley Morehead to Alexander Boyd Andrews, 19 July 1934, Alexander Boyd Andrews Collection (P.C. 125.1), NCA.

52 DePauw et al., eds., *Documentary History of the First Federal Congress,* 13:968; *The Narrative of Whiting Sweeting* (Lansingburgh, N.Y.: Silvester Tiffany, [1791]), 54; *The Life of Abram Antone* (Morrisville, N.Y.: Republican Monitor, 1823), 12.

53 *Life of Michael Martin*, 3d ed. (Boston: Russell & Gardner, 1822), 70; *NYT*, 18 Aug. 1878, 9:3; *Columbian Star*, 8 June 1822, 1:4.

54 *On Bryan Sheehen* ([Boston]: s.n., 1772); *NYT*, 6 Mar. 1869, 8:1, 20 Feb. 1874, 5:3, 19 May 1877, 1:6; *Life and Confession of Amasa E. Walmsley* (Providence: s.n., 1832), 15; Daniel Allen Hearn, *Legal Executions in New York State: A Comprehensive Reference, 1639–1963* (Jefferson, N.C.: McFarland, 1997), 41; Margaretta V. Faugeres, *The Ghost of John Young the Homicide* ([New York]: s.n., [1797]), 4.

55 Caroline Walker Bynum, *The Resurrection of the Body in Western Christianity, 200–1336* (New York: Columbia University Press, 1995); 1 Corinthians 15:13; David E. Stannard, *The Puritan Way of Death* (New York: Oxford University Press, 1977), 100–101.

56 Philippe Ariès, *The Hour of Our Death*, trans. Helen Weaver (1981; New York: Oxford University Press, 1991), 32, 41; Gary Laderman, *The Sacred Remains: American Attitudes toward Death, 1799–1883* (New Haven: Yale University Press, 1996), 82.

57 John Melish, *Travels in the United States of America, in the Years 1806 & 1807, and 1809, 1810, & 1811* (Philadelphia: Thomas & George Palmer, 1812), 1:31.

58 Ariès, *Hour of Our Death*, 356–357, 362–364, 397–400, 476; Frederick C. Waite, "Grave Robbing in New England," *Bulletin of the Medical Library Association* 33 (1945): 292.

59 *VG*, 24 Dec. 1736, 4:1–2.

60 *New-York Gazette*, 20 Apr. 1767, 2:3; *VG* (PD), 30 Apr. 1767, 2:2; Peter Linebaugh, "The Tyburn Riot against the Surgeons," in Douglas Hay et al., *Albion's Fatal Tree: Crime and Society in Eighteenth-Century England* (New York: Pantheon, 1975), 103–105.

61 *God's Tender Mercy and Infinite Compassion Surrounding Man's Severity: In a Remarkable and Surprising Manner Exemplified, in the Following Curious and Very Extraordinary Narrative of the Revivication of Young Joseph Taylor* (Boston: E. Russell, 1788).

62 *The Wonderful and Surprising Resurrection of William Jones* ([Newark, N.J.]: s.n., [1791]).

63 Kumar G. Pradeep and V. Kanthaswamy, "Survival in Hanging," *American Journal of Forensic Medicine and Pathology* 14 (1993): 80–81.

4. The Origins of Opposition

1 Ray W. Irwin and Edna L. Jacobsen, eds., *A Columbia College Student in the Eighteenth Century: Essays by Daniel D. Tompkins* (New York: Columbia University Press, 1940), 23.

2 "On Punishment by Death," *Weekly Magazine of Original Essays* 3 (1798): 42–45; *Memoirs of Jeremiah Mason* (1873; Boston: Boston Law Book Co., 1917), 11–12; William T. Hutchinson et al., eds., *The Papers of James Madison* (Chicago: University of Chicago Press, 1962–1981), 13:94; DeWitt Clinton, *Oration, on Benevolence* (New-York: Friar McLean, [1795]), 17; Julian P. Boyd et al., eds., *The Papers of Thomas Jefferson* (Princeton: Princeton University Press, 1950–), 1:505; Franklin to Benjamin Vaughan, 14 Mar. 1785, in Basil Montagu, ed., *The Opinions of Different Authors upon the Punishment of Death* (London: Longman, Hurst, Rees, and Paternoster, 1809), 164; George W. Corner, ed., *The Autobiography of Benjamin Rush* (Princeton: Princeton University Press, 1948), 209; L. H. Butterfield, ed., *Letters of Benjamin Rush* (Princeton: Princeton University Press, 1951), 628.

3 Robert Zaller, "The Debate on Capital Punishment during the English Revolution," *American Journal of Legal History* 31 (1987): 129–134.

4 Julius Goebel Jr., and T. Raymond Naughton, *Law Enforcement in Colonial New York* (New York: Commonwealth Fund, 1944), 675; Hugh F. Rankin, *Criminal Trial Proceedings in the General Court of Colonial Virginia* (Charlottesville: University Press of Virginia, 1965), 161–162; Donna J. Spindel, *Crime and Society in North Carolina, 1663–1776* (Baton Rouge: Louisiana State University Press, 1989), 124; *A Few Lines upon the Awful Execution of John Ormesby & Matth. Cushing* ([Boston]: s.n., [1734]).

5 *Georgia Gazette*, 19 Aug. 1767, 1:2; *New-York Journal*, 26 Aug. 1773, 4:4; *Theft and Murder!* ([Boston]: s.n., [1773]); Peres Fobes, *The Paradise of God Opened to a Penitent Thief* (Providence: Bennett Wheeler, [1785]), app. 1; Stephen West, *A Sermon: Preached in Lenox* (Pittsfield, Mass.: Elijah Russell, 1787), 4; Montagu, ed., *Opinions of Different Authors*, 164.

6 *Georgia Gazette*, 26 Aug. 1767, 2:2; N.J. 1769, c. 496.

7 Marcello Maestro, *Cesare Beccaria and the Origins of Penal Reform* (Philadelphia: Temple University Press, 1973), 42–43; Gilbert Chinard, ed., *The Commonplace Book of Thomas Jefferson* (Baltimore: Johns Hopkins Press, 1926), 298–316; L. H. Butterfield, ed., *Diary and Autobiography of John Adams* (Cambridge, Mass.: Harvard University Press, 1961), 1:353n2; Paul M. Spurlin, "Beccaria's *Essay on Crimes and Punishments* in Eighteenth-Century America," *Studies on Voltaire and the Eighteenth Century* 27 (1963): 1489–1504; William Blackstone, *Commentaries on the Laws of England* (1765–69), 9th ed. (London: W. Strahan et al., 1783), 4:17.

8 John Locke, *Two Treatises of Government* (1690; London, 1698), ed. Peter Laslett, 2d ed. (Cambridge: Cambridge University Press, 1970), 302, 375; David Heyd, "Hobbes on Capital Punishment," *History of Philosophy Quar-*

terly 8 (1991): 119–134; Jean Jacques Rousseau, *The Social Contract* (1762; Chicago: Encyclopedia Britannica, 1952), 398.

9 Cesare Beccaria, *An Essay on Crimes and Punishments* (1819; Stanford, Calif.: Academic Reprints, 1953), 97, 99, 101, 102, 104.

10 Charles de Montesquieu, *The Spirit of the Laws* (1748; Chicago: Encyclopedia Britannica, 1952), 42; Rousseau, *Social Contract*, 399; Voltaire, *Commentaire sur le Livre Des Délits et Des Peines* ([Geneva]: s.n., 1766); [William Eden,] *Principles of Penal Law*, 2d ed. (London: B. White and T. Cadell, 1771), 306.

11 *Connecticut Courant*, 22 Aug. 1768, 4:1.

12 William Finley Swindler, ed., *Sources and Documents of United States Constitutions* (Dobbs Ferry, N.Y.: Oceana Publications, 1973–), 8:284, 4:373, 8:475, 6:346.

13 Boyd et al., eds., *Papers of Thomas Jefferson*, 2:325, 492–493, 495–501.

14 George Lewis Chumbley, *Colonial Justice in Virginia* (Richmond: Dietz Press, 1938), 125n1; Boyd et al., eds., *Papers of Thomas Jefferson*, 2:505–506.

15 *Pennsylvania Evening Herald*, 30 Apr. 1785, 3:2; *Freeman's Journal*, 7 Sept. 1785, 2:1; *Pennsylvania Packet*, 1 Sept. 1786, 2:4.

16 Pa. 1786, c. 45.

17 Caleb Lownes, "An Account of the Alteration and Present State of the Penal Laws of Pennsylvania," appendix to William Bradford, *An Enquiry Into How Far the Punishment of Death is Necessary in Pennsylvania* (Philadelphia: T. Dobson, 1793), 93; [François Alexandre Frédéric, Duc de La Roche-foucauld-Liancourt], *On the Prisons of Philadelphia* (Philadelphia: Moreau de Saint-Méry, 1796), 27.

18 *Greenleaf's New-York Journal*, 25 Apr. 1795, 2:5; *Washington Patrol*, 27 May 1795, 2:2; *Messages from the Governors* (Albany: J. B. Lyon Co., 1909), 2:335.

19 D. L. Corbitt, ed., "Social Reforms Advocated by 'A Citizen,'" *North Carolina Historical Review* 4 (1927): 312; Philip S. Foner, ed., *The Democratic-Republican Societies, 1790–1800* (Westport, Conn.: Greenwood, 1976), 362.

20 Pa. 1794, c. 257; Va. 1796, c. 2; Ky. 1798, c. 4; N.Y. 1796, c. 30; N.J. 1796, c. 600.

21 James Dana, *The Intent of Capital Punishment* (New-Haven: T. and S. Green, [1790]), 7; Maeva Marcus et al., eds., *The Documentary History of the Supreme Court of the United States, 1789–1800* (New York: Columbia University Press, 1985–), 2:189.

22 Adam Jay Hirsch, *The Rise of the Penitentiary: Prisons and Punishment in Early America* (New Haven: Yale University Press, 1992); Michael Meranze,

Laboratories of Virtue: Punishment, Revolution, and Authority in Philadelphia, 1760–1835 (Chapel Hill: University of North Carolina Press, 1996); David J. Rothman, *The Discovery of the Asylum: Social Order and Disorder in the New Republic* (Boston: Little, Brown, 1971).

23 *Pennsylvania Evening Herald*, 16 July 1785, 2:4.

24 [Benjamin Rush,] "Rejoinder to a Reply to the Enquiry Into the Justice and Policy of Punishing Murder By Death," *American Museum* 5 (1789): 122; "On the Punishment of Death," *New-York Magazine* 5 (1794): 35; Bradford, *An Enquiry*, 21; [Thomas Eddy,] *An Account of the State Prison or Penitentiary House, in the City of New-York* (New York: Isaac Collins and Son, 1801), 16; Samuel Latham Mitchill, *An Oration, Pronounced Before the Society of Black Friars* (New-York: Friar M'Lean, 1793), 32.

25 J. P. Brissot de Warville, *New Travels in the United States of America 1788*, trans. Mara Soceanu Vamos and Durand Echeverria, ed. Durand Echeverria (Cambridge, Mass.: Harvard University Press, 1964), 297; Franklin Bowditch Dexter ed., *The Literary Diary of Ezra Stiles* (New York: Scribner's, 1901), 3:118; Phineas Hedges, *An Oration, Delivered Before the Republican Society, of Ulster County* (Goshen, N.Y.: David M. Westcott, 1795), 13.

26 "Capital Punishments," *Time Piece*, 18 June 1798, 2; *American Minerva*, 6 February 1796, 3:3.

27 James DeWitt Andrews, ed., *The Works of James Wilson* (Chicago: Callaghan and Company, 1896), 2:363; Bradford, *An Enquiry*, 8.

28 [Benjamin Rush,] *An Enquiry Into the Effects of Public Punishments* (Philadelphia: Joseph James, 1787), 12.

29 Donald H. Meyer, *The Democratic Enlightenment* (New York: G. P. Putnam's Sons, 1976), 88–90; Karen Halttunen, *Murder Most Foul: The Killer and the American Gothic Imagination* (Cambridge, Mass.: Harvard University Press, 1998), 41–42, 57–58.

30 *[Speech Delivered in the Virginia House of Delegates, December 1, 1796]* (s.l.: s.n., [1797]), 11.

31 "An Oration Intended to Have Been Spoken at a Late Commencement, On the Unlawfulness and Impolicy of Public Punishments," *American Museum* 7 (1790): 137, 193–94; Rush, *An Enquiry Into the Effects of Public Punishments*, 13.

32 [Benjamin Rush,] "An Enquiry Into the Justice and Policy of Punishing Murder By Death," *American Museum* 4 (1788): 79; "Considerations on Capital Punishments," *Hive* 1 (1803): 69.

33 "On Punishment," *New-York Evening Post*, 16 March 1795, 3:3; M.E., *Essays on the Injustice and Impolicy of Inflicting Capital Punishment* (Philadel-

phia: Democratic Press, 1800), 17; "Friend" to Jefferson, 23 October 1802, RG 59, 893/2/52, NA.

34 William Turner, "An Essay on Crimes and Punishments," *Memoirs of the Literary and Philosophical Society of Manchester* (Warrington: T. Cadel, 1785–90), 2:317.

35 Rush, "An Enquiry Into the Justice and Policy of Punishing Murder By Death," 79–80.

36 "On the Punishment of Murder by Death," *American Monthly Review* 1 (1795): 183; "For the Evening Fire-Side," *Evening Fire-Side* 1 (1805): 220.

37 [Robert Annan,] "Observations on Capital Punishments," *American Museum* 4 (1788): 553, 450; "Remarks on Capital Punishments," *American Museum* 8 (1790): 154.

38 Rush, "An Enquiry Into the Justice and Policy of Punishing Murder By Death," 79; *The Journals of Henry Melchior Muhlenberg*, trans. Theodore G. Tappert and John W. Doberstein (1942–58; Camden, Me.: Picton Press, 1993), 2:235, 2:264.

39 "On the Punishment of Death," 36; Annan, "Observations," 451.

40 Attitudes toward punishment are often produced by perceptions of crime, so it would be useful to know whether crime rates were declining in the late eighteenth century. Little is known, however, about movements in crime rates before the late nineteenth century. Roger Lane, *Murder in America: A History* (Columbus: Ohio State University Press, 1997), 4–7.

41 Louis P. Masur, *Rites of Execution: Capital Punishment and the Transformation of American Culture, 1776–1865* (New York: Oxford University Press, 1989), 54–70; Christopher Adamson, "Wrath and Redemption: Protestant Theology and Penal Practice in the Early American Republic," *Criminal Justice History* 13 (1992): 75–111.

42 John A. Davis, *Conflict and Control: Law and Order in Nineteenth-Century Italy* (Atlantic Highlands, N.J.: Humanities Press International, 1988), 128–29; Carl Ludwig von Bar, *A History of Continental Criminal Law*, trans. Thomas S. Bell (Boston: Little, Brown, 1916), 252; Richard J. Evans, *Rituals of Retribution: Capital Punishment in Germany 1600–1987* (Oxford: Oxford University Press, 1996), 132–35; John T. Alexander, *Catherine the Great: Life and Legend* (New York: Oxford University Press, 1989), 101; John McManners, *Death and the Enlightenment: Changing Attitudes to Death Among Christians and Unbelievers in Eighteenth-century France* (Oxford: Clarendon Press, 1981), 368–408; Leon Radzinowicz, *A History of English Criminal Law* (London: Stevens & Sons, 1948–86), 1:301–607.

43 David Brion Davis, *The Problem of Slavery in Western Culture* (1966) (New York: Oxford University Press, 1988), 488–89; Keith Thomas, *Man and the*

Natural World: Changing Attitudes in England 1500–1800 (Oxford: Oxford University Press, 1983), 173–81.

44 *Georgia Gazette*, 19 August 1767, 1:2; *Report of the Trial of Richard D. Croucher* (New York: George Forman, [1800]), 28; Petition of the Inhabitants of Alexandria, 17 July 1803, RG 59, 893/2/61, NA.

45 Michel Foucault, *Discipline and Punish: The Birth of the Prison*, trans. Alan Sheridan (New York: Random House, 1979), 82.

46 Robert J. Turnbull, *A Visit to the Philadelphia Prison* (Philadelphia: Budd and Bartram, 1796), 88; Rush, *An Enquiry Into the Effects of Public Punishments*, 10–11.

47 Bradford, *An Enquiry*, 9; Rush, *An Enquiry Into the Effects of Public Punishments*, 14.

48 Thomas Bender, ed., *The Antislavery Debate: Capitalism and Abolitionism as a Problem in Historical Interpretation* (Berkeley: University of California Press, 1992); John H. Langbein, "The Historical Origins of the Sanction of Imprisonment for Serious Crime," *Journal of Legal Studies* 5 (1976): 35–60; Michael Ignatieff, *A Just Measure of Pain: The Penitentiary in the Industrial Revolution, 1750–1850* (New York: Pantheon, 1978); George Fisher, "The Birth of the Prison Retold," *Yale Law Journal* 104 (1995): 1235–1324.

49 Bradford, *An Enquiry*, 5.

5. Northern Reform, Southern Retention

1 "The Cabinet, No. LXXV," *Philadelphia Repertory* 2 (1812): 316; "The Question of Capital Punishment," *Livingston's Monthly Law Magazine* 2 (1854): 19.

2 La. 1830, p. 96; Va. 1847–48, p. 125.

3 Philip English Mackey, ed., *A Gentleman of Much Promise: The Diary of Isaac Mickle 1837–1845* (Philadelphia: University of Pennsylvania Press, 1977), 279–280, 357–358.

4 Massachusetts Society for the Abolition of Capital Punishment, *Circular* (Boston: s.n., 1847); Earle D. Ross, ed., *Diary of Benjamin F. Gue in Rural New York and Pioneer Iowa 1847–1856* (Ames: Iowa State University Press, 1962), 120; Frederick Marryat, *A Diary in America* (Philadelphia: Carey & Hart, 1839), 2:54; Alexis de Tocqueville, *Democracy in America* (1835; New York: Vintage, 1945), 2:176; Harriet Martineau, *Society in America* (New York: Saunders and Otley, 1837), 2:287.

5 "For the Repertory," *Philadelphia Repertory* 1 (1810): 228; "Of the Duty of Society in Regard to Criminal Legislation and Prison Discipline," *American Jurist* 24 (1841): 317; *A Faithful Narrative of the Murder of Mrs. Sarah Cross* (Philadelphia: s.n., 1808), iii; "On the Use and Abuse of Capital Punish-

ment," *American Monthly Magazine* 5 (1833): 271; *National Era*, 7 Dec. 1848, 101; "Capital Punishment," *American Jurist* 18 (1838): 334–374; Luther Hamilton, ed., *Memoirs, Speeches and Writings of Robert Rantoul, Jr.* (Boston: John P. Jewett, 1854), 497.

6 *Remarks on Capital Punishments* (Utica: W. Williams, 1821), 17; "Punishment," *New-York Mirror, and Ladies' Literary Gazette* 2 (1825): 335; Joseph Haven, *Moral Philosophy: Including Theoretical and Practical Ethics* (New York: Sheldon, 1859), 293; N.Y. Assembly Doc. 214 (1846), 9; "Capital Punishments," *Christian Telescope* 1 (1825): 91–92; [George Sumner], *Remarks on Capital Punishments and the Penitentiary System* (Boston: Tuttle and Weeks, 1835), 8.

7 [James Richmond], *My Concise Opinion of Published Arguments on the Penalty of Death* (Hudson, N.Y.: P. Dean Carrique, 1847), 23; "Capital Punishment," *United States Magazine and Democratic Review* 20 (1847): 71; "Influence of Penal Laws," *United States Magazine and Democratic Review* 22 (1848): 236; "Capital Punishment in the United States," *Law Reporter* 8 (1846): 494; Charles C. Burleigh, *Thoughts on the Death Penalty* (Philadelphia: Merrihew and Thompson, 1845), 53–54.

8 "Shall the Death Penalty be Abolished?" *Christian Review* 14 (1849): 367; H. A. Boardman, *The Low Value Set on Human Life in the United States* (Philadelphia: Joseph M. Wilson, 1853), 17–18.

9 "An Essay on the Ground and Reason of Punishment," *United States Magazine and Democratic Review* 19 (1846): 90, 98; "Capital Punishments," *Jurisprudent* 1 (1830): 158; J. Sydney Taylor, *A Comparative View of the Punishments Annexed to Crime in the United States of America and England* (London: Harvey and Darton, 1831), 39; *Freedom's Journal*, 2 May 1828, 44.

10 "Capital Punishment," *Biblical Repertory and Princeton Review* 14 (1842): 331; William I. Budington, *Capital Punishment: A Discourse* (Boston: T. R. Marvin, 1843), 4; *Report of the Majority and Minority of the Committee on the Judiciary System, Relative to Capital Punishment* (Harrisburg: M'Kinley & Lescure, 1843), 21; *Daily Democratic Press*, 16 July 1855, 2:1.

11 S. S. Schmucker, *Dissertation on Capital Punishment*, 3d ed. (Philadelphia: Perkins & Purves, 1845), 2; Samuel Lee, *Capital Punishment* (New Ipswich, N.H.: s.n., 1849), 9; Nathaniel West, *An Address on Capital Punishment* (Pittsburgh: J. T. Shryock, 1855), 17; George B. Cheever, *Capital Punishment* (New York: Saxton & Miles, 1843), 11; Frederick Plummer, *A Defence of Capital Punishment* (Philadelphia: Christian General Book Association, 1851), 26; Cornelius C. Cuyler, *The Law of God With Respect to Murder* (Philadelphia: Herman Hooker, 1842), 8.

12 *Christianity Opposed to the "Death Penalty"* (Providence: Knowles, An-

thony, 1852), 8; Roland Diller, *Discourse on Capital Punishment* ([New Holland, Pa.]: s.n., 1825), 5; Milo D. Codding, *Capital Punishment, Shown to be a Violation of the Principles of Divine Government* (Rochester: Jerome & Brother, 1846), 19; "On the Infliction of Capital Punishments," *Christian Monthly Spectator* 2 (1820): 72; *The Bible Against the Gallows* (New York: Edward Walker, 1845), 25; "The Biblical Argument for Capital Punishment as a Divine Ordinance," *Universalist Quarterly* 6 (1849): 343.

13 John Edwards, *Serious Thoughts, on the Subject of Taking the Lives of Our Fellow Creatures, by Way of Punishment for Any Crime Whatever*, 7th ed. (New York: s.n., 1812), 4; *The Impropriety of Capital Punishments* (Philadelphia: John Penington, 1842), 17; Sylvanus Haynes, *A Letter to Dr. Amos G. Hull, in Vindication of Capital Punishments* (Auburn, N.Y.: Thomas M. Skinner, 1822), 11; Joseph P. Thompson, *The Right and Necessity of Inflicting the Punishment of Death for Murder* (New Haven: J. M. Patten, 1842), 12.

14 [Samuel Whelpley], *Letters Addressed to Caleb Strong, Esq.* (Providence: Miller & Hutchens, 1818), 45; Warren Skinner, *Capital Punishment* (Montpelier: George W. Hill, 1834), 18; *Life and Confession of Ann Walters, the Female Murderess!* (s.l.: s.n., 1850), 27.

15 Charles Mason, *Address of the Hon. Charles Mason, Before the Iowa Anti-Capital Punishment and Prison Discipline Society* (New York: New York State Society for the Abolition of Capital Punishment, 1848), 11; "Observations on Penal Jurisprudence," *North American Review* 10 (1820): 247; "Punishment, Its Nature and Design," *American Biblical Repository* 10 (1843): 4; Petition, n.d., RG 59, 893/17/805, NA.

16 Norman Dain, *Concepts of Insanity in the United States, 1789–1865* (New Brunswick, N.J.: Rutgers University Press, 1964); E. H. Chapin, *Three Discourses Upon Capital Punishment* (Boston: Trumpet Office, 1843), 25; *Trial of Capt. John Windsor* (Milford, Del.: J. H. Emerson, 1851), 46.

17 James Richmond, *A Petitioner's Memorial on the Penalty of Death* (Albany: C. Van Kenthuysen, 1847), 3–4; *Report of the Trial of Abner Rogers, Jr.* (Boston: Charles C. Little and James Brown, 1844), 45.

18 *Confessions of Two Malefactors, Teller & Reynolds* (Hartford: Hanmer and Comstock, 1833), 4; L. R. Green collection, CHS.

19 M. B. Sampson, *Rationale of Crime* (New York: D. Appleton, 1846), 2, 43–44.

20 John Dunn Davies, *Phrenology: Fad and Science* (New Haven: Yale University Press, 1955), 98–105; Theodore Parker, *A Sermon of the Dangerous Classes in Society* (Boston: C. & J. M. Spear, 1847), 25–26, 38–39.

21 William Timlow, *Mr. Livingston's Strong Arguments Against Capital Punishment, Reviewed* (Goshen, N.Y.: Clark & Montanye, 1850), 7–8; "Shall

Punishment Be Abolished?" *New Englander* 4 (1846): 566; Elijah Waterman, *A Sermon, Preached at Windham* (Windham, Conn.: J. Byrne, 1803), 20; *United States v. Cornell*, 25 F. Cas. 650, 656 (C.C.D.R.I. 1820).

22 "Capital Punishments," *Carolina Law Repository* 1 (1813): 75–77; "For the Advocates of Capital Punishment," *Harbinger* 4 (1847): 219; William T. Hamilton, *The Last Hours of Charles R. S. Boyington* (Mobile: Commercial Register Office, 1835); Gerald W. McFarland, *The "Counterfeit" Man: The True Story of the Boorn-Colvin Murder Case* (New York: Pantheon, 1990); George Washington Quinby, *The Gallows, the Prison, and the Poor-House* (Cincinnati: G. W. Quinby, 1856), 57–80; Joseph F. Berg, *A Plea for the Divine Law Against Murder* (Philadelphia: James M. Campbell, 1846), 49–50.

23 *Life and Confession of Amos Miner* (Providence: s.n., 1833), 15; *Trial of David F. Mayberry* (Janesville, Wis.: Baker, Burnett & Hall, 1855), 37; *Account of the Short Life and Ignominious Death of Stephen Merrill Clark* (Salem, Mass.: T. C. Cushing, 1821), 3.

24 John N. McLeod, *The Capital Punishment of the Murderer, an Unrepealed Ordinance of God* (New York: Robert Carter, 1842), 22–23; *Remarks of Chief Justice Shaw, When Passing Sentence of Death Upon Nathan Smith* (Lowell, Mass.: Leonard Huntress, 1839), 3; *Trial of Seth Elliot, Esq.* (Belfast, Me.: Fellowes and Simpson, [1824]), 52.

25 *A Brief Review, of the Principles of Capital Punishments* (Philadelphia: s.n., 1816), 12; "Wordsworth's Sonnets on the Punishment of Death," *United States Magazine and Democratic Review* 10 (1842): 280; Jonathan Dymond, *Essays on the Principles of Morality* (New-York: Harper & Brothers, 1834), 330; "Capital Punishments," *Philanthropist* 3 (1820): 242; "Capital Punishment," *Boston Pearl* 5 (1836): 181; *Report of the Trial and Conviction of John Haggerty* (Lancaster, Pa.: s.n., 1847), 80.

26 "Capital Punishments," *Christian Disciple* 5 (1817): 74–75.

27 "Report on the Subject of Capital Punishment," *Southern Quarterly Review* 4 (1843): 81–82; Abel C. Thomas, *A Lecture on Capital Punishment* (Philadelphia: s.n., 1830), 3; *North Star*, 25 May 1849; *Colored American*, 18 July 1840.

28 "Capital Punishment," *Boston Pearl* 5 (1836): 167; *"The Spirit of the Age": Its Tendencies to a Change That is Not Reform* (Albany: C. Van Benthuysen, 1849), 6–11.

29 W. S. Grayson, "Capital Punishment," *Southern Literary Messenger* 33 (1861): 458; William T. Dwight, *A Discourse on the Rightfulness and Expediency of Capital Punishments* (Portland, Me.: Temperance Office, 1843), 13; John C. Hogan, ed., "Joseph Story on Capital Punishment," *California Law Review* 43 (1955): 76.

30 "The New Social Propositions," *Southern Literary Messenger* 20 (1854): 299; "Capital Punishment," *New Englander* 1 (1843): 28; E. B. Hall, *The Punishment of Death* (Cambridge, Mass.: Metcalf, 1845), 4; "The Viviparous Quadrupeds of North America," *Southern Quarterly Review* 12 (1847): 278; Jonathan Cogswell, *A Treatise on the Necessity of Capital Punishment* (Hartford: E. Geer, 1843), 12.

31 Nathaniel Hawthorne, "The New Adam and Eve" (1843), in *Tales and Sketches* (New York: Library of America, 1982), 752.

32 Zephaniah Swift, *A Vindication of the Calling of a Special Superior Court* (Windham, Conn.: J. Byrne, 1816), 11; *Life and Execution of Wilhelms, the Braganza Pirate!* (New York: Sun Office, [1839]); "Review on Penal Law," *Christian Quarterly Spectator* 2 (1830): 509; *Letters from John Pintard to His Daughter* (New York: New-York Historical Society, 1940), 2:144.

33 *Vanity Fair* 1 (1860): 231; Royal Gage, *A Treatise on Resistance and Non-Resistance* (Brattleboro, Vt.: J. B. Miner, 1848), 38.

34 "Capital Punishment," *Methodist Quarterly Review* 28 (1846): 468; "Death Punishment," *Southern Literary Messenger* 18 (1852): 651; Lebbeus Armstrong, *The Signs of the Times* (New York: Robert Carter, 1848), 42–43.

35 C. C. Burr, *Review of Dr. Berg's Three Discourses in Favor of Capital Punishment* (Philadelphia: John H. Gihon, 1845), 6; "Punishment and Penalty," *United States Magazine and Democratic Review* 20 (1847): 300; Robert Rantoul, Jr., *Hon. Robert Rantoul, Jr.'s Letters on the Death Penalty* ([Boston: Robert Rantoul, Jr., 1846]), 5.

36 Henry C. Wright, *John W. Webster, the Murderer, and Joseph Eveleth, the Hangman: The Difference Between Them* (Boston: J. B. Yerrinton & Son, 1855), 29; Walter Whitman, "A Dialogue," *United States Magazine and Democratic Review* 17 (1845): 363–364; *A Brief Statement of the Argument for the Abolition of the Death Punishment* (Philadelphia: Gihon, Fairchild, 1844), 4.

37 "Capital Punishment," *Pathfinder* 1 (1843): 100; "The Gallows and the Gospel," *United States Magazine and Democratic Review* 12 (1843): 227; *Pennsylvania Freeman*, 17 Feb. 1853, 26:6; John Greenleaf Whittier, "The Human Sacrifice" (1843), in *Anti-Slavery Poems: Songs of Labor and Reform* (Cambridge, Mass.: Riverside Press, 1888), 284; Walter M. Merrill and Louis Ruchames, eds., *The Letters of William Lloyd Garrison* (Cambridge, Mass.: Harvard University Press, 1971–1981), 3:149–150.

38 Philip English Mackey, "'The Result May Be Glorious': Anti-Gallows Movement in Rhode Island 1838–1852," *Rhode Island History* 33 (1974): 19–31; Louis Masur, *Rites of Execution: Capital Punishment and the Transformation of American Culture, 1776–1865* (New York: Oxford University Press,

1989), 138; Philip English Mackey, *Hanging in the Balance: The Anti-Capital Punishment Movement in New York State, 1776–1861* (New York: Garland, 1982), 125; Edward W. Bennett, "The Reasons for Michigan's Abolition of Capital Punishment," *Michigan History*, Nov./Dec. 1978, 44–45.

39 Ct. 1801, p. 556; Ma. 1804, c. 131, c. 143; Ind. 1807, c. 6, p. 237; N.H. 1815, pp. 310–11, 317–26; Ohio 1814, c. 28; Conn. 1796, pp. 182, 321, 349; Ind. 1807, c. 6, p. 243; Ind. 1808, p. 667; N.Y. 1808, c. 155; N.Y. 1817, c. 269; Leonard D. Savitz, "A Brief History of Capital Punishment Legislation in Pennsylvania," *Prison Journal* 38 (1958): 50.

40 Me. 1829, c. 430; Ill. 1832, p. 179; Mass. 1852, c. 259; N.H. 1836, c. 273; N.J. 1839, p. 148; Ct. 1846, c. 16; Ind. R.S. 1852, 2:396; Cal. 1856, c. 139, p. 219; Mass. 1858, c. 154; N.Y. 1860, c. 410; *Confession and Execution of Horace B. Conklin* (New York: William Conklin, 1851), 12; *A Voice from Leverett Street Prison, or The Life, Trial and Confession of Simeon L. Crockett* (Boston: s.n., 1836).

41 N.Y. Assembly Doc. 187 (1832), 4–5; N.Y. Senate Doc. 69 (1838); N.Y. Assembly Doc. 378 (1839); John L. O'Sullivan, *Report in Favor of the Abolition of the Punishment of Death By Law*, 2d ed. (New York: J. & H. G. Langley, 1841); Timothy Walker, "Capital Punishment," *Western Law Journal* 2 (1845): 272; Mackey, *Hanging in the Balance*, 192, 233; *Circular* ([New York]: New-York State Society for the Abolition of Capital Punishment, 1848); *Reports and Addresses of James H. Titus Upon the Subject of Capital Punishment* (New York: New-York State Society for the Abolition of Capital Punishment, 1848). The magazine, called *Anti-Draco*, was edited by O'Sullivan. It folded after its initial issue of March 1844.

42 James Richmond, *Petition to the Honourable the Legislature of the State of New-York* ([Livingston, N.Y.]: s.n., 1844); James Richmond, *To the Hon. the Legislators of the State of New York* (Albany: s.n., 1855); N.Y. Assembly Doc. 249 (1845); N.Y. Assembly Doc. 213 (1846); N.Y. Assembly Doc. 95 (1847); N.Y. Assembly Doc. 133 (1848); N.Y. Assembly Doc. 191 (1848); N.Y. Assembly Doc. 109 (1851); N.Y. Assembly Doc. 42 (1859); N.Y. Assembly Doc. 82 (1860).

43 Mass. House Doc. 36 (1835); Mass. House Doc. 32 (1836); Mass. House Doc. 43 (1837); Benjamin Dole, *An Examination of Mr. Rantoul's Report for Abolishing Capital Punishment in Massachusetts* (Boston: Benjamin Dole, 1835), 6; *Enthusiastic Meeting at the Tremont Temple in Behalf of Washington Goode* ([Boston: s.n., 1849]); *Shall He Be Hung?* (Boston: s.n., 1849); Mass. House Doc. 196 (1848); Mass. House Doc. 149 (1851); Philip English Mackey, "An All-Star Debate on Capital Punishment, Boston, 1854," *Essex Institute Historical Collections* 110 (1974): 197; Alan Rogers, "'Under Sen-

tence of Death': The Movement to Abolish Capital Punishment in Massachusetts, 1835–1849," *New England Quarterly* 66 (1993): 27–46; *An Address from the Women of Philadelphia, to the Women of Great Britain* ([Philadelphia: s.n., 1847]); Albert Post, "Early Efforts to Abolish Capital Punishment in Pennsylvania," *Pennsylvania Magazine of History and Biography* 68 (1944): 44; *Report of the Joint Select Committee, on That Part of the Governor's Message Relating to Capital Punishment* (New Haven: Osborn & Baldwin, 1842); *Report of the Joint Select Committee on Capital Punishment* (New Haven: Osborn & Baldwin, 1852).

44 *Report of the Trial of William F. Comings* (Boston: Samuel N. Dickinson, 1844), 127; Quentin Blaine, "'Shall Surely Be Put to Death': Capital Punishment in New Hampshire, 1623–1985," *New Hampshire Bar Journal* 27 (1986): 131–54; Randolph Roth, "'Blood Calls for Vengeance': The History of Capital Punishment in Vermont," *Vermont History* 65 (1997): 16–18; *Report of the Committee of Assembly on the Subject of Abolishing Capital Punishment in the State of New Jersey* (Trenton: Sherman and Harrow, 1847); Albert Post, "The Anti-Gallows Movement in Ohio," *Ohio State Archaeological and Historical Quarterly* 54 (1945): 104–112; *Report of the Debates and Proceedings of the Convention for the Revision of the Constitution of the State of Ohio 1850–51* (Columbus: S. Medary, 1851), 20–22; Edward Archbold, "Report of the Select Committee on Capital Punishment," *Western Law Journal* 5 (1848): 421–429; Clarence Walworth Alvord, ed., *Governor Edward Coles* (Springfield: Illinois State Historical Library, 1920), 281; Dorothy Riker and Gayle Thornbrough, eds., *Messages and Papers Relating to the Administration of James Brown Ray* (Indianapolis: Indiana Historical Bureau, 1954), 575.

45 Tobias Purrington, *Report on Capital Punishment Made to the Maine Legislature in 1836* (Boston: John Wilson & Son, 1852); Me. 1837, c. 292; Edward Schriver, "Reluctant Hangman: The State of Maine and Capital Punishment, 1820–1887," *New England Quarterly* 63 (1990): 271–287; Vt. 1842, no. 5, p. 16; N.H. 1849, c. 855; Mass. 1852, c. 274; N.Y. 1860, c. 410.

46 Mich. R.S. 1846, c. 153, s. 1.

47 R.I. 1852, p. 12; Wis. 1853, c. 103; Mackey, "The Result," 20–26.

48 *Moral Advocate* 1 (1821–1822): title page; *North Star*, 14 Jan. 1848.

49 *Hangman*, 1 Jan. 1845, 2; *Prisoners' Friend*, 7 Jan. 1846, 2; 3 (1851): 194; 8 (1855): preface; Charles Spear, *Circular in Behalf of the Prisoners' Friend* (Boston: s.n., 1846); *Circular: The Prisoners' Friend* ([Boston]: s.n., [1846]). The journal ceased publication in 1861.

50 Allan Nevins and Milton Halsey Thomas, eds., *The Diary of George Templeton Strong* (New York: Macmillan, 1952), 1:312; Patricia G. Holland and Milton Meltzer, eds., *The Collected Correspondence of Lydia Maria*

Child, 1817–1880 (Millwood, N.Y.: KTO Microform, 1979), letter 425; Simeon L. Crockett, *The True Cause of Crime* (Boston: Cassady & March, 1836); *Order of Exercises for the Temperance Convention Meeting* ([New York]: s.n., [1840]), reverse; *NYT*, 11 Oct. 1858, 5:4.

51 S. C. Carpenter, *Report of the Trial of Richard Dennis* (Charleston: G. M. Bounetheau, 1805), 13; Samuel Gaillard Stoney, ed., "The Autobiography of William John Grayson," *South Carolina Historical and Genealogical Magazine* 49 (1948): 29–30; H. M. Wagstaff, ed., *The Papers of John Steele* (Raleigh: North Carolina Historical Commission, 1924), 483.

52 Edward Stanley to Dudley, 9 June 1837, Edward B. Dudley Papers, GP 78, 504, NCA; James P. Leak to Dudley, 22 Apr. 1839, Edward B. Dudley Papers, GP 88, 2327, NCA; Graham to Jesse Rankin, 18 Apr. 1845, Governor William A. Graham Letter Books, GLB 36, 153, NCA; Petition of citizens of Orange County, 30 Apr. 1836, Governor Richard D. Spaight Papers, GP 73, 156, NCA; Petition of citizens of Baltimore, 8 Apr. 1820, RG 59, 893/7/416, NA; Petition of citizens of Alexandria, 18 July 1820, RG 59, 893/7/453, NA.

53 Edward Livingston, *Remarks on the Expediency of Abolishing the Punishment of Death* (Philadelphia: Jesper Harding, 1831); Philip English Mackey, "Edward Livingston and the Origins of the Movement to Abolish Capital Punishment in America," *Louisiana History* 16 (1975): 145–166.

54 Francis Lieber, *Letter to His Excellency Patrick Noble* (s.l.: s.n., [1839]), 46–48; Thomas S. Grimké, "Defensive War," *Calumet* 2 (1835): 140–151; Robert H. White, ed., *Messages of the Governors of Tennessee* (Nashville: Tennessee Historical Commission, 1952–1990), 1:243; G. F. H. Crockett, *An Address, &c., to the Honorable, the Senate and House of Representatives of the Commonwealth of Kentucky* (Georgetown, Ky.: N. L. Finnell, 1823); Benjamin F. Porter, *Argument of Benjamin F. Porter in Support of a Bill . . . to Abrogate the Punishment of Death* (Tuscaloosa: John M'Cormick, 1846); Robert Strange to Graham, 12 Apr. 1846, Governor William A. Graham Letter Books, GLB 36, 498, NCA.

55 Md. 1809, c. 138; La. 1816, p. 182; La. 1818, p. 170; Fla. 1826, p. 34; Del. 1829, c. 190; Del. 1841, c. 346; Del. 1852, c. 127; Tenn. 1829, c. 23; Tenn. 1838, c. 29; Ala. 1841, Jan. 9; Jack Kenny Williams, *Vogues in Villainy: Crime and Retribution in Ante-Bellum South Carolina* (Columbia: University of South Carolina Press, 1959), 100.

56 Ark. 1823, p. 20; Del. 1826, c. 362; Fla. 1826, p. 34; La. 1855, no. 120; Md. 1809, c. 138; *State v. Farmer*, 26 N.C. 224 (1844); Del. R.S. 1852, c. 128; N.C. 1806, c. 6; Miss. 1839, c. 66, title 2; *State v. Bosse*, 41 S.C.L. 276 (1855); Va. 1847, c. 120, p. 99; Ga. 1809, p. 32; Tex. 1838, p. 145; James M. Denham, *"A Rogue's Paradise": Crime and Punishment in Antebellum Florida, 1821–1861* (Tusca-

loosa: University of Alabama Press, 1997), 97; Fla. 1842, no. 22; E. Merton Coulter, "Hanging as a Socio-Penal Institution in Georgia and Elsewhere," *Georgia Historical Quarterly* 57 (1973): 18; Del. 1833, c. 272; *Niles' Weekly Register* 37 (1829): 197.

57 4 Stat. 102, 115 (1825); Thomas Porter, *The Mail Robbers* (Philadelphia: s.n., 1830), 15.

58 Tex. 1858, c. 121; Va. 1847–1848, pp. 125–126; Fla. 1827, p. 109; La. 1818, p. 18; Miss. 1858, c. 98; S.C. 1843, p. 258; Tenn. 1835, c. 19; George M. Stroud, *A Sketch of the Laws Relating to Slavery in the Several States of the United States of America*, 2d ed. (Philadelphia: Henry Longstreth, 1856), 75–87.

59 *NYT*, 2 Oct. 1858, 2:2.

60 Bertram Wyatt-Brown, *Honor and Violence in the Old South* (New York: Oxford University Press, 1986), 187–192; Auditor of Public Accounts, Entry 756, VAA; Philip J. Schwarz, *Twice Condemned: Slaves and the Criminal Laws of Virginia, 1705–1865* (Baton Rouge: Louisiana State University Press, 1988), 27–29.

61 Michael Stephen Hindus, *Prison and Plantation: Crime, Justice, and Authority in Massachusetts and South Carolina, 1767–1878* (Chapel Hill: University of North Carolina Press, 1980), 221–225.

6. Into the Jail Yard

1 26 May 1852, Mary A. Gash Papers, PC 59.1, NCA.

2 16 May 1852, Zebulon Baird Vance-Harriet N. Espy Vance Letters, PC 1255.1, NCA.

3 "Are Capital Punishments Expedient?" *Gleaner* 1 (1809): 117; "Has a Nation the Right to Punish Capitally?" *Gleaner* 1 (1809): 18; "On the Expediency of Capital Punishments," *Gleaner* 1 (1809): 162–163.

4 *Trial of Israel Thayer Jr., Isaac Thayer, and Nelson Thayer* (s.l.: s.n., [1825]), 36; *Connecticut Courant*, 2 July 1816, 3:2; Allen T. and Theodore F. Davidson Papers, PC 100.15, NCA; *Report of the Trial of Martin Posey* ([Edgefield, S.C.]: Advertiser Print, 1850), 52.

5 *Verses, Written on the Trial, Confession, Execution, and Dying Words of Moses Lion* ([Johnstown, N.Y.]: s.n., [1829]); Olive Woolley Burt, *American Murder Ballads* (New York: Citadel Press, 1964), 52.

6 *Essays on Capital Punishments* (Philadelphia: Brown & Merritt, 1811), 9–10; "Thoughts on the Punishment of Death for Forgery," *Christian Examiner* 12 (1832): 29; John Neal, *Logan, a Family History* (Philadelphia: H. C. Carey & I. Lea, 1822), 2:9–10.

7 Thomas Thacher, *The Danger of Despising the Divine Counsel* (Dedham, Mass.: Herman Mann, 1802), 24; "Capital Punishment," *Philanthropist* 1

(1819): 241; "A New Text for the Advocates of the Gallows," *Harbinger* 5 (1847): 120; Elizur Wright, *Perforations in the "Latter-Day Pamphlets" By One of the Eighteen Millions of Bores* (Boston: Phillips, Sampson, and Company, 1850), 30.

8 Ambrose Bierce, "The Death Penalty," in *The Shadow on the Dial and Other Essays* (San Francisco: A. M. Robertson, 1909), 131.

9 "Capital Punishments," *Floriad* 1 (1811): 180; *The Record of Crimes in the United States* (Buffalo: H. Faxon, 1833), viii; *Trial, Sentence, and Execution of Israel Thayer, Jr. Isaac Thayer, and Nelson Thayer*, 2d ed. (New York: J. M'Cleland, 1825), 12.

10 "The Hanging," *Escritoir* 1 (1826): 359.

11 Thomas C. Upham, *The Manual of Peace* (New York: Leavitt, Lord, 1836), 234; Lydia Maria Child, *Letters from New-York* (New York: Charles S. Francis, 1843), 208, 212.

12 *Journal of the Thirty-Fourth House of Representatives of the Commonwealth of Pennsylvania* (Harrisburg: John S. Wiestling, 1823–1824), 707.

13 Jonathan Going, *A Discourse, Delivered at Worcester* (Worcester, Mass.: William Manning, 1825), 11; *Niles' Weekly Register* 47 (1835): 374; *Missouri Republican*, 10 July 1841.

14 *Report on the Expediency of Abolishing Public Executions* (Harrisburg: Henry Welsh, 1833), 7.

15 Lawrence W. Levine, *Highbrow/Lowbrow: The Emergence of Cultural Hierarchy in America* (Cambridge, Mass.: Harvard University Press, 1988); James J. Farrell, *Inventing the American Way of Death, 1830–1920* (Philadelphia: Temple University Press, 1980), 99–116; Randall McGowen, "Civilizing Punishment: The End of the Public Execution in England," *Journal of British Studies* 33 (1994): 257–282; Richard J. Evans, *Rituals of Retribution: Capital Punishment in Germany 1600–1987* (Oxford: Oxford University Press, 1996), 903–904.

16 "The Death Penalty," *Nation* 8 (1869): 167; George Barrell Cheever, *A Defence of Capital Punishment* (New York: Wiley and Putnam, 1846), 50–51; Margaret Fuller Ossoli, *Life Without and Life Within* (New York: Tribune Association, 1869), 199.

17 *Observations on the Penal Code* (Charleston, S.C.: Southern Patriot, 1816), 34; "On Capital Punishments: From Judge Brackenridge's Law Miscellanies," *Carolina Law Repository* 2 (1815): 61.

18 *Trial, Sentence and Execution of James Ransom* (New York: s.n., [1832]), 3; Howard K. Beale, ed., *The Diary of Edward Bates 1859–1866* (1933; New York: Da Capo Press, 1971), 56; Conn. 1830, p. 284; R.I. June Sess. 1833, p. 50; Pa. 1833–34, no. 127; N.J. 1835, p. 170; N.Y. 1835, c. 258; Mass. R.S.

1835, c. 169; N.H. 1836, c. 273, s. 5; Iowa Terr. 1838, p. 170; Miss. 1839, c. 66, title 2; Ala. 1841, c. 8, s. 3; Ohio 1843, p. 71; Vt. 1844, no. 27; Del. 1849, c. 374; Ind. R.S. 1852, p. 2:379; Kan. Terr. 1858, c. 12, p. 190; Colo. 1859, p. 57; Geo. 1859, no. 83, p. 62; Ill. 1859, p. 17; Mont. Terr. 1864, p. 250; Dakota Terr. 1868, c. 1, s. 500; Ore. 1874, p. 115; Nev. 1875, c. 10; Wyo. Comp. L. 1876, c. 14, s. 170; Utah Terr. 1878, p. 136; Minn. 1889, c. 20; Cal. 1891, c. 191; Idaho 1899, p. 342; Neb. 1901, c. 105; Wash. 1901, c. 63; N.M. 1903, c. 76; Ariz. Terr. 1909, c. 28. The Iowa and Colorado statutes gave the trial judge discretion to order a public or a private execution, discretion the states took away in 1860 and 1889 respectively. Iowa R.S. 1860, c. 219; Colo. 1889, p. 118.

19 "Capital Punishment," *Western Law Journal* 7 (1850): 404; Edward L. Ayers, *Vengeance and Justice: Crime and Punishment in the 19th-Century American South* (New York: Oxford University Press, 1984), 46; *NYT*, 24 July 1871, 5:5; 9 Apr. 1872, 5:3; 11 Apr. 1874, 7:1; 27 Nov. 1875, 1:3.

20 Va. 1878–1879, c. 119; Ky. 1880, c. 648; Md. 1882, c. 403; La. 1884, no. 79; Mo. 1887, p. 169; S.C. 1877, no. 362; Tenn. 1883, c. 112; Ark. 1901, no. 58; Ark. 1906, no. 295; Ky. 1920, c. 163; *NYT*, 20 April 1935, 28:2; Ga. 1893, no. 285; Miss. 1916, c. 218; N.C. 1909, c. 443; Okla. 1913, c. 113; Fla. 1923, c. 9169.

21 *NYT*, 15 Mar. 1878, 5:5; 31 Aug. 1911, 4:3; *Springfield Republican*, 1 Aug. 1901, 3:7; "Capitalizing Capital Punishment in Mississippi," *Literary Digest* 51 (1915): 338.

22 "Kentucky Puts On a Hanging," *Christian Century* 53 (1936): 1124; Perry T. Ryan, *The Last Public Execution in America* ([Lexington, Ky.]: Perry T. Ryan, 1992), 179; *Cincinnati Enquirer*, 28 Aug. 1936, 4:1; *NYT*, 23 Aug. 1936, pt. 4, 6:8; 20 Aug. 1936, 4:7; Ky. 1938, c. 131.

23 "A Neglected Art," *Nation* 129 (1929): 402; Wendell Phillips, *Speeches, Lectures, and Letters* (Boston: Lee and Shepard, 1872), 269.

24 *NYT*, 10 Aug. 1867, 8:1; *Boston Daily Globe*, 9 Oct. 1875, 2:1; *Chicago Daily Tribune*, 20 Apr. 1928, 11:1; *Brooklyn Daily Eagle*, 28 Jan. 1902, 7:2.

25 *NYT*, 7 Dec. 1872, 2:1.

26 *NYT*, 7 Dec. 1872, 2:1; 26 Mar. 1878, 5:4; Finley Peter Dunne, "The Majesty of the Law: Impressions of a Boy of Seventeen at a Hanging," *American Magazine* 77 (1917): 12–16; *NYT*, 28 Feb. 1869, 3:5; Michael Madow, "Forbidden Spectacle: Executions, the Public and the Press in Nineteenth-Century New York," *Buffalo Law Review* 43 (1995): 514–515; John D. Bessler, "The 'Midnight Assassination Law' and Minnesota's Anti-Death Penalty Movement, 1849–1911," *William Mitchell Law Review* 22 (1996): 656–657.

27 *NYT*, 7 July 1860, 1:1; 26 Mar. 1878, 5:4; *Chicago Record-Herald*, 27 May 1908, 1:4; 29 May 1908, 8:1; Henry Wadsworth Longfellow, "The Ropewalk" (1854), in *The Complete Poetical Works of Longfellow* (Cambridge, Mass.:

Riverside Press, 1922), 195; *Trial of Thomas J. Armstrong* (Philadelphia: King & Baird, 1861), 9.

28 *NYT*, 20 June 1925, 3:1.

29 A. H. Morris, *The Highland Tragedy: Trial and Execution of James P. Don-nelly* (Freehold, N.J.: Inquirer Print, 1887), 31; *The Trial of Dr. John W. Hughes* (Cleveland: Leader Co., 1866), 57; *John Ward, or The Victimized As-sassin* ([Windsor, Vt.: Vermont Journal Print, 1869]), 96; *NYT*, 13 Jan. 1859, 1:5; 10 Dec. 1875, 5:4.

30 *A Celebrated Case: The Raber Murder* (Lebanon, Pa.: C. M. Bowman, 1879), 55; *NYT*, 20 Apr. 1878, 1:7; 23 Mar. 1867, 1:6; Gale Largey, "The Hanging," *Society* 18(6) (1981): 74; William Francis Kuntz II, *Criminal Sentencing in Three Nineteenth-Century Cities* (New York: Garland, 1988), 60; George Lippard, *The Empire City* (1850; Freeport, N.Y.: Books for Libraries Press, 1969), 186.

31 Eugene T. Sawyer, *The Life and Career of Tiburcio Vasquez* ([San Fran-cisco]: Bacon, 1875), 46; *The Confession of Tom Whittaker* (Pittsburgh: Union Publishing Co., 1874), 77–78; *NYT*, 27 Feb. 1926, 5:5; J. R. S. Pitts, *Life and Confession of the Noted Outlaw James Copeland* (1858), ed. John D. W. Guice (Jackson: University Press of Mississippi, 1980), 142.

32 *Life, Confession, and Letters of Courtship of Jacob S. Harden* (Hackettstown, N.J.: E. Winton, 1860), 43–45; *NYT*, 27 May 1871, 5:2; 25 Mar. 1875, 2:7; 17 May 1873, 5:1; *Buffalo Commercial Advertiser*, 6 Sept. 1872, 3:2; *Philadelphia Inquirer*, 2 Feb. 1871, 2:1.

33 *Trial, Confession, and Execution of Peter Robinson* (New York: The Re-porter, 1841), 16; *Ohio State Journal*, 1 June 1878, 1:6; *Life and Confession of Stephen Dee Richards* (Lincoln: State Journal Co., 1879), 45.

34 Andie Tucher, *Froth & Scum: Truth, Beauty, Goodness, and the Ax Murder in America's First Mass Medium* (Chapel Hill: University of North Carolina Press, 1994); "Editor's Table," *Appletons' Journal* 9 (1873): 505; *Springfield Republican*, 3 Oct. 1901, 8:4; *Harper's Weekly* 1 (1857): 466.

35 Charles Kassel, "Recent Death-Orgies: A Study of Capital Punishment," *South Atlantic Quarterly* 23 (1924): 304.

36 N.Y. 1888, c. 489, s. 7; Colo. 1889, c. 118, s. 3; Minn. 1889 c. 20, s. 5; Va. 1908, c. 298, s. 10; Wash. 1909, c. 249, s. 209; Ark. 1913, no. 55; N.Y. 1892, c. 16; *NYT*, 12 Mar. 1890, 4:5; *Brooklyn Daily Eagle*, 17 July 1891, 4:2; *State v. Pioneer Press Co.*, 110 N.W. 867 (Minn. 1907).

37 Frederika Bremer, *The Homes of the New World* (New York: Harper & Brothers, 1853), 552.

38 *The Life of Andrew Hellman* (Philadelphia: John B. Perry, 1844), 19, 42; *Trial of Mrs. Elizabeth G. Wharton* (Baltimore: Baltimore Gazette, [1872]), 5; *The*

Infernal Machine Case: Trial of William Arrison (Cincinnati: H. H. Robinson, 1854), 15, 21.

39 *Life, Trial, Confession and Conviction of John Hanlon* (Philadelphia: Barclay, 1870), 123; *The Talbotts: History of the Assassination of Dr. P. H. Talbott* (Maryville, Mo.: Republican Steam Job and Book Office, [1871]), 133.

40 *North Star,* 1 June 1849; RG 103.096, William McKinney (1845), ILA; RG 03, Woodson, box 26, file 8, MOA; RG 59, 893/8/513; 893/23/1860, NA; RG 103.096, Andrew J. Nash (1854), ILA; Samuel H. Walker to Hamilton C. Jones, 19 May 1847, Governor William A. Graham Papers, GP 118, NCA; Barron & Lambson to Governor Johnson Hagood, 24 Nov. 1880, S522005, SCA.

41 RG 03, McClurg, box 20, file 1, MOA; Dudley & Newton to Governor Wade Hampton, 22 July 1878, S519013, SCA; RG 03, McClurg, box 19, file 13, MOA; Petition of citizens of LaSalle, 3 Aug. 1854, RG 103.096, Keith Brennan et al. (1854), ILA.

42 *Trial of John C. Colt* ([New York]: Herald Office, [1842]), 4; Petition, 9 Aug. 1878, S519013, SCA.

43 A. Oakey Hall to W. L. Hodge, 13 Aug. 1851, RG 59, 893/44/68, NA.

44 Henry Francisco (1838), RG-26, roll 150, PAA; William Daniel to Governor A. W. Bradford, 9 Dec. 1864, MSA S1274–84–20, MDA.

45 *Confession of Samuel Steenburgh* (Albany: Weed, Parsons, 1878), 19.

46 Charles Spear, *Essays on the Punishment of Death,* 5th ed. (Boston: Charles Spear, 1844), 59; "Theorie des Lois Criminelles," *Southern Quarterly Review* 3 (1843): 396; Thomas Speed Mosby, "The Anomaly of Capital Punishment," *Arena* 38 (1907): 259.

7. Technological Cures

1 *NYT,* 11 July 1889, 4:2; 5 July 1891, 4:1; *NYDT,* 11 July 1891, 6:5; *Thomas A. Edison Papers: A Selective Microfilm Edition* (Frederick, Md.: University Publications of America, 1987–), 126:26.

2 Martin S. Pernick, *A Calculus of Suffering: Pain, Professionalism, and Anesthesia in Nineteenth-Century America* (New York: Columbia University Press, 1985); "On the Use of Chloroform in Hanging," *American Review* 8 (1848): 294; "Killing Kindly," *Harbinger* 6 (1848): 75; George Leib Harrison, *Chapters on Social Science as Connected with the Administration of State Charities* (Philadelphia: Allen, Lane & Scott, 1877), 116.

3 *The Confession of the Terrible Pirate, Charles Gibbs* (New York: s.n., 1831), 2.

4 *Dying Confession of Lewis Wilber* (Morrisville, N.Y.: Madison Observer, 1839), 14; *Thou Shalt Not Kill* ([Boston]: The Hangman, [1845]); *Mrs. Hull's*

Murder (Philadelphia: Old Franklin Publishing House, [1880]), 47; *The Execution and Last Moments of Henry G. Green* (New York: s.n., 1845), 4; *Confession and Execution of Horace B. Conklin* (New York: William Conklin, 1851), 15; *NYT*, 25 Oct. 1858, 2:3; 13 Oct. 1866, 8:1; 23 Mar. 1867, 1:6; 11 Apr. 1874, 7:1; Douglas V. Shaw, "Ethnicity, Politics and Murder: The Hanging of James P. Donnelly," *New Jersey History* 109 (1991): 45; *NYT*, 13 Jan. 1860, 3:1; *The Life and Confession of Bridget Dergan* (Philadelphia: Barclay, [1867]), 30; *NYT*, 15 Nov. 1867, 2:1; 21 Jan. 1866, 1:5; 10 Feb. 1872, 11:7; 28 Feb. 1874, 1:7; 8 May 1875, 1:4.

5 *NYT*, 4 Feb. 1860, 2:3; *Hunter-Armstrong Tragedy: The Great Trial* (Philadelphia: Barclay, 1878), 65; J. Edwards Remault, *The "Car-Hook" Tragedy* (Philadelphia: Barclay, 1873), 73; *NYDT*, 18 Dec. 1875, 2:2.

6 *NYT*, 13 Jan. 1868, 8:1; *Cincinnati Daily Gazette*, 23 Apr. 1877, 6:5; J. H. Dudley, *The Climax in Crime of the Nineteenth Century* (Quincy, Tex.: s.n., 1872), 207; *Trial of Emil Lowenstein for the Murder of John D. Weston* (Albany: William Gould & Son, 1874), 346; *Baltimore Sun*, 13 Mar. 1875, 1:4; *Cincinnati Daily Gazette*, 26 Aug. 1876, 2:2; *Cincinnati Commercial*, 9 Dec. 1877, 4:2.

7 *Missouri Republican*, 28 Jan. 1871, 3:7; *Baltimore Sun*, 23 Aug. 1873, 1:3; *St. Louis Globe-Democrat*, 18 Dec. 1875, 1:4; *Boston Daily Globe*, 27 May 1876, 2:2; H. M. Fogle, *The Palace of Death or The Ohio Penitentiary Annex* (Columbus: H. M. Fogle, 1908), 19–22; August Mencken, *By the Neck* (New York: Hastings House, 1942), 96.

8 *NYT*, 26 Sept. 1877, 5:5; 17 Apr. 1886, 2:4; Homer Thomas, *Six Men Who Were Hanged* (Sacramento: California League to Abolish Capital Punishment, [1932]), 7–8.

9 *NYT*, 24 Jan. 1892, 16:5.

10 Negley K. Teeters, *Hang by the Neck* (Springfield, Ill.: Charles C. Thomas, 1967), 165–166; *NYT*, 18 Dec. 1894, 3:6; "Will Execute Himself," *Popular Mechanics* 7 (1905): 712.

11 *The Interesting Trial of William F. Hooe* ([New York]: s.n., [1826]), 34; *A True Story of Real Life: Seduction, Murder, and a Violent and Premature Death* (s.l.: s.n., 1851), 85; "Horrible Phenomenon. Galvanism," *Port-Folio*, 4th ser., 7 (1819): 523; *The Trial and Confession of John Johnson* (Philadelphia: s.n., [1824]), 5; *The Authentic Confession of Jesse Strang* (New-York: s.n., 1832), 12; *The Life and Adventures of Manuel Fernandez* (New York: New York Sun, 1835), 16; *Trial of Anton Probst* (Philadelphia: T. B. Peterson & Brothers, 1866), 119–20; *NYT*, 1 Sept. 1870, 5:4.

12 *NYDT*, 11 Oct. 1884, 4:4; *NYT*, 31 July 1886, 2:5; *Brooklyn Daily Eagle*, 29 Apr. 1892, 6:8; *NYT*, 19 Apr. 1880, 4:6.

13 *NYT*, 17 Jan. 1888, 4:4; Ohio 1885, pp. 169–170; Colo. 1889, p. 118; Cal. 1891, c. 191; Conn. 1893, c. 137; *NYDT*, 27 May 1882, 8:2; *NYT*, 13 Feb. 1936, 16:5; 15 Aug. 1936, 30:2; 16 Jan. 1875, 2:4.

14 *NYT*, 27 May 1852, 2:3; *NYDT*, 22 Jan. 1876, 5:2; "Torture by the Law's Executioners," *Pittsburgh Legal Journal* 21 (1873): 61; *NYDT*, 6 Apr. 1884, 6:5.

15 Harry James Brown and Frederick D. Williams, eds., *The Diary of James A. Garfield* (East Lansing: Michigan State University Press, 1967–1981), 4:641; David E. Nye, *Electrifying America: Social Meanings of a New Technology, 1880–1940* (Cambridge, Mass.: MIT Press, 1990), 163–165.

16 *NYT*, 23 Feb. 1882, 8:6; Theodore Bernstein, "Theories of the Causes of Death from Electricity in the Late Nineteenth Century," *Medical Instrumentation* 9 (1975): 267.

17 *NYT*, 27 Dec. 1878, 4:6; 24 Feb. 1883, 3:5.

18 N.Y. 1886, c. 352; *Thomas A. Edison Papers*, 138:355–357; N.Y. Senate Doc. No. 17 (1888), 76–77, 81–82.

19 "Electricity and the Death Penalty," *Chicago Law Times* 3 (1889): 310–320; J. Mount Bleyer, *Scientific Methods of Capital Punishment* (New York: J. Fitzgerald, [ca. 1888]), 4; Park Benjamin, "The Infliction of the Death Penalty," *Forum* 3 (1887): 508–509; *NYT*, 14 Jan. 1887, 2:3; 9 Mar. 1888, 5:4.

20 Bernstein, "Theories of the Causes of Death," 270; R. H. Cunningham, "The Cause of Death From Industrial Electric Currents," *New York Medical Journal* 70 (1899): 581–587, 615–622.

21 N.Y. Senate Doc. No. 17 (1888), 49–51, 55, 73, 75, 80–81, 84; N.Y. 1888, c. 489.

22 Elbridge T. Gerry, "Capital Punishment by Electricity," *North American Review* 149 (1889): 325.

23 *NYT*, 31 July 1888, 8:7; 4 Aug. 1888, 8:2; *[New York] Sun*, 25 Aug. 1889, 6:2; Harold P. Brown, "The New Instrument of Execution," *North American Review* 149 (1889): 587.

24 *Thomas A. Edison Papers*, 122:976, 138:356; Theodore Bernstein, "'A Grand Success,'" *IEEE Spectrum* 10(2) (1973): 55.

25 *NYT*, 9 Mar. 1889, 1:5; *Thomas A. Edison Papers*, 122:981–982, 126:41; *The People of the State of New York ex rel. William Kemmler against Charles F. Durston* (s.l.: s.n., [1889]), 33, 68; Thomas P. Hughes, "Harold P. Brown and the Executioner's Current: An Incident in the AC-DC Controversy," *Business History Review* 32 (1958): 156–158.

26 Jacob Spahn, "Kemmler's Case and the Death-Penalty," *Green Bag* 2 (1890): 56; Hugh O. Pentecost, "The Crime of Capital Punishment," *Arena* 1 (1890): 180–181.

27 *In re Kemmler*, 7 N.Y.S. 145 (Cayuga Cty. Ct. 1889), aff'd, 7 N.Y.S. 813 (Sup. Ct. 1889), aff'd, 119 N.Y. 569 (1890), writ of error denied, 136 U.S. 436 (1890).

28 *NYT*, 12 July 1889, 4:1; 13 July 1889, 4:5; 4 May 1890, 4:7.

29 Robert T. Swaine, *The Cravath Firm and Its Predecessors* (New York: Ad Press, 1946–1948), 1:589; *NYT*, 30 Apr. 1890, 1:1–2.

30 *NYT*, 26 Apr. 1890, 2:2.

31 George F. Shrady, "The Death Penalty," *Arena* 2 (1890): 513–523; *NYT*, 7 Aug. 1890, 1:5, 2:1; *NYDT*, 7 Aug. 1890, 1:6, 2:1; *Utica Saturday Globe*, 16 Aug. 1890.

32 *NYDT*, 7 Aug. 1890, 6:2.

33 *NYT*, 4 Sept. 1890, 8:4; 11 Sept. 1890, 8:1; 25 Sept. 1890, 3:3.

34 "Notes on Executions," Samuel B. Ward Papers, SC 17168, box 3, folder 4, NYL; Carlos F. MacDonald, "The Infliction of the Death Penalty by Means of Electricity," *New York Medical Journal* 55 (1892): 505–509, 535–542.

35 *Brooklyn Daily Eagle*, 5 Feb. 1892, 4:2; *NYT*, 28 July 1893, 2:2; 29 July 1893, 4:4; *Brooklyn Daily Eagle*, 27 July 1893, 1:5; *NYDT*, 28 July 1893, 6:3.

36 Paul W. Keve, *The History of Corrections in Virginia* (Charlottesville: University Press of Virginia, 1986), 148; *In re Storti*, 178 Mass. 549 (1901); *State v. Tomasi*, 75 N.J.L. 739 (1908); *Hart v. Commonwealth*, 131 Va. 726 (1921); Ohio 1896, p. 159; Mass. 1898, c. 326; N.J. 1906, c. 79; Va. 1908, c. 398; N.C. 1909, c. 443; Ky. 1910, c. 38; S.C. 1911, no. 402; Ark. 1913, no. 55; Ind. 1913, c. 315; Neb. 1913, c. 32; Okla. 1913, c. 113; Pa. 1913, no. 338; Tenn. 1913, c. 36; Vt. 1912, no. 228; Tex. 1923, 3d Sess., c. 51, s. 14; Ala. 1923, no. 587; Fla. 1923, c. 9169; Ga. 1924, no. 475; 43 Stat. 798–799 (1925) [D.C.]; Ill. 1927, p. 400; N.M. 1929, c. 69; Conn. 1935, c. 266; S.D. 1939, c. 135; La. 1940, no. 14; Miss. 1940, c. 242; W.Va. 1949, c. 37; 50 Stat. 304 (1937); H.R. Rep. 164, 75th Cong., 1st Sess. (29 Jan. 1937).

37 Christine S. Hutson to Charles Angermeyer, 15 Dec. 1986, "Electric Chair" file, TXA.

38 *Malloy v. South Carolina*, 237 U.S. 180 (1915); "Capital Punishment: Two Views," *Pathfinder*, 23 Jan. 1926, 3.

39 *NYT*, 14 Nov. 1894, 5:3; 22 Nov. 1894, 4:5, 9:6; *Brooklyn Daily Eagle*, 19 Nov. 1894, 4:3; *NYDT*, 5 Aug. 1895, 1:1; 11 Aug. 1895, 7:3; Marc J. Seifer, *Wizard: The Life and Times of Nikola Tesla* (Secaucus, N.J.: Citadel Press, 1996), 51–53.

40 Louise G. Robinovitch, "Electrocution: An Experimental Study with an Electric Current of Low Tension," *Journal of Mental Pathology* 7 (1905): 75–85; "Shocked by 13,500 Volts and Lives," *Journal of Mental Pathology* 7 (1905): 179–180.

41 *NYT*, 11 Sept. 1908, 8:5; 12 Sept. 1908, 6:5; 3 Oct. 1908, 6:4; 7 Dec. 1908, 1:4; 8 Dec. 1908, 1:5; 9 Dec. 1908, 1:6; 12 Dec. 1908, 5:4; 14 Dec. 1908, 5:4; 23 Dec. 1908, 1:6; 28 Dec. 1908, 1:4; 8 Jan. 1912, 8:1; 9 Jan. 1912, 4:3.

42 *NYT*, 18 Sept. 1923, 16:2; 30 Jan. 1927, 3:3; Robert E. Martin, "Electric Shocks . . . Do They Really Kill?" *Popular Science Monthly*, July 1938, 44.

43 Earl P. Paulk, *Execution of Six Men*, 5th ed. (s.l.: s.n., 1952), 24–25; Amos O. Squire, *Sing Sing Doctor* (Garden City, N.Y.: Doubleday, Doran, 1935), 212; Amos O. Squire, *Observations Made at Electrocutions of 114 Men at Sing Sing Prison* (s.l.: s.n., [1923]), 4–5; Charles Francis Potter, "I Saw a Man Electrocuted," *Reader's Digest*, Feb. 1938, 70–72; Wade Van Dore, "Charles Monroe—Hill Town Mail Clerk, Philosopher" (1939), 13, *American Life Histories: Manuscripts from the Federal Writers' Project*, American Memory, LC (memory.loc.gov/ammem/wpaintro/wpahome.html, visited 1 Dec. 1999); Oswald Garrison Villard, "Issues and Men," *Nation* 142 (1936): 513; William Dean Howells, "State Manslaughter," *Harper's Weekly* 48 (1904): 198.

44 Ga. 1925, no. 29; S.D. 1943, c. 246; Tenn. 1913, c. 36; 43 Stat. 1322 (1925); La. 1940, no. 14; 1956 (extraordinary session), no. 18; N.Y. 1914, c. 186.

45 Carlos F. MacDonald, "The Trial, Execution, Autopsy and Mental Status of Leon F. Czolgosz," *Journal of Mental Pathology* 1 (1901–1902): 185; Lewis E. Lawes, "Life in the Death House," *World's Work* 56 (1928): 170.

46 David M. Oshinsky, *"Worse Than Slavery": Parchman Farm and the Ordeal of Jim Crow Justice* (New York: Free Press, 1996), 205–207.

47 Robert G. Elliott with Albert R. Beatty, *Agent of Death: The Memoirs of an Executioner* (New York: E. P. Dutton, 1940), 92–95; James F. Penrose, "Inventing Electrocution," *Invention & Technology* 9(4) (1994): 44; Frederic Nelson, "The Executioner-Impresario," *New Republic* 55 (1928): 171–172; *NYT*, 17 Dec. 1920, 24:2; 3 Aug. 1939, 40:3

48 Leo W. Sheridan, *I Killed for the Law: The Career of Robert Elliott and Other Executioners* (New York: Stackpole Sons, 1938); Don Reid with John Gurwell, *Eyewitness* (Houston: Cordovan Press, 1973).

49 Craig Brandon, *The Electric Chair: An Unnatural American History* (Jefferson, N.C.: McFarland, 1999), 226–227; *New York Daily News*, 13 Jan. 1928, 1; *NYT*, 14 Jan. 1928, 8:2; 23 Feb. 1928, 23:5; *Chicago Herald-American*, 26 Nov. 1949, 1; John D. Bessler, *Death in the Dark: Midnight Executions in America* (Boston: Northeastern University Press, 1997), 163.

50 *NYDT*, 30 Aug. 1876, 4:4; 6 Apr. 1878, 4:4.

51 *NYT*, 15 Dec. 1896, 4:4; *NYDT*, 6 Feb. 1897, 6:4; "Methods of Administering the Death Penalty," *West Virginia Bar* 4 (1897): 128–129; *Brooklyn Daily Eagle*, 29 Sept. 1899, 8:3.

52 Loren B. Chan, "Example for the Nation: Nevada's Execution of Gee Jon," *Nevada Historical Society Quarterly* 18 (1975):95.

53 Nev. 1921, c. 246; *Nevada State Journal*, 17 Mar. 1921, 2:2; 20 Mar. 1921, 3:2; *NYT*, 29 Mar. 1921, 9:2; 3 Apr. 1921, pt. 8, 8:1; 30 Jan. 1922, 10:5; "The Infliction of Capital Punishment," *Law Notes* 31 (1927): 64–65.

54 Raymond T. Bye, "Recent History and Present Status of Capital Punishment in the United States," *American Law Review* 60 (1926): 907; *Nevada State Journal*, 29 Mar. 1921, 1:1.

55 Chan, "Example for the Nation," 99–100; P. J. Zisch, "Lethal Gas as a Means of Asphyxiating Capital Offenders," *Medico-Legal Journal*, Jan.–Feb. 1931, 26; Anthony M. Turano, "Capital Punishment by Lethal Gas," *American Mercury* 29 (1933): 92.

56 D. S. Dickerson, *Biennial Report of the Warden of the State Prison 1923–1924* (Carson City: State Printing Office, 1925), 3–4; *Nevada State Journal*, 9 Feb. 1924, 1:6.

57 "Execution by Gas," *Literary Digest*, 1 Mar. 1924, 17; *NYT*, 13 Apr. 1925, 18:5.

58 *State v. Gee Jon*, 46 Nev. 418, 211 P. 676 (1923).

59 Colo. 1933, c. 61; Ariz. 1933 (by referendum, reported in 1933, p. 588, and 1935, p. 577); N.C. 1935, c. 294; Wyo. 1935, c. 22; Calif. 1937, c. 172; Mo. 1937, pp. 221–223; Or. 1937, c. 274; Miss. 1954, c. 220; Md. 1955, c. 625; N.M. 1955, c. 127.

60 *Hernandez v. State*, 43 Ariz. 424 (1934); *People v. Daugherty*, 40 Cal. 2d 876 (1953); Raymond Hartmann, "The Use of Lethal Gas in Nevada Executions," *St. Louis Law Review* 8 (1923): 168.

61 *Rocky Mountain News*, 23 June 1934, 1:8; *Colorado Springs Gazette*, 23 June 1934, 1:7; *Daily Capital News*, 4 Mar. 1938, 1:5; 6 Mar. 1938, 1:1; *Oregonian*, 21 Jan. 1939, 1:2; *Oregon Statesman*, 21 Jan. 1939, 1:1.

62 *Tucson Daily Citizen*, 6 July 1934, 1:8; *Arizona Republic*, 6 July 1934, 1:8; *NYT*, 27 Nov. 1943, 15:4; *Raleigh News and Observer*, 25 Jan. 1936, 1:3; *Charlotte Observer*, 25 Jan. 1936, 1:7; *Los Angeles Times*, 3 Dec. 1938, 1:2; *San Francisco Chronicle*, 3 Dec. 1938, 1:3.

63 Turano, "Capital Punishment by Lethal Gas," 92–93; "Pro or Con: Execution by Lethal Gas?" *Reader's Digest*, Dec. 1937, 56–58.

64 "Nevada's Gas House," *Outlook* 155 (1930): 256; *NYT*, 1 Oct. 1939, 21:2.

65 "Pro or Con," 58–59.

66 RG 213, box 1, file 6, MOA.

67 *NYT*, 28 Feb. 1911, 10:2; 12 Feb. 1912, 20:4; 26 June 1930, 15:4.

68 Martin R. Gardner, "Mormonism and Capital Punishment: A Doctrinal Perspective, Past and Present," *Dialogue* 12(1) (1979): 9–26; Utah Terr. 1851–1852, pp. 142–143; 1878, p. 135; Nev. R.S. 1912, s. 7281; *Springfield Republican*,

27 Nov. 1903, 6:4; *NYT*, 15 Sept. 1894, 1:7; 9 Feb. 1913, pt. 3, 2:2; 1 Nov. 1938, 22:4.

69 Witness list, RG 213, box 1, file 2, MOA; Ben Abelson to James D. Carter, 12 Jan. 1965, and W. P. Steinhauser to Abelson, 15 Jan. 1965, RG 213, box 1, file 2, MOA; Frank Maudlin to E. V. Nash, 5 Feb. 1957, and Nash to Maudlin, 7 Feb. 1957, RG 213, box 1, file 12, MOA; G. W. Lane to Ben B. Stewart, 28 Feb. 1947, and Stewart to Lane, 3 Mar. 1947, RG 213, box 1, file 14, MOA.

70 Dorothy Turner to R. N. Eidson, 30 June 1953, and Eidson to Turner, 2 July 1953, RG 213, box 1, file 8, MOA.

71 Clinton T. Duffy with Al Hirshberg, *88 Men and 2 Women* (Garden City, N.Y.: Doubleday, 1962), 101.

72 Harry Jones Jr. to Harold R. Swensen, 28 Sept. 1966, and Swensen to Jones, 29 Sept. 1966, RG 213, box 1, file 2, MOA.

73 Ky. 1920, c. 163.

8. Decline

1 *NYT*, 2 Nov. 1912, 2:4.

2 Arthur E. Fink, *Causes of Crime: Biological Theories in the United States 1800–1915* (Philadelphia: University of Pennsylvania Press, 1938); John Stolz, *Murder, Capital Punishment, and the Law* (Chicago: Union Publishing Co., 1873), 88; Nicole Hahn Rafter, *Creating Born Criminals* (Urbana: University of Illinois Press, 1997); Robert L. Dugdale, *"The Jukes": A Study in Crime, Pauperism, Disease, and Heredity* (New York: G. P. Putnam's Sons, 1877); Cesare Lombroso, *Crime: Its Causes and Remedies*, trans. Henry P. Horton (Boston: Little, Brown, 1918).

3 Charles Wiley, "Retributive Law and Capital Punishment," *American Presbyterian Review* 3 (1871): 418.

4 *NYT*, 1 Nov. 1912, 12:7; J. A. Fogarty, "Considerations against Capital Punishment," *Catholic Charities Review* 9 (1925): 102; "Legal Laughs," *Albany Law Journal* 59 (1899): 313.

5 *Clarence Darrow on the Death Penalty* (Evanston, Ill.: Chicago Historical Bookworks, 1991), 58; Harry Elmer Barnes, "The Case against Capital Punishment," *Current History* 24 (1926): 366; Clifford Kirkpatrick, *Capital Punishment* (Philadelphia: Committee on Philanthropic Labor of the Philadelphia Yearly Meeting of Friends, 1925), 16.

6 Philip H. Burkett, "Ought Capital Punishment to be Abolished?" *Catholic Charities Review* 4 (1920): 75; *NYT*, 17 Jan. 1915, pt. 3, 2:4; Duke C. Bowers et al., *Life Imprisonment vs. the Death Penalty* (Nashville: s.n., [1913]), 16–17.

7 Francis Wayland, *Opening Address Before the American Social Science Association* (New Haven: Hoggson & Robinson, 1883); Herbert Harley, "Segre-

gation vs. Hanging," *Journal of the American Institute of Criminal Law and Criminology* 11 (1921): 512–527; Howard C. Forbes, "The Death Penalty from a Scientific Point of View," *Scientific Monthly* 25 (1927): 80–83; David Guest, *Sentenced to Death: The American Novel and Capital Punishment* (Jackson: University Press of Mississippi, 1997), 19, 169.

8 Irwin Ross Beiler, "'For the Abolition of the Death Penalty': A Needed Clause in Our Social Creed," *Methodist Review* 111 (1928): 221; George W. Kirchwey, "Capital Punishment," *Prison Journal*, Oct. 1923, 14; W. J. Roberts, "The Abolition of Capital Punishment," *International Journal of Ethics* 15 (1905): 281.

9 Frank Cavanaugh, "Considerations for Retaining the Death Penalty," *Catholic Charities Review* 9 (1925): 100; John H. A. Whitman, "Capital Punishment and Irresistible Impulse as a Defense," *Notre Dame Lawyer* 5 (1930): 193; Leigh H. Irvine, *By Right of Sword: A Defense of Capital Punishment* (New York: Baker & Taylor, 1915), 7; H. L. Mencken, "Men in Cages," *American Mercury* 16 (1929): 125.

10 Brand Whitlock, "'Thou Shalt Not Kill,'" *Reader* 9 (1907): 387; S. S. Nehru, "Some Aspects of the Sentence of Death," *Chicago Legal News* 48 (1916): 215; W. Duncan McKim, *Heredity and Human Progress* (New York: G. P. Putnam's Sons, 1900), 192; Robert Cloutman Dexter, *Social Adjustment* (New York: Alfred A. Knopf, 1927), 327–28; Edwin H. Sutherland, *Criminology* (Philadelphia: J. B. Lippincott, 1924), 373.

11 George Cheever, Samuel Hand, and Wendell Phillips, "The Death Penalty," *North American Review* 133 (1881): 544; C. H. Eaton, "Can Capital Punishment Be Longer Justified?" *Criminal Law Magazine and Reporter* 10 (1888): 2.

12 James T. Rice to Benjamin Gratz Brown, 24 Apr. 1872, RG 03, Brown, box 23, file 4, MOA; Abram E. Adelman, "Capital Punishment," *Public* 10 (1907): 103; "Sadism Will Out," *New Republic* 46 (1926): 264.

13 James C. Mohr, *Doctors and the Law: Medical Jurisprudence in Nineteenth-Century America* (1993; Baltimore: Johns Hopkins University Press, 1996), 170–172; *The Official Report of the Trial of Henry K. Goodwin for the Murder of Albert D. Swan* (Boston: Wright & Potter Printing Co., 1887), 14; *Speech of Henry L. Clinton, Esq., to the Jury, on the Part of the Prosecution on the Trial of Isaac V. W. Buckhout* (s.l.: s.n., [1871]), 5.

14 Tenn. 1837, c. 29; Ala. 1841, Jan. 9; La. 1846, no. 139; Ga. 1866, no. 208 (all capital crimes); Fla. 1872, c. 1877 (all capital crimes); Miss. 1872, c. 76 (all capital crimes); Tenn. 1865, c. 5 (horse-stealing, robbery, burglary, and arson); Texas 1866, c. 137 (rape); Va. 1866, c. 14 (rape), c. 25 (burglary), c. 26 (robbery).

15 Ill. 1867, p. 90; Minn. 1868, c. 88; Neb. 1869, p. 94; W.Va. Code 1870, c. 159; Fla. 1872, c. 1877; Miss. 1872, c. 76; Ky. Gen. Stat. 1873, c. 29, art. 3; Calif. 1873–1874, c. 508; Utah Terr. R.S. 1876, p. 586; Iowa 1878, c. 165; Ind. 1881, c. 37; Dakota Terr. 1883, c. 9; Ariz. Terr. 1885, no. 70; Okla. Terr. 1890, p. 446; S.C. 1894, no. 530; 29 Stat. 487 (U.S. 1897); Ohio 1898, p. 223; Colo. 1901, c. 64; N.H. 1903, c. 114; Mo. 1907, p. 235; Mont. 1907, c. 179; Nev. 1907, c. 93; Md. 1908, c. 115 (judge's discretion); Md. 1916, c. 214 (jury's discretion); Wash. 1909, c. 249; Vt. 1910, no. 225; Idaho 1911, c. 68; Texas 1913, c. 116; Va. 1914, c. 240; Ark. 1915, no. 187; Wyo. 1915, c. 87; N.J. 1916, c. 270; Del. 1917, c. 266; Ore. 1921, p. 6; Pa. 1925, no. 411; Kan. 1935, c. 154; N.M. 1939, c. 49; N.C. 1949, c. 299; Conn. 1951, no. 369; Mass. 1951, c. 203 (still mandatory if murder committed in connection with rape or attempted rape); 76 Stat. 46 (D.C. 1962); N.Y. 1963, c. 994.

16 Michael von Moschzisker, "Capital Punishment in the Pennsylvania Courts," *Pennsylvania Bar Association Quarterly* 20 (1949): 188; Robert E. Knowlton, "Problems of Jury Discretion in Capital Cases," *University of Pennsylvania Law Review* 101 (1953): 1099–1136.

17 Robert Ralston, *The Delay in the Execution of Murderers* ([Philadelphia]: Pennsylvania Bar Association, 1911); Lawrence M. Friedman and Robert V. Percival, *The Roots of Justice: Crime and Punishment in Alameda County, California, 1870–1910* (Chapel Hill: University of North Carolina Press, 1981), 303–307; James W. Marquart, Sheldon Ekland-Olson, and Jonathan R. Sorensen, *The Rope, the Chair, and the Needle: Capital Punishment in Texas, 1923–1990* (Austin: University of Texas Press, 1994), 95; Donald M. McIntyre, *Delays in the Execution of Death Sentences* (Chicago: American Bar Foundation, 1960), 3.

18 James H. Fairchild, *Moral Philosophy* (New York: Sheldon, 1869), 173; Jerome W. Turner, "Capital Punishment," *Michigan Law Journal* 1 (1892): 291; Lewis E. Lawes, *Meet the Murderer!* (New York: Harper & Brothers, 1940), 177–178.

19 Thomas Speed Mosby, "Does Capital Punishment Tend to Diminish Crime?" *Harper's Weekly* 50 (1906): 1029; "Capital Punishment," *Law Notes* 31 (1928): 224–225.

20 Harold A. Phelps, "Effectiveness of Life Imprisonment as a Repressive Measure against Murder in Rhode Island," *Journal of the American Statistical Association* 23 (1928): supp. 174–181; George B. Vold, "Can the Death Penalty Prevent Crime?" *Prison Journal*, Oct. 1932, 4–9; Robert H. Dann, *The Deterrent Effect of Capital Punishment* (Philadelphia: Committee on Philanthropic Labor of Philadelphia Yearly Meeting of Friends, 1935);

Charles T. Jerome, "The Death-Penalty," *Potter's American Monthly* 18 (1882): 152; *Does the Death Penalty Deter? A Ten-Year Statistical Comparison* (New York: American League to Abolish Capital Punishment, [1930]). For the state of the art at midcentury, see Thorsten Sellin, *The Death Penalty: A Report for the Model Penal Code Project of the American Law Institute* (Philadelphia: American Law Institute, 1959).

21 Maynard Shipley, "Results of the Practical Abolition of Capital Punishment in Belgium," *Publications of the American Statistical Association* 9 (1905): 307–314; N.Y. Assembly Doc. no. 79 (1890), 7–9; "Growing Tendency in Latin America to Abolish the Death Penalty," *Bulletin of the Pan American Union* 58 (1924): 362–365; "Capital Punishment," *Law Notes* 32 (1928): 43; E. Roy Calvert, "Murder and the Death Penalty," *Nation* 129 (1929): 406.

22 Marcus A. Kavanagh and Lewis Lawes, *Does the Death Penalty Curb Crime?* (Girard, Kan.: Haldeman-Julius, 1931), 15; *NYT*, 18 Nov. 1912, 10:7.

23 "The Death Penalty in the United States," *Green Bag* 9 (1897): 130–131; John J. Ford, "Capital Punishment," *Catholic Mind* 13 (1915): 134–135; "Argument against Capital Punishment," *Nation* 16 (1873): 213; "Shall the State Continue to Take Human Life?" *Pathfinder*, July 1927, 4; *Capital Punishment: Hearings Before the Subcommittee on Judiciary of the Committee on the District of Columbia, House of Representatives* (Washington: Government Printing Office, 1928), 60.

24 Arthur Macdonald, "Death Penalty and Homicide," *American Journal of Sociology* 16 (1910): 88–116; E. H. Sutherland, "Murder and the Death Penalty," *Journal of the American Institute of Criminal Law and Criminology* 15 (1925): 522–529; Frederick L. Hoffman, "Murder and the Death Penalty," *Current History* 28 (1928): 408–410.

25 Lawrence M. Friedman, *Crime and Punishment in American History* (New York: Basic Books, 1993), 210; Sheldon Amos, "Right and Wrong in Politics," *Princeton Review* 1 (1882): 288–289; James H. Vahey, "The Abolition of Capital Punishment," *Green Bag* 19 (1907): 359; C. F. Fanning, ed., *Selected Articles on Capital Punishment* (Minneapolis: H. W. Wilson Co., 1909); C. F. Fanning, ed., *Selected Articles on Capital Punishment*, 2nd ed. (Minneapolis: H. W. Wilson Co., 1913); C. F. Fanning, ed., *Selected Articles on Capital Punishment*, 3rd ed. (White Plains, N.Y.: H. W. Wilson Co., 1917); Lamar T. Beman, ed., *Selected Articles on Capital Punishment* (New York: H. W. Wilson Co., 1925); Julia E. Johnsen, ed., *Capital Punishment* (New York: H. W. Wilson Co., 1939); George W. Phillips and Fremont Older, "The Death Penalty?" *Sunset Magazine*, Jan. 1928, 18–21; Henry Barrett Chamberlin and Clarence Darrow, "Capital Punishment?" *Rotarian*, Nov. 1933, 12–15.

26 *The Sacredness of Human Life* (Philadelphia: Friends' Book Store, 1905); William Q. Judge, "Theosophy and Capital Punishment," *Theosophical Path* 19 (1920): 210; *NYT*, 21 Dec. 1919, pt. 10, 6:2.

27 Iowa 1872, c. 242; 1878, c. 165; Me. 1876, c. 114; 1883, c. 205; 1887, c. 133; Richard Acton, "The Magic of Undiscouraged Effort: The Death Penalty in Early Iowa, 1838–1878," *Annals of Iowa* 50 (1991): 721–750; Edward Schriver, "Reluctant Hangman: The State of Maine and Capital Punishment, 1820–1887," *New England Quarterly* 63 (1990): 271–287.

28 Colo. 1897, c. 35; 1901, c. 64; "The Death Penalty," *Public Opinion* 13 (1892): 33; *NYT*, 31 May 1868, 4:4; Connecticut legislative card file, CTL; C. G. Garrison, "The Failure of the Death Penalty," *Arena* 21 (1899): 469; John D. Bessler, "The 'Midnight Assassination Law' and Minnesota's Anti-Death Penalty Movement, 1849–1911," *William Mitchell Law Review* 22 (1996): 677–689; *Debates and Proceedings of the Constitutional Convention of the State of Illinois* (Springfield: E. L. Merritt & Brother, 1870), 1573; *Debates in the Convention for the Revision and Amendment of the Constitution of the State of Louisiana* (New Orleans: W. R. Fish, 1864), 459; "Capital Punishment in Foreign Countries," *American Law Record* 10 (1881): 72.

29 *NYT*, 26 Dec. 1911, 6:2; 12 Jan. 1912, 6:3; 14 Dec. 1912, 3:4; Edward F. Dunne, *Address of Governor Edward F. Dunne of Illinois at the Governors' Conference* (s.l.: s.n., [1915]); George W. P. Hunt, *A Paradox of Progress* (Phoenix: R. A. Watkins, [1914]), 17–18, 22; Orben J. Casey, "Governor Lee Cruce, White Supremacy and Capital Punishment, 1911–1915," *Chronicles of Oklahoma* 52 (1974–75): 456–475; George W. P. Hunt to Titus M. Coan, 8 Dec. 1914, Titus M. Coan Papers, NYHS; Frank Marshall White, "A Function of State," *Outlook* 114 (1916): 389; *NYT*, 20 Nov. 1914, 1:5; 8 Jan. 1915, 5:6; 18 Feb. 1915, 6:2; 4 Mar. 1915, 7:2; Thomas Mott Osborne and Robert E. Crowe, "The Death Penalty—A Debate," *Forum* 73 (1925): 156–168.

30 Kan. 1907, c. 188; Harvey Richard Hougen, *The Strange Career of the Kansas Hangman: A History of Capital Punishment in the Sunflower State to 1944* (Ph.D. diss, Kansas State University, 1979), 86; Minn. 1911, c. 387; Wash. 1913, c. 167; Ore. 1915, p. 12; N.D. 1915, c. 63 (abolished except for prisoners already serving life sentences for murder); S.D. 1915, c. 158; Ariz. 1917, p. 4; Mo. 1917, p. 246; Tenn. 1915 (extra session), c. 181.

31 Ariz. 1919, p. 17; Ore. 1921, p. 6; Mo. 1919, extra session, p. 778; Wash. 1919, c. 112; Ellen Elizabeth Guillot, "Abolition and Restoration of the Death Penalty in Missouri," in Thorsten Sellin, ed., *Capital Punishment* (New York: Harper & Row, 1967), 124–131; Loren Holcombe Milligan, *The Influence of the Press of the State of Washington on the Commonwealth's Criminal Code* (M.A. thesis, University of Washington, 1927), 23–24; Tenn. 1919, c. 4;

Kans. 1935, c. 154; S.D. 1939, c. 30; Bessler, "Midnight Assassination Law," 706n899.

32 James J. Barbour, "Efforts to Abolish the Death Penalty in Illinois," *Journal of the American Institute of Criminal Law and Criminology* 9 (1919): 502; *NYDT*, 11 Dec. 1902, 5:3; *NYT*, 28 May 1909, 1:6; 7 Mar. 1911, 1:6; 3 Mar. 1915, 10:5; 8 Apr. 1915, 22:1; Jacob Goldstein, "Shall Capital Punishment Be Abolished? How Pennsylvania Is Answering the Question," *Outlook* 116 (1917):18–19; "Capital Punishment Day," *Law Notes* 15 (1911): 3; 1915 Constitutional Convention (L0076), Committee Correspondence, Minutes and Proposal Files, box 1 (Bill of Rights Committee), NYA; Richard B. Dressner and Glenn C. Altschuler, "Sentiment and Statistics in the Progressive Era: The Debate on Capital Punishment in New York," *New York History* 56 (1975): 197–208; Connecticut legislative card file, CTL; *Chicago Record-Herald*, 23 June 1912, 8:2; Samuel J. Barrows, "Legislative Tendencies as to Capital Punishment," *Annals of the American Academy of Political and Social Science* 29 (1907): 181; *Report of the Committee to Inquire into the Subject of Capital Punishment* (Trenton, N.J.: MacCrellish & Quigley, 1908); *NYT*, 13 Feb. 1913, 4:1; Samuel Untermyer, *Resolved, That Capital Punishment Be Abolished* (New York: League to Abolish Capital Punishment, 1928), 9; Louis Filler, "Movements to Abolish the Death Penalty in the United States," *Annals of the American Academy of Political and Social Science* 28 (1952): 134; J. D. Bibb Jr. to Westmoreland Davis, 11 Feb. 1918, Governor Westmoreland Davis (1918–1922), Executive Papers, box 7, folder marked "Death Penalty, Abolition of," VAA.

33 Ill. 1917, p. 351; Vt. 1917, no. 236; Colo. 1919, extraordinary session, c. 1.

34 *NYT*, 23 Dec. 1920, 2:7; 2 Feb. 1921, 16:3; 29 Apr. 1925, 10:3; 23 Jan. 1931, 3:5; 21 Feb. 1935, 15:5; Ernest Kahlar Alix, *Ransom Kidnapping in America, 1874–1974: The Creation of a Capital Crime* (Carbondale: Southern Illinois University Press, 1978).

35 "Abolishing the Death Penalty," *Literary Digest*, 22 Aug. 1925, 29; Franklin Hirchborn, *13 Minutes at the End of a Journey* (New York: League for the Abolition of Capital Punishment, [1920s]); *NYT*, 7 Oct. 1929, 18:6; 28 May 1930, 16:6; 29 Dec. 1931, 2:5; 30 Jan. 1932, 5:4; William Randolph Hearst, *We Cannot Cure Murder by Murder* (New York: J. J. Little and Ives Co., 1926); Henry Ford, *Henry Ford on Capital Punishment* (New York: League to Abolish Capital Punishment, [1927]), 2; *NYT*, 6 June 1927, 14:3; S. J. Duncan-Clark, "Clarence Darrow Opens His Fight against the Death Penalty," *Success*, Dec. 1924, 28; Clarence Darrow, "The Futility of the Death Penalty," *Forum* 80 (1928): 327.

36 *NYT*, 12 Jan. 1936, part 2, 2:6; *Complete Presidential Press Conferences of*

Franklin D. Roosevelt (New York: Da Capo Press, 1972), 2:446; Mrs. Herbert B. Ehrman to M. A. LeHand, n.d., and LeHand to Ehrman, 10 Jan. 1934, President's Personal Files, file 1156, FDR.

37 Harry L. Davis, *Death By Law* (Columbus: Federal Printing Co., 1922); *NYT*, 8 Apr. 1923, 3:6; 30 Jan. 1928, 24:8; 7 Mar. 1939, 4:4; 29 Aug. 1923, 8:3; 9 Mar. 1948, 25:6; Henry F. Pringle, *Wardens Oppose Execution as No Deterrent to Crime* (New York: League for the Abolition of Capital Punishment, n.d.); "To Kill or Not to Kill," *Independent* 115 (1925): 143.

38 *NYT*, 26 Oct. 1929, 20:2; 9 Mar. 1928, 27:5; 12 Oct. 1925, 24:5; 18 Feb. 1926, 22:8; 12 Apr. 1926, 25:6; 25 Apr. 1927, 26:8; 6 Feb. 1928, 22:6; 19 Mar. 1928, 24:1.

39 "The Loeb-Leopold Sentence," *World's Work* 49 (1924): 12–13; Leonard Blumgart, "The New Psychology and the Franks Case," *Nation* 119 (1924): 261–262; "Rich and Poor Murderers," *Literary Digest*, 27 Sept. 1924, 10–11; "Murder Most Foul," *Outlook* 138 (1924): 115–116; *NYT*, 13 Sept. 1924, 12:5; 19 Sept. 1924, 22:6; "Questions From Chapman's Grave," *Literary Digest*, 24 Apr. 1926, 30–31; RG5, box 324a, CTA; *Message of Governor Friend Wm. Richardson Regarding Acts of Executive Clemency* (Sacramento: California State Printing Office, 1926), 2.

40 "The Death Penalty," *Nation* 127 (1928): 472; "Delay in Executing Death Sentence," *Law Notes* 31 (1927): 141; *NYT*, 2 Jan. 1928, 12:2; 17 Feb. 1929, 24:6; "New York Kills Again," *Nation* 126 (1928): 85; "The Death Penalty: Pro and Con," *Literary Digest*, 4 Feb. 1928, 13; Courtenay Terrett, "Hangman's Holiday," *Outlook* 148 (1928): 166–167; *New York Evening Post*, 3 Mar. 1928, 1:2; James Goodman, *Stories of Scottsboro* (New York: Pantheon, 1994); Richard C. Cortner, *A "Scottsboro" Case in Mississippi: The Supreme Court and Brown v. Mississippi* (Jackson: University Press of Mississippi, 1986); "Hauptmann's Death Sentence," *New Republic* 85 (1936): 325–326.

41 "Capital Punishment," *Christian Century* 53 (1936): 591; "Inhuman America," *Living Age* 350 (1936): 348.

42 For these figures and others that follow I have allocated the following states to the south (and the rest to the north): Alabama, Arizona, Arkansas, Delaware, Florida, Georgia, Kansas, Kentucky, Louisiana, Maryland, Mississippi, Missouri, New Mexico, North Carolina, Oklahoma, South Carolina, Tennessee, Texas, and Virginia.

43 John F. Marszalek, ed., *The Diary of Miss Emma Holmes 1861–1866* (Baton Rouge: Louisiana State University Press, 1994), 455; William Kauffman Scarborough, ed., *The Diary of Edmund Ruffin* (Baton Rouge: Louisiana State University Press, 1972–1989), 3:562; George W. Hays, "The Necessity for Capital Punishment," *Scribner's Magazine* 81 (1927): 581.

44 Richard Reifsnyder, "Capital Crimes in the States," *Journal of Criminal Law, Criminology and Police Science* 45 (1955): 691.

45 W. Fitzhugh Brundage, *Lynching in the New South: Georgia and Virginia, 1880–1930* (Urbana: University of Illinois Press, 1993), 8; *Chicago Record-Herald*, 1 Aug. 1906, 1:4; 23 Nov. 1906, 7:2; George C. Wright, *Racial Violence in Kentucky, 1865–1940: Lynchings, Mob Rule, and "Legal Lynchings"* (Baton Rouge: Louisiana State University Press, 1990), 71, 227.

46 J. E. Cutler, "Capital Punishment and Lynching," *Annals of the American Academy of Political and Social Science* 29 (1907): 622–625; Raymond T. Bye, *Capital Punishment in the United States* (Philadelphia: Committee on Philanthropic Labor of Philadelphia, 1919), 70–71; "The Death Penalty as a Preventive of Crime," *Annals of the American Academy of Political and Social Science* 17 (1901): 366–369; Andrew J. Palm, "Capital Punishment," *American Journal of Politics* 2 (1893): 326; Stewart E. Tolnay and E. M. Beck, *A Festival of Violence: An Analysis of Southern Lynchings, 1882–1930* (Urbana: University of Illinois Press, 1995), 98–113; Charles David Phillips, "Exploring Relations among Forms of Social Control: The Lynching and Execution of Blacks in North Carolina, 1889–1918," *Law & Society Review* 21 (1987): 361–374.

9. To the Supreme Court

1 *Time*, 10 July 1972, 37; *Newsweek*, 10 July 1972, 20.

2 *New Republic*, 15 July 1972, 7.

3 William Finley Swindler, ed., *Sources and Documents of United States Constitutions* (Dobbs Ferry, N.Y.: Oceana Publications, 1973–), 10:49, 2:198, 4:373, 7:402, 5:95, 6:347, 8:293, 8:481; Merrill Jensen et al., eds., *The Documentary History of the Ratification of the Constitution* (Madison: State Historical Society of Wisconsin, 1976–), 13:239, 13:350, 13:466, 13:527, 15:18, 16:59, 18:43, 18:202, 18:298, 18:316; Linda Grant De Pauw et al., eds., *Documentary History of the First Federal Congress of the United States of America* (Baltimore: Johns Hopkins University Press, 1972–), 11:1290–91.

4 Leonard W. Levy, *Origins of the Bill of Rights* (New Haven: Yale University Press, 1999), 231–236; Anthony F. Granucci, "'Nor Cruel and Unusual Punishments Inflicted': The Original Meaning," *California Law Review* 57 (1969): 856–860.

5 Lois G. Schwoerer, *The Declaration of Rights, 1689* (Baltimore: Johns Hopkins University Press, 1981), 92–94; Jensen et al., eds., *Documentary History of the Ratification of the Constitution*, 16:381.

6 Jonathan Elliot, ed., *The Debates in the Several State Conventions on the*

Adoption of the Federal Constitution, 2d ed. (Washington: Jonathan Elliot, 1836–1845), 2:111, 3:447; William Blackstone, *Commentaries on the Laws of England* (1765–1769), 9th ed. (London: W. Strahan et al., 1783), 4:377.

7 Joseph Story, *Commentaries on the Constitution of the United States* (Boston: Hilliard, Gray, 1833), 710–711.

8 *Wilkerson v. Utah,* 99 U.S. 130 (1878); *State v. Burris,* 190 N.W. 38 (Iowa 1922); *State v. Butchek,* 253 P. 367 (Ore. 1927).

9 *State v. Stubblefield,* 58 S.W. 337 (Mo. 1900); *Territory v. Ketchum,* 65 P. 169 (N.M. 1901); *Gibson v. Commonwealth,* 265 S.W. 339 (Ky. 1924); *Robards v. State,* 259 P. 166 (Okla. 1927); *Brookman v. Commonwealth,* 145 S.E. 358, 361 (Va. 1928); *In re Finley,* 81 P. 1041 (Cal. 1905); *Dutton v. State,* 91 A. 417 (Md. 1914); *Hart v. Commonwealth,* 109 S.E. 582 (Va. 1921); *Tomlinson v. Commonwealth,* 87 S.W.2d 376 (Ky. 1935); *Lee v. State,* 150 So. 164 (Ala. 1933); *People v. Tanner,* 44 P.2d 324 (Cal. 1935); *United States v. Rosenberg,* 195 F.2d 583 (2d Cir. 1952).

10 *Weems v. United States,* 217 U.S. 349, 365, 372–373, 380–381 (1910).

11 "Cruel and Unusual Punishment," *University of Pennsylvania Law Review* 59 (1910): 43–46; "Cruel and Unusual Punishment," *Virginia Law Register* 16 (1910): 222–223; Larry Charles Berkson, *The Concept of Cruel and Unusual Punishment* (Lexington, Mass.: Lexington Books, 1975), 71–73; *Robinson v. California,* 370 U.S. 660, 667 (1962).

12 *Weems,* 217 U.S. at 373; "What Is Cruel and Unusual Punishment," *Harvard Law Review* 24 (1910): 55; Henry Schofield, "Cruel and Unusual Punishment," *Illinois Law Review* 5 (1911): 335.

13 Harold Burton Papers, box 171, LC.

14 *Trop v. Dulles,* 356 U.S. 86, 100–101, 126–127 (1958).

15 *Pervear v. Commonwealth,* 72 U.S. 475 (1866); *Louisiana ex rel. Francis v. Resweber,* 329 U.S. 459 (1947); *Johnson v. Dye,* 175 F.2d 250 (3d Cir. 1949); *Harper v. Wall,* 85 F. Supp. 783 (D.N.J. 1949); *In re Middlebrooks,* 88 F. Supp. 943 (S.D. Cal. 1950); *Robinson v. California,* 370 U.S. 660 (1962).

16 Unpublished draft concurring opinion, Robert Jackson Papers, box 138, file "No. 142 Louisiana ex rel. Francis v. Resweber," LC; *NYT,* 12 Mar. 1961, 64:1; 6 July 1968, 42:1; *Haley v. Ohio,* 332 U.S. 596, 602 (1948) (Frankfurter, J., dissenting); Felix Frankfurter, "The Problem of Capital Punishment" (1950), in Philip Elman, ed., *Of Laws and Men: Papers and Addresses of Felix Frankfurter* (New York: Harcourt, Brace, 1956), 81.

17 Joseph E. Browdy and Robert J. Saltzman, "The Effectiveness of the Eighth Amendment: An Appraisal of Cruel and Unusual Punishment," *New York University Law Review* 36 (1961): 859–860; Nancy-Nellis Warner, "Cruel and Unusual Punishments," *Catholic University Law Review* 3 (1953): 119;

Alexander M. Bickel, *The Least Dangerous Branch: The Supreme Court at the Bar of Politics* (Indianapolis: Bobbs-Merrill, 1962), 240–242.

18 *Williams v. New York,* 337 U.S. 241, 248 (1949); *People v. Oliver,* 134 N.E.2d 197, 201–202 (N.Y. 1956); Herbert L. Packer, *The Limits of the Criminal Sanction* (Stanford: Stanford University Press, 1968), 10; *Model Penal Code and Commentaries* (Philadelphia: American Law Institute, 1980–), pt. I, 3:16.

19 Robert G. Caldwell, "Why Is the Death Penalty Retained?" *Annals of the American Academy of Political and Social Science* 284 (1952): 52; 10 Jan. 1958, MSA S97–14, MDA.

20 Robert M. Bohm, "American Death Penalty Opinion, 1936–1986: A Critical Examination of the Gallup Polls," in Bohm, ed., *The Death Penalty in America: Current Research* (Cincinnati: Anderson Publishing Co., 1991), 113–145.

21 Arthur Koestler, *Reflections on Hanging* (1956; New York: Macmillan, 1957); Albert Camus, *Reflections on the Guillotine,* trans. Richard Howard (Michigan City, Ind.: Fridtjof-Karla Publications, 1959); Michael V. DiSalle with Lawrence G. Blochman, *The Power of Life or Death* (New York: Random House, 1965); *NYT,* 26 Mar. 1959, 23:6; 28 July 1959, 17:4; 23 Apr. 1960, 48:4; 25 Apr. 1960, 3:6; Governor Terry Sanford, General Correspondence 1961, box 106; General Correspondence 1963, box 340; General Correspondence 1964, box 443, NCA; *NYT,* 10 Apr. 1960, 57:1; 1 Oct. 1962, 11:1; 24 July 1965, 1:5; Walter E. Oberer, "Does Disqualification of Jurors for Scruples against Capital Punishment Constitute Denial of Fair Trial on Issue of Guilt?" *Texas Law Review* 39 (1961): 545.

22 *What Do the Churches Say on Capital Punishment?* 4th ed. (West Hartford, Conn.: Friends Committee on Social Order, 1960); *NYT,* 26 Apr. 1959, 61:4; 7 May 1960, 23:1; 30 June 1966, 26:3; Trevor Thomas, *This Life We Take: The Case against the Death Penalty,* rev. ed. (Washington: Friends Committee on Legislation, 1959); Roland B. Gittlesohn, "A Contemporary Jewish View of Capital Punishment," in Ruth Leigh, *Man's Right to Life* (New York: Commission on Social Action of Reform Judaism, 1959), 37–38; John Howard Yoder, *The Christian and Capital Punishment* (Newton, Kan.: Faith and Life Press, 1961).

23 RG03, Hearnes, box 362, file 4568; box 379, file 4857; box 404, file 5208; box 448, file 5810; box 476, file 6117, MOA; RG 5, box A-233, two files "Capital Punishment," CTA; Harold H. Punke, "Capital Punishment—Pro and Con," *Clearing House* 35 (1960): 103–107.

24 Brian P. Block and John Hostettler, *Hanging in the Balance: A History of the Abolition of Capital Punishment in Britain* (Winchester: Waterside Press, 1997); David Chandler, *Capital Punishment in Canada* (Toronto:

McClelland and Stewart, 1976); Roger Hood, *The Death Penalty: A World-Wide Perspective*, 2d ed. (Oxford: Clarendon Press, 1996), 241–245.

25 RG 204, 1004/1–2, NA; *NYT*, 19 Feb. 1960, 16:2; 22 Feb. 1960, 38:5; 27 Oct. 1959, 20:4; 7 Apr. 1960, 11:8; 10 Apr. 1963, 19:6.

26 Mary L. Dudziak, *Cold War Civil Rights: Equality as Cold War Policy, 1946–1968* (Princeton: Princeton University Press, 2000); RG 59, 711.341/8–2658, NA; *Sunday Express* [London], 24 Aug. 1958, 7; *NYT*, 27 Aug. 1958, 16:7; 2 Sept. 1958, 13:3; 4 Sept. 1958, 15:3; 6 Sept. 1958, 7:1; 14 Sept. 1958, 56:3; 25 Sept. 1958, 20:4; 30 Sept. 1958, 1:5.

27 Alaska 1957, c. 132; Haw. 1957, no. 282; Del. 1958, c. 347; 1961, cc. 309–10; Ore. 1965, p. 6 (reporting results of 1964 referendum); N.Y. 1965, c. 321 (retained for murder of police officer on duty or murder committed by life prisoner); Iowa 1965, cc. 435–446; Vt. 1965, no. 30 (retained for unrelated second murder or murder of law enforcement official); W.V. 1965, c. 40; N.M. 1969, c. 128 (retained for second murder or murder of police officer or prison guard).

28 *NYT*, 14 Mar. 1965, 74:3; 19 Apr. 1963, 22:1; 13 Mar. 1964, 65:4; Illinois Committee to Abolish Capital Punishment, *The Death Penalty* (Chicago: Illinois Committee to Abolish Capital Punishment, [1959]); *NYT*, 10 May 1957, 53:4; 17 Apr. 1967, 23:1; *Report and Recommendations of the Special Commission Established for the Purpose of Investigating and Studying the Abolition of the Death Penalty in Capital Cases* (Boston: Wright & Potter Printing Co., 1959); *Report of the Subcommittee of the Judiciary Committee on Capital Punishment Pertaining to the Problems of the Death Penalty and Its Administration in California* ([Sacramento]: Assembly of the State of California, 1957); Pennsylvania General Assembly, *Report of the Joint Legislative Committee on Capital Punishment* ([Harrisburg]: s.n., 1961); *Report of the Committee on Capital Punishment to the Legislative Council of Maryland* ([Annapolis]: s.n., 1962); *NYT*, 28 Feb. 1965, pt. 4, 10:1.

29 Statistics in the following paragraphs come from Margaret Werner Cahalan, *Historical Corrections Statistics in the United States, 1850–1984* (Rockville, Md.: U.S. Department of Justice, 1986), 18–19; from U.S. Department of Justice, *National Prisoner Statistics: Executions* (Washington: U.S. Dept. of Justice, 1961–1968), National Prisoner Statistics nos. 26, 28, 32, 34, 37, 39, 41, and 42; and from U.S. Department of Justice, *National Prisoner Statistics: Capital Punishment* (Washington: U.S. Dept. of Justice, 1969 and 1971), National Prisoner Statistics nos. 45 and 46.

30 *Capital Punishment in North Carolina* (Raleigh: North Carolina State Board of Charities and Public Welfare, 1929), 19; Margaret Vandiver, "The

Quality of Mercy: Race and Clemency in Florida Death Penalty Cases, 1924–1966," *University of Richmond Law Review* 27 (1993): 322.

31 Lester Bernhardt Orfield, *Criminal Appeals in America* (Boston: Little, Brown, 1939), 225–227; "Criminal Appeals in Southern States," *Michigan Law Review* 21 (1923): 584–586; Grant Foreman, "The Law's Delays," *Michigan Law Review* 13 (1914): 108–109n8.

32 Robert A. Kagan et al., "The Business of State Supreme Courts, 1870–1970," *Stanford Law Review* 30 (1977): 146; Federal Courts Study Committee, *Working Papers and Subcommittee Reports* (Philadelphia: Federal Courts Study Committee, 1990), 1:469.

33 *Brown v. Allen*, 344 U.S. 443 (1953); *Griffin v. Illinois*, 351 U.S. 12 (1956); *Douglas v. California*, 372 U.S. 353 (1963); *Fay v. Noia*, 372 U.S. 391 (1963).

34 *Shelley v. Kraemer*, 334 U.S. 1 (1948); *Sweatt v. Painter*, 339 U.S. 629 (1950); *McLaurin v. Oklahoma State Regents*, 339 U.S. 637 (1950); Eric W. Rise, *The Martinsville Seven: Race, Rape, and Capital Punishment* (Charlottesville: University Press of Virginia, 1995), 99–132.

35 *Hampton v. Commonwealth*, 58 S.E.2d 288 (Va. 1950); *State ex rel. Johnson v. Mayo*, 69 So. 2d 307 (Fla. 1954); *State ex rel. Copeland v. Mayo*, 87 So. 2d 501 (Fla. 1956); *Thomas v. State*, 92 So. 2d 621 (Fla. 1957); *Williams v. State*, 110 So. 2d 654 (Fla. 1959); *Williams v. State*, 335 S.W.2d 224 (Tex. 1960); *Mitchell v. State*, 337 S.W.2d 663 (Ark. 1960); *Rudolph v. State*, 152 So. 2d 662 (Ala. 1963).

36 *In re Ernst*, 294 F.2d 556 (3d Cir. 1961); *State v. White*, 374 P.2d 942 (Wash. 1962); *State v. Latham*, 375 P.2d 788 (Kan. 1962); *State v. Leland*, 227 P.2d 785 (Ore. 1951); *United States v. Puff*, 211 F.2d 171 (2d Cir. 1954); *People v. Carpenter*, 150 N.E. 100 (Ill. 1958); *United States v. Sain*, 297 F.2d 799 (7th Cir. 1962); *Turberville v. United States*, 303 F.2d 411 (D.C. Cir. 1962); Gerald H. Gottlieb, "Testing the Death Penalty," *Southern California Law Review* 34 (1961): 268–281; Jack Greenberg and Jack Himmelstein, "Varieties of Attack on the Death Penalty," *Crime and Delinquency* 15 (1969): 114–115.

37 Arthur J. Goldberg, "The Death Penalty and the Supreme Court," *Arizona Law Review* 15 (1973): 363; Alan M. Dershowitz, *The Best Defense* (New York: Random House, 1982), 307.

38 The memorandum was not published until much later, as Arthur J. Goldberg, "Memorandum to the Conference *Re:* Capital Punishment, October Term, 1963," *South Texas Law Review* 27 (1986): 493–506.

39 Ian Gray and Moira Stanley, *A Punishment in Search of a Crime: Americans Speak Out against the Death Penalty* (New York: Avon Books, 1989), 330; Melvin I. Urofsky, ed., *The Douglas Letters: Selections from the Private Pa-*

pers of Justice William O. Douglas (Bethesda, Md.: Adler & Adler, 1987), 189; *Rudolph v. Alabama*, 375 U.S. 889 (1963) (Goldberg, J., dissenting from the denial of certiorari).

40 Dorothy Goldberg, *A Private View of a Public Life* (New York: Charterhouse, 1975), 178.

41 Jack Greenberg, *Crusaders in the Courts: How a Dedicated Band of Lawyers Fought for the Civil Rights Revolution* (New York: Basic Books, 1994), 442; Michael Meltsner, *Cruel and Unusual: The Supreme Court and Capital Punishment* (New York: Random House, 1973), 86–105.

42 Aryeh Neier, *Only Judgment: The Limits of Litigation in Social Change* (Middletown, Conn.: Wesleyan University Press, 1982), 198.

43 *Maxwell v. Bishop*, 398 F.2d 138, 147 (8th Cir. 1968); Meltsner, *Cruel and Unusual*, 108–109.

44 Meltsner, *Cruel and Unusual*, 107.

45 *United States v. Jackson*, 390 U.S. 570 (1968); Meltsner, *Cruel and Unusual*, 117.

46 Motion for Leave to File Brief *Amici Curiae* and Brief *Amici Curiae* of the NAACP Legal Defense and Educational Fund, Inc., and the National Office for the Rights of the Indigent, *Witherspoon v. Illinois*, 391 U.S. 510 (1968); Meltsner, *Cruel and Unusual*, 120–122.

47 *Witherspoon v. Illinois*, 391 U.S. 510 (1968).

48 Brief for the N.A.A.C.P. Legal Defense and Educational Fund, Inc., and the National Office for the Rights of the Indigent, as *Amici Curiae*, 25, *Boykin v. Alabama*, 395 U.S. 238 (1969).

49 Thurgood Marshall Papers, box 58, folder 3, LC; William J. Brennan, Jr., Papers, box I:417, folder 5, box I:416, folder 6, LC.

50 William J. Brennan, Jr., Papers, box I:417, folder 5, LC; *Maxwell v. Bishop*, 398 U.S. 262 (1970).

51 Douglas's conference notes, 13 Nov. 1970, William O. Douglas Papers, box 1514, LC.

52 *McGautha v. California*, 402 U.S. 183, 204 (1971).

53 Urofsky, ed., *Douglas Letters*, 193–194; William J. Brennan, Jr., "Constitutional Adjudication and the Death Penalty: A View from the Court," *Harvard Law Review* 100 (1986): 321; Douglas memorandum to conference, 3 June 1971, Thurgood Marshall Papers, box 64, folder 5, LC; John C. Jeffries Jr., *Justice Lewis F. Powell, Jr.* (New York: Scribner's, 1994), 408.

54 Brennan and White memorandum to conference, 8 June 1971, William O. Douglas Papers, box 1486, LC.

55 Brief for Petitioner, *Aikens v. California*, 68–5027, 10, 39, 42, 53.

56 Dennis J. Hutchinson, *The Man Who Once Was Whizzer White* (New York: Free Press, 1998), 363. The account of the conference is drawn from the notes taken by Douglas and Brennan. William O. Douglas Papers, box 1542, LC; William J. Brennan, Jr., Papers, box I:420A, folder 4, LC. I have made silent insertions to convert the notes into grammatically correct sentences.

57 Notes, spring 1972, *Furman v. Georgia*, 69–5003, LFP.

58 *Furman v. Georgia*, 408 U.S. 238 (1972).

59 Austin Sarat and Neil Vidmar, "Public Opinion, the Death Penalty, and the Eighth Amendment: Testing the Marshall Hypothesis," in Hugo Adam Bedau and Chester M. Pierce, eds., *Capital Punishment in the United States* (New York: AMS Press, 1976), 190–223.

60 *Miranda v. Arizona*, 384 U.S. 436 (1966); *Aguilar v. Texas*, 378 U.S. 108 (1964); *United States v. Wade*, 388 U.S. 218 (1967); *Gideon v. Wainwright*, 372 U.S. 335 (1963).

61 *Swann v. Charlotte-Mecklenburg Board of Education*, 402 U.S. 1 (1971); *Regents of the University of California v. Bakke*, 438 U.S. 265 (1978).

62 *Chicago Tribune*, 9 Oct. 1972, 8:1.

63 Meltsner, *Cruel and Unusual*, 290; Greenberg, *Crusaders*, 451.

10. *Resurrection*

1 *NYT*, 1 July 1972, 10:1; John Ehrlichman to Nixon, 4 Aug. 1972, Nixon Presidential Materials Project, White House Central Files, box 12, file 18, LC; Walter E. Switzer, "Capital Punishment," *Pacific Historian* 23 (1979): 68; *Gregg v. Georgia*, 428 U.S. 153, 179–180nn23,24 (1976).

2 Robert M. Bohm, "American Death Penalty Opinion, 1936–1986: A Critical Examination of the Gallup Polls," in Robert M. Bohm, ed., *The Death Penalty in America: Current Research* (Cincinnati: Anderson Publishing Co., 1991).

3 *Model Penal Code and Commentaries* (Philadelphia: American Law Institute, 1980–), pt. II, s. 210.6.

4 Tracy L. Snell, *Capital Punishment 1998* (Washington: Bureau of Justice Statistics, 1999), 13.

5 Robert H. Bork, *The Tempting of America: The Political Seduction of the Law* (New York: Free Press, 1990), 219–221; Brief for the United States as Amicus Curiae, *Fowler v. North Carolina*, 73–7031, 31.

6 *Fowler v. North Carolina*, 422 U.S. 1039 (1975).

7 AA to Douglas, 15 May 1975, and James B. Ginty to the Conference, 10 Sept. 1975, William O. Douglas Papers, box 1706, LC; James B. Ginty to the Conference, 15 Jan. 1976, William J. Brennan, Jr., Papers, box I:363, folder 5, LC.

8 Brief for Petitioner, *Jurek v. Texas*, 75–5394, 23.

9 *Landmark Briefs and Arguments of the Supreme Court of the United States* (Washington: University Publications of America, 1975–), 90:624–625, 632–633.

10 I have reconstructed the conference from the notes of Powell and Brennan, silently adding words to make grammatical sentences. General Files—Capital Cases—1975 Term, LFP; William J. Brennan, Jr., Papers, box I:429, folder 5, LC.

11 *Gregg v. Georgia*, 428 U.S. 153 (1976).

12 Kathleen Maguire and Ann L. Pastore, eds., *Sourcebook of Criminal Justice Statistics—1998* (Washington: Bureau of Justice Statistics, 1999), 134–135.

13 William J. Bowers, Margaret Vandiver, and Patricia H. Dugan, "A New Look at Public Opinion on Capital Punishment: What Citizens and Legislators Prefer," *American Journal of Criminal Law* 22 (1994): 77–150.

14 Peter G. Bourne, *Jimmy Carter* (New York: Scribner, 1997), 212; Griffin Bell, Stuart Eizenstat, and Annie Gutierrez to Carter, 10 Nov. 1977, White House Office of Counsel to the President, box 12, file "death penalty," JC; Huron to Eizenstat, 19 Oct. 1977, Domestic Policy Staff—Civil Rights & Justice Cluster, Annie Gutierrez Files, box 15, file "Death Penalty [1]," JC; 306-WNET-428, 28 May 1987, NA.

15 Bureau of Justice Statistics, *Homicide Trends in the U.S.: Regional Trends*, www.ojp.usdoj.gov/bjs/homicide/region.htm (visited 17 Feb. 2000).

16 Snell, *Capital Punishment 1998*, 10, 15.

17 *Rates of Compensation for Court-Appointed Counsel in Capital Cases at Trial: A State-By-State Overview*, 1999 (West Newton, Mass.: Spangenberg Group, 1999); Stephen B. Bright, "Counsel for the Poor: The Death Sentence Not for the Worst Crime but for the Worst Lawyer," *Yale Law Journal* 103 (1994): 1835–83.

18 Isaac Ehrlich, "The Deterrent Effect of Capital Punishment: A Question of Life and Death," *American Economic Review* 65 (1975): 397–417.

19 David C. Baldus and James W. L. Cole, "A Comparison of the Work of Thorsten Sellin and Isaac Ehrlich on the Deterrent Effect of Capital Punishment," *Yale Law Journal* 85 (1975): 170–186; William J. Bowers and Glenn L. Pierce, "The Illusion of Deterrence in Isaac Ehrlich's Research on Capital Punishment," *Yale Law Journal* 85 (1975): 187–208.

20 Kenneth L. Avio, "Capital Punishment," in Peter Newman, ed., *The New Palgrave Dictionary of Economics and the Law* (London: Macmillan, 1998), 1:201–206.

21 *Capital Punishment: Hearings Before the Committee on the Judiciary*, U.S. Senate, 97th Cong., 1st Sess., S. 114 (Apr. and May 1981), 37; George

Deukmejian, *Murder & the Death Penalty: A Special Report to the People* ([Sacramento]: California Department of Justice, [1981]), 8.

22 Phoebe C. Ellsworth and Samuel R. Gross, "Hardening of the Attitudes: Americans' Views on the Death Penalty," *Journal of Social Issues* 50 (1994): 19–52.

23 *Public Hearing Before Senate Judiciary Committee on Senate No. 112* (N.J. Senate, 26 Feb. 1982), 4.

24 Walter Berns, *For Capital Punishment: Crime and the Morality of the Death Penalty* (New York: Basic Books, 1979), 173.

25 *Public Hearing Before Assembly Judiciary Committee on Senate Bill No. 799 and Assembly Bills 556 and 1318* (N.J. Assembly, 27 June 1972), 1.

26 *Coker v. Georgia*, 433 U.S. 584 (1977); *Enmund v. Florida*, 458 U.S. 782 (1982); *Tison v. Arizona*, 481 U.S. 137 (1987).

27 *Stanford v. Kentucky*, 492 U.S. 361 (1989); *Ford v. Wainwright*, 477 U.S. 399 (1986); *Penry v. Lynaugh*, 492 U.S. 302 (1989); *Herrera v. Collins*, 506 U.S. 390 (1993).

28 *Godfrey v. Georgia*, 446 U.S. 420 (1980); *Maynard v. Cartwright*, 486 U.S. 356 (1988); *Arave v. Creech*, 507 U.S. 463 (1993).

29 *Lockett v. Ohio*, 438 U.S. 586 (1978); *Eddings v. Oklahoma*, 455 U.S. 104 (1982).

30 *Zant v. Stephens*, 462 U.S. 862 (1983); Mo. Stat. s. 565.032.

31 *Payne v. Tennessee*, 501 U.S. 808 (1991).

32 *Morgan v. Illinois*, 504 U.S. 719, 751 (1992) (Scalia, J., dissenting); *Callins v. Collins*, 510 U.S. 1141 (1994) (Blackmun, J., dissenting); John C. Jefferies, Jr., *Justice Lewis F. Powell, Jr.* (New York: Scribner's, 1994), 451–452.

33 Laurie E. Ekstrand et al., *Death Penalty Sentencing: Research Indicates Pattern of Racial Disparities* (Washington: General Accounting Office, 1990).

34 David C. Baldus, George Woodworth, and Charles A. Pulaski Jr., *Equal Justice and the Death Penalty: A Legal and Empirical Analysis* (Boston: Northeastern University Press, 1990), 154.

35 Brief for Petitioner, *McCleskey v. Kemp*, 481 U.S. 279 (1987), 26; Powell to Leslie, 16 Sept. 1986, *McCleskey* file, LFP; Summary notes for conference, n.d., *McCleskey* file, LFP.

36 *McCleskey v. Kemp*, 481 U.S. 279, 312, 319 (1987); Scalia to conference, 6 Jan. 1987, Thurgood Marshall Papers, box 425, folder 7, LC.

37 Margaret Vandiver, "The Quality of Mercy: Race and Clemency in Florida Death Penalty Cases, 1924–1966," *University of Richmond Law Review* 27 (1993): 315–343; Hugo Adam Bedau, "The Decline of Executive Clemency in Capital Cases," *New York University Review of Law & Social Change* 18 (1990–1991): 255–272.

38 Lassers to Illinois Coalition Against the Death Penalty, 15 Dec. 1977, Illinois Coalition Against the Death Penalty collection, CHS; *St. Petersburg Times*, 5 July 1979.

39 Snell, *Capital Punishment 1998*, 12.

40 Powell to Burger, 31 Jan. 1984, Subject Files—Capital Cases, 1984, LFP; 110 Stat. 1214 (1996); *Teague v. Lane*, 489 U.S. 288 (1989); *McCleskey v. Zant*, 499 U.S. 467 (1991).

41 RG 301, box 1989/158–10, file "Capital Murder Seminar," TXA.

42 Philip J. Cook and Donna B. Slawson, *The Costs of Processing Murder Cases in North Carolina* (Durham: Terry Sanford Institute of Public Policy, Duke University, 1993); Robert L. Spangenberg and Elizabeth R. Walsh, "Capital Punishment or Life Imprisonment? Some Cost Considerations," *Loyola of Los Angeles Law Review* 23 (1989): 45–58.

43 *Brooklyn Daily Eagle*, 13 Feb. 1892, 1:9.

44 Patrick Malone, "Death Row and the Medical Model," *Hastings Center Report*, Oct. 1979, 5; *The Death Penalty and North Carolina Department of Correction* ([Raleigh]: North Carolina Department of Correction, 1994), 7.

45 RG 301, box 1991/141–9, file "Death Penalty," TXA; *Time*, 20 Dec. 1982, 29; Stephen Trombley, *The Execution Protocol: Inside America's Capital Punishment Industry* (New York: Crown, 1992), 277.

46 *Heckler v. Chaney*, 470 U.S. 821 (1985).

47 Robert Johnson, *Death Work: A Study of the Modern Execution Process* (Pacific Grove, Cal.: Brooks/Cole, 1990); *NYT*, 17 Dec. 2000, 1:1.

48 Trombley, *Execution Protocol*, 79, 113.

49 Roger Hood, *The Death Penalty: A World-wide Perspective*, 2d ed. (Oxford: Clarendon Press, 1996).

50 Franklin E. Zimring and Gordon Hawkins, *Crime Is Not the Problem: Lethal Violence in America* (New York: Oxford University Press, 1997), 22, 53, 55.

51 Hood, *The Death Penalty*, 213–214; Franklin E. Zimring and Gordon Hawkins, *Capital Punishment and the American Agenda* (Cambridge: Cambridge University Press, 1986), 12.

52 *USA: The Death Penalty: Amnesty International Briefing* (London: Amnesty International, 1987); *Administration of the Death Penalty in the United States* (Chenôve, France: International Commission of Jurists, 1996); *NYT*, 26 Feb. 2000.

53 *Soering v. United Kingdom*, 11 E.H.R.R. (1989); *State v. Makwanyane*, CCT/3/94, 16 H.R.L.J. 154 (1995); United Nations document E/CN.4/1998/68/Add.3 (22 Jan. 1998); Commission on Human Rights resolution 1999/61 (28 Apr. 1999).

54 *Paraguay v. United States*, ICJ 1998/99; *Germany v. United States*, ICJ 1999/104; *Breard v. Greene*, 523 U.S. 371 (1998); *Federal Republic of Germany v. United States*, 526 U.S. 111 (1999).

55 *Death Penalty Legislation: Hearing Before the Committee on the Judiciary*, U.S. Senate, 99th Cong., 1st Sess., S. 239 (Sept. 1985), 35; Gallup News Service, "Support for Death Penalty Drops to Lowest Level in 19 Years, Although Still High at 66%" (24 Feb. 2000), www.gallup.com/poll/releases/pr000224.asp (visited 9 Mar. 2000).

Epilogue

1 *St. Louis Post-Dispatch*, 18 May 2000, B7.

2 *St. Louis Post-Dispatch*, 23 Oct. 1997, C4; *Pantagraph* [Bloomington, Ill.], 22 Oct. 1997, A1.

ACKNOWLEDGMENTS

For FINANCIAL ASSISTANCE, I thank the Woodrow Wilson International Center for Scholars, for a fellowship that cut years off the time necessary for research and writing. Thanks also to three successive deans at the Washington University School of Law, Dan Ellis, Dan Keating, and Joel Seligman, for generous research support.

For research assistance, I thank four extraordinary law students at Washington University, Mark Leinauer, Amy Poth, Holly Stone, and Adam VanGrack. I would also like to express my gratitude to the archivists and librarians at the American Antiquarian Society, the Jimmy Carter Library, the Chicago Historical Society, the Connecticut State Archives, the Connecticut State Library, the Georgia Department of Archives and History, the Illinois State Archives, the John F. Kennedy Library, the Library of Congress, the Maryland State Archives, the Massachusetts Archives, the Missouri Historical Society, the Missouri State Archives, the National Archives, the New-York Historical Society, the New York Public Library, the New York State Archives, the New York State Library, New York University, the North Carolina State Archives, the Pennsylvania State Archives, the Franklin D. Roosevelt Library, Rutgers University, the South Carolina Archives and History Center, the Texas State Archives, the Library of Virginia, Washington and Lee University, and the Woodrow Wilson Center—and most of all to the librarians at Washington University, especially Mark Kloempken, Rebecca Ryan, and Katrina Stierholz.

I thank those who took the time to give suggestions on drafts of chapters: Ellen Blau, Tamara Detloff, George Fisher, Lawrence Friedman, David Gerber, Tom Green, Pauline Kim, David Konig, David Lieberman, Louis Masur, Michael Meranze, Austin Sarat, Bob Thompson, and

Bob Weisberg; many colleagues at Washington University; and participants in colloquia at the Woodrow Wilson Center, Northwestern Law School, Yale Law School, Vanderbilt Law School, and at the annual meetings of the Working Group on Law, Culture and Humanities, the Law and Society Association, and the American Society for Legal History. Glenn Kroog and Phil Lee provided anatomical advice in response to some very odd questions. Joyce Seltzer, David Lobenstine, and Camille Smith at Harvard University Press helped turn a mass of anecdotes into a book.

Space constraints have forced me to omit any critical engagement with secondary literature. For the same reason I have been unable to make explicit the theoretical presuppositions that specialists will recognize all too clearly. My greatest misgiving in this regard is that the notes do not reflect how much my thought has been shaped by the work of others, especially that of Richard Evans, V. A. C. Gatrell, Peter Linebaugh, and Louis Masur. If my book is half as good as theirs are, I'll be happy.

INDEX